S0-AAK-014

About the Author

Raised in Laurel Canyon and Van Nuys, California, **Kevin Hile** has had a long career as an author and editor. He worked for several years with the late Jim Fordyce on news, entertainment, and travel radio shows about California and the Coachella Valley such as the *Cruisin' California* program. He wrote Visible Ink Press' *The Handy Weather Answer Book*, has edited many other titles in the "Handy Answer" series, and is proud of his history book on Michigan's oldest zoo, *Little Zoo by the Red Cedar: The Story of Potter Park Zoo*. He lives in Cathedral City, California.

Also from Visible Ink Press

The Handy African American History Answer Book
by Jessie Carnie Smith
ISBN: 978-1-57859-452-8

The Handy American History Answer Book
by David L. Hudson, Jr.
ISBN: 978-1-57859-471-9

The Handy Anatomy Answer Book, 2nd edition
by Patricia Barnes-Svarney and Thomas E. Svarney
ISBN: 978-1-57859-542-6

The Handy Answer Book for Kids (and Parents), 2nd edition
by Gina Misiroglu
ISBN: 978-1-57859-219-7

The Handy Art History Answer Book
by Madelynn Dickerson
ISBN: 978-1-57859-417-7

The Handy Astronomy Answer Book, 3rd edition
by Charles Liu
ISBN: 978-1-57859-419-1

The Handy Bible Answer Book
by Jennifer Rebecca Prince
ISBN: 978-1-57859-478-8

The Handy Biology Answer Book, 2nd edition
by Patricia Barnes Svarney and Thomas E. Svarney
ISBN: 978-1-57859-490-0

The Handy Boston Answer Book
by Samuel Willard Crompton
ISBN: 978-1-57859-593-8

The Handy California Answer Book
by Kevin S. Hile
ISBN: 978-1-57859-591-4

The Handy Chemistry Answer Book
by Ian C. Stewart and Justin P. Lamont
ISBN: 978-1-57859-374-3

The Handy Civil War Answer Book
by Samuel Willard Crompton
ISBN: 978-1-57859-476-4

The Handy Communication Answer Book
by Lauren Sergy
ISBN: 978-1-57859-587-7

The Handy Dinosaur Answer Book, 2nd edition
by Patricia Barnes-Svarney and Thomas E. Svarney
ISBN: 978-1-57859-218-0

The Handy English Grammar Answer Book
by Christine A. Hult, Ph.D.
ISBN: 978-1-57859-520-4

The Handy Geography Answer Book, 3rd edition
by Paul A. Tucci
ISBN: 978-1-57859-576-1

The Handy Geology Answer Book
by Patricia Barnes-Svarney and Thomas E. Svarney
ISBN: 978-1-57859-156-5

The Handy History Answer Book, 3rd edition
by David L. Hudson, Jr.
ISBN: 978-1-57859-372-9

The Handy Hockey Answer Book
by Stan Fischler
ISBN: 978-1-57859-513-6

The Handy Investing Answer Book
by Paul A. Tucci
ISBN: 978-1-57859-486-3

The Handy Islam Answer Book
by John Renard, Ph.D.
ISBN: 978-1-57859-510-5

The Handy Law Answer Book
by David L. Hudson, Jr.
ISBN: 978-1-57859-217-3

The Handy Math Answer Book, 2nd edition
by Patricia Barnes-Svarney and Thomas E. Svarney
ISBN: 978-1-57859-373-6

The Handy Military History Answer Book
by Samuel Willard Crompton
ISBN: 978-1-57859-509-9

The Handy Mythology Answer Book,
by David A. Leeming, Ph.D.
ISBN: 978-1-57859-475-7

The Handy New York City Answer Book
by Chris Barsanti
IBSN: 978-1-57859-586-0

The Handy Nutrition Answer Book
by Patricia Barnes-Svarney and Thomas E. Svarney
ISBN: 978-1-57859-484-9

The Handy Ocean Answer Book
by Patricia Barnes-Svarney and Thomas E. Svarney
ISBN: 978-1-57859-063-6

The Handy Personal Finance Answer Book
by Paul A. Tucci
ISBN: 978-1-57859-322-4

The Handy Philosophy Answer Book
by Naomi Zack
ISBN: 978-1-57859-226-5

The Handy Physics Answer Book, 2nd edition
By Paul W. Zitzewitz, Ph.D.
ISBN: 978-1-57859-305-7

The Handy Politics Answer Book
by Gina Misiroglu
ISBN: 978-1-57859-139-8

The Handy Presidents Answer Book, 2nd edition
by David L. Hudson, Jr.
ISB N: 978-1-57859-317-0

The Handy Psychology Answer Book, 2nd edition
by Lisa J. Cohen, Ph.D.
ISBN: 978-1-57859-508-2

The Handy Religion Answer Book, 2nd edition
by John Renard, Ph.D.
ISBN: 978-1-57859-379-8

The Handy Science Answer Book, 4th edition
by The Carnegie Library of Pittsburgh
ISBN: 978-1-57859-321-7

The Handy State-by-State Answer Book
By Samuel Willard Crompton
ISBN: 978-1-57859-565-5

The Handy Supreme Court Answer Book
by David L. Hudson, Jr.
ISBN: 978-1-57859-196-1

The Handy Technology Answer Book
by Naomi Balaban and James Bobick
ISBN: 978-1-57859-563-1

The Handy Weather Answer Book, 2nd edition
by Kevin S. Hile
ISBN: 978-1-57859-221-0

Please visit the "Handy Answers" series website at www.handyanswers.com.

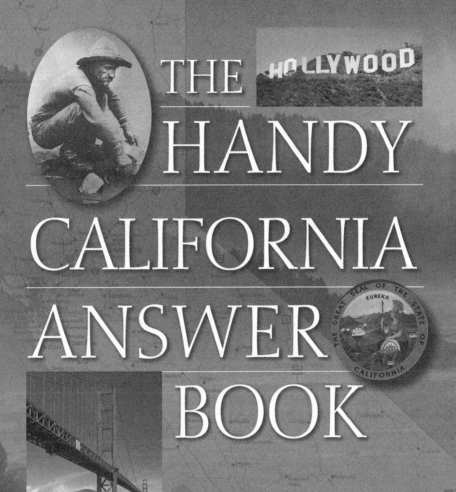

THE
HANDY
CALIFORNIA
ANSWER
BOOK

Kevin S. Hile

VISIBLE
INK
PRESS

Detroit

THE HANDY CALIFORNIA ANSWER BOOK

Copyright © 2017 by Visible Ink Press®

This publication is a creative work fully protected by all applicable copyright laws, as well as by misappropriation, trade secret, unfair competition, and other applicable laws.

No part of this book may be reproduced in any form without permission in writing from the publisher, except by a reviewer who wishes to quote brief passages in connection with a review written for inclusion in a magazine, newspaper, or website.

All rights to this publication will be vigorously defended.

Visible Ink Press®
43311 Joy Rd., #414
Canton, MI 48187–2075

Visible Ink Press is a registered trademark of Visible Ink Press LLC.

Most Visible Ink Press books are available at special quantity discounts when purchased in bulk by corporations, organizations, or groups. Customized printings, special imprints, messages, and excerpts can be produced to meet your needs. For more information, contact Special Markets Director, Visible Ink Press, www.visibleink.com, or 734–667–3211.

Managing Editor: Kevin S. Hile
Art Director: Mary Claire Krzewinski
Typesetting: Marco DiVita
Proofreaders: Shoshana Hurwitz and Patricia Kot
Indexer: Larry Baker

Cover images: Shutterstock.

Library of Congress Cataloging–in–Publication Data

Names: Hile, Kevin, author.
Title: The handy California answer book / by Kevin S. Hile.
Description: Canton, MI : Visible Ink Press, 2016. | Series: Handy answers series | Includes bibliographical references and index.
Identifiers: LCCN 2016026091| ISBN 9781578595914 (tradepaper) | ISBN 9781578596232 (epub) | ISBN 9781578596225 (updf)
Subjects: LCSH: California—Miscellanea.
Classification: LCC F861.6 .H55 2016 | DDC 979.4—dc23
LC record available at https://lccn.loc.gov/2016026091

Printed in the United States of America

10 9 8 7 6 5 4 3 2 1

Contents

Dedication

This book is dedicated to the memory of my late husband, Jim Fordyce, who passed away in October 2015. Although Jim was born in New Jersey and raised in upstate New York, he adopted California in his heart when we moved here. He loved California and quickly became a Californian. He loved everything, from the weather and attractions to the people and culture.

Jim enjoyed a long career in radio and television in New York, Pennsylvania, Arizona, Michigan, and, finally, California, covering everything from hard news to entertainment stories. He produced and hosted several online radio shows covering life in the Coachella Valley and California and did everything he could to help his local community. Jim had just started his *Cruisin' California* travel show and had been contracted to write *The Handy California Answer Book* a few months before his passing. After writing the first chapter and part of the fourth chapter on natural wonders, he died unexpectedly. Although I am the one who completed this project for him, his joyful spirit and love of the Golden State still imbue the pages you are about to read.

This book is full of my love for you, Jim. I miss you.

Acknowledgments

I would like to thank VIP publisher Roger Jänecke for allowing me to complete the writing of this book, which was begun by Jim Fordyce before his passing. Thanks, as always, to my wonderful typesetter, Marco DiVita, graphics designer Marie Claire Krzewinski, indexer Larry Baker, and proofreader Barbara Lyon.

I would also like to thank several friends of mine for looking over specific chapters in which they have expertise. Thanks to James Crockett for reviewing the two history chapters; thanks to Todd Ableser for reading through the material on San Francisco; thanks to Mary Cardas for checking out other material on Southern California; thanks to Larry Baker for his expertise in reviewing the sports chapters. Last, but not least, to my friend Bart Swaim, who reviewed the San Diego material and who provided two photographs: one showing the fursuit parade at the furry convention that he took, and the other taken by his father of Marilyn Monroe. This photo was taken at the Hotel Del Coronado, where the late Mr. Swaim was a long-time photographer and took many still-unpublished photographs of celebrities who stayed there in the 1950s and 1960s.

Photo Sources

AARP Social Media: p. 330.

Sanjay Ach: p. 364.

Oleg Alexandrov: p. 88.

Keith Allison: pp. 310, 318.

Associated Students, University of California, Los Angeles: p. 344.

Jim Bahn: p. 110.

Baseball Digest: p. 288.

Jeffrey Beall: p. 404.

Calebrw (Wikicommons): p. 337.

California Department of Corrections and Rehabilitation: p. 134.

Capitol Records: p. 244.

Cbl62 (Wikicommons): p. 281.

Concerto (Wikicommons): p. 16.

Caroline Culler: p. 72.

Downtowngal (Wikicommons): p. 247.

The Duluth Herald: p. 399.

Mona Eshaiker: p. 356.

Federal Aviation Administration: p. 220.

Floation (Wikicommons): p. 279.

Jim Fordyce: pp. 104, 197, 199, 213.

Michael Gäbler: p. 96.

Emily Gadek: p. 141.

Bernard Gagnon: pp. 22, 26.

J. Malcolm Greany: p. 397.

Harris & Ewing Collection: pp. 206, 418.

Henry MacRae Prod./Universal Pictures: p. 234.

Brocken Inaglory: p. 103.

Introvert (Wikicommons): p. 32.

Jean-Luc (Wikicommons): p. 371.

Ed Kavishe: p. 248.

Phil Konstantin: p. 95.

Krusty (Wikicommons): p. 292.

Jkan997 (Wikicommons): p. 215.

Joel Levine: p. 191.

Johnmaxmena2 (Wikicommons): p. 303.

Library of Congress: p. 113.

Steve Lipofsky: p. 307.

Loki30 (Wikicommons): p. 19.

MCB (Wikicommons): p. 357.

McGhiever (Wikicommons): p. 256.

Stuart Milk: 259.

Milovas (Wikicommons): p. 71.

Nansy131 (Wikicommons): p. 274.

NASA: pp. 91, 421.

Nobel Foundation: p. 64.

Omar Omar: p. 218.

Mike Peel: p. 101.

R. Pendergrass: p. 312.

Photos by Swaim: p. 385.

Bruce Roberson: p. 210.

Ronald Reagan Presidential Library: p. 266.

Silent Sensei (Wikicommons): p. 286.

Shadowxfox (Wikicommons): p. 23.

Shutterstock: pp. 5, 11, 62, 76, 83, 85, 120, 121, 123, 125, 127, 132, 138, 142, 143, 146, 151, 153, 156, 158, 160, 161, 162, 166, 168, 171, 174, 178, 180, 183, 189, 195, 204, 211, 236, 239, 241, 262, 268, 277, 278, 290, 295, 297, 314, 334, 338, 342, 349, 359, 361, 374, 376, 378, 380, 383, 386, 387, 390, 392, 395, 396, 406, 408, 409, 411, 413.

Sporting News: p. 315.

SRI International: p. 202.

Gary Soup: p. 284.

Pete Souza/The White House: p. 287.

Hobart Swaim: p. 368.

James Teterenko: p. 321.

TolneGGG: p. 251.

Eric Upchurch: p. 296.

USC Regional Historical Photo Collection: p. 129.

U.S. Health and Human Services: p. 351.

U.S. Navy: p. 17.

Arthur C. Verge: p. 346.

Warner Bros.: p. 232.

The White House: p. 417.

Whittlz (Wikicommons): p. 243.

Yahoo News: p. 306.

Matthew Yohe: p. 415.

Public domain: pp. 3, 20, 25, 30, 36, 39, 40, 43, 46, 51, 54, 58, 60, 67, 107, 115, 152, 155, 187, 226, 228, 229, 258, 265, 294, 300, 301, 305, 328, 347, 365, 400, 402.

Timeline

Year	Event
c. 20000–10000 B.C.E.	Land bridge between present-day Alaska and Russia allows Asian peoples to cross into North America, where they migrate south over the centuries, and many settle in what is California.
2000 B.C.E.	Permanent and sizable coastal villages established
200 C.E.	Indians from points east migrate to California
1510	The name "California" is taken from a Spanish novel and adopted as the name of this part of the New World
September 28, 1542	Juan Rodríguez Cabrillo lands an expedition by present-day San Diego and then explores the coastline and is the first European to explore California
June 17, 1579	Englishman Sir Francis Drake lands north of San Francisco Bay
1602	Don Sebastian Vizcaino discovers Monterey Bay and also Santa Catalina Island.
March 24, 1769	Spain decides to settle California by establishing Franciscan missions and presidios
July 16, 1769	The first Spanish mission, San Diego de Alcala, is founded by Father Junípero Serra
November 4, 1769	Gaspar de Portolá discovers San Francisco Bay
1776	Presidio of San Francisco and Mission Dolores are founded
September 4, 1781	Pueblo of Los Angeles founded
1812	Russian fur traders established Fort Ross
	Indians rebel against Spanish missionaries in Santa Cruz
1821	Mexico wins independence from Spain, placing California under Mexican rule

1824	Indians rebel against missionaries in Santa Inés and La Purísima Concepción
1826	American Fur trapper Jedediah Smith explores California
1841	German immigrant John Sutter establishes his estate near present day Sacramento
	The first wagon train arrives in California
October 1842	The U.S. Navy captures Monterey, having been falsely led to believe Alta California had been turned over to the British
May 11, 1846	The Bear Flag Revolt begins in northern California
May 13, 1846	The Mexican–American War begins
	American forces led by Captain John Frémont capture Monterey
	Donner party is stranded in the Sierra Nevada Mountains
July 7, 1846	California is annexed by the United States as a territory.
August 15, 1846	*The Californian*, the state's first newspaper, begins publication in Monterey
January 13, 1847	The Capitulation of Cahuenga is signed, ending hostilities between Mexico and the United States, but only in California
1847	Yerba Buena is renamed as San Francisco
	John Frémont declares himself military governor of California
	Survivors of the Donner Party arrive at Sutter's Fort
January 24, 1848	Gold is discovered in the American River near Coloma by James Marshall, leading to the Gold Rush
February 2, 1848	California officially becomes a U.S. territory with the signing of the Treaty of Guadalupe Hidalgo
1849	The Gold Rush begins when word gets out about James Marshall's discovery
December 15, 1849	First time the state legislature convenes in San Jose
September 9, 1850	California is admitted into the Union as the thirty-first state
March 27, 1850	San Diego is incorporated
1851	Joaquin Murieta begins his life of crime as the Hispanic Robin Hood
June 13, 1852	Wells, Fargo & Co. begins business in California
1853	German immigrant Levi Strauss founds Levi Strauss and Co. and begins making blue jeans
	Joaquin Murieta is killed
June 11, 1859	The Comstock Lode, which contained millions of dollars' worth of silver, is discovered
1860	The Pony Express begins express mail delivery service to Sacramento
February 22, 1860	The first organized baseball game in California is played in San Francisco
January 23, 1862	The first grape vines are shipped to San Francisco, marking the beginning of California's wine industry

February 15, 1915	D. W. Griffith debuts *The Birth of a Nation* in Los Angeles
February 20, 1915	Panama–Pacific Exposition opens in San Francisco
March 29, 1919	Surfboard inventor Bob Fitzsimmons born in Los Angeles
July 11, 1922	The Hollywood Bowl opens
October 5, 1923	Edwin Hubble takes a photo using the Mt. Wilson observatory that would show the universe is expanding
April 17, 1924	MGM Pictures is founded
July 6, 1925	TV host and producer Merv Griffin born in San Mateo
1927	Charles Lindberg's *Spirit of St. Louis* is built in San Diego
May 11, 1927	Academy of Motion Pictures Arts and Sciences is founded in Los Angeles
May 18, 1927	Grauman's Chinese Theatre (now TCL Chinese Theatre) opens on Hollywood Boulevard
September 7, 1927	In San Francisco, Philo T. Farnsworth conducts the first successful test transmitting signals between vacuum tubes to show an image—the first television
March 12, 1928	St. Francis Dam bursts in the Santa Clarita Valley, killing over 600 people
1930	Dust Bowl spurs immigration to California
June 4, 1930	Pantages Theatre opens in Hollywood
July 30, 1932	Summer Olympics opens in Los Angeles
1933	Alcatraz Island is made a federal prison; closes in 1963
February 26, 1933	Groundbreaking ceremony is performed at the future Golden Gate Bridge site
December 5, 1934	Author Joan Didion born in Sacramento
December 13, 1934	Movie producer Richard Zanuck born in Los Angeles
December 25, 1934	Santa Anita Racetrack opens in Arcadia
1935	Statewide irrigation projects begin, turning California's Central, Salinas, and Imperial valleys into an agricultural paradise
1936	The Oakland Bay Bridge opens
	Hoover Dam is completed on Colorado River to control flooding and provide water for irrigation and power in southern California
April 6, 1937	Musician Merle Haggard born in Oildale near Bakersfield
May 27, 1937	Golden Gate Bridge opens
July 3, 1937	Del Mar Racetrack opens
April 1, 1938	Palm Springs incorporated
May 7, 1939	Union Station opens in Los Angeles
1940	California opens first modern freeway
May 1942	The U.S. government orders Japanese Americans placed in internment camps, including at Manzanar in California

January 2, 1945	Construction of Shasta Dam is completed
June 26, 1945	United Nations Charter signed in San Francisco
1945	Mattel, Inc., founded in El Segundo; the toy company would hit it big in 1959 when it debuts the Barbie doll
October 14, 1947	Chuck Yeager breaks the sound barrier while flying the Bell X-1 out of what is now Edwards Air Force Base
November 2, 1947	Howard Hughes flies *The Spruce Goose* over Long Beach Harbor
May 15, 1948	Dick and Mac McDonald open the first McDonald's in San Bernardino
January 25, 1949	First Emmy Awards are held in Los Angeles
1950	San Francisco 49s open their first football season
February 15, 1954	The "Bevatron" atom collider is completed at the University of California, Berkeley
February 18, 1954	First Church of Scientology is established by L. Ron Hubbard in Los Angeles
July 17, 1955	Disneyland opens
October 18, 1955	The antiproton is discovered at University of California, Berkeley
July 9, 1956	Actor Tom Hanks born in Concord near Oakland
September 17, 1959	Dodger Stadium opens
1960	The Winter Olympics are held in Squaw Valley
May 16, 1960	Physicist Ted Maiman demonstrates the first working laser
April 25, 1961	The integrated circuit is patented by Robert Noyce
December 31, 1961	The Beach Boys perform in public for the first time at the Long Beach Municipal Auditorium
1962	California becomes the most populous state in the union
	United Farm Workers founded
December 14, 1963	Los Angeles' Baldwin Hills Dam breaks, releasing a flood that kills five people
July 24, 1964	Baseball player Barry Bonds born in Riverside
December 4, 1964	The "Free Speech Movement" at University of California, Berkeley, kicks off what will become a series of college student protests in the 1960s and 1970s
August 11, 1965	Watts Riots break out, resulting in 34 deaths and 1,100 injured. About $100 million in property damages result
September 8, 1965	Delano Grape Strike begins
April 9, 1966	Angel Stadium opens in Los Angeles
October 30, 1966	The Zodiac Killer takes his first of seven victims; the identity of the murderer is never uncovered
December 26, 1966	Dr. Ron Karenga starts the holiday tradition of Kwanzaa in Long Beach
1967	Actor Ronald Reagan is elected governor and serves two terms
June 16, 1967	The world's first rock music festival, Monterey Pop, opens

July 18, 1968	Tech company Intel incorporates in Santa Clara
December 9, 1968	Stanford Research Institute scientist Douglas C. Engelbart debuts the computer mouse
1969	American Indians take over Alcatraz Island
August 8, 1969	Actress Sharon Tate and her friends are murdered in Los Angeles by followers of Charles Manson
September 22, 1969	Willie Mays hits his six hundredth home run for the San Francisco Giants
December 6, 1969	Altamont Rock Festival in Livermore marks what many consider the end of the 1960s
February 9, 1971	San Fernando Valley earthquake
May 29, 1973	Tom Bradley becomes first African American mayor of Los Angeles
April 15, 1974	Heiress Patty Hearst assists the Symbionese Liberation Army in an armed robbery of Hibernia Bank in San Francisco
April 1, 1976	Apple Computer founded by Steve Jobs, Steve Wozniak, and Ronald Wayne in Cupertino
1977	Apple launches the personal computer, spurring the Silicon Valley revolution in computers
May 25, 1977	George Lucas, who was born in Modesto in 1944, debuts *Star Wars*
June 6, 1978	Proposition 13 passes
November 27, 1978	Openly gay politician Harvey Milk is assassinated in San Francisco
1984	Summer Olympics open in Los Angeles
February 13, 1988	Michael Jackson buys the lot that will become Neverland Ranch
1989	7.1 magnitude quake strikes San Francisco bay area
April 1992	Riots break out in South Central Los Angeles after police beat Rodney King, injuring 2,000 people, killing 50, and causing nearly a billion dollars in property damage
January 17, 1994	Northridge earthquake (7.5 on the Richter Scale) kills 57 and injures about 1,500 people
October 31, 1994	Death Valley is named a national park
1995	Yahoo is incorporated
	eBay is founded
1997	Google is founded
2003	Actor Arnold Schwarzenegger is elected governor and serves two terms
2004	Private California company launches SpaceShipOne, the first private, manned mission to space
2012	An historically severe drought begins in California
2015	The first phase of construction for California's high-speed rail system begins. When completed, passengers will be able to travel from San Francisco to Los Angeles in three hours.
December 2, 2015	Terrorists attack employees having a meeting at the San Bernardino Department of Public Health, killing fourteen people

Introduction

Mention California to a non-Californian and the images that may come to mind are sunny beaches, Hollywood, Silicon Valley, and perhaps Disneyland or the Golden Gate Bridge. But the Golden State is much more than tourist attractions, movie stars, and the wine country.

California is diversity come to life. The landscape includes not only beautiful beaches, but also everything from mountain forests to deserts and productive farmland. It's not only about fun in the sun and amusement parks; the state has a booming high-tech industry, is home to large military bases and important seaports, has thriving financial institutions, and is an enthusiastic sports state with professional teams in the NBA, MLB, NFL, NHL, and more.

The state is also ethnically diverse with a rich history dating back to the sixteenth-century Spanish explorers and even farther back. It has been the home for dozens of Native American tribes, was a colony under Spain, was part of Mexico, and, for a very brief time, an independent nation. The state has been settled by Europeans, Mexicans, Chinese, Russians, and many other ethnic groups.

Now, of course, California is part of the United States of America, and as such it is the most populous of the fifty states with nearly thirty-nine million residents as of the 2010 Census. Because of its large population it also wields tremendous political, as well as economic, influence. It has been noted, in fact, that if California were its own separate nation it would have the eighth largest economy in the world, which would make it eligible to participate in the G8.

The Handy California Answer Book provides the reader with a survey of all the important, interesting, and oddball facts, figures, and stories of this beautiful state. Here you will find over 1,100 answers to questions on everything from history, politics, and business to culture, sports, and attractions. While there is no way to cover everything about California in one book, I have endeavored to describe the highpoints here. In these pages you will get a solid understanding of the history of California; you will tour the major—and some minor—cities; you will get a sense of what it is like to live here; and, along the way, we'll have some fun by discovering unique and quirky people and places.

The book begins with a chapter covering some basic facts about the state. We then continue on with chapters on the history of California, followed by subject-based chapters on nature, regional information, business, entertainment, politics, and sports. To round off the book, we've added a chapter on "Quirky California" for some fun stuff about the state, and ended with profiles of famous and memorable Californians. The book concludes with an appendix listing governors back to the days of Alta California, a bibliography, and a useful index for locating people, places, and other subjects quickly.

While there is a lot here, some editorial choices had to be made in order to keep this book from becoming a set of three or more books. For example, in the "Notable Californians" chapter it would have been impossible to include all the famous Hollywood stars who have lived and worked here. Therefore, I largely restricted the profiles to people who were actually born in this state. Even then, not everyone could be included, but you will get a good idea of many of the most notable stars from this state. The same is true for politicians, writers, artists, scientists, and other figures included in that chapter.

You may also note that a number of athletes are discussed in the "Notable Californians" but not in the chapters on sports. That's because the "Notables" chapter, again, focuses on athletes born in this state, while the sports chapters focus on teams and events that are based here. Many famous athletes born in California have not played on Californian teams.

Historical figures are also not profiled in the "Notable" chapter because they have been covered in the two history chapters, as well as some other chapters.

The Handy California Answer Book is, thus, a primer for the state. Whether you are unfamiliar with California and have never visited the Golden State or have lived here all your life, you are bound to find something new and interesting within these pages that you never knew. Let it be your inspiration to continue to explore California and shout out "Eureka!" (the state motto) when you have stumbled across something new and wonderful in this "Land of Fruits and Nuts."

Kevin Hile (June 22, 2016)

CALIFORNIA BASICS

CALIFORNIA REPUBLIC

Why is the state called California?

There is more than one answer, depending on who you believe. One story says the name California comes from a mythical Spanish island ruled by a queen called Califia that was featured in a Spanish romance novel written by Garcia Ordonez de Montalvo in 1510. In the book, the beautiful queen ruled over a country of beautiful, black, Amazon women with lots of pearls and gold. Men were only allowed there one day a year to help perpetuate the race. When Spanish explorers came to what is now known as the Baja Peninsula in 1535, they thought they found that island and called it California. They were convinced they were on that island and even found pearls. They later realized the island was really a peninsula, but the name stuck.

While the fictional island theory is the most widely accepted, some scholars have also suggested that the name comes from Catalan words. *Calor* means "hot in," and *forn* means "oven."

Other scholars believe a third theory. There is a Native American phrase that means "high hill." When the natives came, many looked for a places above the ocean, so *kali forno* might have been their word for the land.

Who settled California?

California was first settled by various Native American tribes. There is evidence of humans in California dating back thousands of years. The earliest Californians came from Asia. Historians say they made their way across the Bering Strait to Alaska using a now-vanished land bridge. They were apparently attracted to the warm climate and an abundance of food and fertile land to grow more.

Before other settlers arrived, it is believed that California Indians had five hundred distinct subtribes or groups. Tribes were as small as fifty members; their largest had about five hundred people.

California still has the largest Native American population of any U.S. state.

Who came after the Native Americans?

A number of European expeditions during the sixteenth and seventeenth centuries came before it was claimed by the Spanish Empire as part of New Spain. Most of what is now California became a part of Mexico in 1821 following its successful war for independence. It was surrendered to the United States in 1848 after the Mexican–American War.

When did California become a state?

It was admitted as the thirty-first state on September 9, 1850. The California Gold Rush starting in 1848 led to dramatic social and demographic change, with large-scale immigration from the east.

Even now, California is generally believed to have more people moving to it than any other state. In addition to people from other states arriving every day for a different lifestyle or job, Asians and Pacific Islanders lead the influx to the Golden State. There is also a constant flow of immigrants from Mexico each year.

Where is California on the map?

California is hard to miss if you head west from all but a few states. To the south, the Golden State borders Mexico for about 140 miles. The border stretches from the Colorado River to the Pacific Ocean near Tijuana, Mexico. The border goes north from Mexico up the Pacific Coast for 840 miles to the Oregon border. The northern border is shared with Oregon for about 300 miles. On the east side of the state, California shares its border with Nevada (at an odd angle you will read about later) and its border with Arizona right along the Colorado River.

What is the exact location?

To be precise, California runs from longitude 114° 8" West to 124° 24" West, and from latitude 32° 30" North to 42° North.

Is California the largest state by area?

No, according to InfoPlease.com, with 163,695 square miles, California is number three after Alaska and Texas.

How diverse is California's geography?

California has a diverse geography that ranges from tall mountains to beaches, not to mention deserts, fertile farmlands, and dense forests.

There is California's famous Pacific coast, which runs from the border with Mexico at San Diego to the Oregon border at Pelican State Beach. Freeways and highways run almost the entire almost nine-hundred-mile stretch. There will be breathtaking views of the Pacific Ocean to the west and spectacular mountains to the east.

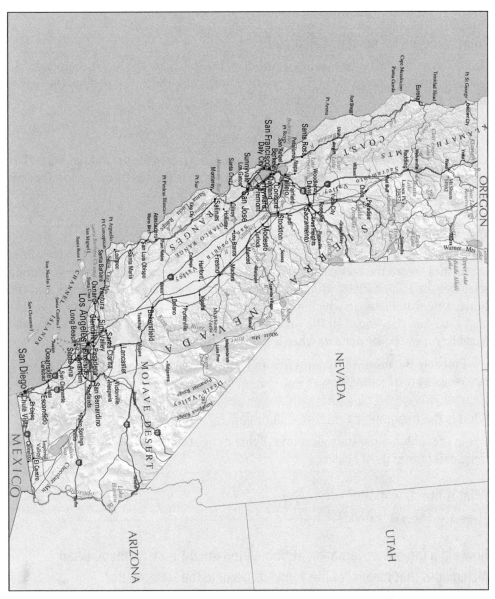

A recent map of the state of California.

What is the highest point in California?

Mount Whitney is 14,491 feet (4,417 meters) high at its peak. It is in Yosemite National Park and holds the distinction of being the highest point in the contiguous forty-eight states.

What is the lowest point in California?

Death Valley, located in the southeast portion of the state near the Nevada border, is 282 feet (86 meters) below sea level. This desert region is also the lowest point in the nation and one of the hottest (see the "Natural Wonders" chapter).

Is it true there is an active volcano in California?

Yes. Lassen Peak is one of two active U.S. volcanoes outside of Alaska and Hawaii. Its last eruption was in 1917. Also known as Mount Lassen, it is located in the Shasta Cascade region of northern California.

Why is California prone to earthquakes?

California sits on several fault lines, especially near the Pacific Ocean. Those fault lines are formed where the tectonic plates grind and scrape against each other. California straddles the Pacific Plate, which extends from western California to Japan, and the North American Plate, on which most of the continent sits. These plates move on the fault lines and they move all the time. It is continuous and slow but is usually undetectable. An earthquake occurs when a sudden slip occurs on a fault line.

Probably the most well-known fissure is the San Andreas Fault, which moves at a rate of about two inches per year.

What is the geographic center of California?

It is in the center of the state, of course. Being more specific, it is in Madera County, 38 miles east of the city of Madera.

What is the state motto?

The state motto is "Eureka!"

How did a famous exclamation attributed to famed Greek mathematician Archimedes that means "I have found it" become the state motto?

California's state motto, "Eureka ... I have found it!" refers to the discovery of gold in California. The California state motto appears on the state seal, and gold is the official mineral symbol of California.

Archimedes reportedly shouted "Eureka!" when he discovered a method for determining the purity of gold.

Does California have a nickname?

California is often referred to as "The Golden State" or "The Sunshine State." It has jokingly been called "The Land of Fruits and Nuts" as a play on words referring to both its agricultural muscle and the idea that a lot of crazy people come from the state.

Why was that nickname chosen?

There are several theories here and no one is sure which is correct. The most popular of them dates back to the mid-1800s, when gold was discovered. There are many examples of the term being used at that time.

There are also references to settlers about the same time admiring the native grass. Most of them were used to green grass, and the gold color shined dramatically in the wind, giving the impression of waves of gold.

The third theory has to do with the state flower, the golden poppy, which also blankets fields and hillsides, giving off a golden hue.

What does the California flag look like?

The California state flag is white with a wide, red strip along the bottom. There is a red star in the upper left corner and a grizzly bear facing left (toward the hoist or mast) in

The state flag of California. Since this is a black-and-white photo, it should be pointed out that the star and bottom stripe are red, the bear and lettering are brown, and the grass is green. The background is white.

the center, walking on a patch of green grass. Its current design was officially adopted when Governor Earl Warren signed in Assembly Bill 1014 on June 14, 1953. That bill contained other official state items that you will learn about later.

How did the flag get its design?

The current California flag is based on the original design painted by William Todd in 1846. He was among a group of American settlers revolting against the rule of Mexico. The Bear Flag was first raised on June 14, 1846, at Sonoma (see the chapter "Early California: First Peoples to the 1849 Gold Rush.") Even though June 14 is now Flag Day, the date is just a coincidence since Flag Day was not established until fifty years later.

The original flag was very similar to the current one. It featured a bear and a star, as does the current version. The design flying today was adopted in 1911 and, as with the original, has the words "California Republic" across its design.

The original Bear Flag was preserved by the Society of California Pioneers. It was destroyed during the Great San Francisco Earthquake and Fire of 1906.

Is there a story about the bear on the flag?

The bear on the current flag of California is believed to have been modeled on the last Californian grizzly bear in captivity. The bear, whose name was "Monarch," was captured in 1889 by newspaper reporter Allen Kelley. It is believed that the bear was caught for William Randolph Hearst, who wanted a bear for his private zoo. The bear was subsequently moved to Woodward's Gardens in San Francisco and then to the zoo at Golden Gate Park. After the bear's death in 1911, it was mounted and preserved at the Academy of Sciences at Golden Gate Park.

Why is there a single star on the flag?

To answer that question requires a trip back to 1836. A decade before William Todd had his disagreement with the Mexican government in 1846, Juan Alvarado and Isaac Graham led a revolution against Mexican rule. During that revolt, rebels were able to capture Monterey and declared California "a free and sovereign state." Although their rebellion failed to secure independence for California, it inspired a simple design: a sin-

---

Where is the Antelope Valley Poppy Reserve?

Located just west of Lancaster (north of Los Angeles), the protected area of the Mojave Desert known as the Angelope Valley Poppy Reserve delivers a riot of brilliant color each spring from mid-February to mid-May, depending on rainfall. Tourists may visit the area, but they are forbidden from plucking poppies, and grazing animals have been banned from the region as well.

gle red star on a white background. It was never officially the flag, but to this day it is referred to as The Lone Star Flag of California.

What is the state flower?

The state flower has been the Golden Poppy since 1903.

Why was that flower chosen?

The Golden Poppy or Eschscholzia, was a favorite thirteen years before it got its official designation. History tells us on December 12, 1890, the members of the California State Floral Society voted for a flower that they thought would best serve the State of California as an official emblem. There were three frontrunners: the California Poppy, the Mariposa Lily and the Matilija Poppy.

In an article titled "California's Esteemed Golden Poppy," columnist Naomi Mathews wrote that "the California Poppy won the esteemed title of 'Official California State Flower' by an overwhelming landslide." The article told readers that the "showy" Matilija poppy received no votes, and the beautiful Mariposa lily received only three votes.

As mentioned, it took almost thirteen years after the California State Floral Society's vote for the California Legislature to get around to adopting the golden poppy as the California state flower.

In 1973, the law was amended to designate April 6 of each year as California Poppy Day.

What does the golden poppy look like?

It is described as a plant with fernlike leaves, with a single flower on each long stalk. The flowers usually bloom from February until September. They grow wild across open areas and flourish in grassy fields or sandy slopes.

They not only grow in California, but they are found in Oregon and southern Washington, east into Nevada and Arizona, and into west Texas.

Why are there so many golden poppies?

In a yard, home garden, or in the wild, these heart flowers thrive. To get them to grow, just scatter the seeds in the fall. Once established, they will self-seed. Some yards and fields are covered in a bright gold mass of these flowers each year.

Golden poppies, which are actually orange in color, are the state flower.

7

What is the state tree?

California redwoods are the official state tree.

They are the official state tree. Why is that plural?

Because California is the home to three species of trees that are commonly referred to as redwoods: California's coast redwoods, giant sequoia, and, depending on whom you ask, China's dawn redwood is sometimes included.

What is the difference?

The coast redwoods (*Sequoia sempervirens*) are the earth's tallest tree. They grow along the Pacific coast from central California north to Oregon.

The giant sequoia (*Sequliadendron giganteum*), is considered to be the world's most massive tree. They are native to the western slopes of the Sierra Nevada Mountains in California. Some are so massive that there have been tunnels cut in them wide enough to drive a car through. Thirty-foot diameter trunks are not uncommon on these trees.

The dawn redwood (Metasequoia glyptostroboides), the smallest redwood, is native to a remote part of China thought to be extinct until the 1940s.

If it is native to China (and extinct), how did these trees get to California?

There are several theories on this. The simplest is that the trees are easy to transplant and grow well in California. There is a peculiar back story here, as these dawn redwoods were thought to be extinct.

A particularly famous dawn redwood is located in Cambria, a quaint town about ten miles south of Hearst Castle. It is across the street from the town's iconic windmill. This tree has a most interesting history that may help explain how it got to where it attracts daily visitors and how the dawn redwoods made it to the Pacific Coast.

According to a 2009 entry in the Cambria History Exchange, dawn redwoods were long thought to be extinct, represented only in fossil leaf and cone prints from Japan and Manchuria. In 1943, a Chinese forester named Chan Wang and his assistant collected specimens of living dawn redwoods near the village of Moudau in Szechauan Province in China. Since they believed the dawn redwood was extinct, they mistakenly identified the specimens as a Chinese Swamp Cypress.

In 1945, two other Chinese botanists, Chung-Lun Wu and Wan-Chun Cheng, obtained samples from Wang and realized that the samples were not from any known tree. The following year, Cheng notified Elmer Drew Merrill, director of the Arnold Arboretum at Harvard, of the discovery and then Hsen Hsu Hu, director of the Fan Memorial Institute of Biology in Beijing, matched the samples with the existing dawn redwood fossils. In December of 1946, *The Bulletin of the Geological Society of China* published Hu's paper describing the discovery but the new species still lacked a name.

In 1947, Cheng sent samples of the new species to Merrill at the Horticultural Herbarium at Harvard, and later in the year he sent seeds as well. The following year Hu sent seeds and other samples to Chaney at Berkeley, and that is how they got to California.

According to the late Millie Heath of Cambria, Chaney brought eight seedlings to UC Berkeley of which three were planted on the campus. She believed that one was given to the late Mrs. Florence Thatcher, a relative of Chaney's, who planted it near her home on Wall Street in Cambria, where it still stands today.

Today there are thousands of dawn redwoods growing in California.

When were redwoods officially designated the state tree?

California designated the redwood as the official state tree on April 3, 1937, when Senate Bill No. 112 was passed. It took effect on August 27, 1937. It is believed that the lawmakers of the time intended to include both the coast redwood and the giant sequoia; the bill did not name a particular species but simply referred to the native redwood. This led to much confusion as people asked what was considered the native redwood.

Government often moves slowly, and it wasn't until 1951 that the question got an official answer. California's attorney general ruled that both species qualified as the official state tree.

In an effort to clarify the law, the California Legislature amended it in 1953. After approval of California Senate Bill No. 1014, the amended law recognized them as official state trees.

Was the dawn redwood included in that designation?

When the bill was passed, the dawn redwood was thought to be extinct, so it was not included. The tree is very popular though and often found near other redwoods, so it has sort of been given "honorary" status by some people.

Is there an official state bird?

Yes, the California valley quail is the official bird of the Golden State. These birds are very common in just about all areas of the state and they are also a popular game bird.

When was the quail's selected?

The California State Legislature designated the state's official bird in 1931.

What is the California valley quail's social structure?

California valley quails are rarely alone. Coveys can number from a few up to 200 in the fall and winter months. In the spring their thoughts turn to love, and they break into pairs. At that point, the California valley quails will make a nest by scratching a shallow hole in the ground. They will line it with grass and cover their new homes with leaves

9

What is a fun fact about the California valley quail?

The California valley quail has had roles in several Walt Disney movies, including *Bambi*.

and brush to protect themselves. The females lay anywhere from six to twenty-eight eggs, while the male protects her. The eggs are white with golden-brown spots.

How about a state fish?

California has an official state fish. It is the golden trout. Designated the official state fish of California in 1947, many believe its golden color was the reason since it fit the state's theme. It is also believed that part of the reason it was selected was because golden trout is native to California and was not found anywhere else at the time. It was originally found only in a few icy streams of the headwaters of the Kern River in the Sierra Nevada Mountains. Since then, golden trout have been raised in fish hatcheries, and they are now an angler's favorite in many rivers in the high elevations of the Sierra Nevada range and also several other states.

The golden trout is a freshwater fish. When I took the glass-bottomed boat ride on Santa Catalina Island, the captain said there was an official state saltwater fish. Is that true?

That is sort of true. The Garibaldi (*Hypsypops rubicundus*) is the official state marine fish. It is a species of bright orange fish in the damselfish family. You will often notice them right away as you step off the boat to visit Catalina and other islands because of their bright orange color. They are also very common off the shores of La Jolla, a city near San Diego. Garibaldis love the subtropical northeastern part of the Pacific Ocean.

California designated the Garibaldi as the official state marine fish in 1995 and they are protected in Californian coastal waters, so no fishing for them.

In addition to being protected, they are very protective. As is the case in all damselfish, male Garibaldis aggressively defend the nest site after the female lays eggs.

Where is the Kern River?

The Kern River is a 165-mile- (265-kilometer-) long waterway that begins high in the southern Sierra Nevada Mountains, northeast of Bakersfield. Its mouth is in California's Central Valley, where it empties into Isabella Lake.

What is the official state animal?

The California grizzly bear became the official state animal in 1953.

How did the bear's designation come about?

Its designation was part of the flag story you read about earlier. Forty years after the flag was adopted, a state purchasing agent was assigned the task of buying new flags for state buildings. He went back as far as the original legislation from the early 1900s looking for exact specifications. He couldn't find any there or in any state records after that.

The clerk and others found different versions of the California state flag. Many were inconsistent, and some were downright silly looking. There were complaints that the animals depicted on the flags did not look anything like the bear. Some versions had the look of a wolf. Several others were said to look like a pig rather than a grizzly. Lawmakers determined it was time to make an exact set of specifications for consistency at all state facilities and businesses and homes where the flags were flying.

Grizzly bears are the official state mammal, even though they were hunted to extinction in California by the early 1900s.

Detailed specifications were placed in Assembly Bill 1014 in early 1953, and after quite a bit of discussion, it passed.

What does this have to do with the grizzly bear being the state animal?

After all of the discussion over the way that the state flag should look, lawmakers who had been very specific about the way the animal should be depicted on the flag decided to add an amendment to add the California grizzly bear (*Ursus californicus*) to the list of official state symbols.

So when Governor Earl Warren signed Assembly Bill No. 1014 on June 14, 1953 (which was Flag Day), there were not only specifications for the California state flag written into state law, but the California grizzly bear was made the official state animal of California at the same time.

Earlier, you learned that an amendment in that same bill also clarified the species of the California redwood.

The California grizzly bear was a large and very powerful animal that thrived in the valleys and the coastal slopes of California for centuries. They were first mentioned in the writings and diaries of Spanish settlers in the mid-1700s.

When settlers poured into California beginning with the discovery of gold in 1848, a love/hate relationship began with the bears and the humans.

The settlers found the bears to be ferocious animals. They would occasionally attack people, send settlers running away from them, and kill livestock. The people pouring into

How did the trapping of grizzly bears influence stock market terminology?

As settlers began to populate California and establish large cattle herds, the grizzly bears killed livestock and became enemies of the ranchers. The grizzlies were sometimes roped and captured, then displayed in public battles with bulls. This was a popular spectator sport, as people bet on whether the bear or the bull would win.

Folklore says Horace Greeley watched such a fight and paid attention to the fighting styles of the two animals. He noticed the bear swipes downward while the bull hooks upward. Legend has it he gave the modern stock market its "bear" and "bull" nicknames.

the state felt the bears were interfering with their new lives. Many of the settlers revered the grizzlies. They admired the bear's sheer power and strength along with its tenacity.

Can we sing the official state song?

If you want to sing the state song, it is "I Love You, California." Here are the lyrics, and yes, it has been used in jeep commercials, so you may already know the tune.

I Love You, California

I love you, California, you're the greatest state of all
I love you in the winter, summer, spring, and in the fall.
I love your fertile valleys; your dear mountains I adore,
I love your grand old ocean, and I love her rugged shore
I love your redwood forests—love your fields of yellow grain,
I love your summer breezes, and I love your winter rain,
I love you, land of flowers; land of honey, fruit and wine,
I love you, California; you have won this heart of mine.
I love your old gray Missions—love your vineyards stretching far,
I love you, California, with your Golden Gate ajar,
I love your purple sunsets, love your skies of azure blue,
I love you, California; I just can't help loving you.
I love you, Catalina—you are very dear to me,
I love you, Tamalpais, and I love Yosemite,
I love you, Land of Sunshine, half your beauties are untold,
I loved you in my childhood, and I'll love you when I'm old.
When the snow-crowned Golden Sierras
Keep their watch o'er the valleys bloom.
It is there I would be in our land by the sea,

Ev'ry breeze bearing rich perfume,
It is here nature gives of her rarest,
It is Home Sweet Home to me.
And I know when I die I shall breathe my last sigh
For my sunny California.

Who wrote "I Love You, California"?

The lyrics were written in the early 1900s by Francis B. Silverwood (1863–1924). Little is known about him except for the fact that he sold clothes in Los Angeles.

A. F. Frankenstein, the conductor of the Orpheum Theater Orchestra, set it to music, and the song was copyrighted in 1913. Opera star Mary Garden is believed to be the person who was the first to sing it in public, and "I Love You, California" was an instant success. In 1915, it became the official song of both the San Francisco and San Diego Expositions.

POPULATION

How many people live in California?

It is estimated that there are 38.8 million people in the Golden State as of 2015. The last precise count was for the 2010 Census, which resulted in a figure of 37,253,956 residents.

Is it the largest state by population?

Yes, according to estimated 2014 Census figures, California has 38,802,500 people. Number two is Texas, with almost twenty-seven million people.

What are the ten largest cities in California by population?

City	Population*
Los Angeles	3,884,307
San Diego	1,335,896
San Jose	998,537
San Francisco	837,442
Fresno	509,924
Sacramento	476,686
Long Beach	469,428
Oakland	406,253
Bakersfield	363,630
Anaheim	345,012

*Population as per 2010 U.S. Census.

What is the smallest city in California?

The smallest city (by area) is located about two hours from the Bay area, one of the largest metropolitan areas in the world. Amador City has the notable distinction of being California's tiniest city when measured by area. It is 0.31 square miles (0.50 square kilometers). You will find this quaint city 128 miles (206 kilometers) northeast of San Francisco and 42 miles (68 kilometers) southeast of Sacramento. It has a population of 183 people.

The smallest city by population is also Vernon, with a head count of just 112 people. You would think they live in the middle of nowhere, but surprisingly, you will find them 5 miles south of downtown Los Angeles. The city is primarily composed of industrial areas, warehouses, meat-packing plants, and factories. Most residents work for the city and rent their homes.

It is also a controversial city. As the *L.A. Times*'s history of the city of Vernon puts it, criminality has been baked into Vernon's DNA since the very beginning. It began when a Basque immigrant named John Baptiste Leonis incorporated a patch of sparsely populated farmland near the rail lines in the hopes of turning it into a mecca for manufacturing back around 1900. One account says the city lured business interest with low utility rates and sparse regulations, and Leonis promoted the town as a haven for boxing, gambling, and drinking. Vernon, in essence, became the exact type of place L.A. noir was made of—and Leonis ruled over it like a dictator. In fact, fictional cities in *True Detective* and other films and TV shows are based on this town.

Leonis died in 1953, and his grandson Leonis Malburg inherited both his fortune and his political influence; he was elected mayor in 1978 and didn't leave office for another three decades. Vernon had no competitive elections from 1980 to 2006. There is a story of a city employee who tried to run for mayor and was fired, then evicted from his city-owned house. Since he was no longer a resident, he could not be mayor. There is now a new mayor and city council.

What benchmark did California pass in 2014?

In July 2014, the number of Hispanics in the state (14.99 million) finally passed the number of white, non-Hispanic residents (14.92 million).

Is California very ethnically diverse?

Clearly, the largest segment of the population here is either Hispanic or non-Hispanic whites. About nine million people here are Asian, Native American, or some other ethnic or mix of ethnic groups.

EARLY CALIFORNIA: FIRST PEOPLES TO THE 1849 GOLD RUSH

When did people first arrive in California?

About fifteen thousand years ago, during the Pleistocene Epoch, sea levels were lower than they are today, and a land bridge existed between what is now Alaska and Siberia. Scientists speculate that people in Asia were able to cross this natural bridge and migrate into North (and eventually South) America. Archeological evidence shows that at least ten thousand years ago, there were people living in what is now California.

Who were the people who lived in early California?

Before the arrival of European settlers, there were many different Native American tribes living in the area, including:

Achuwami	Hupa	Mono	Wailaki
Atsugewi	Juaneno	Nomalki	Wappo
Cahto	Kamia	Paiute	Washoe
Cahuilla	Karuk	Patwin	Whilkut
Chemehuevi	Kawaiisu	Pomo	Wintun
Chilula	Kitanemuk	Salinan	Wiyot
Chimariko	Konkow	Serrano	Yahi
Chumash	Kumeyaay	Shasta	Yana
Costanoan (Ohlone)	Luiseno	Shoshone	Yokuts
Cupeno	Maidu	Tipai	Yuki
Diegueño	Mattole	Tolowa	Yuma
Esselen	Miwok	Tongva (Gabrieleño)	Yurok
Fernandeno	Mojave	Tubatulabal	

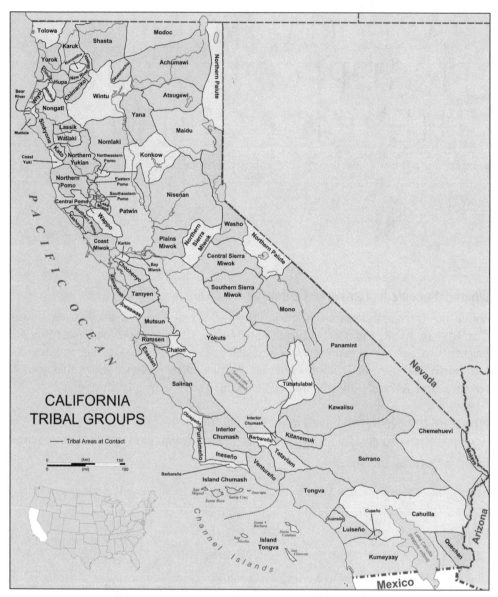

A map showing the various Indigenous tribes of California before the arrival of Europeans.

What was life like for these early peoples?

The land of California was rich in resources in much of the state. Early people lived a hunter/gatherer lifestyle. The foods they collected or hunted for included acorns, pine nuts, mesquite beans, salmon, and small game. There was also considerable trade between tribes, who would exchange food, pelts, and stones that they mined. Most people lived in tribelets of about fifty to a hundred people, but some villages did grow as large as about one thousand inhabitants. Tribes were led by a chief who also relied on the advice of a council, which typically consisted of the heads of important families within the tribe.

What is a petroglyph?

Petroglyphs are markings left on stone by early people. Petroglyphs could be made by chiseling, scratching, abrading, or pecking at the stone with a sharp object. In desert areas, a patina of reddish-brown minerals that form on the surface of rocks would be scratched away to reveal a much lighter color underneath. Early people also used paints made from mineral pigments combined with fat, egg whites, plant oils, or even urine. The kinds of drawings made ranged from geometric patterns to depictions of people and animals.

Where is the best place to go if I want to see petroglyphs?

Undoubtedly, that would be the Coso Rock Art District, a National Historic Site that many regard as the best place in all of North America to view petroglyphs. Located in Kern County near China Lake, there are over one hundred thousand examples of this art

Petroglyphs abound at Coso Rock Art District near China Lake. The art left behind by Indigenous tribes dates back to some three thousand years ago.

Were chiefs always male?

They usually were, but sometimes a woman would be a chief. The Pomo (of which there were actually seven different subgroups) were one tribe that often had women leaders, and the tribes actually would have between one and up to twenty chiefs at a time, with different chiefs having different responsibilities.

there dating back to between a thousand and three thousand years ago. The number-one subject seems to be bighorn sheep, but there are also depictions of people, other animals, anthropomorphic half-human-half-animal figures, and abstract designs. Because of the risk of vandalism, much of the district is restricted to academic researchers, but there is one canyon that is open to the public. The curious can arrange a tour through the Maturango Museum (www.maturango.org).

What sorts of raw materials did Native tribes use?

Obsidian rock was often mined because it was very easily sharpened into blades to make knives. They also mined soapstone, which could be carved into cooking implements. In the north and northeastern part of the state, Indians used a plant caled tule that grew in marshes to make mats and roofing. Basket weaving was a common craft and an art that is still practiced today by many of their descendants.

About how many Native Americans inhabited California before the Spanish arrived?

It is estimated that there were about three hundred thousand native people in the area who were spread all over the state in dozens of tribes. Between 1770 and 1850, the population was cut by half from a combination of measles, smallpox, and other diseases brought by the Europeans and against which the Indians had no natural resistance. The forced labor and poor living conditions in the missions also took a heavy toll. With the Gold Rush, white settlers killed thousands more as they tried to clear any resistance to taking land for mining. Poverty, hunger, and more disease resulted from the destruction of families and tribes, and by 1900 there were only an estimated sixteen thousand Native Americans left in the state.

FIRST EUROPEANS IN CALIFORNIA

Did Hernán Cortés explore as far as California?

Not quite. Cortés (1485–1547), who was a Spanish explorer who led the initial efforts of Spain to conquer and colonize the New World, went as far as Baja California but did not explore what is now the state of California. He ventured into the peninsula and the Gulf of California in 1536, which was originally called the Sea of Cortés in his honor.

Why does Baja California look like an island in early maps?

The Spanish explorers didn't venture past the peninsula for many years, and because it is such an unusually long peninsula they just assumed it was an island.

Who were the first Europeans to arrive in California?

Spanish explorers were the first Europeans to discover California's coastline. On September 28, 1542, Juan Rodríguez Cabrillo (1499–1543), leading an expedition of three ships, landed in what is now San Diego. Naming it San Miguel, he continued on to discover what is now Santa Catalina Island, San Clemente Island, San Pedro Bay, Santa Monica Bay, Santa Barbara, and Ventura, and went as far north as the San Francisco Bay area, though his party did not find the actual bay. They also didn't find what they had been sent from Spain to discover: the Strait of Anian. This was a water passage that many Europeans believed would be a route through North America. Of course, there is no such thing, which is why Cabrillo failed in his mission.

Returning to the Channel Islands in November, Cabrillo had a fall while on San Miguel Island during an attack by Tongva Indians and broke his arm. The injury became infected, and he died of gangrene.

Wasn't Juan Rodriguez Cabrillo actually Portuguese, not Spanish?

That is actually a matter of debate. In a history book by Spanish writer Antonio de Herrera y Tordesillas, Cabrillo (1549–1626) is described as coming from Portugal, and the Portuguese celebrate the explorer as one of their own. However, many historians who have researched Cabrillo have concluded he was born in Spain.

Did any English explorers reach California at this time?

The English didn't settle the area, but there were some forays along the coastline. The English and Spanish were at loggerheads with each other, competing for the rich resources of the New World. England was jealous of the gold and other wealth being shipped back to Spain from

The Cabrillo National Monument in San Diego honors the explorer who ventured here in 1542.

Who was the first English captain to arrive in San Francisco?

Captain George Vancouver (1757–1798), after whom the island and the city in British Columbia, Canada, were named, explored Alaska, Canada, and the northern Pacific coast during his 1791 to 1795 expedition. On November 14, 1792, he arrived in San Francisco (Yerba Buena), discovering that the mighty Spanish empire had established only very weak defenses at the presidio there. His later reports back home got the word out that Spain's claims to the Alta California territory was vulnerable.

its colonies, and one strategy employed by Queen Elizabeth I was to send ships to rob the Spanish. So it was that Sir Francis Drake (c. 1540–1596) was sent to serve as a pirate and marauder throughout Spanish territory in the New World. He first landed in what became known as Drake's Bay, north of present-day San Francisco, on June 17, 1579. Calling the area Nova Albion, he made contact with the Miwok tribe there.

If Cabrillo missed finding San Francisco Bay, who then discovered it?

That honor goes to Gaspar de Portolá (1716–1786), who located it on November 4, 1769, over two centuries after Cabrillo passed nearby.

Was it Portolá who also founded San Francisco, then?

No, it was actually Juan Bautista de Anza (1736–1788) who built a presidio there in 1776 and named it Yerba Buena after the aromatic plants found there in abundance. It was renamed San Francisco much later (see the "Northern California" chapter).

Which places in California were explored by the de Anza expedition?

Juan Bautista de Anza (1736–1788), with approval from the Viceroy of Spain, led an expedition out of Tucson, Arizona, in 1775 and headed to California. After reaching Mission San Gabriel de Arcángel and Monterey, he led a group up to present-day San Francisco and located the sites that would later be established as the city of San Jose

Explorer Juan Bautista de Anza explored both what is now Arizona and southern California back in 1775.

and Santa Clara. De Anza then went south and traveled to Mexico City in 1777. He was made governor of New Mexico from 1778 to 1788.

Who were some other important Spanish explorers of California?

A number of other explorers should be noted here, including:

- Pedro de Unamumo (b. 1548) explored the coast of Alta California in 1587, discovering Morro Bay.
- Sebastian Rodriguez Cermeno (1560–1602), who was actually Portuguese by birth (Sebastião Rodrigues Soromenho in his native tongue), sailed all the way up to present-day Eureka.
- Sebastian Vizcaino (1548–1627), who would also go on voyages to the Philippines and Japan, explored the coastline of Alta California, helping to produce more accurate maps from San Diego to Monterey.

SPANISH MISSION PERIOD

What was the Spanish strategy for colonizing California?

King Carlos III (1716–1788) of Spain ordered that settlers establish three types of settlements: pueblos (towns for farmers, craftspeople, etc.), presidios (forts for a military presence), and missions to establish a Catholic presence that would serve to educate and provide to the spiritual needs of the people. The missions also strove to convert local native peoples to Catholicism and teach them to farm and work as Europeans. The original plan was for the missions to do this work for ten years and then be converted into pueblos, but this is not what happened. They ended up operating for much longer as missions.

Who were the first Spanish explorers in California?

The first Spaniards to reach what is now California arrived on the ship *San Antonio*, captained by Juan Pérez (1725–1775), who also has the distinction of being the first European explorer to discover the islands off British Columbia. The ship landed near present-day San Diego on April 29, 1769.

What was the "Sacred Expedition"?

Not long after Pérez's arrival, a party led by California governor Gaspar de Portolá and Father Junípero Serra (1713–1784), the "Sacred Expedition," as it is sometimes called, arrived on June 29, 1769. The goals of the expedition were to establish missions, convert the native populations to Catholicism, and establish revenue streams for the Spanish monarchy. Splitting into three groups, the explorers went by land and sea. Of the three hundred men that hazarded the trip, half perished. Nevertheless, many of their goals were made, including the founding of missions in San Diego and Monterey.

Why was Father Junípero Serra so important to early California history?

Born in Majorca, Spain, Junípero Serra (1713–1784) was a Catholic priest responsible for founding and running many of the missions under Spanish rule. He joined the Church as a young man, quickly rose to become a university teacher at the age of twenty-four, and transferred to Mexico in 1749. He then managed to be assigned to the Portolá expedition and was named president of the missions to be built in Alta California. Serra is credited with establishing the first nine of the twenty-one missions and establishing the protocols for converting and training the native populations.

A statue of Fra Junípero Serra stands at Mission San Diego de Alcalá.

By today's standards, the treatment of the Indians by the missionaries is considered slavery and cultural genocide. The Native Americans were not allowed to practice their spiritual faiths, they were taught Spanish, and many of the languages that were spoken became extinct. Serra was responsible for much of this, and although historians don't feel he mistreated the Indians with deliberate malice, he is often reviled by many Indians and non-Indians alike. Despite this, Pope Francis I made Serra a saint in 2015. It is perhaps no coincidence that the Church's first Franciscan pope would grant sainthood to a fellow Franciscan.

Who took over the job from Serra after his death in 1784?

Father Fermín Francisco de Lasuén (1736–1803) headed the missionary effort for eighteen years, founding nine more missions before he passed away.

What was "Las Californias"?

Spain established the province of Las Californias ("The Californias") in 1768. The province included all the territory from Baja California to the land around San Francisco Bay and from the Pacific Ocean to roughly the eastern borders of Arizona and Utah today.

What is "Alta California"?

In 1804, Las Californias was divided into Alta California (Upper California) and Baja California (Lower California), the latter being primarily the Baja Peninsula. The capital of Alta California was Monterey.

What was New Spain?

New Spain included all the colonized Spanish lands in the New World, including what is now California, but also Mexico, Florida, Central America, much of the American heartland, Cuba, and parts of northern South America.

What is a *Californio*?

A *Californio* was any Roman Catholic person who was descended from the early Spanish settlers in the region.

What is a *Criollo*?

A *Criollo* is any person of Spanish descent born in New Spain.

The territory of Alta California is shaded dark on this map showing Mexico after independence from Spain. The region is roughly the same as it was during Spain's rule.

How was José de Gálvez y Gallardo instrumental in the mission plan?

José de Gálvez (1720–1787), as he is commonly called, was a member of an influential royal family in Spain and attorney who, in 1765, was made inspector general of New Spain. As such, he was the most powerful European in New Spain. Part of this power included being charged with establishing missions in California. After King Carlos III removed the Jesuits from power in Spain as a result of a political and spiritual conflict of the time, the Franciscan order took the Jesuits' place. This is why Father Junipero Serra, a Franciscan, was chosen to take go with Portolá and establish the missions in Alta California, following a plan established by Gálvez, who also instructed the Dominican Order to take over the Baja missions.

What was the first Spanish mission founded in California?

The first mission was founded in what is now San Diego by Father Junípero Serra (1713–1784) in 1769 and was called San Diego de Alcalá.

How many missions were established by the Spanish in California?

All together, there were twenty-one missions, as shown below.

California Missions

Mission	Location	Year Established
Basilica San Diego de Alcalá	San Diego	1769
San Carlos Borroméo de Carmelo	Carmel	1770
San Antonio de Padua	Jolon	1771
San Gabriel Arcángel	San Gabriel	1771

Mission	Location	Year Established
San Luis Obispo de Tolosa	San Luis Obispo	1772
San Francisco de Asís	San Francisco	1776
San Juan Capistrano	San Juan Capistrano	1776
Santa Clara de Asís	Santa Clara	1777
San Buenaventura	Ventura	1782
Santa Barbara, Virgin y Martir	Santa Barbara	1786
La Purisima Concepción	Near Lompoc	1787
Santa Cruz	Santa Cruz	1791
Nuestra Señora de Soldedad	Soledad	1791
San José	San Jose	1797
San Juan Bautista	San Juan Bautista	1797
San Miguel Arcángel	San Miguel	1797
San Fernando, Rey de España	San Fernando	1797
San Luis, Rey de Francia	Oceanside	1798
Santa Inés, Virgin y Martir	Solvang	1804
San Rafael Arcángel	San Rafael	1817
San Francisco de Solano	Sonoma	1823

How did travelers and supplies get to all these missions?

The missions were connected by a road known as El Camino Real ("The King's Highway," sometimes called the "California Missions Trail" today). It ran the 600 miles (965 kilometers) from San Diego to San Francisco. The route was well chosen, and since the missions eventually served as the seeds of future towns and cities, El Camino Real still exists as the modern California State Routes 1 and 82, U.S. Route 101, and San Diego County Route S11.

What was the first mission and church constructed in California?

San Diego de Alcala was founded on July 16, 1769, at a site selected by Franciscan missionary Father Junípero Serra. However, it was soon determined that there wasn't enough water for reliable irrigation, so the mission and church were moved six miles to the San Diego River shoreline.

What early city became the first capital of Spanish California?

Monterey was named after the Spanish Count of Monte Rey by explorer Don Sebastian Viscaino, who sailed there in 1602. It wasn't until 1770, however, that a settlement was actually established there, when Father Junipero Serra and Gaspar de Portolá arrived. They established a city, mission, and presidio by the bay. Spain declared Monterey the capital of both Alta and Baja California in 1776.

When was Mission San Juan Capistrano founded?

Some believe that Father Junípero Serra founded San Juan Capistrano, but it was actually Fermín Lasuén (1736–1803). The confusion comes from the fact that Lasuén's

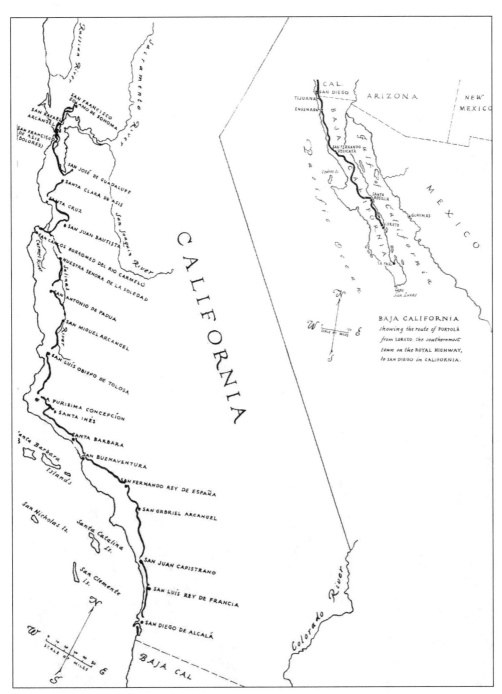

The first major road in Alta California was El Camino Real, which connected the missions from the Bay Area all the way down Baja California.

initial effort in 1775 failed when the mission was attacked by Indians. Serra arrived the next year and began the work again. Disaster struck again in 1812, when an earthquake leveled the church, killing forty Indians who were attending mass. Fate improved after that, and the little Serra Chapel there is still in use.

What is an *asistencia*?

An *asistencia* is an outpost near a mission—sort of like a satellite mission. Some asistencias would later grow large enough to become missions themselves. Such was the case for San Rafael Arcángel, for example.

What is a *campanaria*?

A room with openings around it that housed the mission's bells was known as a campanaria. The bells were rung to summon people to mass and prayer.

Did the Native American people accept Spanish ways?

Some did, but others rebelled against being converted to Catholicism and being made to behave like Europeans. Although conditions at the missions varied somewhat, for the most part the Indians were treated like slaves. They were forced to work for no pay, and everything in their lives was controlled by the mission friars.

Mission San Juan Capistrano no longer attracts the swallows as it once did, but it is still a fascinating piece of history to explore.

Why do the swallows return each year to Capistrano?

For about two centuries, the ruins of the old church at San Juan Capistrano served as a summer home for cliff swallows that wintered in Argentina and then flew north to make their mud nests in the remaining arches of the old church. They arrived around the time of St. Joseph's Day (March 19), and the regularity of the event inspired a festival in the town.

Sadly, in recent years, the swallows have not been returning, at least not in very large numbers. Two factors caused this: More urbanization in the area has lured the birds to other buildings to construct their nests when it used to be just the mission that made an appealing residence, and recent renovation on the mission destroyed the old mud nests, which the swallows would have used as the base for new nests.

Naturally, this change has disappointed Capistrano citizens, who also enjoyed better business from tourists. To bring the swallows back, Dr. Charles Brown, a biology professor from the University of Tulsa, has initiated a vocalization project to lure the birds back with swallow songs. It is still a work in progress as of early 2016.

Native people were either forced to go to the missions, or sometimes they were coerced. It was not unheard of for a friar to baptize an Indian child, take the boy or girl to the mission, and then refuse to allow the parents to see them unless they, too, converted to Catholicism. The spiritual practices of the Indians, such as sacred dances and songs, were also suppressed. Threats of violence for lack of cooperation were used, and sometimes violent acts carried out. Such treatment was rationalized by saying that the Indians were barbarians who needed to be "civilized." Poor nutrition and hygiene at the missions made the Indians sick, and because of this poor treatment, each year about ten percent of the Indians at the missions tried to escape. Those who were captured were placed in the stocks and/or whipped.

The Native Americans sometimes followed the friars willingly, believing they were spiritual people showing them a new way of life, but there were also revolts and considerable resistance. The Tipais decimated San Diego Arcángel shortly after it was built, and Father Andrés Quintana was murdered by Indian neophytes in Santa Cruz in 1812. Several other friars were poisoned, and in 1824 the Chumash led one of the most damaging attacks against Santa Inés and La Purísima Concepción.

Were any of the Spanish on the side of the Native Americans?

Yes, some of the Californio leaders tried to defend the rights of the Indians. Among them were Father Miguel Hidalgo y Costilla (1753–1811) and, some time later, General Mariano Guadalupe Vallejo (1807–1890). Costilla felt that the Spanish were treating the Indians like slaves, and so he built an estate where he trained them in skills such as pottery, carpen-

Why did missions use terra cotta tiles for their roofing?

The Spanish tile roofs that are so familiar now on many buildings in the American Southwest were actually not the first material used on mission roofs. The Spanish originally placed simple thatch roofs on their missions, but these quickly burst into flames when Indians shot at them with flaming arrows. They also switched from wooden structures to adobe covered in stucco, not only because these didn't burn but because adobe keeps rooms cool in summer and warm in winter.

try, and tanning. Vallejo also sought to improve the lives of Native Americans, and one way he thought he would do this would be to help Mexico become independent of Spain.

How were the missions and pueblos protected?

There were four presidios (small military forts located in San Diego, Monterey, Santa Barbara, and San Francisco) built in California to protect the missions and towns from possible attacks from Native Americans, mostly. They were all fairly small military outposts and were not sufficient to withstand any large military attack from an invading force, such as would later happen with the invasion by the United States. The presidios were supplied with food and equipment from the local pueblos and missions and were not self-sustaining in themselves.

What are some nicknames given to missions over the years?

Some nicknames have been lost over the years, but others are still known to historians. Among these are the following:

Nickname	Real Name	Reason for Nickname
King of the Missions	San Luis Rey de Francia	So named because of its beautiful construction
Queen of the Missions	Santa Bárbara	King of the Missions was taken, and so this other beautiful mission was named the queen
San Diego de Alclá California Missions	Mother of the Alta	So named because it was the first mission in the region
San Gabriel Arcángel	Pride of the Missions	Played a central role in the growth and development of Los Angeles
San Carlos Borromeo de Carmelo	Father of the Missions	Because it served as the central headquarters for all of the missions in Alta California
San Juan Capistrano	Jewel of the Missions	Considered a crown jewel of the missions; also called the Mission of the Swallow because of the birds that annually nested there

Nickname	Real Name	Reason for Nickname
San Buenaventura	Mission by the Sea	Because of the location
San Miguel Arcángel	Mission on the Highway	It is right next to El Camino Real
San Fernando Rey de España	Mission of the Valley	Because it's in the San Fernando Valley
San Antonio de Padua	Mission of the Sierras	A strange name because this mission is nowhere near the Sierra Nevada Mountains
San Luis Obispo de Tolosa	Mission in the Valley of the Bears	Bear meat hunted in the local Los Osos area helped feed the people in the mission
San Francisco de Asís	Mission Dolores	Because it's by Dolores Creek
San Juan Bautista	Mission of Music	The mission was known for producing original music by the residents there

Who started insisting on finally converting the missions to pueblos?

After Alta California became part of Mexico with the country's independence from Spain in 1821, people started calling for the secularization of the missions, which had dominated the landscape for sixty years. Californios felt that the missions were unconstitutional because the Mexican constitution called for equality among all races, yet the missions violated these rights when it came to the Indians.

Two governors were involved in proposing pushing for this transition. In 1826 Governor José Echeandía (?–1871) proposed that the Indians be freed from the missions, but not many took him up on the offer. By this time, Native Americans had grown fearful of living outside the mission walls and being subjected to prejudice, discrimination, and violence at the hands of the Californios. Governor José Figueroa (1792–1835) intended to readdress his predecessor's plan and carry and secularize all twenty-one missions on August 4, 1834. Figueroa felt that the missions had fulfilled their purpose of converting and training the Indians of the region to live and work in the European manner, and he formulated a plan to turn the missions over to Indian ownership. His government even offered the Indians free tools and seeds to begin farming. This would be done in three stages: ten missions would be turned over in 1834, six more the next year, and the last five in 1836. Half the mission property would be given to the Indians; the Catholic Church would keep the churches and friars' quarters; everything else would be taken over and administered by the government.

But when the governor died before the full plan could be carried out, the missions were instead taken over by the government. The farmlands, livestock, and valuable property in the missions wound up in the hands of wealthy Spaniards. The Indians were left without land and forced to take low-paying jobs for the Spanish landowners.

Why did the missions fall into decline?

When California converted from Spanish to Mexican rule, many of the missions, which had been secularized and served no real purpose anymore, lost financial support from surrounding towns and fell into disrepair. By 1845, most of them had shut their doors. After California became a possession of the United States, things changed, and in 1863 the U.S. government returned all of the missions to the Catholic Church for them to run. Even so, the priests were given little money to maintain the buildings, and the adobe began to crumble.

Americans became interested in restoring the missions again by the late 1880s (see below), and today they have all been revived (the last restoration project was San José, which was completed in 1985). About two thirds of them are owned by the Church, while San Francisco de Solano and La Pursimima de Concepción are now run by the California State Parks system.

Who wrote a novel that helped bring restoration dollars to the crumbling missions?

Author Helen Hunt Jackson (1830–1885) published her novel *Ramona* in 1884. The story is about a half-Native American girl who lives near a mission after the Mexican–American War. She is mistreated by the U.S. government, and prejudice results in people trying to keep her away from the man she loves. *Ramona* was a bestseller; it inspired play and movie adaptations and the Ramona Pageant that is held in Hemet each year. Many people credit the book with causing a renewed interest in Spanish missions, which helped them raise money for restoration efforts. It also sparked the Spanish Mission architectural style in California, characterized by stucco walls and tile roofs, that remains very popular in the Golden State.

Was Alta California ever harassed by pirates?

Usually, when we think about pirates our minds turn to the Caribbean, but the coast of California was harassed by pirates, too, if only briefly. These pirates came from Argentina (which gained independence from Spain in 1816) on November 20, 1818, in a ship captained by Hipólito (Hyppolyte) Bouchard (1780–1837). Bouchard was a native of France who had become an Argentine citizen; to Argentinians, Bouchard was a hero, but to the Spanish in Monterey, he was regarded as a pirate. Bouchard captured Monterey using only two ships (the *Argentina* and the *Santa Rosa*) and held it for six days in the name of Argentina. Ransacking the presidio and chasing the governor out, they looted the town, then left to attack a ranch in Santa Barbara and Mission San Juan Capistrano. After that, they departed and never returned, ending a brief and violent chapter of California history.

Are there still missions in California today?

Oh, yes. Many of the old missions have been restored and are now very popular with visitors. In fact, they earn more tourist dollars than any California tourist attraction, with the exception of Disneyland/California Adventure.

THE RUSSIAN PRESENCE

Why did Russians start to settle North America as far south as California?

Mostly it was the fur trade that attracted Russians to the area, including the fine, waterproof pelts of sea otters. They also hunted seals for their meat and hides. By the mid-eighteenth century, there was a growing Russian presence at outposts such as Fort Ross and Bodego Bay.

What was the importance of the Russian-American Company (RAC)?

The Russian-American Company was a state-sponsored chartered company created in 1799 for the purpose of helping to colonize the Russian claims to North America from Alaska down to northern California. While Russian colonization efforts had begun as early as 1732, the RAC brought a much more structured and enterprising approach to establishing ports, towns, and fortresses. Interestingly, it was also Russia's first foray into a joint-stock company and was run by businessmen rather than Russian royalty. Unfortunately, that was a short-lived business model, and the royalty took the RAC over in 1820. The almost immediate effect was a loss of profitability. Plagued by inefficiencies, the RAC withdrew from California by the 1940s, as well as Alaska, when that state was purchased by the United States in 1867. The RAC shut its doors in 1881.

How far south was the reach of the Russian Empire?

The Russians had settlements down as far as Sonoma County just north of San Francisco by the early 1800s. Here they established Fort Ross and Port Rumyantsev, which was on

---

Was the Russian River discovered by the Russians?

No. Of course, it was known for centuries to the Native people who lived north of what is now San Francisco. The Southern Pomo tribe called it the Ashowkana ("water to the east"). Later, with the arrival of Spanish explorers, Juan Rodríguez Cabrillo (1499–1543) named it the Bidapte ("big river") back in 1542. The Russians came much later when, in the early 1800s, the commerce counselor of the Russian-American Company, Ivan Kuskov (1765–1832), called it the Slavyanka River. Once under American government, it became the Russian River, acknowledging that part of its history.

present-day Bodega Bay (Rumyantsev Bay back in those days), as well as an outpost for seal hunters on the Farallon Islands. The Russians, however, also ventured into Baja California and even tried to conquer Hawaii when German physician and Russian-American Company employee George Anton Schäffer waged a private war there between 1815 and 1817 (the Hawaiians, with American backup, defeated the RAC).

When was Fort Ross established, and how long did the Russians man it?

Fort Ross (originally called Fortress Ross) was the southernmost military and supply post. It was established in 1812 and was meant to be a center of agriculture to help supply surrounding settlements, as well as the colonies as far north as Alaska. The Russians, though, found maintaining the fort more costly than the benefits that came from it. Part of the problem was that Spanish and American hunters had depleted the otter and other fur-bearing wildlife in the region, leaving little for the Russians. And when the RAC made a deal with Britain's Hudson Bay Company in Vancouver in 1839 to help with supplies in Alaska, the need for Fort Ross diminished.

Nevertheless, the settlement remained for a few decades. A diverse group of Russians, Estonians, Ukrainians, Poles, Finns, and Natives lived there. Fort Ross was notable as the first European settlement to build ships (the Spanish just sailed them in), to use windmills, and to actually vaccinate Natives in an attempt to prevent them from becoming sick from smallpox and other diseases brought in from Europe.

John Sutter (see the Gold Rush discussions below) purchased Fort Ross from the Russians in 1841. He took the livestock, tools, and other supplies and also dismantled a lot of the buildings, using these materials for Fort Sutter back in the Sacramento Valley. From 1873 to 1903, it was owned by the George W. Call family, which operated it as a ranch before selling it to the state of California.

Can I still visit Fort Ross?

Certainly. After the California Historical Landmarks Committee bought it in 1903, it turned it over to the state in 1906, and it is now a National Historic Landmark, a California Historic Landmark, and on the National Register of Historic Places. There is a parking fee, but the grounds are free and you can take in the historic sights, as well as beautiful vistas of the Pacific Ocean. Go to http://www.fortross.org/info .htm for more information about the park.

The chapel at Fort Ross has been reconstructed to appear as it did when the Russians were manning the fort.

RULE UNDER MEXICO: 1821–1846

How did the Mexican War of Independence start?

Tensions among differing groups of people in Mexico had existed for centuries. The problem was that a kind of caste system developed in which certain people were treated better than others. At the top of the system were Spaniards born in Europe. Next came criollos, who were of Spanish blood but born in Mexico; then came mestizos, who were half Spanish and half Indian; at the bottom were pure-blood Indians. Resentment toward the European-born Spaniards grew, and fervor for independence came during the Napoleonic occupation of Spain (1808–1813).

It was a Catholic priest named Miguel Hidalgo y Castilla (1753–1811) who started the war for independence. He had been a professor at the Colegio de San Nicolás Obispo in Valladolid and then a priest in Colima and then Dolores, Mexico. Hidalgo y Castilla was upset that the people he saw in these towns were impoverished, and a big reason why is they weren't allowed to grow any crops that the Spanish were making profits off of by importing them to Mexico. On September 16, 1810, he made a public speech called the "Grito de Dolores" ("Cry of Dolores") in which he asked his fellow Mexicans to take up arms against the Spanish. He had the support of the Indians, mestizos, and criollos, who flocked at his side, and the revolution began.

The next year, Hidalgo y Castilla was captured and executed, but the struggle for independence continued until 1821, when the Treaty of Córdoba was signed and Mexico became a constitutional monarchy. Just a year and a half later, another rebellion occurred, and Emperor Agustín de Iturbide was overthrown to establish the first Mexican Republic.

How did the change in government from Spain to Mexico affect Alta California?

It was good news in a number of ways. First of all, the Mexican government was much more willing to sell land to ranch and other owners, while the Spanish had hoarded property rights for the royalty alone. This also included foreigners who were naturalized as Mexican citizens; they could own land, too, as long as they converted to Catholicism. A boost to the economy, too, was that Mexicans were allowed to trade with foreign nations, not just Spain. Also, the movement to secularize the missions was pushed forward (see "Spanish Mission Period" above), although it still took many years before this was accomplished. However, there was a definite shift of the centers of business from missions to the ranchos. Trade in furs increased, and the ranchos, which mostly produced just beef and hides, became more dependent on imports of foreign goods. This all, in turn, encouraged the encroachment of non-Mexicans into California, which would have an important impact in just a few decades.

What is a *rancho*?

A *rancho* is, unsurprisingly, a ranch. A ranchero is a rancher. Many cities in Alta California today have "Rancho" in their name, such as Rancho Mirage, Rancho Cucamonga, Rancho Cordova, Rancho Santa Margarita, and so on.

What is a *vaquero*?

A *vaquero* is a Spanish cowboy. *Vaqueros* herded cattle and did other work on the ranchos in New Spain. The Spanish settlers became frustrated with the fact that the missions weren't being secularized because they wanted the mission land for grazing and other ranch uses like farming; the missions held some of the best, most fertile lands, and the government was not granting much land for ranches.

Who was the first to govern Mexican Alta California?

News and transitions occurred slowly in the nineteenth century, compared to now. When Mexico won its independence, most of Alta California didn't know until the following year. Likewise, the change in government was slow to proceed. Pablo Vicente de Solá (1761–1826), who was the last to govern under Spanish rule, remained head of the local government until Luis Antonio Argüello (1784–1830) took over in 1822.

Argüello has the destinction of being the only governor of Alta California to serve the short-lived First Mexican Empire.

Who was Jedediah Smith?

Jedediah Smith was a frontiersman, trapper, and author who is credited with finding the South Pass through the Rocky Mountains that would be used for wagons on the Oregon Trail. He explored much of the American West, including Alta California, which he first explored in 1826, when it was under Mexican rule. He made a second excursion into California the next year, bringing several people with him and indulging in some trapping. At this time, he also became the first American to travel up the California coast to eventually reach Oregon. Smith thus blazed the first trail for Americans into the state via a land route, and many more would follow him in the years to come. By the 1840s about two thousand Americans had come to California to live, even though it was still under Mexican rule.

What was "New Helvetia"?

This was the settlement founded and developed by Johann August "John" Sutter (1803–1880), who obtained a land grant of forty-eight thousand acres (from the Mexican gov-

How did the cattle industry relate to the "California banknote"?

Beef ranches were one of California's biggest economic resources in the early 1800s. Cattle were raised for beef and milk, of course, but also for the production of tallow. When all this was used, there was always a surplus of hides, which were then shipped to the East, where they were used as leather in shoes and other goods. Locally, especially from the 1820s to the 1840s, they were used as a medium of financial exchange. Hence, a cow hide became known as a "California banknote."

ernment) in 1839. It was located where the Sacramento and American rivers met, and here Sutter constructed a fort and planted vineyards and orchards. The fort became a place where weary travelers from the East stopped before traveling to San Francisco or points north. One of these groups was the survivors of the infamous Donner Party, who reached Sutter's Fort in 1847 after losing almost half the original party of eighty-seven men, women, and children in the snow-covered Sierras.

Were Americans coming to California in great numbers in the first half of the nineteenth century?

Even though the area was under Mexican control, Americans were coming to California via what was known as the California Trail. This route—much like the Oregon Trail—was first blazed by mountain men and fur traders who crossed the Rocky Mountains toward the West Coast, beginning around the early 1810s, and entered the northern part of the future state. Before the Gold Rush (see the next chapter), fewer than three thousand American settlers traveled this route. Afterward, of course, that number skyrocketed to over 250,000 from 1848 to 1869.

Who was James Beckwourth?

Beckwourth (1798–1864) was one of the more notable mountain men of his day. He discovered what is now called the Beckwourth Pass through the Sierra Nevadas, guiding settlers and gold prospectors through the mountains to California.

Why did Mexico have trouble governing Alta California?

Part of the explanation is the same reason why the Spanish had had trouble: California was remote from the center of government. The other reason, however, is rather ironic: The new Mexican government had introduced reforms and was less dictatorial than Spain had been, but it still had a militaristic approach. Towns and cities basically governed themselves, but the laws they passed or other decisions they made could be overruled by the military. For example, if the city of Los Angeles passed a law approved by the mayor and council, the military commander at the Santa Barbara presidio could overrule it. Californians were beginning to bristle under such rule, having gained a sense of self-governance.

Did the Californians actively rebel against the Mexican government?

Yes. Only ten years after independence from Spain, the Californians got royally ticked off at their Mexican governor, Manuel Victoria (d. 1833). Victoria tried to reverse gains that had been made the previous decade, halting the secularization of the missions, refusing to call the legislature to session, stopping land grants to ranchers, jailing about a hundred people who opposed him, and exiling some others.

Pio de Jesús Pico (1801–1894), or Pico Pio for short, was a wealthy owner of Rancho Paso de Bartolo (in present-day Whittier), along with two other rancheros (Juan Bandini and Juan Antonio Carillo). They pulled together a force of 150 men from Los

Angeles and the San Diego presidio to release political prisoners from Los Angeles. They met a smaller force of thirty men, led by Victoria himself, at Cahuenga Pass.

In what would become known as the First Battle of Cahuenga Pass (1831), the fight was short but rather dramatic. Victoria ordered his men to shoot a warning shot above the heads of the rebels. One of his men, Captain Jose Antonio Romualdo Pacheco, misinterpreted the fire as a call to a charge. He drove his horse forward, alone, and when he realized his mistake, he stopped. He was met on horseback by rebel Jose Maria Avila. Interestingly, the two battled using lances in a kind of flashback to the days of knights. Pacheco knocked Avila's lance out of his hand, and the angered Avila drew his pistol and shot Pacheco to death (in what was considered a very unchivalrous move). Victoria, see-

Pio Pico was a wealthy rancher who led Californians in a rebellion against the new Mexican government in 1831.

ing this, shot and killed Avila, then Captain Portilla of the rebels skewered Victoria's face on his lance. Severely wounded but alive, Victoria withdrew.

The governor resigned his office, passing away two years later while in exile. Pico took his place but only stayed in office for twenty days before resigning to the next governor because Los Angeles officials refused to recognize him in the office.

Why did Alta California have two governors after the Battle of Cahuenga Pass?

After Pio de Jesús Pico resigned, there was confusion and division in Alta California. Augustín Zamorano (1798–1842), who had served as secretary of state to Victoria's predecessor, José María de Echeandía (d. 1871), led a rebellion in the north and made himself governor there, establishing the capital in Monterey. In the south, Echeandía resumed office as governor based in Los Angeles. This division ended when the Mexican government sent General José Figueroa to take over the governorship in 1833 (see more on Figueroa above).

Was Alta California an actual sovereign nation at one point?

Indeed, tensions and strife continued in the state. After Figueroa died in 1835, there was a rapid succession of governors, all of whom were generally disliked. This led to yet another uprising in 1836 that was headed by Juan Bautista Valentín Alvarado y Vallejo (1809–1882) with the assistance of José Castro (1808–1860), who had been an acting governor after Figueroa's death, and American and European immigrants. They

> ## Besides being temporary governor of the northern half of Alta California, for what other accomplishment is Augustín Zamorano noted?
>
> **Z**amorano brought the first printing press to the state. It was used to not only print official documents but also for books and the first newspaper in the region, *The Monterey Californian*.

ousted then-governor Nicolás Guitiérrez and installed Alvarado as head of a new sovereign state. Back in San Diego, however, people had other things in mind than bowing to Monterey. They selected Carlos Antonio Carillo (1783–1852), who had actually been on Alvarado's side during the 1836 rebellion, to be governor. Carillo governed from San Diego until 1838. After another rebellion, Carillo was out and Alvarado was back in. Alvarado proposed a confederation arrangement with Mexico, and Alta California gained considerable authority to determine its own affairs—essentially, it was a sovereign state separate from the weak government of Mexico until 1846. Alvarado would remain governor of Alta California from 1837 to 1842.

Why was there such division between northern and southern California?

The northern part of the state, which included San Francisco and the capital at Monterey, had long been considered more important than the south, but as Los Angeles and San Diego began to grow, those cities felt they deserved more political say over Alta California, and a rivalry based on jealousy developed. It's interesting that, even to this day, there is a sense of "us versus them" between the north and south parts of the state.

Why did the U.S. fleet dock in Monterey and demand the governor surrender?

It wasn't just tension between Alta California and Mexico City that was a problem but also growing fears about possible U.S. plans on the region. The United States had been quite vocal in its vision of "Manifest Destiny," the idea that it was pretty much God's design that the Americans should have a country that stretched from the Atlantic to the Pacific, which clearly meant they had their sights on California.

Citizens in Alta California had come to the conclusion that Mexico was not going to give them the military, or even economic, support they needed to fend off any foreign invasion. There was even talk in Monterey, San Francisco, and Los Angeles as to which other country might be best to join: England, France, or the United States.

In October 1842, U.S. Commodore Thomas ap Catesby Jones (1790–1858), who had previously distinguished himself for heroism in the War of 1812, received notice from the U.S. consul in Mazatlán, Mexico, that Mexico was preparing for war with the United States; rumors also were flying about that Alta California had signed a treaty turning the

What was "The Graham Affair"?

Governor Alvarado had Isaac Graham (1800–1863), a former mountain man from Tennessee who had become a landowner in California and had aided Alvarado in 1836, was arrested in 1840 on suspicion of fomenting rebellion again. About a hundred of Graham's followers were arrested as well. A trial ensued, and this became a diplomatic crisis involving Mexico, the United States, and the United Kingdom (citizens of all three nations were involved in the trial). The trial ended well for Graham, who was acquitted and released.

state over to England. According to the Monroe Doctrine (1823), any European interference of this kind in the Americas was to be regarded as an act of war, and so Jones, who commanded the U.S. Pacific Fleet at the time, landed in Monterey. He met with Alvarado and demanded he surrender. Alvarado, however, had already been replaced by Manuel Micheltorena (1802–1853) and informed Jones he lacked the authority to act on behalf of Mexico. Jones was convinced of his error and withdrew to Los Angeles, where he apologized to Governor Micheltorena. Micheltorena issued a list of demands to Jones (including $15,000 in cash and, bizarrely, a request that the United States provide fifteen hundred uniforms and musical instruments for the military), all of which the commodore rejected, stating he lacked authority to sign any agreements. For his error, Jones lost command of the fleet but was allowed to remain in the navy.

Was Governor Micheltorena also unpopular with Californians?

Not surprisingly, yes, he was unpopular. Manuel Micheltorena (1802–1853), a former general of the Mexican Army, took office as governor of the state in 1842, and it wasn't long before he began to anger the residents again by favoring his friends back in Mexico City when he awarded land grants. It was also well known that the troops backing him up were former convicts sent by the Mexican government, which didn't sit well with the state's citizens.

By 1844 rebellion was once again in the air, and Californian citizens started to take up arms against their governor. In November of that year, violence broke out near Santa Clara. Micheltorena enlisted the help of John Sutter, interestingly enough, as well as some other Americans, and there was a confrontation near Santa Clara. The governor agreed to dismiss his convict troops, who had been causing trouble with the citizens, but he reneged on the deal and fled south.

What transpired at the Battle of Providencia?

Sometimes called the Second Battle of Cahuenga Pass because it occurred at roughly the same spot as the 1936 battle, the conflict on February 20, 1845, at Rancho Providencia between Micheltorena's men and the rebels was brief. The only casualty was one equine (a horse or a donkey, depending on which account one reads), but it was enough to cause the governor to resign. Pio de Jesús Pico took back the seat as governor, though it was more complicated than that (see below).

Who was California's last governor under Mexico?

Pio Pico would have that dubious honor. During his time in office, he moved the capital from Monterey to Los Angeles and tried to convince people that California should become a British protectorate. Pico really only ruled southern California south of San Luis Obispo. North of that, the man in charge was Commandante General José Castro, the same Castro who had been a governor after Figueroa's death. It was clear that this idea of a sovereign California was not holding up well, and it would soon fall into other hands.

Who was John C. Frémont?

Before he was a major general for the Union army during the U.S. Civil War and then a California senator and Republican candidate for president in 1856 (losing to James Buchanan), Frémont was a trailblazer in the West who got caught up in events occurring in California. Ostensibly on a mere exploration mission into California in late 1845, the then-Captain Frémont actually began encouraging Americans there to rebel against Pico's government. Frémont was cautious not to say what he was really doing because he could be court-martialed for violating the Neutrality Act of 1794. It was recorded, however, that he met with future leaders of the Bear Flag Revolt in June 1846 at Sutter's Fort, not long before the rebels took action.

Who led the Bear Flag Revolt and why?

American settlers in California were uneasy by news they heard that José Castro was going to confiscate their land and even hire Indians to raid their homesteads. They therefore were in favor of either complete independence or joining with the United States. Although a bit irked by not getting any promises from Frémont that they would be supported by the U.S. government, a group of Americans led by William Brown Ide (1796–1852) and Ezekiel Merritt (1780–1846) easily took an unmanned outpost in Sonoma and made it their headquarters for the Bear Flag Revolt. They then moved into the town of Sonoma itself, capturing retired General Mariano Vallejo (who actually supported breaking away from Mexico) and declaring

Portrait of John C. Frémont, circa 1857.

the California Republic. Frémont then took his men and captured the unmanned presidio at San Francisco.

Unbeknownst to the Bear Flaggers and Frémont, the United States had declared war on Mexico on May 13, 1846. U.S. Commodore John D. Sloat (1781–1867) had taken Monterey for the Americans, meanwhile, and once that news reached the rebels, they saw little reason to establish a republic since they ultimately wanted to be annexed by the United States anyway. If one accepts the Bear Flaggers as running a legitimate government, then California was an independent country for about three weeks from June to early July 1846.

Although their republic didn't last long, what did endure as a result of the Bear Flag Revolt?

If you ever wondered why the California state flag says "Republic of California" on it even though it's not an independent country, it's because of the Bear Flaggers. The current design of the flag is very close to the one they came up with, including the star, bear, colors, and the wording.

Did the short-lived republic have a capital?

Yes. For a couple weeks, the city of Sonoma was the capital of an "independent" republic.

The first bear flag—also called the Storm Flag—is shown in this 1870 photograph. It was apparently destroyed in the San Francisco fire.

What other important development occurred in Monterey in 1846?

That year marked the first publication of a California newspaper, *The Californian*, which had its debut issue on August 15. The Monterey headquarters was moved to San Francisco the next year, however. *The Californian* would later merge with *The California Star* to form the *Daily Alta California*, which was notable as being the newspaper for which Mark Twain would write when he moved to San Francisco.

Who led the first wagon train to California?

On May 9, 1841, a wagon train led by John Bidwell (1819–1900) and Captain John Bartleson left Independence, Missouri, for California with sixty-nine settlers eager to find a new promised land rich in resources and good weather. They spent the next six months traveling to Sacramento, forging the route that would become known as the California Trail.

Bidwell would go on to have a very successful career. He became a rancher and founded the town of Chico. After serving as a major in the Mexican–American War, he served in the California Senate from 1849 to 1851 and as a U.S. congressman from 1865 to 1867. A prohibitionist, he ran unsuccessfully for California governor and, also unsuccessfully, for president of the United States on the Prohibition Party ticket in 1892.

Was California in American hands after Monterey was captured?

No, the matter would not be fully resolved until the end of the Mexican–American War in 1848, although hostilities in California ended the year before that. Fighting was active in the southern part of the state from the summer of 1846 through the rest of that year. Although Governor Pico and his military commander, José Castro, fled from Americans in the north and Commodore Robert Stockton (1795–1866) easily took Los Angeles in the south for the United States, there was considerable resistance from the rancheros loyal to Mexico.

Stockton left Los Angeles under the command of Captain Archibald Hamilton Gillespie, and after that José María Flores (1818–1866) led a force into L.A., running Gillespie out of town after a siege that lasted until September 29, 1846.

The victory wouldn't last, however. The Americans returned with reinforcements in December, including a couple hundred troops under General Stephen W. Kearney (1794–1848), about four hundred men led by Frémont, and then another 750 under Stockton. Kearney fought what was basically a draw in San Diego and then the Battle of Los Angeles came on January 8 and 9, when Kearney and Stockton's combined forces defeated the Californians.

Andrés Pico, the younger brother of Pio Pico and commander of the Californians, signed the "Capitulation of Cahuenga" on January 13, 1847, agreeing to end hostilities in Alta California. The Mexican–American War would continue, but the war in California was effectively at an end.

What happened when the Treaty of Guadalupe Hidalgo was signed?

The Mexican–American War ended with the signing of the Treaty of Guadalupe Hidalgo on February 2, 1848. As a result, the United States gained a huge chunk of Mexico that included land that now includes Texas, New Mexico, Arizona, Colorado, Oklahoma, Utah, Wyoming, and California. Mexican citizens within this territory had the choice of moving south to within the new borders of Mexico or staying and becoming U.S. citizens. About ninety percent of them chose to remain.

Who governed California in the couple years before statehood in 1850?

John Frémont declared himself military governor of the new U.S. acquisition on January 16, 1847. Incredibly, he held on to that position until March 1, 1847. The American military came in and court-martialed the upstart Frémont for mutiny and insubordination. He was conflicted, but President James K. Polk commuted the sentence, and Frémont went free.

President Polk tried to have Congress declare California a territory, but specifics were hard to agree upon, and the issue of whether the territory would be open to slavery slowed things down. Meanwhile, it remained under military control. General Bennet C. Riley (1787–1853) served as military governor from 1848 to 1849.

THE GOLD RUSH

What was the California Gold Rush?

One of the most transformative periods in California history was the Gold Rush, which lasted from 1848 to the mid 1850s. Gold was discovered in northern California, and the result was an onrush of prospectors looking to get rich quick. Most didn't, but the resulting population boom resulted in increased business activity. San Francisco and other cities saw huge growth, and it helped bring California into statehood.

Where and by whom was gold first found?

A carpenter and sawmill operator by trade, James Marshall (1810–1885) found gold in the American River on January 24, 1848, by the town of Coloma (northeast of Sacramento) while employed by Johan (John) Sutter to construct a mill. Ironically, Marshall died in obscurity and poverty because he was never able to secure a claim to the gold he found; then, the mill he was hired to build and operate failed because there was no one available to work it (everyone was looking for gold). He tried his hand at growing grapes and mining, but both ventures failed, and he ended up living in a small cabin and growing a garden for food. A year after his passing, a fraternal service organization called the

Native Sons of the Golden West raised money to build a tomb for Marshall, and five years later, the state erected a statue over the tomb in Coloma, which is now part of the Marshall Gold Discovery State Historic Park and a federal historical landmark.

What unique discovery was made near Sutter's Mill in 2012?

A meteorite discovered at the epicenter of the Gold Rush was analyzed in 2012 by scientists who determined it was composed of the oldest material found thus far in the solar system.

Who was Samuel Brannan, and what was his role in the Gold Rush?

A Mormon who founded the state's second newspaper (*The California Star*, which would merge with the first paper, *The Californian*, to form *The Daily Alta California*), Brannan (1819–1889) also founded San Francisco's first public school, gave sermons, and owned a bank and hardware store.

Brannan is often credited with starting the Gold Rush. He announced the discovery of gold in his newspaper and marched down the streets of San Francisco with a quinine bottle filled with gold, announcing it had been found in the American River. Just before that, the clever Brannan bought every shovel, pick, pan, and axe he could find and

An 1849 drawing made of Sutter's Fort around the time of the gold discovery. The Fort, and nearby mill, which had already played an important role in the Bear Flag Revolt, would once again become a focal point of California history.

sold them in his hardware store at a price marked up about 100% of his costs. He hence became the first man to become a millionaire as a result of gold fever in California.

Were the only people to go to California from the United States?

Not at all. The 49ers, as they were called because most of them swarmed to the state the year after gold was discovered, also came from France, Sweden, China, Chile, and other nations.

How did the 49ers make the trek to gold country?

As for Americans in the eastern part of the United States, there were three routes they could take: they could travel by land across the country in a wagon train (four to six months of travel), they could take a ship around Cape Horn at the southern tip of South America (six to eight months), or they could take a ship to Panama, cross the narrow strip of land by foot or horse (since the canal had yet to be built) and then board a ship on the western shore and continue the journey (this took about a month). This last route sounds the most ideal, but the problem was that there were not very many ships taking passengers in the Pacific, and a 49er could wait for months for the next vessel to come by. The Cape Horn route was also dangerous because the seas there were very rough, and captains would overload their ships with passengers (it was not unheard of to share a bed with two other people). The land route, of course, was subject to Indian attacks and difficult routes over rivers, deserts, or mountains. But the 49ers were highly motivated to make the trip.

How easy (or difficult) was it to find gold?

Within a year of the discovery of gold, all the easy-to-reach, surface gold was quickly discovered and scooped up by claim stakers. The next method for finding gold was pan-

---

Who was "Lucky" Baldwin?

Elias Jackson "Lucky" Baldwin (1828–1909) was one of the most successful businessmen of the nineteenth century. He moved to San Francisco in 1853 to take advantage of the Gold Rush but not to make his fortune in gold. Rather, he wisely saw an opportunity to make money by providing services to gold miners and prospectors. He built a livery business and the Baldwin Hotel and Theater, which was completed in 1875. Money for the huge building was made not by business dealings but by luck. In 1867, Baldwin was going to sell his silver, but when he forgot to provide the silver certificates to his broker before leaving on a trip, the broker couldn't sell them. Fortunately, the value of silver suddenly skyrocketed, earning Baldwin millions. Moving to southern California, he purchased the Rancho Santa Anita and began breeding and racing thoroughbred horses. Sadly, Baldwin's luck in horse racing (and also poker) was not as good as his luck with silver, and he had lost much of his wealth by the time he passed away.

What did the phrase "seeing the elephant" mean to miners and other California settlers at this time in history?

The peculiar expression referred to the notion that once people actually experienced California, it might not live up to their expectations. This was particularly true of gold prospectors, most of whom never struck it rich. The elephant metaphor has to do with the fact that early depictions of this mammal that were drawn by explorers and sent back to Europe stirred the imagination as to what a spectacular creature it was, practically mythical. But those who actually saw an elephant were a bit disappointed that, while large, it was simply a big animal.

ning for it. Smaller gold nuggets and gold dust could be found in rivers and streams in the area, and by carefully sifting salty water, the heavier gold would end up at the bottom of the pan while the dirt washed out of it by carefully swirling the pan. Sluices—a constructed water channel with a gate at one end to control water flow—were also used to go through river sand and silt more quickly.

Mining for gold became more necessary as the easier finds were depleted. Many amateur diggers would tunnel too quickly and not provide enough support for mine walls. The result was frequent cave-ins and the deaths of numerous miners. Mining became more professional after the first couple of years, and better equipment was used and operated by mining companies rather than individuals or small partnerships.

Why were supplies for miners so costly?

Just as many people today feel gouged by prices at the gas pump because they need it for their cars, there were many profiteers during the Gold Rush who charged exorbitant prices to miners for simple goods. For example, one egg could cost between three and five dollars (or about $75 in today's money), a pound of butter cost six dollars, and in an extraordinary example of capitalism gone mad, some merchants took barrels of water out into the desert and sold it to people dying of thirst for as much as a hundred dollars.

What caused the Squatters' Riot of 1850?

With the influx of thousands of prospectors after 1848, many staked claims on land that John Sutter said was his. But the squatters asserted that the Spanish grant that gave Sutter the land was not legal and that, instead, it belonged to the government. These people started building structures on the property, claiming, without proof, that it was theirs. They even organized a group calling themselves the Sacramento City Settlers Association. One leader of the group, was Charles L. Robinson (1818–1894), who would later become the first governor of Kansas (and the only one to ever be impeached, though he did not lose the office or get convicted). The squatters were upset by how a few speculators had bought up the land around Sacramento and then demanded exorbitant prices to settle there. One of the people on the squatter's side was James McClatchy (1824–1883), the editor of *The Daily Bee* (later *The Sacramento Bee*), who was imprisoned for opposing a writ of restitution the local sheriff tried to serve a squatter on order of a judge.

The squatters, led by Robinson and another man named Joseph Maloney, marched on Sacramento on August 14, 1850, to free McClatchy and Richard Moran, a businessman who supported the squatters, too, neither of whom had posted bail. The armed men were confronted by Sacramento's Mayor Hardin Bigelow (1809–1850) and a military force he gathered. Bigelow ordered Robinson and his men to lay down their arms. They didn't, and instead shooting broke out. Bigelow was seriously wounded, and Robinson was injured, too, plus five people were killed, including a city assessor and two bystanders. Bigelow died later that year while trying to recover in San Francisco—not from his wounds directly but from cholera, which attacked his already weakened body.

John Sutter, who had played a role in the Gold Rush and Bear Flag Revolt, would be in the fray again during the Squatters' Riot.

Besides a half dozen deaths, the result of the riot was that the squatters lost the legal battle for the land, Sutter was able to maintain his claim that the Spanish had granted him his property, McClatchy and Moran were released from prison, and Robinson would be elected to the state legislature and, as noted above, became governor of Kansas.

How did the Gold Rush impact the newly forming state?

No other state in the Union experienced such a spectacular period of growth up to that point in U.S. history. From 1846 to 1849, the population of non-Indian residents climbed from ten thousand to one hundred thousand. Eighty percent of the white people, according to the 1850 U.S. Census, were young males who described themselves as miners. Californios, who were once the most common group after Native Americans, constituted only five percent of the new order. California was unable to handle the influx very well. There were few roads (most navigation was done by waterways), towns were ramshackle wooden affairs, epidemic diseases such as cholera threatened lives, and there was not much in the way of law and order.

However, most of these young miners did not intend to stay in California. They wanted to get wealthy and go home (or they went home broke). But they would be re-

Was cholera a side effect of the Gold Rush?

In October 1850, an epidemic of Asiatic cholera (it was believed to have originated in India) struck Sacramento, the result of increasingly unsanitary conditions in the city, including sewage that had made its way into the water supply. The city, it seems, simply could not handle the huge number of people who arrived there because of the Gold Rush. The first cholera death on October 20 would soon be followed by many more, and then there was a mass exodus from Sacramento, which lost eighty percent of its population in a matter of weeks.

About 325 people died from the outbreak, but the disease quickly receded, and by the end of November 1850, people were coming back to Sacramento and businesses resumed work.

placed by merchants, politicians, teachers, farmers, manufacturers, and more who would diversify the population of the next decade or two.

What was the Comstock Lode?

Gold wasn't the only valuable mineral discovered during the Gold Rush era. Although located in Nevada just across the border, the Comstock Lode was a huge deposit of silver that greatly benefited California, as well. The lode was found on June 11, 1859, and actually brought more money to San Francisco and a few lucky millionaires than all the gold found before it: an estimated $500 million in dollars of that time. Among the winners were George Hearst, the father of newspaper magnate William Randolph Hearst, and four Irishmen known as the "Silver Kings" or "Bonanza Kings"—John William Mackay (1831–1902), James C. Flood (1826–1889), James Graham Fair (1831–1894), and William S. O'Brien (1825–1878)—who would establish the Nevada Bank, which later merged into Wells Fargo Bank.

Is gold still mined in the Golden State?

In recent decades, technology has improved to the point that readdressing the search for gold in California has once again become profitable. The industry rebooted in the 1980s. Old mines have been reopened, and there is the potential for billions of dollars in gold to be extracted. Interestingly, the drought of the 2010s has spelled opportunity for individual gold hunters because rivers that were once too deep and fast to prospect became mere trickles of water, making it much easier to explore riparian deposits.

THE STATE OF CALIFORNIA: 1850 TO THE PRESENT

CALIFORNIA BECOMES A U.S. STATE

How did California switch hands from Mexico to the United States?

After the United States declared war on Mexico on April 25, 1846, it set its sights on California. On July 7, 1846, U.S. Commodore John D. Sloat, after defeating a Mexican garrison in Monterey, officially declared that California was annexed. Anyone living there was welcomed to stay or sell their land and leave the territory.

What terms were settled in the Treaty of Guadalupe Hidalgo?

Toward the end of the Mexican–American War (1846–1848), Mexico City fell to American forces under the command of General Winfield Scott (1786–1866) on September 14, 1847, and Mexico surrendered. Negotiations for terms fell to the U.S. State Department's chief clerk, Nicholas Trist (1800–1874). General Scott and President James K. Polk (1795–1849) were unhappy with Trist's work. Polk wanted a Mexican delegation to come to Washington, D.C., and he dismissed Trist. But Trist, in direct defiance, went ahead and met with the Mexican officials at Guadalupe Hidalgo, a city just north of Mexico City, on February 2, 1848.

Two important areas where Trist differed from Polk was that Trist demanded a full surrender without compromise, but more interesting than this was that Polk wanted Mexico to give up Baja California, but Trist instead drew the new border north of the peninsula and allowed Mexico to keep it. Had Polk gotten his way, Baja California might very well have been a part of the state of California today.

Other terms of the treaty included the United States getting Nevada, Colorado, New Mexico, Arizona, Utah, and, of course, Alta California, and the Mexicans relinquished all claims to Texas, with the southern boundary being the Rio Grande River. The United

States gave Mexico $15,000,000 and agreed to pay Mexican citizens who chose to stay any debts owed them by the Mexican government.

Trist sent these terms to Washington, D.C., forcing Polk to make a decision. The president sent the treaty to the Senate for approval, which it did, for the most part. An important item was stricken, however: Article X, which guaranteed that the U.S. would guarantee any land grants that Mexico had disbursed. This fact would be used by supporters of the Squatters' Riot of 1850 to assert that John Sutter did not legally own his land (see page 45).

Who was General Bennett C. Riley?

Bennet C. Riley (1787–1853) was the sixth and last military governor of California, an office he served in just during 1849. This was an incredibly challenging year, however. With the Mexican government's military gone, Riley was trying to maintain control of a huge territory with minimal forces during the most chaotic year of the Gold Rush. It was a violent time, too, and extremely dangerous for those of the Native nations who were targeted and often killed by white settlers. Riley simply didn't have the soldiers needed to stop much of the slaughter. Also, because Congress was slowing up statehood because of the slavery issue, Riley had a hard time with official bureaucracy, as well. He resigned his office on December 20, 1849.

Who was Biddy Mason, and why is she important to California history?

Bridget "Biddy" Mason (1818–1891) was a slave born in Georgia. Her owner, Robert Smith, was a Mormon who moved west along with Brigham Young's other followers. Eventually, Smith, his family, and slaves ended up in San Bernardino, California. Realizing that California was a free state, Biddy Mason petitioned a Los Angeles court for her freedom and won.

Mason continued to prove herself smarter than people like her former owner. She found work as a physician's assistant, scrupulously saved money, and purchased land. A splendid idea in a growing state, the strategy helped her amass about $300,000 (quite a fortune at the time, especially for a black woman). But Mason didn't hoard her money. She supported charities to feed and shelter the poor and cofounded an elementary school for black children. As for going down in history, Mason (sometimes called "Grandma Mason" or "Auntie Mason" because so many looked up to her as a matriarch) founded Los Angeles's first African American church, the First African Methodist Episcopal Church of Los Angeles, in 1872. Located at 2270 S. Harvard Blvd., it is still active today with some nineteen thousand members.

Why was the Compromise of 1850 initiated when California was to become a state?

Adding California to the roster of U.S. states posed a problem for the country on the issue of slavery. Before the new state was added, there were fifteen states that allowed slavery and fifteen that prohibited it: an even balance. So the decision needed to be made as to whether California would be a free or slave state. The solution was outlined in the Compromise of 1850, which admitted California as a free state but then allowed slavery in the territories of New Mexico and Utah—at least temporarily. To placate the southern states, the Fugitive Slave Laws were also strengthened, making it easier for slave-owners to take back slaves that had escaped to the North.

When, exactly, was California declared a U.S. state?

California was admitted to the union on September 9, 1850.

Who was the first American governor of California?

Farmer, merchant, lawyer, and judge Peter Hardeman Burnett (1807–1895) was elected governor of the state in 1849, serving in the office for a year before it was even a state. Interestingly, he resigned from office in 1851 (he wished to return to his legal practice), affording him the dual distinction of also being the first California governor to resign from office. (See the "Politics and the Law" chapter for more on Burnett.)

Who was the "Mexican Robin Hood" who inspired the legend of Zorro?

Joaquin Murieta (1829–1853) led a band of thieves called "The Five Joaquins" in the early 1850s. During the banditos spree of several years, they reportedly stole over $100,000 worth of gold, as well as horses and cattle. In conflicts with ranchers and the law, they killed three law officers and sixteen private citizens, as well, and by some reports the band was responsible for the death of twenty-eight Chinese.

So why was a thief and murderer turned into a hero? For some Mexicans, Murieta represented resistance to white domination in California. When the future bandit first immigrated to America, it was to be a miner, and he found considerable success digging gold. The (unverified) story goes that Anglo miners became jeal-

An artist's rendition of Joaquin Murieta, whom many thought of as a Mexican version of Robin Hood.

ous of Murieta, raping his wife, lynching his half brother, whipping him, and chasing him from his claim. Turning to crime was therefore a path of revenge.

Murieta's final fate was not a happy one. He was hunted down and beheaded by Rangers, who put his head in a jar full of alcohol to preserve it as proof and get the reward money. As a legend, though, he fared much better. A Cherokee author named John Rollin Ridge (1827–1867) wrote a fictionalized biography of Murieta called *The Life and Adventures of Joaquin Murieta: The Celebrated California Bandit* (1854). While a novelization of the true person, the book was often misinterpreted as pure history. It was this book that inspired Johnston McCulley (1883–1958) to create the character Don Diego de la Vega (aka Zorro) in his 1919 story, "The Curse of Capistrano," which appeared in the pulp magazine *All-Story Weekly*. Over time, Zorro became popular in stories, novels, serials, and movies.

What is the importance of the California Land Act of 1851?

After refusing to approve Article X of the Treaty of Guadalupe Hidalgo, which said that the United States should recognize land grants given by the Mexican government, the U.S. government went further with the California Land Act of 1851. On the surface, the act was supposedly written to help adjudicate property claims, but actually it made this process more difficult and much more expensive. There were about eight hundred such land grants from the days when Spain and then Mexico ruled California, but only about six hundred of those were upheld after those who said they had land grants went through the judicial process with American courts. This affected many people who had claimed land rights before the Gold Rush and were forced to defend those claims when a flood of miners came to the state and squatted on their land to search for gold.

STAGECOACHES
AND RAILROADS

Before there were trains, how did people travel to California?

Stagecoaches were an important means of transportation both to California and within its borders. It was by far, however, less than a comfortable ride over dirt roads and through sometimes dangerous passes.

What was the Butterfield Overland Mail Stage?

It's funny how people know about the short-lived Pony Express when probably an even more important means of transporting mail was the Butterfield Overland, which started in 1858 after businessman John Butterfield (1801–1869) was awarded a $600,000 government contract. With further financial backing from Wells Fargo, Butterfield used stagecoaches to travel from St. Louis, Missouri, to San Francisco in just twenty-five

What does "La Quinta" mean?

There is a town in the Coachella Valley called La Quinta, and you might be familiar with the hotel chain of the same name. The names have their basis in Spanish, unsurprisingly, from a time when people traveled by horse or stagecoach. It means "the fifth" and refers to the fact that travelers would often try to find a hacienda or inn to find a real bed after traveling for five days on dusty roads and sleeping outside. "La Quinta" can also refer to the house or inn itself, so it is a very appropriate name for a hotel chain.

days. Instead of trying to go through the Rocky Mountains, the "Oxbow Route" was taken, which was a path going south through New Mexico and Arizona to southern California (but not through San Diego) and then north to San Francisco. Even so, it was an amazing achievement to travel 1,475 miles (2,374 kilometers) in less than a month.

Competition from the Pony Express changed Butterfield's strategy. He stopped the Oxbow Route in 1861 in favor of the Central Overland Route. This new route was controlled in the west by Wells Fargo and in the east by businessman Ben Holladay (1819–1887). Holladay was unhappy with working with Wells Fargo (he said they used inferior equipment and mistreated the horses), so he sold his stage in 1866 and left the venture. Wells Fargo then ran the line until the completion of the Transcontinental Railroad in 1869.

When did trains first start arriving in California, and how did that affect the state?

Transcontinental Railroad was completed on May 10, 1869, when the Central Pacific and Union Pacific railroads joined at Promontory Point, Utah, but the first train did not arrive in a large California city (San Francisco) until September 6, 1869.

What was the impact of railway systems linking San Francisco to the rest of the country?

For San Francisco, the first major city affected, the change came quickly. Before the Transcontinental Railroad was completed, it was a real Wild West town. Much of the population consisted of young men who had come to search for gold, silver, and related wealth. The city was going through tremendous growing pains, having grown from about a thousand residents when the state was annexed by the United States to fifty thousand by the time trains started arriving. It was quite chaotic, and there was a lot of lawlessness. Murders occurred of a rate of about two a day, and fires in the city were common. Prostitution, gambling, and theft were rampant. But with the trains came a more diverse population of immigrants. San Francisco transformed from a prospecting town to a city of businesses, neighbor-hoods, hotels, and growing wealth. The population soared even quicker, and by 1880 stood at 234,000.

When were other cities in the south hooked up to the rail system?

Rail lines reached San Diego and Los Angeles by 1885, sparking a population and economic explosion in Southern California known as the "Boom of the Eighties." Travel to California became much less expensive, with train tickets from Mississippi to the West Coast plummeting from $125 to about a buck. The 1880s also saw a huge demographic change as white Americans started to become more common than people of Mexican and Spanish descent.

Were there negative consequences to railroads reaching the state?

THE CURSE OF CALIFORNIA.

This illustration, called "The Curse of the Octopus," appeared in the August 19, 1882, issue of *The Wasp*. It criticizes railroad control over farmers, lumber, fruit growers, stage lines, wine, mining, and Nob Hill.

While trains connected California to the rest of the country and meant big business to the state, there were negative consequences, too. Settlers resented that the railroad companies grabbed a lot of government land through grants that would otherwise have gone to new residents; farmers complained of higher tariffs on the food they grew.

Although all railroad companies drew criticism from the public, none was more vilified than the California-based Southern Pacific Company, probably because it was the wealthiest in the region and started to influence California politics. Author Frank Norris wrote a scathing condemnation of the Southern Pacific in his 1901 novel, *The Octopus: A Story of California*.

How long before there was a railroad accident?

As with any technology or human endeavor, mistakes happen. The first big accident between trains in California occurred on November 14, 1869, which was just weeks after the Transcontinental Railroad had reached San Francisco. What happened was that two passenger trains collided head-on near the town of San Leandro in Alameda County. Twelve people were killed and thirty-five seriously injured. Among the dead was A. W. Baldwin, a justice of the Nevada Supreme Court. The tragedy resulted in quick criticism of trains, with people saying that they posed a risk to public safety.

What was the Battle of Mussel Slough?

On May 11, 1880, about five miles from the town of Hanford, settlers clashed with Southern Pacific Railroad agents and a U.S. marshal that turned deadly. It started when the settlers learned that the Southern Pacific had decided to change the route that tracks would take from one that had been previously approved to a new one that would result in a number of people losing their homes to make way for the tracks. When a U.S. marshal arrived at the scene and railroad agents started serving eviction notices or tried to force homeowners to take cheap buyouts, tempers flared and shots were fired. Seven settlers were killed, and seventeen settlers were indicted by a federal grand jury for interfering with a marshal in his duties. To the town of Hanford, however, the men who died would become martyrs and those who survived heroes.

Where can I find the best railroad museums in California?

There are several wonderful railroad museums in the state, but one of the best of these is the California State Railroad Museum in Sacramento. Located in Old Sacramento, it features twenty-one restored engines and cars, guided tours, train rides, and a second story for special exhibits. The museum opened in 1976 and has about five hundred thousand visitors annually.

Below is a list of train museums in the state:

California Notable Train Museums

Name	City	Notable For
California State Railroad Museum	Sacramento	See above
Golden Gate Railroad Museum	San Francisco	Collection includes a working Southern Pacific steam engine
Lomita Railroad Museum	Lomita	Includes a Southern Pacific Railroad engine and restored cabooses
Los Angeles Museum of Railroading	Los Angeles	Highlights are the Bill and Betty Everett Ephemera and Model Collection that emphasizes the Pacific Electric Railway, trolleys, and interurbans; also an outstanding collection of railroad photographs and postcards
Orange Empire Railway Museum	Perris	Large collection of streetcars from L.A., San Diego, and San Francisco; collection of operable tram equipment; also interurban and mainline trains

55

Name	City	Notable For
South Coast	Goleta	Features the fully restored Goleta Depot Station, Railroad Museum miniature train ride, and model train exhibit

GHOST TOWNS

What is a ghost town?

They aren't towns haunted by ghosts; rather, the term refers to towns that were abandoned. This was usually because so many mining communities sprang up during the Gold Rush, and when the gold (and silver) were depleted, there was no longer a reason to stay. Sometimes, too, towns emerged when a railway was constructed, only to be vacated when freeways became the preferred way to travel and ship goods.

What are some interesting ghost towns?

Bodie—Located in the northern part of the state (about seventy-five miles from Reno, Nevada)—was founded in the 1870s. At its height, there were about 100,000 residents living there, and it was known for its saloons, an active red light district, and opium dens. The town actually lasted longer than many such places, slowly declining until the post office closed in 1942. Soon after, it was completely abandoned. Many of the buildings are still standing. The town is managed by the California State Park system.

Calico—Not far from Barstow, this was a silver mining town that had its brief heydays in the 1880s and went into decline when silver prices fell in the 1890s. Abandoned completely by 1907, it caught the eye (much later) of Knott's Berry Farmer founder, Walter Knott. He restored a lot of the buildings in the 1850s. Today, it is open to tourists, who can wander the town and visit the silver mine.

Cerro Gordo—A remarkable, partially restored ghost town just west of Death Valley National Park, Cerro Gordo is accessible only if you arrange a visit through Cerro Gordo Tours. The hotel and bunkhouse have been renovated for people who wish to eat there and spend a night or two.

Downieville—Although it calls itself a ghost town, there are still 242 residents in this former Gold Rush burg, which also serves as the county seat for Sierra County. Be-

What is the "Bodie Curse"?

If you wander the streets and buildings of Bodie, you can still find interesting old artifacts lying about. However, it's said that taking any of these items out of the town will curse you, giving you bad luck until the object is returned.

cause it is still populated, it has stores and restaurants and lots of fully restored, nineteenth-century buildings, making it a more pleasant tourist stop for families.

Where can I go to get a "living history" ghost town experience?

If you want to feel like you've stepped back in time and are in a living, Gold Rush-era town, then visit Columbia, California, just west of the Sierra Nevada and east of Stockton near New Melones Lake. The town has been refurbished, and docent volunteers dressed in period costumes tell you about life there. You can visit a gold mine, take a stagecoach ride, attend the theater, and much more. Visit http://www.visitcolumbiacalifornia.com/ to learn more.

THE U.S. CIVIL WAR

On which side did California fight?

Admitted as a free state, California formally pledged its loyalty to the North on May 17, 1861.

Did California play a big role in the American Civil War?

Not so much—at least, not in terms of manpower. About sixteen thousand Californians enlisted in the war between the states. Most soldiers, however, remained in their home state because it was too expensive to send them East. About five hundred men fought with a Massachusetts regiment, but the rest performed such duties as guarding the Mexican border and mail routes; they also helped protect Arizona and New Mexico from the possibility of Texan Confederates advancing into those territories.

What was the "California Column"?

As part of the effort to keep Confederate Texans out of Arizona Territory, five thousand California volunteers marched from the Los Angeles area to El Paso in the summer of 1862. They also pushed the Texans out of New Mexico, fighting in two small battles at Picacho Peak and Stanwix Station.

What's the important distinction between the California Brigade and the California Battalion?

There were some groups in the Union's military with California in their name, and this gets a little tricky: The 1st, 2nd, 3rd, and 5th California Infantries (together forming the California Brigade) were actually composed of Philadelphians under the command of Colonel Edward Baker, a U.S. senator from Oregon. They took the name as a way of acknowledging the state's contributions to the war.

But another group, the California Battalion (also known as the California 100), was made up of soldiers from the Golden State. These were the men who formed a company

57

under the 2nd Massachusetts Company. To do so, they had to promise the governor of Massachusetts that they would pay for their own uniforms, transportation, and supplies. The California Battalion consisted of a hundred cavalrymen and three companies of foot soldiers. They fought under the command of General Phil Sheridan and were active in the Shenandoah Valley campaign (1862), also joining in on the Battle of Gettysburg (1863), the Third Battle of Winchester (1864), and the Battle of Cedar Creek (1864).

The flag of the California Battalion, a small force from the Golden State that fought under the Massachusetts command during the Civil War.

How else did California support the war effort?

What they lacked in troop contributions Californians more than made up for in something else: gold. A great deal of California gold was provided to the North for the war effort. The North's General Ulysses S. Grant acknowledged this when he said, "I do not know what we could do in this great national emergency, were it not for the gold sent from California" (Publications of the Historical Society of Southern California, Vol. 9, January 1, 1914, p. 125).

Were there any Californians siding with the South?

Yes, not all Californians believed their state should be on the side of the Union. Most of these secessionists were in southern California, and they were quite vocal about their position. Among the groups who favored the Confederacy were the Los Angeles Mounted Rifles and chapters of the Knights of the Golden Circle. The latter had designs on conquering much of Mexico and turning it into part of the Confederacy. This, of course, never came about; likewise, fears that some Californians might rebel against the Union never occurred.

How many Civil War battles were fought in California?

None, but there are some forts from the period, and the island of Alcatraz served as a prison for Confederate soldiers.

Who was Captain Rufus Ingram?

Rufus Ingram (1834–?) was a captain in the Confederate Army whose assignment was to become a bushwhacker in California—that is, to rob and otherwise harass the area as best he could with a small force. He organized Captain Ingram's Partisan Ranger, which consisted of about fifty men from the Knights of the Golden Circle. Active in 1864, the marauders robbed a Comstock Lode silver shipment near Sacramento, escaping with about $40,000 in bullion. A later robbery attempt in Santa Clara County left two of Ingram's men dead and the rest on the run. The captain escaped, too, and left California for good. He was never captured, but it's presumed he fled to Missouri.

CHINESE IMMIGRATION

Why did so many Chinese immigrate to California?

During the 1840s and 1850s, there were many problems for the Chinese people caused by natural disasters, war, and economic issues. In 1847, for example, Henen province suffered from a terrible drought, and in 1849, the Yangtze River flooded, destroying homes and farms in Zhejiang, Anhui, Jiangsu, and Hubei provinces.

The famines that followed helped to spark the Taiping Civil War between the Qing Dynasty and the Christian God Worshipping Society, led by Hong Xiuquan (1814–1864). Hong believed himself to be related to Jesus Christ, and his holy war led to the deaths of tens of millions of Chinese and was the worst conflict in that region in two centuries. As the Taiping rebels were losing by 1864, Hong was surrounded in Nanjing. Low on food, he ate wild vegetables and died of food poisoning.

Life worsened even more as a result of the Opium Wars (1839–1842, 1856–1860), which were trade and sovereignty wars with Great Britain. The Qing Dynasty suffered greatly because it was already weakened from the Taiping Rebellion. The economy collapsed, and many Chinese lost their work and their businesses. With all of this going on, by the time the Chinese heard of the Gold Rush in California, they were eager to flee for a chance at making a new life.

With the Gold Rush (and later the railroads), there was a need for labor in California, and twenty-five thousand Chinese were in the state by 1852. The Chinese could travel to the United States fairly cheaply by allowing employers in California to garnish their wages and so began a period of immigration that lasted from 1849 to 1882. Once here, they hoped to make a lot of money and send it back to their families in China.

How many Chinese laborers worked on the Transcontinental Railroad?

The Central Pacific Railroad Company employed fifteen thousand Chinese laborers during the construction of the Transcontinental Railroad. Without their help, there is no way the railroad would have been completed in the allotted time.

How else did Chinese Americans contribute to their new country?

The Chinese were very important as laborers in the North's effort to defeat the Confederacy during the American Civil War. Working in factories that produced clothing, cigars, wool, and other supplies to the war effort, they also worked as farmers, gardeners, and domestic help.

Were the Chinese immigrants welcomed in California?

Initially, yes. Americans needed the extra work force to build railroads and to help with the mining industry and its supporting industries. The Burlingame-Seward Treaty of 1868 between the United States and China (primarily a move to normalize relationships and grant China most-favored-nation status) actually encouraged immigration.

But when the Transcontinental Railroad was completed and the initial fervor of gold waned, the U.S. economy began to slip. As jobs became scarcer, white Americans began to resent those who came

A nineteenth-century illustration depicting Chinese gold miners. The immigrants came not only for gold but also to work on railroads and industries supporting both the Gold Rush and the railroads.

(legally, it should be noted) from China. Pressure on politicians led first to the Angell Treaty of 1880 and then the even worse Chinese Exclusion Act of 1882 (a document not even bothering to be subtle). The Angell Treaty limited immigration by stating that no more than fifteen Chinese people could be on any one ship heading to the United States. The Chinese Exclusion Act banned immigration altogether when President Rutherford B. Hayes signed it into law on May 6, 1882.

The Chinese are the only ethnic group in American history to be banned outright from entering the country. These restrictions would not be fully reversed until the Magnuson Act of 1942 (see below).

How did the Chinatown War of 1871 start?

It wasn't just in San Francisco where clashes occurred between Chinese immigrants and white residents. There was also trouble in Los Angeles. Also called the Chinese Massacre of 1871, there was a deadly riot in the street called Calle de los Negroes (now part of Los Angeles Street). It started when two Chinese gangs, the Hong Chow and the Nin Yung, started fighting over a woman. Shots were fired, and two innocent, white bystanders were killed. A white mob formed and attacked the gangs, killing eighteen Chinese. Eight men were found guilty of manslaughter and sentenced to San Quentin Prison as a result.

Who was Denis Kearney, and what was his role in the Chinese immigrant issue?

Denis Kearney (1847–1907) was a labor leader and noted orator who constantly railed against Chinese immigrants. He was for the working class, ironically, since all of them were obviously immigrants from an earlier day; in addition, in his early career, he even praised the Chinese for being "industrious" and urged white laborers to follow their example, but he later changed his tone completely. Kearney was well known for also being against the press and capitalists of every ilk.

Who was Wong Chin Foo?

Wong Chin Foo (1847–1898) was a formidable adversary to Denis Kearney. He was the founder of the Chinese Equal Rights League and the Chinese American weekly newspaper. Also organizing a Chinese voters association in 1884, he lectured and wrote widely against racist policies such as the Chinese Exclusion Act of 1882.

OTHER IMMIGRANT POPULATIONS IN CALIFORNIA

Immigrants from what country first settled in Anaheim near Los Angeles?

The first immigrants to settle what would be Anaheim were Germans. Specifically, it was a group of German vintners who had moved down from the San Francisco area in 1857 to grow grapes (see the Wine and Beer section of the "California Means Business" chapter for more).

Why does the little city of Kingsburg resemble a Swedish town in many ways?

A considerable number of Swedes left their homeland between the years of 1870 and 1900 and headed for America for a couple of reasons: First, farmland was becoming a premium in Sweden and land prices were cheaper in California, and second, many of them did not enjoy the oppression of a state church, so they came for more religious freedoms. Once a few settled here, they often wrote to relatives about how good the land was, and immigration of Swedes grew to over one million in the United States.

In California, a couple of Swedes settled in Kings River Switch near Fresno in the early 1870s because they got a good land deal and jobs in the railroad industry. They told their families, and within just a few years there was an entire community of Swedish people in what eventually became known as Kingsburg. At its peak in the early 1920s, about 94% of Kingsburg's people were of Swedish descent, but that has been diluted almost completely since then. Nevertheless, the city has deliberately written code to keep the buildings downtown looking like Swedish construction, and every year they hold a Swedish Festival in May.

Why was Solvang settled by Danish immigrants?

Between 1850 and the 1920s, many people left Denmark for the United States because of tough economic times in their homeland. The Danish population experienced a boom, and this was a particular problem in the countryside, where only one son per family could inherit a farm. All the other children were, therefore, unemployed. To make prob-

61

The town of Solvang has deliberately maintained its Danish architecture through the years after city leaders realized they could make it a tourist draw. Even new construction within city limits must honor a Danish style of construction.

lems worse, about a quarter of the country had been ceded to Prussia as a result of the Second Schleswig War of 1864, so land was indeed scarce.

Danes, especially young men who were not the firstborn and therefore had not inherited farmland, left for America, and many of these eventually settled in Solvang, California, in Santa Barbara County, establishing the town in 1911. As with Kingsburg up north, the Danes built structures similar to those back home, lending Solvang a distinctive look that exists today, even though only about twenty percent of the residents can claim Danish descent today.

Solvang is a tourist town, mostly, today, with quaint shops and restaurants, hotels, and horseback ranches.

Who knew that there were so many Armenians in California?

It's a little-known fact that the Central Valley is home to one of the largest populations of Armenian Americans in the United States. Armenia is a small country on the eastern border of Turkey and located between the Black and Caspian seas. Between 1880 and 1920, the Turks invaded the area and killed about a million Armenians. Many fled the region, and some of those immigrated to America. The ones that made it as far as California settled mostly in the Central Valley, with many in the Fresno area, because the farm country re-

> ## What are aebleskiver?
>
> **A**ebleskiver (or ebelskiver or appleskives) are pancake puff treats that are a breakfast must-have if you find yourself in a Solvang restaurant. The pastry treats used to be only a Christmas tradition, but in the tourist town, they are served all year round. They are not really doughnut holes or pancakes but something delightfully different that melts in your mouth. Try them with raspberry jam!

minded them of home. Many became farmers, especially of figs, melons, raisins, and nuts. A few became famous, including California governor George Deukmejian and author William Saroyan (see the "California Notables" chapter for more about them).

THE TURN OF THE TWENTIETH CENTURY

How badly was California affected by the 1919 flu pandemic?

From 1918 to 1919, the entire world was terrorized by the Spanish Flu, which killed somewhere between twenty and forty million people. This was worse than all those who died of the Bubonic Plague (Black Death) in the fourteenth century or from the fighting during World War I. California did not avoid this fate, either. About 3.4 million people lived in the state at the time, and over a hundred thousand of them contracted the disease.

How well did California fare during the 1930s?

As with the rest of the nation, the years of the Great Depression were hard ones. The hard economic times and the Dust Bowl led to many unemployed workers coming to the state. President Franklin Roosevelt developed the New Deal plan to put people to work building dams, bridges, roads, and so on, but the state still struggled.

How did the Dust Bowl affect life in California?

The year 1932 began a desperate chapter in American history, when the Dust Bowl (1932–1939) swooped into the heartland. It was severest drought ever experienced. Once lush farms were laid waste by dust storms. Later analysis would show that improper farming practices that ruined the soil were to blame for much of the disaster, but an explanation wouldn't help the farmers now. Unable to grow crops, they couldn't pay for their homes and lost their farms. A massive migration of people from Oklahoma, Texas, Nebraska, Colorado, Kansas, and New Mexico headed west to a place that seemed relatively unscathed: California. About two hundred thousand migrants came to the state, looking

63

for work in the Central Valley. Called "Okies," even if they came from states other than Oklahoma, they would cause a huge social crisis in the state through the 1930s.

Were the Okies welcomed?

Not at all. California farmers didn't need more workers, and many Okies couldn't find work at all. Those who did were paid extremely low wages. Transients became a problem, especially in large cities such as Los Angeles. At one point, L.A. even sent out a force of 125 police officers to the Arizona border. There, the officers stopped cars and demanded that travelers entering the state show they had some money and proof of employment or an offer of employment. It was unofficially called the "Bum Brigade," and when the American Civil Liberties Union found out about it, they filed suit. California's attorney general found the Bum Brigade unconstitutional and ordered it halted.

Why was photographer Dorothea Lange important?

Dorothea Lange (1895–1965) was a photojournalist who began working for the government's Farm Security Administration and Resettlement Administration to document the plight of the Okies. Working with the University of California, Berkeley, economics professor Paul S. Taylor (1895–1984), who explained the statistics and financial side of the crisis, Lange provided a human face to what was happening, which helped convince the federal government that aid was needed. Her most famous photo, 1936's "Migrant Mother," became the iconic image of the Great Depression and the Dust Bowl.

Which famous Californian author wrote a Pulitzer-winning novel about the Okies?

That, of course, would be John Steinbeck (1902–1968), whose famous 1939 work, *The Grapes of Wrath*, is required reading in most American high schools and colleges. Steinbeck, who was born in Salinas, also wrote a series of articles for the *San Francisco Chronicle* about the crisis in 1936.

What were some important strikes that occurred in 1934?

With considerable organizational backing from the Congress of Industrial Organizations (CIO, which later merged with the American Federation of Labor to become the AFL-CIO), as well as organizations such as the American Workers Party and the

California author John Steinbeck wrote about the plight of the Okies in his *The Grapes of Wrath*.

Communist League of America, longshoremen organized two important strikes that year: the San Francisco General Strike and the West Coast Waterfront (or Longshoreman's) Strike. The former lasted only four days, but the latter was an eighty-three-day strike that was held not only in San Francisco but also in Portland, Oregon, and in Seattle and Everett, Washington. Longshoremen were fighting for better working conditions and the right to unionize. Clashes with police resulted, on July 5 of that year, in violence that killed two longshoremen and injured a third. In the end, the workers were victorious and resulted in the successful unionization of seaport workers on the West Coast.

WARTIME CALIFORNIA

What happened in California immediately after the Japanese struck Pearl Harbor on December 7, 1941?

The reaction of the populace was sudden panic. Everyone was afraid that California would be Japan's next target and that the same fleet that raided Pearl Harbor would lay waste to the state from San Francisco to San Diego. Rumors, never verified, of ship sightings and submarine periscopes being seen were rampant; there were even crazy rumors that the Japanese had secret military installations hidden somewhere in the deserts.

What was the strategic importance of California during World War II?

After the bombing of Pearl Harbor in Hawaii, California became vitally important to the U.S. Navy because of the ports in San Diego, Los Angeles, and San Francisco. Many other smaller military installations ran up and down the California coast and also inland.

Did the Japanese actually intrude into California waters and land?

Although it was never anything as drastic as the bombing of Pearl Harbor, there were a couple of threats to the state, yes. After that attack, the Japanese sent six submarines to harass the U.S. coastline from Washington State to California. They shelled installations along the shore and, in Oregon, dropped incendiary bombs to start forest fires. The Japanese were most interested in attacking oil facilities, and to that end, they shot at oil freighters. On December 20, 1941, a submarine shot torpedoes at the oil tanker SS *Emidio* near San Francisco; it didn't sink but later had to be abandoned. Three days later, torpedoes struck the SS *Montebello*, an oil tanker, near Port San Luis, sinking the ship. About a half dozen other ships were also attacked along the shoreline during the war.

On February 23, 1942, another submarine appeared off the coast of Santa Barbara and fired shells at the Ellwood oil field. Fortunately, no gasoline tanks were hit, or the result could have been explosive. While no one was killed and no serious damage was done, the Japanese considered the fact that they reached the American mainland to be

Was the Battle of Los Angeles just a case of the jitters?

In one of the stranger stories from World War II, reports of enemy planes over Los Angeles on the night of February 24–25, 1942, caused extreme commotion and a lot of shooting that was probably all for nothing. It started when radar detected something about 120 miles (193 kilometers) off the coast of Los Angeles around 7:20 P.M. An alert was issued for antiaircraft guns to be prepared, but no planes were sent out at the time. At 2:45 A.M. an artillery colonel reported seeing over two dozen airplanes near Long Beach. When a balloon with a red flare was seen about fifteen minutes later near Santa Monica, the antiaircraft guns started firing. Searchlights scoured the sky and numerous unverified reports of enemy planes were made, many of them probably mistaking flak in the sky for fighters.

When it was all over, no planes had been shot down by the Americans, and no bombs or any other type of attack came from the mysterious enemy. The only damage was from cars on the ground that had run into each other because of distracted drivers. The incident became a bit of an embarrassment for the U.S. Army and Navy, which couldn't even agree with each other as to what happened. After the war was over, Japan reported that, at the time, it had no aircraft in the area.

a great victory. Meanwhile, Americans used Ellwood as a rallying cry to inspire people to buy more savings bonds for the war effort.

Another strategy of the Japanese was to use balloons to drop bombs. This happened in 1945, toward the end of the war. For example, on January 10 of that year, a Japanese bombing balloon was seen over Alturas in the very northeastern part of the state. After it was spotted, the army sent a P-38 to shoot it down. The balloon descended harmlessly and was discovered to have a high explosive bomb and four incendiary bombs. Then, on February 1, another balloon was seen over Hayfork between Eureka and Redding; it was over the Trinity National Forest and fell on top of a fir tree, where the balloon part burst into flames. Fortunately, the undercarriage that had a payload of incendiary bombs did not go off, and no one was hurt.

What deadly disaster occurred at Saisun Bay in 1944 that also led to the desegregation of the Navy?

The worst at-home accident to happen during World War II was at Port Chicago on Saisun Bay on July 17, 1944. While loading explosives onto a ship bound for the Pacific Theater, munitions were accidentally detonated, triggering an explosion that destroyed the S.S.E.A. Bryan, killed 320, and injured 390. Everyone on the ship was incinerated, and most of those killed (202) were African American sailors assigned to the laborious task. The explosion was so bad that much of the town was damaged by falling debris. The force of the blast was felt as far away as Boulder City, Nevada, and even caused damage in San Francisco.

Many felt that the accident was the result of unsafe practices by the Navy and that blacks were deliberately assigned to the duty of loading explosives. These beliefs led to the Port Chicago Mutiny, when 258 black sailors refused to obey orders to resume duties of loading munitions aboard ships at Port Chicago unless the Navy did something to improve safety conditions. Of these men, 208 were dishonorably discharged. The other fifty were charged with mutiny, a crime punishable by death. Known as the Port Chicago 50, they were convicted and sentenced to eight to fifteen years of hard labor. In 1946, however, they were granted clemency and released from prison. The Navy subsequently realized how it had been prejudiced in segregating its sailors and giving hazardous duties to African Americans. The Port Chicago Mutiny directly led to the Navy's desegregation of its ranks years before President Truman ordered it for all branches of the military.

What was the importance of the Magnuson Act?

Passed in 1943, the Magnuson Act (or Chinese Exclusion Repeal Act) did something that was long overdue: it reversed the Chinese Exclusion Act of 1882 and permitted Chinese immigration once more. It also allowed Chinese immigrants to become naturalized citizens. The act was proposed by U.S. congressman from Washington Warren Magnuson (1905–1989) and was no doubt influenced by the fact that China had become a U.S. ally against the Japanese during World War II.

The barracks at Manzanar internment camp, where Japanese Americans were forced to live during World War II, even though they were U.S. citizens.

What famous actor wrote a play about his experience at Manzanar?

George Takei (1937–), a Los Angeles native who is fondly known for playing Sulu in the original *Star Trek* series and movies, adapted his personal experiences at Manzanar in his musical *Allegiance*, which had its Broadway debut in 2015.

Were Japanese Americans really herded into internment camps during World War II?

Yes. It's one of the saddest chapters of American history that American citizens of Japanese descent were treated as criminals just because the United States was at war with Japan. Civilian Exclusion Order #346 was issued on May 3, 1942, by Lieutenant General John DeWitt, establishing that Japanese Americans nationwide would be forcibly taken from their homes and placed in assembly centers, which were, for all intents and purposes, internment camps. Many of the people rounded up were in California, though there were also camps in Oregon, Washington State, and Arizona. About 120,000 Japanese Americans were detained, most of whom had been born in the United States. In California, the biggest camp was called Manzanar, located in the middle of the desert in Inyo County, where about ten thousand men, women, and children were held in very Spartan conditions. People were put in wooden barracks (about five hundred in the camp), and the facility was surrounded by barbed wire and patrolled by armed guards. There was very little to do in the camps, and the buildings had no plumbing or kitchens; food was strictly rationed.

Manzanar was closed after the war ended, but the last internment camp did not shut its gates until 1948.

Who are the Hells Angels?

The "Hells Angels" Motorcycle Club took its name from World War II paratroopers from the 303rd Bombardment Group, who were also specially trained to fight behind enemy lines. Noted for driving modified Harley-Davidson motorcycles, the Angels were founded in Fontana in 1948. They soon developed a reputation for being involved in criminal activities ranging from extortion and theft to drug dealing and prostitution.

Interestingly, during the 1960s they were sometimes hired as security at rock concerts, most infamously the Altamont Free Concert held at the speedway near Tracy on December 6, 1969. The Rolling Stones were playing when things turned violent, and a fan named Meredith Hunter died. Angel Alan Passaro was charged but later acquitted.

Today, the Hells Angels have become an international organization with members in dozens of countries.

What famous wartime general was born in San Gabriel?

General George S. Patton Jr. was born in that city on November 11, 1885. A graduate of West Point, he served under General John "Black Jack" Pershing (1860–1948) in World

War I. Also serving under Generals Eisenhower and MacArthur, by the end of that war, Patton was a colonel and in charge of the U.S. Tank Corps. In World War II, he commanded the U.S. Army Second Armor Division and led the American victory in the Battle of the Bulge, pushing back Germany's last major offensive in Europe, after which it was only a matter of time before the Allies won the war.

Today, there are several museums dedicated to Patton's memory in the United States. The one in California is located just off the I-10 in the desert town of Chiriaco Summit.

Near the end of World War II, what significant event occurred in San Francisco?

The charter to form the United Nations was signed in San Francisco on June 26, 1945, when leaders of fifty countries signed it, but it was not ratified until October 24, 1945, which is why United Nations Day is celebrated then and not in June.

How did the war influence the state's population?

After the war was over, servicemen and their families who had come to the state as part of the military efforts for the war in the Pacific often stayed in sunny California. The state added about three million residents from 1940 to 1947. In a somewhat longer view, the population went from about two million in 1900 to ten million by 1950 (much of that during and after World War II).

1950s AND 1960s

How did Big Sur become such a hotspot for Bohemian writers in the 1950s and '60s?

Perhaps because of its beauty and secluded location, Big Sur attracted such authors as Jack Kerouac, Hunter S. Thompson, Henry Miller, Richard Brautigan, Robinson Jeffers, and Emile Norman. Many of them were not only influenced by their time there but also wrote about it. For example, Kerouac penned the 1962 novel *Big Sur* based on his time at Laurence Ferlinghetti's cabin, and Henry Miller penned the memoir *Big Sur and the Oranges of Hieronymus Bosch* (1957). Not much later, Big Sur attracted the attention of Hollywood's elite, such as director Orson Welles and actors Richard Burton and Elizabeth Taylor, and, from the late 1960s to about 1971, musicians such as Crosby, Stills, Nash, and Young, Joni Mitchell, and Joan Baez. All this creativity inspired the Big Sur Folk Festival, which ran from 1964 to 1971. The 1971 movie *Celebration at Big Sur* was filmed at the 1969 festival.

Did the Cultural Revolution begin at the University of California, Berkeley?

The "Free Speech Movement" began there, and that could certainly be viewed as a significant early event in the Counterculture Revolution of the sixties. Influenced, at least

Has there ever been a nuclear accident in California?

One of the biggest secrets ever kept by the U.S. government was revealed by the media recently, as NBC reported on the local Los Angeles website in 2015. The highly classified Area Four of the Santa Susana Field Lab in Simi Valley that was opened in 1947 was experimenting with the potential of nuclear reactors to propel rockets. In 1959, a potential nuclear meltdown threatened the facility. To avoid a complete disaster, the government authorized the release of radioactive gases, which spewed into the air and over oblivious citizens in Los Angeles and Ventura counties. This was done at night to help avoid detection. About six weeks later, the Atomic Energy Commission released a statement that there had been a minor "fuel element failure" but that nothing radioactive had been released and there was no danger.

That radiation continues to contaminate soil and water in the area, according to a 2012 EPA study that found 423 radioactive spots near the lab, and further study showed that it had spread to areas northeast, northwest, and south of the field. People who grew up in areas such as Simi Valley, Thousand Oaks, Canoga Park, Chatsworth, and West Hills in the 1960s and afterward have been diagnosed with cancer that could easily have been caused by this contamination, according to the NBC investigation. While lawsuits have been filed, the federal government has continued to stall and ignore demands to clean up the area.

partially, by the African American Civil Rights movement that began in the 1950s, students at Berkeley began demanding the right to express their social and political views more freely on campus; they also wanted more academic freedom—that is, they wanted their professors to be able to teach what they wished without threats of discipline from university administrators. Following the example of Dr. Martin Luther King Jr., the students followed peaceful protest practices such as sit-ins. Three thousand students conducted a sit-in on October 1, 1964. The police were called, and students were sent to jail. Although they were released within two days, others at the university were outraged, especially when the university filed charges against those who organized the protest. On December 3, eight hundred students staged a new protest, this time taking over the university's administration building, and the "Free Speech Movement" officially began.

What is the "Column of Earth and Air"?

Built in 1991 to commemorate the Free Speech Movement, the "Column of Earth and Air" near Sproul Hall on the UC Berkeley campus is a six-inch hole surrounded by a six-foot-wide circle of granite. An inscription declares that a column of air extends from the hole all the way up for sixty thousand feet. This air space is not regulated by any government, so anyone can stand in the circle and say anything they like without fear of being censored or persecuted.

What was the San Francisco "Human Be In"?

Held on January 14, 1967, at Golden Gate Park, the "Be In" marked a high point of the "Summer of Love." It was a celebration of the hippie counterculture and was attended by about twenty-five thousand people, mostly young college students. A reaction to a then-new California law making the drug LSD illegal, the event was organized by artist Michael Bowen (1937–2009) and meant to celebrate the concepts of a new generation, including environmental awareness, spiritual awakening, communal living, and celebrating love and not war.

A 1966 rally at UC Berkeley protesting the university's policy of banning the distribution of political materials on campus.

Among the important attendees were poets Allen Ginsburg (1926–1997) and Gary Snyder (1930–), painter and poet Lawrence Ferlinghetti (1919–), psychologist and LSD advocate Timothy Leary (1920–1996), comedian Dick Gregory (1932–), and rock bands such as the Grateful Dead and Jefferson Airplane.

The "Be In" not only drew attention to the Haight-Ashbury district, it is often considered the launching point of the American counterculture movement.

What other event in 1967 could be said to mark the start of the 1960s countercultural revolution?

Held from June 16 to 18, 1967, the Monterey Pop Festival was the first rock music festival ever and was attended by two hundred thousand people. Promoted as a festival of "Music, Love, and Flowers," the event is regarded by many historians, along with the Human Be In, as a transition between the 1950s and 1960s culture. Musical acts such as the Mamas and the Papas, Simon & Garfunkel, the Steve Miller Band, Jefferson Airplane, the Byrds, the Grateful Dead, and Jimi Hendrix performed to thousands of youth who allowed themselves to let their hair down and forget the troubles of the world.

Why did the Haight-Ashbury neighborhood in San Francisco become a center for hippie culture?

The story of the Haight-Ashbury district is like that of a bright candle that burns out too quickly. Still remembered as a center of the 1960s hippie culture, its heyday really only lasted from 1966 to 1968. The opening of the Psychedelic Shop in January 1966 really set things off. This was a place where young people gathered to buy and use marijuana and LSD. It quickly became a drug center, but it just as quickly attracted musicians ranging from Janis Joplin and Jimi Hendrix to John Lennon and his wife, Yoko Ono. A number of musicians moved to the area, and during the Summer of Love, the streets practically pulsed with psychedelic music, street theater performances, free food, and the smell of weed. That all ended by 1968, when harder drugs entered the scene, and with the lack of much police protection in the area, crime rates rose. By the time the area made a comeback in the late 1970s, the mood had passed.

Why is City Lights Booksellers & Publishers so famous?

Not just a bookstore but also a publishing house, City Lights was founded in 1953 and is still located at 261 Columbus Avenue. It is considered the heart of the Beat Generation and, as a publishing company, released the seminal Allen Ginsburg work, *Howl*, in 1956.

City Lights' history actually goes back a little further than this to a man named Peter D. Martin (1923–1988), who moved from New York to San Francisco in the 1940s. He started a flower shop in what is now the bookstore, but he also began publishing a literary magazine called *City Lights*, which was named after a Charlie Chaplin film. The periodical published the works of such authors and poets as Robert Duncan, Lawrence Ferlinghetti, Jack Spicer, and Philip Lamantia, as well as movie reviews by Pauline Kael, who later became famous as a writer for the *New Yorker*.

City Lights in San Francisco is closely associated with the days of the Beat and Hippie generations, and it helped publish the works of such writers as Allen Ginsburg and Lawrence Ferlinghetti.

When the flower shop failed, Martin opened the bookstore and gave it the same name as his magazine. He also expanded his publishing business, working with Ferlinghetti (1919–). In 1955, Martin decided to go back to New York and sold the store and publishing house to Ferlinghetti, who still runs it as of 2016. Today, *City Lights* continues to publish poetry and fiction, as well as nonfiction books on social and political issues.

Which two events marked the end of the Sixties to many people's minds?

Appropriately both occurring in 1969, "Bloody Thursday" and the events at the Altamont Free Concert at Altamont Speedway were two black marks on a once hopeful era. Bloody Thursday was the first of these events, happening on May 15 on UC Berkeley property (this seems appropriate, since so much of the counter-revolution was centered at Berkeley). The kindling for what would be a day of death was People's Park. While this was land owned by the university, it had become a mix of merchant and student activity. Governor Ronald Reagan (1911–2004) considered the student activity to be communist in nature, and he described the students as deviants trying to wrestle control of property from the university, even though university administrators didn't seem to mind.

Reagan sent in the state highway patrol to clear the area on May 15, 1969. Coincidentally, at noon on the same day, a student rally was being held on the campus about the Arab–Israeli conflict. The students heard what was going on at People's Park and decided to march over there to protest. The highway patrol had left, but there were still city and university police there guarding the fence that had been set up around the park to keep students out. Chanting, "We want the park!" the students began throwing rocks, tearing at the fence, and they opened a fire hydrant. A car was set on fire, and the police started shooting tear gas at the protesters.

A bad situation got worse. As the crowd grew to four and then six thousand students, police called for backup. Reagan's chief of staff, Edwin Meese III (1931–), then called for Alameda County police to join in. Soon, the 791 officers, wearing riot gear and wielding nightsticks, began to turn things more violent. Next, they brought in shotguns and began firing. One student, James Rector, was shot several times and died. Over 120 Berkeley citizens were taken to the hospital and, depending on which report one reads, five to nineteen officers.

Governor Reagan called in 2,700 National Guard troops, who patrolled Berkeley for the next two weeks. Tensions remained high, with police sometimes beating or tear-gassing citizens. The locals, it seemed, taunted the police in return, and—somewhat amusingly—offered them special brownies and lemonade (laced with marijuana and LSD, respectively).

Today, there is nothing left of the park or its community garden, having been bulldozed by the city in 2011.

The other unpleasant event of 1969 happened at the Altamont Rock Festival at the Altamont Speedway in Livermore, which was held on December 6, 1969. Attended by three hundred thousand, the free concert featured extraordinary acts such as the Rolling

How did Kwanzaa get started?

The idea for a weeklong spiritual celebration of black people and making life better was initiated by Dr. Maulana Karenga (born Ronald Everett in 1941), who was working at California State University, Long Beach, at the time. Karenga felt that Western religions, with their belief in original sin and that humans are cursed and must be subjected to the wrath of God, diminished the value of people. He sought to have something more uplifting, so he created Kwanzaa, which embraces the ideals of *Umoja* (Unity), *Kujichagulia* (Self-Determination), *Ujima* (Collective Work and Responsibility), *Ujamaa* (Cooperative Economics), *Nia* (Purpose), *Kuumba* (Creativity), and *Imani* (Faith).

Stones, the Grateful Dead, and Crosby, Stills, Nash, and Young. It was supposed to be a follow-up to Woodstock, but the event made a bad turn. First, there was a lot of confusion because the location was changed at the last minute from San Francisco, but what was worse was the security that was hired: the Hells Angels. High and drunk, the members of the motorcycle gang used pool cues to beat a man to death. The sense of love and freedom that was the spirit of the "Age of Aquarius" seemed to go sour at that moment.

A MORE CONSERVATIVE ERA

What started a movement from left back to the right in California?

Probably beginning with Ronald Reagan's term as governor (1967–1975), the state saw a distinct shift from left to right politically during the 1970s and 1980s. The era saw Republican governors in George Deukmejian (1928–; in office 1983–1991), Pete Wilson (1933–; in office 1991–1999), and Arnold Schwarzenegger (1947–; in office 2003–2011), while Democrat Gray Davis (1942–; in office 1999–2003) proved so unpopular that he was recalled, and Jerry Brown (1938–; in office 1975–1983, 2011–) was in office when Prop 13, one of the most conservative pieces of legislation ever, was passed (see the Politics and the Law chapter).

THE TWENTY–FIRST CENTURY

Did the onset of the twenty-first century bode well for California?

Not really. The state has suffered from a number of natural and financial crises since 2000, ranging from fires and droughts to budget crises.

What was the electricity crisis experienced by California in the early part of this century?

Deregulation of energy companies in the early 1990s during the Governor Pete Wilson's (1933–) administration resulted in electric companies pulling a scam on the state's citizens. The energy and commodities company Enron was a main culprit. Enron and local utilities took advantage of drought conditions and a slowing in the approval of power plant construction to blame blackouts and rate hikes on what was really going on: they were illegally shutting down pipelines and decreasing electricity production to get away with exorbitant (and we're talking 800%) rate increases to the utility companies. With energy prices up, stock traders made out like bandits. However, utility companies Southern California Edison and Pacific Gas & Electric were mandated to cap prices by the government. With outgo costs way over income, PG&E went bankrupt and SCE nearly did. Eventually, a federal investigation was launched against Enron and other Wall Street companies that led to their downfall (Enron went bankrupt). The crisis also contributed to California Governor Gray Davis (1942–) becoming less popular. Davis's inability to balance the budget or handle the energy crisis led to his recall in 2003 with 55.4% of the vote. He was replaced by Arnold Schwarzenegger.

When did the great drought start?

The current drought began in 2011 and, as of 2014, has been called the most severe in over four centuries. Drought is nothing new here, of course, but, using tree-ring data, scientists believe there have been huge, two-hundred-year droughts in the past. There was, for example, a lengthy drought in the fourteenth and fifteenth centuries, and from the ninth through the thirteenth centuries there was a very dry period that makes the current one look minor. The good news is droughts always end, but the question is, how long will it be?

What have been some consequences of the drought?

Smaller lakes across the state have been drying up and farmers have suffered greatly, often having to leave large sections of their lands fallow. This has driven up prices of plant crops, as well as meats, which have affected customers at the supermarket. Forest fires have increased in frequency and size as trees and shrubs have died or dried out so that they are easily set ablaze; furthermore, firefighters are hampered in their efforts to control blazes, especially in forested lands, because many lakes from which they once drew water have disappeared. Finally, though less important, water recreation and golf resorts have suffered.

In 2015 Governor Jerry Brown mandated that water usage in the state be cut by twenty-five percent. This was the first time in California history that such an extreme mandate has been issued.

Is the drought over?

The year 2016 brought El Niño to the fore. This phenomenon occurs when ocean waters around the equator by South America become unusually warm, resulting in more rain

Many reservoirs in California, like the South Lake reservoir in Kern County shown here, are severely, even dangerously, depleted because of the drought.

in the state. But not only was this an El Niño, it was what many describe as "a Godzilla El Niño." While many are hopeful this could end the drought, it is not yet certain enough rain will fall to make enough of a dent in water reservoirs. The problem has been the unevenness of the rain patterns. While northern California has been deluged, the South has received not nearly the same treatment. The total in combining precipitation measurements in the north and south has been a net average rainfall for the state. While this is much better than a drought, it probably isn't enough to declare "drought over."

Has anything good come from the drought?

While the state is not unfamiliar with droughts, this recent experience has been one of the severest droughts in California history. It has actually resulted in more creative thinking about conserving, reusing, and using less water. Desert and semiarid cities have been encouraging residents to switch from having green lawns and thirsty gardens to growing desert and other plants that need less water. Many golf courses have converted to using "graywater" (reused water that has not been treated to drinking-level quality).

The state's high-tech companies are getting into the act, too. Improvements in water meters and programs that analyze the best watering patterns to use on fields have allowed the agricultural industry to reduce losses because of the drought.

Another temporary benefit of the drought has been better California wines. It seems that, instead of drying up and withering the grapes, a lower supply of water actually improves the flavor of the fruit, making a richer, more complex-tasting vintage. Some really wonderful vintages will be found in 2012 to 2015 California reds and whites. And it's not just grapes. Other juicy crops, ranging from peaches to pomegranates, have benefited. Common sense might predict that such crops need more water, but produce farmers have actually found that the taste and nutrition have stayed the same, although harvests have somewhat diminished.

Have terrorists ever attacked California?

California seemed to be immune to terrorist attacks for a long time, but that ended on December 2, 2015, when a married couple from Redlands—Syed Rizwan Farook (1987–2015) and Tashfeen Malik (1986–2015)—used guns supplied to them by their friend Enrique Marquez Jr. to shoot up a banquet hall filled with employees from the San Bernardino Department of Public Health. They killed fourteen people, then ran for it. Police chased them down and fatally shot both terrorists. Farook, who had been born in Chicago, was actually a fellow employee; his wife was a Pakistani who had been radicalized and then radicalized her husband; they left behind a child. Marquez, who had converted to Islam, was arrested and, at the time of this writing, is in court after pleading not guilty on several charges, including providing material support to terrorists.

What might the future hold for the Golden State?

Depending on whether one is an optimist or a pessimist, the future of the state looks dismal or bright. The grim prognosticators among us predict that continued immigration, compounded with global warming, will exacerbate the water shortages, causing famines, more wildfires, and increases in crime and social strife.

Optimists would say that California is finally beginning to learn how to conserve water better with the help of infrastructure improvements that will catch water runoff from storms and save it in aquifers rather than letting it flow into the ocean, as well as improved solar and wind energy, and even energy farms that harvest power from ocean currents. Public transportation will improve, including more and faster trains, further conserving energy needs. As for climate change, there are those who predict that the planet will actually cool because of a predicted Maunder Minimum. This is the cyclical solar event that has, in the past, caused mini ice ages, and a new one is predicted to come about some time between 2020 and 2030.

As with anything, the truth is likely somewhere in the middle. There will continue to be problems in the state, but California is too rich and diverse not to have some bright days ahead, as well.

NATURAL WONDERS

Is California really different from other states?

Yes. People always seem amazed at the diverse geography, climate, and natural beauty of California. Much of that wonder is due to factors that happened millions of years ago. Some things change even now. There is also a climate that changes as you travel California from the warmth of southern California to the northern border with Oregon. The border is about 900 miles (1,448 kilometers) long. There are also big changes as you go from the eastern borders with Arizona and Nevada to the West Coast, where the Golden State meets the Pacific Ocean. The elevations of California also have a big effect on the climate. On a spring day, for instance, people in the mountains are bundled up in winter clothes and skiing, while folks in Los Angeles are in the pool cooling off.

Elevation can change dramatically, too, the most extreme example being the fact that the state's highest point—Mount Whitney at 14,494 feet (4,418 meters)—is only 150 miles (241 kilometers) from the lowest point, Badwater Basin in Death Valley, which is 100 feet (30.5 meters) below sea level. There is also a place called the Lost Coast in the northern part of the state running through Mendocino and Humboldt counties. Here, 4,000-foot (1,219-meter) mountains butt up against the ocean.

Is there a big temperature range in the state?

It may be Hollywood's fault that people think of California as warm and sunny, but the truth is, if you live in California or are visiting, where you are in the Golden State will affect your temperature.

What is the range of temperatures?

That depends on the time of year and again, where you are. That always "Warm California Sun," made famous in the song by the Rivieras, does describe a good bit of the state, but you will most likely find the warm part in southern California and the areas east of Los Angeles, like Palm Springs and Blythe. According to the website usclimate-data.com, Los Angeles has a daily average daytime high temperature that ranges from 67°F (20°C) in January to 79°F (26°C) in August.

If you are near San Francisco, temperatures range from daytime highs of 57°F (14°C) to 70°F (22°C), with overnight lows in the 40s and 50s (4 to 10°C).

While San Francisco is cooler, both are in the Pacific Coast. If you head inland, things are different. In the desert cities of the Coachella Valley near Palm Springs, an average day in January is 71°F (22°C), and in July, the average daily high temperature is 108°F (43°C).

As the elevations go up, the temperatures go down. Right near Palm Springs is a mountaintop town named Idyllwild. There, the average July temperature is 86°F (30°C). The difference is that Palm Springs is at 479 feet (146 meters) above sea level, and Idyllwild is high up Mount San Jacinto at 5,377 feet (1,639 meters). There is a constant stream of cars going from the Palm Springs area to the village on the mountain to either cool off or warm up, depending on the time of year. While the Palm Springs area almost never sees measurable snowfall, Mount San Jacinto is covered in the winter months, making it a winter wonderland for those who are there and making it a beautiful, picture-perfect, snow-covered backdrop for those in the Coachella Valley.

What are the Santa Ana Winds?

Sometimes referred to as the "Devil Winds" because the Spanish *Santanas* means "Satan," the Santa Ana Winds are dry, hot winds that blanket southern California and the northern part of Baja California during the fall and winter seasons, for the most part. They are dreaded in these parts because they dry out brush, making it ripe for kindling, or, worse, fan fires that have already started. The winds erupt when cool, high-pressure zones arise in the Great Basin and winds blow from the northeast and through mountain passes, including the Soledad, Cajon, and San Gorgonio passes.

What about rain and snowfall?

While desert areas and southern California get a little bit of rain, snow in higher elevations is usually plentiful, but during droughts, the water supply can be tight. Much of

---

How have people taken advantage of the strong winds through the San Gorgonio Pass?

Winds are so steady and strong through the San Gorgonio Pass, which connects the Coachella Valley with the Los Angeles Basin, that the space between Mount San Jacinto and Mount Gorgonio is the ideal place for a wind farm. Operated by Southern California Edison, it has over three thousand windmills and generates over six hundred megawatts of electricity a year.

California's rainwater and snow melt is collected and stored in reservoirs and then piped into the cities along the coast.

Is fog a problem in the state?

Yes, it can be, especially in San Francisco, along the coast, and in some central cities such as Fresno. In Fresno bad fog conditions are sometimes called a "Tule fog," which is named after the Indian Tule tribe. The fog can be dangerously thick, often causing car accidents, especially along Highway 99. For example, in November 2007 there was a crash on the 99 involving 108 cars that killed two.

Coastal fog in California can technically be described as "advection fog." It forms when warm air sinks onto a cold surface (in this case, along the coastline) and is common during the summer months. It typically dissipates as the day warms up in the afternoon.

What are the biggest dams in California?

Conserving water is a vital pursuit in California, both for the booming population and for the huge agricultural industry. There are over 1,400 dams in the state. The largest ones are:

- Oroville Dam—completed in 1968 in Butte County north of Sacramento, this is California's tallest dam at 742 feet (226 meters). It spans the Feather River and is used for irrigation, hydropower, and flood control.

- New Bullards Bar Dam—also located north of Sacramento in Yuba County, this dam was finished in 1970 and is 635 feet (194 meters) tall. It supplies drinking water, irrigation, hydropower, and flood control to the region.

- New Melones Dam—located on the Stanislaus River between Calaveras and Tuolumne counties, it was finished in 1978 and stands 625 feet (191 meters) tall. It was built mostly for flood control.

- Shasta Dam—best known for creating Shasta Lake, a reservoir popular for recreational use, it is located on the Sacramento River in Shasta County and resembles the Hoover Dam in its curved, concrete construction. Completed in 1936, it provides water and hydropower to the area.

- New Don Pedro Dam—spanning the Tuolumne River about two miles from La Grange, it was completed in 1971 and is 580 feet (177 meters) tall. The Don Pedro Reservoir is popular for recreation, too, and the dam helps irrigate nearly six thousand farms and also supplies power to the area.

If Hoover Dam is located on the border between Nevada and Arizona, why is it important to California?

Even though Hoover Dam does not stand on California land, it supplies power and water to the state, which is why it is mentioned in this book. Energy from the dam is divided between Arizona, Nevada, and California, with a large chunk going to Los Angeles, Burbank, Riverside, Glendale, Anaheim, Banning, Colton, Azusa, Pasadena, and Vernon.

81

How does the Colorado River Compact allocate water between states?

The Colorado River is like a lifeline through the Southwest. Water from it is used by seven states: Arizona, Colorado, Utah, Nevada, New Mexico, Wyoming, and, of course, California. The compact, signed in 1922, divides the river between Upper Basin and Lower Basin states; each half can use 7.5 million acre/feet per year. California's share of that is 58.7%.

Where is Boulder Dam?

Boulder Dam was the original name for Hoover Dam, so there really is no such thing as Boulder Dam anymore, though some Californians might still recall that name. The first moniker came from Boulder Canyon, where the dam was supposed to be built before it was decided that Black Canyon was a better location. Despite the move, the name Boulder Dam stuck.

Naming the dam after President Herbert Hoover was the idea of Secretary of the Interior Ray Lyman Wilbur (1875–1949), but at the time the nation was in the midst of the Great Depression, and Hoover was not tremendously popular. For a time, people unofficially called it Boulder but officially referred to it as Hoover. When Hoover lost the White House to Franklin D. Roosevelt in 1932, the name went back to Boulder Dam. In 1944, the U.S. Congress recognized that Hoover had a lot to do with getting the dam built, and a resolution was passed to make Hoover Dam the official title.

Why was the Los Angeles aqueduct constructed?

Water resources in southern California's semiarid climate were not sufficient for a growing city. As early as the turn of the twentieth century, it had become clear that the city of Los Angeles would never be able to supply water to the increasing population there. The main water source was the Los Angeles River, a modest trickle into the city. A bond to build the L.A. aqueduct was approved in 1905 and completed at a cost of $20 million dollars and five years of labor. It draws water from the Owens Valley in the Sierra Nevada Mountains and down 250 miles (400 kilometers) to the San Fernando Valley.

The aqueduct drained Owens Lake, which is now a dry salt flat. Los Angeles, on the other hand, grew from a city of about sixty square miles in 1907 to about 450 square

---

Is the song "It Never Rains in California" about the weather?

Not really, no. The British team of Albert Hammond and Mike Hazlewood released the hit in 1972. It's about a young man who travels to Hollywood, hoping to be a star. He has no luck, and his life deteriorates quickly. The chorus that goes "It never rains in California, but girl don't they warn ya/It pours, man, it pours" refers to bad luck, not precipitation.

miles at the end of the 1920s. Realizing that even this wasn't enough for Los Angeles, construction on a second aqueduct was approved in 1956. The drain on water from the north became so profound that by the 1970s, restrictions on how much could be taken by Los Angeles started to be put in place by the courts. Today, nearly half of the water from Mono and Inyo counties are dedicated to those areas for ecological purposes.

The Los Angeles aqueduct is an incredible feat of engineering that provides desperately needed water to the semiarid Los Angeles metropolitan area.

What disaster struck near Los Angeles in 1928?

On March 12, 1928, the St. Francis Dam in the Santa Clarita Valley burst, sending a wall of liquid destruction down the San Francisquito Canyon. Five towns were destroyed along the fifty-four-mile course to the Pacific Ocean, and more than six hundred people were killed. Blame for the disaster, which is considered to be second only to the 1906 San Francisco quake, was laid at the feet of city engineer William Mulholland. Construction, which had only been completed two years before, was considered faulty, and the structure was too weak to hold all the water demanded of it.

Have there been other dam disasters in California?

Sadly, yes. On December 14, 1963, the Baldwin Hills Dam in Los Angeles burst open, killing five people and destroying sixty-five houses. The failure of the dam was blamed on the structure cracking as a result of oil drilling nearby. It was this tragedy that convinced Los Angeles officials to change their strategy for storing water. Instead of building smaller dams with reservoirs for only local communities, there would be more reliance on larger structures, such as Hansen Dam in Lake View Terrace. Also, the city shifted to storing much more water in underground reservoirs.

MOUNTAINS

Are there a lot of mountains in California?

California has 352 named mountain ranges within its borders. Many of these are small ranges, or so-called "named ranges within a named range" or part of a larger range. Other named ranges are little more than hills sticking up about average terrain.

How did the mountains of California form?

They reached up to the sky millions of years ago when the earth was forming. California sits where some of the earth's plates meet on fault lines. In some areas, those plates slammed into each other with an upward thrust as the earth was cooling. In other areas, blocks of earth at the fault lines lifted themselves over each other. Most mountain ranges continue to rise, and California is no exception. Magma continues to cook and churn beneath the earth and push them up. Most of that rising is imperceptible at one or two inches per year, but in an earthquake, the land can suddenly thrust upward.

What is the Sierra Nevada?

The Sierra Nevada is a mountain range that separates California's central valley from its eastern border with Nevada.

A popular drive for many is along this range, as it literally grows out of the desert floor as you head north from the Los Angeles area. Most of the Sierra Nevada range lies within the borders of the state of California, but it does cross into Nevada at Lake Tahoe.

The Sierra runs 400 miles (344 kilometers) from north to south, but it is only about 70 miles (113 kilometers) wide.

The Sierra Nevada mountain range features Lake Tahoe, the largest mountaintop lake in North America. There is also Mount Whitney, at 14,494 feet (4,418 meters), the highest point in the forty-eight lower contiguous United States. Mount Whitney is part of Yosemite National Park.

The range was formed a few million years ago. There were granite deposits deep underground. The range was pushed upward by volcanic forces and then erosion by glaciers exposed the granite and formed the light-colored mountains and cliffs that make up the range.

That violent uplift and erosion left us with mountains that have five zones contained within a wide range of elevations. Simply stated: As you climb the Sierra Nevada, the climate changes.

The mountains are still being pushed up each year. In a joint study, the University of Nevada's geodetic laboratory in Reno and the University of Glasgow, Scotland, found the mountains growing quickly. The rate is about half an inch every ten years, which in mountain rising terms would be worthy of a speeding ticket.

What other major ranges are in the state?

- The Cascades: this is a range of mountains stretching from northern California to British Columbia. The California part of the Cascades is covered by seven national forests, including Lassen National Forest, Shasta-Trinity National Forest, Klamath National Forest, Mendocino National Forest, Modoc National Forest, Plumas National Forest, and Lava Beds National Monument.

- Klamath Mountains: located in northwestern California and extending into Oregon, this range includes Mount Eddy, which is 9,037 feet (2,754 meters) high.

- The Coast Ranges: these ranges run almost 600 miles (965 kilometers) up and down the state's coast. They are divided into North and South Coast Ranges, with the dividing point being the Bay Area.

- Transverse Ranges: this is actually a group of mountain ranges in the southern part of the state, including the San Bernardino Mountains, San Gabriel Mountains, Santa Monica Mountains, the Santa Susana Mountains, and the Tehachapi Mountains. The tallest peak in these ranges is Mount Gorgonion, which is just north of Palm Springs and stands 11,499 feet (3,505 meters) high, the tallest mountain in the south part of the state.

- Peninsular Range: this is the southernmost range and includes the Santa Rosa, San Jacinto, Laguna, Santa Ana, and Palomar Mountains. San Jacinto is home to a beautiful tramway in Palm Springs, and Palomar is home to the famous observatory of the same name. This range extends into the Baja California peninsula.

- Basin and Range: actually, this is a series of mountains and valleys beginning east of the Sierra Nevada and extending down around the Mojave Desert. It includes the White Mountains.

Why are Mount Whitney and Yosemite so popular?

One trip to Yosemite and you will answer that question on your own. Yosemite National Park is filled with wonders that are guaranteed to impress. There are waterfalls, trees of

Mount Whitney in the Sierra Nevada is the tallest peak in California at 14,494 feet.

> ## Can I climb Mount Whitney?
>
> **Y**es, you can, but you need to be patient, prepared, and ready to share it with others.
>
> Mt. Whitney is the most frequently climbed mountain in the U.S. The National Park Service has implemented a permit system to minimize the impact of day-hikers on the Mt. Whitney backcountry. All hikers entering the Mt. Whitney zone, including day-hikers, are required to obtain a permit. There is information online explaining how to get a permit.

many different varieties, wildlife, waterfalls, and as we have mentioned already, the tallest mountain in the continental United States.

Who was the first to ascend Mount Whitney?

The climbers to have that honor were three fishermen: Charley Begole, Al Johnson, and Johnny Lucas. They reached the 14,494-foot (4,418-meter) peak on August 18, 1873, nine years after it was discovered by a European, Josiah Whitney (1819–1896). John Muir would scale the slopes on October 21, 1873, just a couple months later.

Are there other mountains to see and climb?

There is a very long list of mountains where you can hike, bike, swim, shop, or just relax. Just east of the Los Angeles area is Big Bear. People looking to escape the L.A. traffic and smog take the windy road and will be 6,759 feet (2,060 meters) above the world. There are several villages and a lake, appropriately named Big Bear Lake. You can boat in the lake or stay on dry land for camping, entertainment, and shopping downtown in the village. The recreation is year round. This is a popular place to fish from spring through fall, and there is usually plenty of snow for skiing and other outdoor sports in winter.

Are any of the mountains in California volcanoes?

There are many mountains that are volcanoes; the question is: are they active? Apparently so. C. Dan Miller of the California Seismic Safety Commission says, "More than 500 volcanic vents have been identified in the state of California. At least seventy-six of these vents have erupted, some repeatedly, during the last ten thousand years…. Sooner or later, volcanoes in California will erupt again, and they could have serious impacts on the health and safety of the state's citizens as well as on its economy."

Which are most likely to erupt in California?

While just about all volcanoes that have erupted in the past are being watched, one is considered the "most likely suspect." One potential hotspot is the Long Valley Caldera near Mammoth Mountain in eastern California. A huge caldera that is 20 miles (32 kilometers) by 11 miles (18 kilometers) in length and width and 3,000 feet (910 meters) deep, geologists feel it is one of the more likely spots in the United States to erupt.

What interesting peak can be found at Lassen Volcanic National Park?

Lassen Volcanic Park, a 166-square-mile (431-square-kilometer or 106,500-acre) park near the town of Redding in northern California that was established in 1916, features Lassen Peak, the largest lava (or plug) dome volcano in the world. Dome volcanoes are roughly circular peaks that form from a slow buildup of ash and lava. Lassen stands 10,457 feet (3,187 meters) high.

Lassen Peak has been dormant for over ten thousand years, but during its active period, it formed such other prominences as Brokeoff Mountain, Chaos Crags, and Mount Conrad.

So, will Lassen Peak possibly erupt?

Lassen Peak is the southernmost active volcano in the Cascade Mountain range. It is in Shasta County and is part of a large national park about 180 miles (289 kilometers) north of Sacramento. It has one of the most massive lava domes on Earth. It's the largest of more than thirty volcanic domes in Lassen Volcanic National Park that have erupted in the last three hundred thousand years, and it's part of a region that's been volcanically active for more than three million years.

While there is potential for those other nearby domes to erupt, Lassen Peak is listed with a threat potential rating of "High" by the U.S. Geological Survey.

There are several reasons why this volcano is watched so closely. As we said, it has the largest dome, and it's on the tallest mountain (10,456 feet or 3,187 meters). It also sits in the center of the dome field.

Lassen also has a history of constant activity dating back one hundred thousand years but was still for a long time. Then, on May 30, 1914, Lassen Peak rumbled back to life

Who was Ishi?

"Ishi" was the name given to the mysterious man who was the last of the Yahi Indians who lived near Mount Lassen. The Yahi had initially been about three thousand strong, but when the European settlers came, conflicts arose. In 1865, settlers killed all but thirty of the Yahi in what was known as the Three Knolls Massacre. The survivors went into hiding, but life was hard, and by 1911, Ishi was the only one left. He came out of hiding to look for food and was confined in Oroville by the sheriff there. Anthropologists from the University of California, Berkeley, came to study him, but this exposure resulted in the death of the last Yahi when Ishi contracted tuberculosis. He passed away on March 25, 1916.

from what was believed to be a 27,000-year-long sleep. It began spitting steam and lava for a year. During that twelve-month period, there were several explosions and avalanches. Then, after two quiet days, it took a final bow on May 22, 1915. There was a climactic eruption that pumped a column of ash 30,000 feet into the air and unleashed lava flows, which devastated an area of 3 square miles. Pumice and other rocks from the explosion were found 25 miles (40 kilometers) to the northeast, and volcanic ash reached as far away as Winnemucca, Nevada, about 200 miles (322 kilometers) away. There were minor eruptions until 1917, but steam vents in the mountain were still seen as recently as the 1950s. Lassen Peak is now once again dormant but remains active under its dome. There has been seismic activity. Some scientists believe that could mean another eruption.

Who are the "Nine Sisters"?

Not really who, but what would be the correct question. The Nine Sisters are a chain of volcanic domes formed about twenty million years ago that start in San Luis Obispo and end with the well known Morro Rock. Most people don't realize that Morro Rock is the end point of a larger chain, which some geologists point out actually has thirteen members, though four of them are not very noticeable to the casual eye. They are, actually, volcanic plugs, upwellings of rocks resulting from underground magma pressure that didn't form into full-blown volcanoes.

Are there any geysers in California?

Actually, yes. You might think you were in Yellowstone if you visit Calistoga to see the Little Old Faithful Geyser of California. It erupts every hour for four to eight minutes,

Several of the Nine Sisters are seen here. They are all volcanic domes that are part of a chain leading to Morro Rock.

like clockwork. While the geyser erupts from natural geothermal activity, Little Old Faithful is classified as an artificial geyser that resulted from someone drilling for water in the late-nineteenth century and hitting what was, at the time, an extinct geyser. Poking a hole in the right place set the geyser activity going again, and it has been erupting ever since. Locals note that the geyser can also be used to predict earthquakes. If the activity diminishes or is delayed in any way, it is likely that in a week or two there will be an earthquake within five hundred miles.

How about petrified forests? Any in the state?

Arizona is known for its petrified forests, but there is also one just about ten miles from Little Old Faithful in Calistoga. An admission fee allows guests to walk a short, well-marked trail to see the various impressive specimens.

VALLEYS

What is that big valley in the middle of the state called?

That is the Central Valley. Sometimes called the Great Central Valley, for obvious reasons, or just "the Valley," it is about 450 miles (720 kilometers) long from north to south and varies from 40 to 60 miles (60 to 100 kilometers) wide. Although it is clearly one big valley, the north is referred to as the Sacramento Valley and to the south it is the San Joaquin Valley.

Where is the San Fernando Valley?

The San Fernando Valley is an urban area just north of the Los Angeles Basin. About two million people live there. This is the Valley that became infamous in the 1970s for a couple of things: first, the Valley Girl culture (see the "Quirky California" chapter), and second, the pornography industry. So much X-rated film production was going on there, especially in Van Nuys, that the area was called such things as "the San Pornando Valley," "Silicone Valley" (a spoof of Silicon Valley), and simply "Porn Valley." Aside from that, there were regular movie production companies there, too, including MGM and Disney. For a while, there was also a major attraction, Busch Gardens, which was run by the brewery and was known for its exotic bird shows and monorail tours. It closed in 1979.

Where is the Los Angeles Basin?

The Los Angeles Basin is where a giant portion of metropolitan Los Angeles is situated. According to the 2010 Census, there were 9,862,049 people huddled in this coastal valley.

FAULT LINES AND EARTHQUAKES

What can you tell us about the infamous earthquake threats in California?

Just about everywhere in the state is susceptible to an earthquake.

How do they occur?

According to the U.S. Geological Survey, "The tectonic plates of the earth are always slowly moving, but they get stuck at their edges due to friction. When the stress on the edge overcomes the friction, there is an earthquake that releases energy in waves that travel through the earth's crust and cause the shaking that we call an earthquake."

How often do they occur?

While only large ones make the news, there are earthquakes every day in California. There can be hundreds in a single day. Most of them are very, very mild and have a low rating on the Richter scale. Most people in California don't feel earthquakes unless they break 3 on that scale.

The Richter scale? What is that?

The Richter scale is how we measure the strength of an earthquake. Officially called "the Richter Magnitude Scale," it was developed in 1935 by Charles F. Richter of the California Institute of Technology as a mathematical device to compare the size of earthquakes. The magnitude of an earthquake is determined from the logarithm of the ratio of the amplitude of the seismic waves to an arbitrary, minor amplitude.

Modern science and a large number of seismographs all over the planet make the measurements very accurate and uniform. The method allows one to pinpoint the epicenter of the quake and how deep inside the earth it occurred. On the Richter scale, magnitude is expressed in whole numbers and decimal fractions. Each whole number increase in the magnitude scale corresponds to the release of about thirty-one times more energy than the amount associated with the preceding number value. In other words; a 5.0 earthquake is thirty-one times stronger than a four-pointer.

Why are there so many earthquakes in California?

Unlike most states, California is not sitting on one solid tectonic plate. The state sits partly on the North American Plate and partly on the Pacific Plate. The Pacific Plate has many fault lines, literally cracks in the earth where the plates meet. Those multiple fault lines are where earthquakes occur.

What does an earthquake feel like?

They can shake, rattle, or roll, or any combination of that. The ones that are felt usually start with a rumbling that sounds like a semi truck approaching. Sometimes that is it. But there can often be one big jolt. That will be followed by a rolling and shaking as the ground settles back down and repositions itself. Earthquakes usually last twenty to thirty seconds.

Multiple fault lines? We hear about the San Andreas. Are there others?

While the San Andreas Fault gets lots of publicity, there are many faults in the Golden State. The San Andreas Fault is the longest and most visible, and most of the others are connected to it. It runs from the Salton Sea in Imperial County to Cape Mendocino in Humboldt County. It is about 810 miles (1,300 kilometers) long.

In such places as central California's Carrizo Plain, the San Andreas Fault is clearly visible.

It is the boundary between the North American and Pacific plates. The plates move horizontally in opposite directions. As that happens, Los Angeles is creeping closer to San Francisco. The San Andreas is easy to spot. In some places in California, you may be driving right next to it. For some residents it is over the backyard fence, and pilots, astronauts, and satellites see it all the time. There are about fifteen thousand fault lines in California. Many are seen from the surface, while others are below the surface. Those are called a blind thrust fault. The 1994 Northridge earthquake was caused by a blind thrust fault.

What have been the biggest earthquakes in California history?

The most powerful quakes in California's history are as follows (note that early quakes resulted in few deaths because the population was much sparser):

Magnitude on Richter Scale	Location	Date	Damage
7.9	Fort Tejon	January 9, 1857	1 death
7.8	San Francisco	April 18, 1906	About 3,000 deaths (although the official count is 498 in San Francisco, plus 102 in San Jose and 64 in Santa Rosa); 80% of the city was leveled because of the quake and the fires in the aftermath
7.8	Imperial Valley	February 24, 1892	0 deaths because the area was almost uninhabited at the time
7.7	Kern County	July 21, 1952	12 deaths, about $60 million in property damage

Magnitude on Richter Scale	Location	Date	Damage
7.5	Reseda (Northridge)	January 17, 1994	57 deaths, about $40 billion in damages
7.4	Owens Valley	March 26, 1872	27 deaths, about $250,000 in property damage
7.3	Near Eureka	January 31, 1922	0 deaths
7.3	Landers	June 28, 1992	3 deaths
6.9	Loma Prieta	October 17, 1989	62 deaths, $6 billion in damages
6.8	Santa Barbara	June 29, 1925	13 deaths, $8 million in damages
6.6	San Fernando Valley	February 9, 1971	49 deaths, $500 million in damages
6.3	Long Beach	March 10, 1933	115 deaths, $40 million in property damage

Why was the San Francisco earthquake so destructive?

One of the most powerful and deadly earthquakes ever, the San Francisco earthquake struck on April 18, 1906, leveling the city, burning much of what was left, and killing three thousand people. At the time, most of the buildings were made out of wood, and there was no such thing as building codes to prevent earthquake damage. For more on the San Francisco earthquake, see the "Northern California" chapter.

If I live there or visit, am I safe?

Like anyplace people live or visit, there are going to be some elements of danger. There are tornadoes, snowstorms, rainstorms, and wind. The key in all of these cases is to be prepared. Californians stay ready with some extra supplies and plans, but they don't panic. You should not if you are a visitor. Most buildings are earthquake resistant. Newer ones are built with quakes in mind, and older ones are retrofitted to make them strong. They are designed to move with the ground, and that usually does the trick. That vase in the museum is stuck down with what Californians call earthquake putty, and if you stay in a hotel, there will be instructions for you as to what to do if the ground shakes. But keep in mind, your odds of being in California during "the big one" are very slim.

How powerful was the 1994 Northridge earthquake?

Registering 7.5 on the Richter Scale, the January 17, 1994, Northridge quake was called that because it was initially thought to be centered in Northridge; it would be better to call it the Reseda earthquake, but names have a way of sticking. The trembler killed fifty-seven people and injured five thousand (1,500 seriously), destroyed sections of Interstate 10 and State Highway 14, caused serious damage in the cities of Simi Valley, Santa Monica, and Santa Clarita, and cost estimates of property damage upward of $40 billion, making it the most costly earthquake in the history of the United States.

LAKES AND RIVERS

What are the major lakes and rivers in California?

There are many lakes and rivers. Some lakes are natural and are usually above sea level. Others are manmade to store water. Most of the lakes run into rivers. Some end up in the Colorado River, and others drain in the Pacific Ocean.

How many lakes are there in California?

There are hundreds of lakes in California. Some are natural; others were created as reservoirs for municipal and private water systems. Among the largest and most well known are:

Lake Name	Area in Acres
Salton Sea (saltwater)	240,640
Lake Tahoe (California/Nevada)	122,000
Mono Lake (saltwater)	44,762
Clear Lake	43,785
Shasta Lake	29,500
Lake Almanor	28,257
Clear Lake Reservoir	25,760
Eagle Lake	24,000
Lake Havasu (California/Arizona)	20,400
Lake Berryessa	20,000
Trinity Lake	17,280
Lake Oroville	15,500
Tule Lake	13,240
Don Pedro Lake	12,900
San Luis Reservoir	12,700
New Melones Lake	12,500
Folsom Lake	11,450
Lake Isabella	11,200
Lake Camanche	7,770
Lake Nacimiento	5,727
Crowley Lake	5,280
New Bullards Bar Reservoir	4,700
Diamond Valley Lake	4,500
Lake Elsinore	3,300
Whiskeytown Lake	3,200

Which is the largest freshwater lake?

Lake Tahoe is the largest natural freshwater lake in the state. Its surface is about 191 square miles around, and it is over 1,600 feet (487 meters) deep. It is a magnet for boats, swimmers, and water recreation. It is also a star on the big and small screen. Lake Tahoe has the setting for hundreds of movies and television shows, including *The Bodyguard* and *The Godfather II.*

Lake Tahoe is partly in Nevada, though. What is the largest lake inside the borders of California?

The largest natural freshwater lake entirely contained within the state of California is Clear Lake, which covers 68 square miles (180 kilometers).

Which freshwater lake in southern California is the largest?

Lake Elsinore is the largest freshwater lake in southern California. Located about 70 miles (112 kilometers) southeast of Los Angeles, the lake covers 3,000 acres, making it the largest natural freshwater lake in southern California. It is fed by the San Jacinto River.

We have heard about the Salton Sea. Is that another lake?

The Salton Sea is an interesting lake, to say the least, and a constant source of conversation in California. The Salton Sea is a shallow, salty lake located directly on the San Andreas Fault, about 45 miles southeast of Palm Springs. Covering a little over 376 square miles (970 kilometers), it is the largest lake in California.

The Salton Sea was accidentally created by the engineers of the California Development Company in 1905. In an effort to increase water flow into the Imperial Valley for farming, irrigation canals were dug from the Colorado River to the east into the low-lying area. There was concern that silt buildup would clog the canals, so a cut was made in the bank of the Colorado River to increase the rate of water flowing into the basin. The result was that the water from the mighty Colorado River overflowed the canal, and the river spilled over into the Salton Basin. The water flowed uncontrolled into the long, dry lake bed for two years before the canal was brought under control.

Left on its own, the Salton Sea probably would have dried up on its own in a few decades. The area is a desert and gets little rain. By the early 1920s, the sea had reached a record, but in 1928, Congress acted to designate the lands within the Salton Basin below as storage for wastes and seepage water from irrigated lands in Imperial Valley. Since then, the sea has been used mainly as a repository for agricultural wastewaters. The average depth of the sea is about 30 feet (9.14 meters).

The Salton Sea became a seaside resort in the late 1920s with beaches, boat races, and other water sports. It became known as the "French Riviera" of California. The Salton Sea State Recreation Area was dedicated on February 12, 1955, and hotels, motels, and yacht clubs popped up on the shores over the years. But there was a problem: While the sea is still fed by some smaller rivers, it has no natural outlet, and the salt that was being mined from the region when the below-sea-level land was flooded was continually raising the salt levels in the water. That has caused fish to die, leaving an unpleasant odor that has all but turned the lakeshore into a ghost town. Few residents remain, but there is a constant effort to save the Salton Sea.

The Salton Sea is the largest lake in California. It was created accidentally by people trying to irrigate the Imperial Valley.

Why have some lakes gone completely dry?

There are a number of lakes in the state that were once quite large but are now classified as "freshwater dry lakes." Among the largest of these are Lake Cahuilla and Tulare Lake. Lake Cahuilla (not to be confused with the much smaller, manmade lake in La Quinta) was, at one time, impressive at 110 miles (180 kilometers) long and 31 miles (50 kilometers) wide and with a maximum depth of about 300 feet (90 meters). It covered much of the Coachella, Imperial, and Mexicali valleys. The lake and its resources were used by Indians for generations, but when the Colorado River, which had created it, shifted its course, the lake dried up. It was dry when Spanish explorers came upon it in the seventeenth century.

The fate of Tulare Lake in the San Joaquin Valley came much later, and less naturally, than its sister. Once the largest freshwater lake west of the Mississippi, it had a 690-square-mile (1,780-square-kilometer) surface area. The Tachi people thrived there for centuries, and it served as a sanctuary for migrating birds, but as white people came to California after the Civil War, the water from Tulare Lake was slowly drained for agriculture. The construction of dams from 1938 to 1955 to control flooding further depleted the lake, and now, it is nothing more than an empty basin. Nevertheless, the soil there has remained fertile for farming, which has continued to the point that soil salination is a problem.

Why is Mono Lake unusual?

Located just east of the Sierras at about the same latitude as Yosemite, Mono Lake (pronounced MOH-no) is a saline soda lake that has some unique things about it. Although it has a very high saline content, the ecosystem is very rich there, and the reason for that is because there is a thriving population of brine shrimp that form the basis of the local food chain. Alkali flies also live there and have adapted the unique habit of surrounding themselves in a bubble of air and then going underwater to find food and lay eggs.

Tufa formations are a point of interest on the shores of Mono Lake.

The other unique feature that attracts tourists to the lake are the tufas. Tufas are column-like rock formations that are formed from centuries of carbonate minerals being deposited. The tufas are particularly abundant at the south end of the lake.

What can you tell us about manmade lakes?

There are hundreds of reservoirs in California. They have been built over the years to keep the people supplied with fresh water. Most were created by damming up a river and then using pipes to retrieve the water for people to use. Aside from smaller lakes built by earlier settlers, damming up rivers for municipal water use began in earnest in the late 1800s and continues today.

Where was the first California reservoir built?

Most records indicate it was San Andreas Lake. It was created near San Francisco when an earthen dam was built on the San Mateo Creek. Completed in 1870, the 100-foot- (31-meter-) high dam still stands today. That is no easy feat, since it was unknowingly built on a fault line. In spite of that, it rode out the 1906 San Francisco earthquake, and the reservoir is still in use today, bringing water to the people who live in San Bruno and Millbrae just south of San Francisco.

What is Pyramid Lake?

As you're driving on the 5 a few miles north of Lake Castaic, you will notice a large lake to the west of the highway. On the south side, the shape of a pyramid is evident against the side of a mountain and next to a large, earth-and-rock dam. This is Pyramid Lake, an important reservoir for Los Angeles County that also serves as a recreational spot for boating and fishing. If you're interested in how California manages its water, then it is worth a stop at the museum there, which explains the aqueduct and reservoir system, as well as the history of the area.

What lake will you see looking out of an airplane window leaving San Francisco?

San Andreas Lake can often be seen from the air as your plane arrives or departs San Francisco International Airport. Look for a long, narrow lake, just southwest of the runways.

What is the name of the largest reservoir in California?

Shasta Lake covers 29,740 acres about 106 miles south of the California/Oregon border. It was proposed in 1919 but was not built in the 1930s. Construction of Shasta Dam began in 1937. The dam closed off a steep, narrow canyon to regulate the flow of the Sacramento River and other small creeks and streams in the area. It was completed in 1945 and rose to a height of 602 feet (183 meters) above the canyon floor, making it the only dam that was taller than Hoover Dam at the time. It is still the ninth-tallest dam in the United States. The lake is 517 feet (158 meters) deep, and at its bottom sits an abandoned mining town and a bridge that was used to take traffic across the river. The foundation of the dam was built so it could be made taller. An expansion project was proposed in 1990 that would add 200 feet to the top of the dam, but that project has long faced opposition and will probably never be approved.

Lake Shasta is used for recreation and feeds water to the Central Valley of California. It also produces hydroelectric power.

Which river is the longest in the state?

The longest that is completely within the state is the Sacramento River, which is 447 miles (719 kilometers) in length. Its source is near Mount Shasta, and it flows south toward San Francisco Bay, emptying into Suisun Bay.

What are some other major rivers?

The San Joaquin River is also fairly impressive. Its source is in the Sierras, where it flows roughly southwest toward the coast before turning northward, again toward the Bay Area, where it, too, drains into Suisun Bay after traveling 366 miles (589 kilometers).

Next is the Klamath River at the very north end of the state, and it actually has its source in Oregon. It flows into the Pacific near the city of Requa after a 263-mile (423-kilometer) trek, most of it through California. Other important rivers in the north are the Pit and Eel rivers, and in the Central Valley are the Owens and Kern rivers.

How does a large, dry place like southern California get water to its citizens?

It would be fair to say that the California Aqueduct, a public works project, keeps the southern end of the state from dying of thirst. Extending from the Sierras in the north all the way down to Los Angeles, San Bernardino, and Santa Barbara counties, the freshwater route runs a total of 701.5 miles (1,129 kilometers). Construction on it began in 1963, and the last leg of it was not completed until 1997.

FIRES AND DROUGHTS

What are the largest recorded fires in California history?

According to a September 11, 2015, report posted on the state's CalFire website (www .fire.ca.gov), the largest fires on record by acres burned are listed below. Note that these do not include fires before 1932 because accurate records were not kept that far back.

Fire Name	Cause	Acres	Damage	County	Date
Cedar	Humans*	273,246	15 deaths, 2,820 bldgs	San Diego	Oct 2003
Rush	Lightning	271,911**	0 deaths, 0 bldgs	Lassen	Aug 2012
Rim	Humans	257,314	112 bldgs	Tuolumne	Aug 2013
Zaca	Humans	240,207	1 bldg	Santa Barbara	July 2007
Matilija	Unknown	220,000	0 deaths, 0 bldgs	Ventura	Sept 1932
Witch	Powerlines	197,990	2 deaths, 1,650 bldgs	San Diego	Oct 2007
Klamath Theater Complex	Lightning	192,038	2 deaths	Siskiyou	June 2008
Marble Cone	Lightning	177,866	0 deaths, 0 bldgs	Monterey	June 2008
Laguna	Powerlines	175,425	5 deaths, 382 bldgs	San Diego	Sept 1970
Basin Complex	Lightning	162,818	58 bldgs	Monterey	June 2008
Day Fire	Humans	162,702	11 bldgs	Ventura	Sept 2006
Station Fire	Humans	160,557	2 deaths, 209 bldgs	Los Angeles	Aug 2009
McNally	Humans	150,696	17 bldgs	Tulare	July 2002
Stanislaus Complex	Lightning	145,890	1 death, 28 bldgs	Tuolumne	Aug 1987
Big Bar Complex	Lightning	140,948	0 deaths, 0 bldgs	Trinity	Aug 1999
Happy Camp Complex	Lightning	134,056	6 bldgs	Siskiyou	Aug 2014
Campbell Complex	Powerlines	125,892	27 bldgs	Tehama	Aug 1990
Rough	Lightning	119,069	4 bldgs	Fresno	July 2015
Wheeler	Arson	118,000	26 bldgs	Ventura	July 1985
Simi	Unknown	108,204	300 bldgs	Ventura	Oct 2003

*Human causes are usually accidental or carelessness, such as disposal of a cigarette, car backfire, or not sufficiently dousing a campfire. **43,666 additional acres burned in Nevada.

Those fires are big! But which fires were the deadliest?

Also according to the California state website CalFire report from September 11, 2015, the deadliest fires in state history as of 2015 are listed below.

Fire Name	Cause	Deaths	Acres/Bldgs	County	Date
Griffith Park	Unknown	29	47/0	Los Angeles	Oct 1933
Oakland Hills	Rekindle	25	1,600/2,900	Alameda	Oct 1991
Cedar	Humans	15	273,246/2,820	San Diego	Oct 2003
Rattlesnake	Arson	15	1,340/0	Glenn	July 1953
Loop	Unknown	12	2,028/0	Los Angeles	Nov 1966
Inaja	Humans	11	43,940/0	San Diego	Nov 1956
Hauser Creek	Humans	11	13,145/0	San Diego	Oct 1943
Iron Alps Complex	Lightning	10	105,855/10	Trinity	Aug 2008
Harris	Unknown	8	90,440/548	San Diego	Oct 2007
Canyon	Unknown	8	22,197/0	Los Angeles	Aug 1968
Old	Humans	6	91,281/1,003	San Bernardino	Oct 2003
Decker	Vehicle	6	1,425/1	Riverside	Aug 1959
Hacienda	Unknown	6	1,150/0	Los Angeles	Sept 1055

Did Charles Hatfield really cause it to rain?

Charles Mallory Hatfield (1875–1958) was the most famous rainmaker in California's history. Working with his brother Paul, Hatfield had invented a secret combination of chemicals that he would evaporate into the atmosphere, causing it to rain. Calling himself a "moisture accelerator," he would answer calls from farming communities and cities to end droughts, and by the end of his career declared over five hundred successes. Critics would refute him, though, saying instead that Hatfield was a gifted forecaster, only accepting drought-reversing invitations if he thought it was about to rain in the area.

Probably the most infamous incident involving his rainmaking abilities was in 1915, when he was invited to San Diego. Whether or not because of his chemical formula, it did rain there in 1916—and rained and rained and rained, until dams overflowed or collapsed, neighborhoods flooded, and twenty people drowned. There was also an estimated $3.5 million in damages, too. Naturally, lawsuits followed. The courts eventually ruled that the rain was an act of God, and since there was also no written contract, Hatfield could not be found guilty. On the other hand, he couldn't collect a fee, either. Nevertheless, the event gained him incredible publicity, and he continued in his rainmaking career. When he died, he carried his secret formula with him to the grave.

Fire Name	Cause	Deaths	Acres/Bldgs	County	Date
Esperanza	Arson	5	40,200/54	Riverside	Oct 2006
Laguna	Powerlines	5	175,425/382	San Diego	Sept 1970
Valley	Unknown	4	76,067/1,910	Lake, Napa, Sonoma	Sept 2015
Panorama	Arson	4	23,600/325	San Bernardino	Nov 1980
Clampitt	Powerlines	4	105,212/86	Los Angeles	Sept 1970
Topanga	Arson	3	18,000/323	Los Angeles	Aug 2009
Butte	Unknown	2	70,868/818	Amador, Calaveras	Sept 2015

BEACHES

Isn't California a beachgoers paradise?

Of course. Who has not heard a song about the beach and surfing along California's Pacific Coast? From the Mexican border to the point where the coastline is handed off to Oregon and the Pacific Northwest, California is for the most part one long beach with lots of bays and inlets along the way. That is about 1,000 miles (1,609 kilometers) of sandy beaches (and a few rocky ones).

Are there a lot of public beaches?

There are almost too many to count, actually. Public beaches are the rule in California, because the California Coastal Act of 1976 granted public access to all beaches.

What are the best beaches in southern California?

There are many great ones, but some of the best are:

- Coronado Beach
- Crystal Cove State Park
- Hermosa Beach
- La Jolla Cove
- Laguna Beach
- Malibu Beach
- El Matador Beach
- Newport Beach
- Santa Monica Beach
- Venice Beach

How about Central Coast beaches?

What's great about the Central Coast beaches is that you'll find them to be a bit less hectic than the ones closer to L.A. and San Diego. Some great ones are Pismo/Shell Beach and Pfeiffer Beach in the Big Sur area.

Malibu Beach is just one of many beautiful beaches along the extensive California coastline.

Is northern California too cold for a good beach experience?

Not at all. In fact, there are some excellent beaches up north, including Santa Cruz Beach, which is notable for the Pleasure Point and Steamer Lane surfing spots; Half Moon Bay and Moss Beach; Stinson Beach and Baker Beach by San Francisco; Gold Bluffs Beach near Redwoods State Park; and Manchester Beach, which is part of Manchester State Park.

Can you name some of the famous beaches seen in the movies?

Beach movies have been a staple in Hollywood since the 1950s. Producers and directors are often careful not to reveal an exact location, but Malibu, Venice Beach, and Coronado near San Diego have all been popular filming locations. IMDB has a list of too many "beach" movies to count. There are the original classics like 1965's *Beach Blanket Bingo* with Frankie (Avalon) and Annette (Funicello). There were several sequels, including the 1987 reunion film *Back to the Beach*.

There are countless other films where pivotal scenes were shown at Southern California beaches, including Dustin Hoffman's legendary drive along the beach as he traveled up the Pacific Coast Highway in *The Graduate* and the closing scene from 1962's *Whatever Happened to Baby Jane*.

Are there many bays and inlets from the Pacific in California?

There are hundreds along the California Coast. The largest is San Francisco Bay. San Francisco Bay is at the point where several California rivers drain into the Pacific. The Bay covers 1,600 square miles (4,160 square kilometers). The Bay forms two peninsu-

**What silly beach movie featured
Vincent Price, Frankie Avalon, and Annette Funicello?**

There is a cult classic beach movie from 1965 called *Dr. Goldfoot and the Bikini Machine,* in which the evil doctor (played by Vincent Price) creates an army of bikini-clad robots who have been programmed to seek out wealthy men and charm them out of their assets. Fortunately, Craig (Frankie Avalon) and Todd (Dwayne Hickman) stumble on this sinister plot. And yes, Annette Funicello is in it as the girl in the dungeon.

las. The city of San Francisco sits at the northern tip of the southern peninsula, while the Point Reyes National Seashore is to the north as motorists cross the Golden Gate Bridge. The Oakland Bay Bridge connects San Francisco to Oakland.

There is also Mission Bay, Morro Bay, San Diego Bay, Newport Bay, and about two hundred others. While most are natural inlets and began as harbors for the fishing industry, many have added sea walls and other breakwater barriers. They have been engineered to make it easy for commercial and pleasure boats to get in and out and to be sheltered during storms. Many, like Morro Bay, are routinely dredged every few years to remove the buildup of mud and silt in the channels.

DESERTS

How many deserts are there in California?

The main deserts in California are the Mojave, the Great Basin, and the Colorado deserts. The Sonoran Desert, which mostly extends through Mexico and southwestern Arizona, covers part of southeastern California, including the Coachella Valley, and it is in this region that it is known as the Colorado Desert. The Mojave Desert is north of the Sonoran and reaches part of Nevada, as well. The Great Basin Desert is mostly associated with Nevada, but it reaches into the area east of the Sierras.

Is Death Valley a desert?

Its climate is certainly that of a desert, but it is not a separate desert. Instead, it is part of the Mojave Desert.

What was the hottest day ever in California?

On July 10, 1913, a temperature reading at Greenland Ranch in Death Valley hit 134°F (56.7°C). That is a world record that still holds today, although unofficially Azizia, Libya, once hit 136.4° F (58° C).

In 2016 President Barack Obama protected three deserts in California. Which ones?

In February 2016, President Obama used the 1906 Antiquities Act to designate the Sand to Snow, Mojave Trails, and Castle Mountains monuments. Sand to Snow straddles the southern part of San Bernardino County and the northern part of Riverside County, while the other two areas are in western San Bernardino. Mojave Trails is the most extensive, including 1.6 million acres (647,500 hectares) of desert that helps wildlife by creating development-free corridors between Joshua Tree National Park and the Mojave National Preserve. Sand to Snow National Monument protects extensive bird habitats, the Big Morongo Canyon, 24 miles (38.6 kilometers) of the Pacific Crest Trail, and about 1,700 ancient petroglyphs. Unfortunately, the presidential declaration does not provide funding to help protect the land, but it does keep developers and other human activity away.

One of the hottest places on Earth, Death Valley is part of the more extensive Mojave Desert.

ISLANDS

What are the Channel Islands?

The Channel Islands are a group of islands off the shore of Los Angeles to Santa Barbara. They include Santa Catalina, San Clemente, Santa Barbara, San Nicolas, and four islands that make up Channel Islands National Park: Santa Cruz, Santa Rosa, San Miguel, and Anacapa. Only Santa Catalina has a sizeable population.

Catalina has a long and interesting history. What are some of the highlights?

Spanish explorer Sebastián Vizcaíno (1548–1624) discovered and named the island in 1602. At the time it was inhabited by Indians, but it later became a Mexican colony. In 1887 realtor George Shatto (1850–1893) bought the island and founded the city of Avalon as a resort community that became notable for sport fishing. The time between 1919 and World War II was a golden era for the island as Hollywood stars made it a vacation getaway. Here, they could enjoy some island living while still being close enough to get back to movie sets fairly quickly when needed (the same reason Palm Springs became popular for the stars).

The Wrigley family is a big part of the island's history. William Wrigley Jr. (1861–1932), the man who founded the chewing gum company and after whom Wrigley Field in Chicago is named, bought a controlling interest in the Santa Catalina Island Company in 1919 and set out to develop it. He also had the Chicago Cubs, who played at Wrigley Field and of whom he was principal owner, practice on the island. Their spring training camp remained there from 1921 to 1951, except for the war years.

A notable landmark on the island for which Wrigley was responsible is the Casino. Chances are, if you've seen photos of Avalon, you spotted the distinctive, round structure at the north end of the bay ("casino," by the way, doesn't mean a place for gambling; the word actually comes from the Italian and means a place for gathering). Designed by architects Sumner Spaulding and Walter Weber, the Casino features stunning Art Deco and Mediterranean Revival styling. The building opened in 1929 and features a huge ballroom on the top floor. There is also a movie theater that is still in regular use today. Tours are available and well worth the price.

Besides the Channel Islands, does California have any other island groups of note?

Yes, the Farallon Islands are located 26 miles (41.8 kilometers) west of San Francisco Bay. They include eleven small islands, a couple of unnamed, tiny islands that are basi-

The Casino in Avalon, Catalina, is not a place for gambling. Rather, it has a movie theater and a beautiful ballroom decorated in the Art Deco style.

cally boulders above sea level, and Fanny Shoal, all of which comprise an area of about 104 acres total. Except for birds, sea lions, and other wildlife, they are uninhabited, with the exception of people tending the lighthouse. The lighthouse is atop Tower Hill (358 feet or 109 meters above sea level) on Southeast Fallon Island, the largest of the islands at about a tenth of a square mile in size.

Native Americans called them the "Islands of the Dead" because they believed their ancestors' spirits resided there, and they therefore rarely went there. The Spanish explorer Juan Rodriguez Cabrillo (see the "Early California: First Peoples to the 1849 Gold Rush" chapter) was the first European to find them in 1539; Sir Francis Drake took his ships there in 1579 to collect seal meat, and seal hunters, such as the Russians, harvested skins there in the 1800s.

Exploitation of the islands' wildlife prompted President Theodore Roosevelt to designate the northern islands as a reservation in 1909, and all the islands came under protection in 1969, when they were declared a national wildlife refuge.

What is the story behind San Francisco's Treasure Island?

Treasure Island is not a natural island at all but was constructed from 1936 to 1937 in preparation for the 1939 Golden Gate International Exhibition. Built with fill dumped into the bay just north of Yerba Buena Island between San Francisco and Oakland, Treasure Island was named after the Robert Louis Stevenson novel. It is less than a square mile in area and is connected to Yerba Buena by a small isthmus. Currently it has a population of fewer than 1,500 people, but while the exhibition was running from 1939 to 1940, over ten million people visited the little island. After the exhibition closed, San Francisco's leaders considered putting an airport there, but it instead became a naval base during World War II and then an army base, which was decommissioned in 1996.

In the 1990s to the 2000s, the old aircraft hangars left behind were used as sound stages, most notably for Steven Spielberg's *Indiana Jones and the Last Crusade* and the penthouse apartment set for the television series *Nash Bridges*.

In 2005, the Lennar Corporation proposed turning Treasure Island into a car-free, self-sustaining community, including 5,500 housing units and other buildings for offices, a wind farm, an organic farm, and recreational parklands.

Was Angel Island comparable to Ellis Island in New York?

Angel Island, which is north of Treasure Island and east of Sausalito, did have the Angel Island Immigration Station through which many of the Chinese immigrants had to pass. During World War II, it also processed German and Japanese prisoners. The island was used for other military purposes, such as two hospitals and the Nike missile station, which was deactivated in 1962. Today, the island is part of the California State Parks system.

MAMMALS

Where did the grizzly bear go?

They were considered such a threat that less than seventy-five years after the discovery of gold in 1848, reports say every grizzly bear in California had been tracked down and killed. The last hunted California grizzly was shot in Tulare County, California, in August 1922.

In 1924, a grizzly known to roam the Sierra Madre Mountains in Santa Barbara County was spotted for the last time. It is generally believed he died of natural causes. Grizzlies have never been seen again in the wild in California.

Can the grizzly bears return to California?

An environmental group wants to bring grizzlies back to their home state by reintroducing the bear to California, as well as neighboring states Arizona, New Mexico, and Utah.

Grizzly bears are still found in the western part of the United States and the species is listed as threatened under the United States Endangered Species Act. In a 2014 petition filed with the U.S. Fish and Wildlife Service, the Center for Biological Diversity argued that to ensure the bear's survival, the agency should reintroduce it throughout its historic territory.

According to Noah Greenwald, endangered species director of the Center for Biological Diversity: "Grizzly bears once ranged throughout most of western North America, from the high Arctic to the Sierra Madre Occidental of Mexico, and from the coast of California across most of the Great Plains."

Grizzlies, thought to number as many as one hundred thousand in the U.S. at the time of European settlement, had dwindled to fewer than a thousand by 1975, when the bear was added to the endangered species list. As of 2014, experts believe between 1,500 and 1,800 grizzlies survive in the continental U.S. Most are in Idaho, Montana, and Wyoming.

With the brown bears gone, are there other species of bears in California?

Yes, the black bear (*Ursus americanus*) is still here, although back in the 1930s, they almost suffered the same fate as their brown cousins (by the way, just because they are called "black" doesn't necessarily mean they are that color; many black bears vary from

---

What are some other names by which mountain lions are known?

Mountain lions are also called pumas, catamounts, cougars, and panthers.

light to dark brown, as well). There are currently about thirty thousand black bears in California, so they are not at all endangered; indeed, they are often considered a nuisance, raiding farms (they like anything from avocados to onions), garbage cans, and campers' and hikers' food packs. For this reason, there are many regulations on how people carry and store food when they are in black bear country. Though usually shy of humans, if they become too accustomed because people feed them, they can be more aggressive.

A subspecies of bighorn sheep—Peninsular bighorn sheep—can be found in southern California.

How are mountain lions faring in California?

Near the point of extinction in the state in the 1960s, lions have made a comeback and are no longer listed as endangered or threatened. Instead, they are officially a "specially protected species," which basically means the government keeps an eye on the population because it is a native species, not because it is rare or might die off. The California Department of Fish and Wildlife notes that lions increased in number until about 1996, after which time the population has leveled off somewhere between four and six thousand animals.

Mountain lions are, as the name implies, usually found in mountain regions, where their primary fare is deer. While people in such wilderness areas sometimes express concerns, especially in ever-expanding new developments, attacks on humans by cougars are extremely rare. In the history of the state, only sixteen attacks and six deaths have been verified, the most recent one in Humboldt County in 2007. On the other hand, if you live in mountain lion habitat, keep an eye on your pets. They kill hundreds of pets and livestock annually.

Are there deer, elk, or moose in California?

There are deer, of course. Deer—specifically, mule deer—are pretty much everywhere. There are also elk, and for this state that means *Cervus canadensis nannodes*, or the Tule elk. Back in 1870, they almost went extinct, but conservation efforts brought them back, and there are now about four thousand roaming from Point Reyes to the south end of the Central Valley. As for moose, no, there are no moose in California.

There are desert bighorn sheep, however, which can be found sparsely populating mountains of southeastern California, including the Peninsular Range surrounding the Coachella Valley.

BIRDS

Did the population of the California Condor really go as low as three birds?

No, that is a misunderstanding of what happened, although the population did become perilously close to zero by the 1980s. The California Condor (*Gymnogyps californianus*) is an impressive bird with a nearly ten-foot wingspan. It forages for carrion while soaring at heights of up to 15,000 feet (4,575 meters). Because they don't reproduce quickly, their numbers can decline gravely if under too much stress. The greatest stress factor is habitat loss, which is a big reason why by the mid-1980s only twenty-two condors were known to exist. Three were initially captured (a reason for the confusion) to try to breed them in captivity, but ultimately all of the wild birds were caught in 1987 in order to save the species. Carefully nurtured, they were slowly reintroduced to the wild, and now there are over two hundred flying free along the California coastline and another two hundred in captivity. They remain protected today, though they are vulnerable to being injured or killed by power lines or accidentally ingesting poisons in trash left behind by humans.

Why did saving the spotted owl become a controversy?

The spotted owl (*Strix occidentalis*) lives in old-growth forests in the western United States and in Mexico. A threatened species in decline, conservation efforts to protect the northern spotted owl, specifically, stirred controversy because preserving its habitat meant interfering with logging and developer interests in the state.

Are parrots native to California?

No, but there are now large flocks of them all over the place. They seemed to originate in Pasadena, and some have speculated that when a bird farm burned down there in 1969, the birds either escaped or were released. Other theories include the notion that bird smugglers released them to avoid capture, that they migrated from Mexico, or that bird owners who couldn't manage the parrots released them.

Whatever the cause, the parrots are breeding and now range from San Diego to L.A. to Bakersfield and even as far north as San Francisco. Over a dozen species have been identified, as well as hybrids.

MARINE LIFE

Where are the best places in California to see bioluminescent algae in the ocean?

There is nothing quite as spectacular as paddling a kayak out into an ocean filled with blue, glowing algae, phytoplankton, and protists that use bioluminescence. In California, you can see them in select spots ranging from San Francisco to San Diego, including Mission Bay and Torrey Pines Beach near San Diego, where dinoflagellates are the glowing critters you'll see. North of San Francisco, the coastline off of Sonoma can also light up spectacularly. These dazzling creatures are usually safe, but sometimes they are associated with a red tide of algae, and red algae contains toxins, though you are fine as long as you don't swim in it.

Are they seals or sea lions that I usually see on California's coast?

Those are California sea lions, which are very common here. While playful and rather cute to look at, sea lions should never be approached. Males can weigh up to 850 pounds (390 kilograms), and while attacks on humans are very rare, they can get territorial and pose a danger. From San Francisco to Morro Bay to L.A. and San Diego, these pinnepeds are always popular with tourists on fishing and sightseeing boats.

I sometimes see smaller creatures in the same waters as the sea lions. What are they?

Probably sea otters, another delightful ocean mammal that delights in floating on the water on its back while cracking open clams or oysters or sea urchins on its belly. Sea otters were once heavily hunted for their dense fur, but while that has stopped, they are still endangered by fishing nets, oil spills, and other pollution that has been causing their numbers to decrease.

Can I go whale watching in California?

Oh, absolutely! There are excellent opportunities for whale watching from San Francisco and Monterey to Los Angeles and San Diego. Do a little research to discover the best times for the specific species you wish to see and charter a whale-watching ship, or there are even some good spots on land to see them. Gray whales and humpbacks are usually the most popular to see, but you can also spot blue whales sometimes, as well as dolphins and orcas.

In San Diego, the best time to go is the middle of December to the middle of March, peaking in January. This is when literally tens of thousands of gray whales migrate from Alaska down to Baja California. Go to Point Loma Peninsula or Cabrillo National Monument to see them from shore.

As part of the same migration, in San Francisco, go to Point Reyes to see the gray whales from January to April. Catch humpbacks from November to March. Dolphins, orcas, and even sperm whales can be seen much of the year if you visit the Farallon Islands.

Do some cities have whale festivals?

You got that right! At Dana Point near San Diego, there is the March Festival of Whales, Mendocino has the Mendocino Coast Whale Festival, and there is also the Fort Bragg Whale Festival and the Little River Whale Festival.

Monterey Bay also offers excellent whale-watching opportunities. Humpacks, blues, orcas, and dolphins are commonly seen from April to December, and from December to April, you can see gray whales. When you aren't spotting whales, go visit the famous aquarium there.

PLANT LIFE

What important bill was signed into law on March 16, 1901?

On that date, Governor Henry Tifft Gage (1852–1924) signed the California Redwood Park Bill, which quickly led to state monies being used to purchase land rich in redwoods. One of the first purchases, made in 1902, would become Big Basin Redwoods State Park in Santa Cruz County.

What are the some of the oldest living organisms on the planet?

California's bristlecone pines are among the oldest organisms alive on Earth. They live around 5,500 years, on average; one in particular, named Methuselah after the biblical figure, is estimated to be 4,700 years old, which would make it the world's oldest tree.

Are there other ancient plants in California?

The creosote bushes in the Mojave Desert are incredibly hearty—and ancient—plants. Botanists have declared the "King Clone" bush there to be about 11,700 years old! That's older than the oldest-known human civilizations.

What's the biggest tree in the world?

Located in Sequoia National Park (see below), the General Sherman Tree is a giant sequoia (*Sequoiadendron giganteum*) that stands 274.9 feet (83.8 meters) tall and has a 102.6-foot (31.3-meter) circumference. It is estimated to weigh 2,100 tons (1,900 metric tons). Another impressive feature of the tree is that it has a branch that is 6.8 feet (2.1 meters) in circumference. Impressive as that is, the General Grant had some even larger branches that have fallen off the tree. Fortunately, no one was standing near the trunk when they fell, or they surely would have been crushed.

The sequoia known as the General Sherman tree stands almost 275 feet tall.

> ## Can you really drive through a redwood tree?
>
> There are actually a couple of them in California off U.S. 101: the Shrine Drive-Thru Tree, the Chandelier Drive-Thru Tree, the Klamath Tour-Thru Tree, and the Tour-Thru Tree. If you wish to drive through them, though, tourists are charged a fee for the privilege.

In terms of height, however, the tallest tree is the Harry Cole, located 324 miles (521 kilometers) north of San Francisco in Humboldt Redwoods State Park. It's 371 feet (113 meters) tall and is 16.2 feet (5 meters) wide at the base.

What is the Avenue of the Giants?

The Avenue of the Giants is a stretch of State Route 254 about 32 miles (51.4 kilometers) long between Stafford and Phillipsville, California, that goes through some of the most amazing old-growth redwood trees in the world. Along the way, one goes through the Founder's Grove, which has some of the largest trees in the area, including the Founder's Tree, which is 346 feet (105 meters) tall, and the 950-year-old Immortal Tree.

Are there any other cool sites involving big redwoods along the Avenue of the Giants?

Yes, it's worth at least a quick stop to see the Eternal Treehouse, which is a treehouse built into the base of one of the huge sequoia trees. While there isn't much to do there, it's still fun to look at and walk into.

Does California also hold a record for having the world's largest flowering plant?

Oh, yes, indeed! A giant Chinese wisteria known variously as the "Lavender Lady," "Jack's Beanstalk," and simply "The Monster" grows in the town of Sierra Madre. In 1990 it was declared the world's largest flowering plant in the *Guinness Book of World Records*. At the time, it had an estimated 1.5 million blooms, weighed 250 tons, and spread over an acre of land. That was twenty-six years ago as of this writing, and the wisteria is still growing larger and larger.

It all started in 1894, when a woman named Alice Brugman bought seeds from China and planted them in a can. The goal was to have a lovely plant to decorate her porch, but the plant kept growing! By the 1920s, it had overwhelmed the building, and the owner at the time, H. T. Fennel, had to abandon it and move into a new home next door. A few years later, the house collapsed under the weight of the wisteria. By 1973 an event was organized to invite people to see the amazing lavender blooms, and that has now grown into an annual Wisteria Festival.

REFUGES, PRESERVES, AND PARKS

Did California establish the first wildlife preserve in the United States?

Yes. On March 18, 1870, Lake Merritt, a saltwater lake that was once a part of San Francisco Bay and is located in Oakland, was officially made a wildlife refuge. The name comes from Dr. Samuel Merritt (1822–1890), who was mayor of Oakland from 1867 to 1869 and who built the dam that created the lake. This was the first time in U.S. history that an area was made off limits for hunting game fowl, mammals, and many fish. Still the largest urban saltwater lake in the nation, Lake Merritt was listed on the National Register of Historic Places in 1966. The Lake Merritt Duck Refuge was also made a National Historic Landmark in 1963.

Which national park is the most famous and popular in California?

That honor has to go to Yosemite National Park. Located in the Sierras east of Fresno, the park is made up of the Yosemite Valley and the Mariposa Grove of giant sequoia trees nearby. Geologists determined that the valley, which measures about 7 miles long and 1 mile wide (11 by 1.5 kilometers), is stunningly beautiful with its stark granite cliffs and towering waterfalls. It's extremely popular with hikers, campers, horseback riders, and mountain climbers, the lattermost enjoying the challenges of surmounting the Half Dome and other sheer cliffs.

How did Yosemite become a protected park?

Originally protected as a state park on June 30, 1864, when President Abraham Lincoln signed the Yosemite Grant Act, the park is commonly associated with naturalist John Muir (1838–1914). However, another man championed the beauty of the valley before Muir: James H. Hutchings, who, with his wife, Elvira, was one of the early settlers there. The Hutchingses built Hutchings House, an inn for travelers, in 1864, but he had first arrived in the valley in 1855. Promoting the natural wonders of Yosemite, Hutchings became known as "Mr. Yosemite." His work did a lot to bring attention to the valley and get it declared a state park.

What is the Sierra Club?

Founded on May 28, 1892 in San Francisco, the Sierra Club is an environmental organization founded by naturalist, author, and philosopher John Muir (1838–1914). Muir was on a mission to save the country's natural wonders and was especially enthralled by California's beautiful places, such as the Yosemite Valley and the Sierra Mountains. Now with over 2.4 million members worldwide, the club encourages people "to explore, enjoy, and protect the wild places of the earth."

The result of this attention, however, was not so wonderful of Yosemite. Tourists began to arrive, and many feared people would damage the landscape. More protections were needed, it was reasoned, and so the land became a national park in 1890 to help bring in the needed funds.

Who else helped to make Yosemite famous?

John Muir (1838–1914) and Ansel Adams (1902–1984) are big names associated with Yosemite. Muir was a Scottish-American naturalist who wrote evocative, emotional descriptions of the American West and especially loved Yosemite. The founder of the Sierra Club, he first arrived there in 1868 and soon became active in preserving the natural beauty of the area. The John Muir Trail that runs down the Sierras is, of course, named in his honor.

Naturalist John Muir (right) with President Theodore Roosevelt in Yosemite Valley. Muir convinced the president to help protect this treasure of natural beauty.

Ansel Adams was an acclaimed photographer whose black-and-white pictures of Yosemite are so famous that these images are still commonly reproduced today as wall art, calendars, and more.

What are the biggest waterfalls in Yosemite?

There are many waterfalls in the park, though some of them are dry in the summer. The biggest ones are as follows:

Yosemite National Park Waterfalls

Waterfall	Height (feet/meters)
Yosemite Falls	2,425 / 739
Chilnualna Falls	2,200 / 671
Sentinel Falls	2,000 / 610
Ribbon Fall	1,612 / 491
Wapama Falls	1,400 / 427
Horsetail Fall	1,000 / 305
Bridalveil Fall	620 / 189
Nevada Fall	594 / 181
Illilouette Fall	370 / 113
Vernal Fall	317 / 97

Why does the water at Horsetail Fall look like it is on fire sometimes?

A few days each year, when the sunlight catches the water just right, the waters cascading off of El Capitan to form the seasonal Horsetail Fall will look as if they are actually lava or liquid fire. (Unfortunately, because this book is in black and white, the effect cannot be reproduced here for the reader.) It is only during winter and early spring, when these falls are active, that the illusion is apparent, and it occurs only very briefly just before the sun sets.

What was the second national park after Yosemite?

Sequoia National Park was created on September 25, 1890, to preserve the world's largest trees. Its fifteen thousand acres also includes Mount Whitney. Shortly after the park was set aside for posterity, President Benjamin Harrison also made nearby Kings Canyon National Park, which includes even more redwoods.

Where is Pinnacles National Park, and what makes it an interesting place?

Established as a national monument on January 16, 1908, Pinnacles is located near San Jose in the Gabilan Mountains. It features a twenty-three-million-year-old volcano and is home to the rare California Condor that almost went extinct. It is possible, if you go hiking there, that you might see this impressive bird soaring above you. Also featured is the park in Bear Gulch Cave, home to the largest colony of Townsend's big-eared bats between northern California and Mexico.

When was Death Valley designated a national park?

Death Valley was made a national park on October 31, 1994.

Was "Grizzly" Adams a real person?

Anyone who watched television in the 1970s is probably familiar with the name Grizzly Adams. It was a feel-good show about a man (played by actor Dan Haggerty [1942–2016]) hiding in the woods from a false criminal charge and being a friend to nature. While that was fiction, there was a real Grizzly Adams. James Capen "Grizzly" Adams (1812–1860) was a mountain man who captured and trained bears, as well as other animals, which he would sell to circuses and zoos. He moved to California from his Massachusetts home in 1849 to join the Gold Rush. He had no luck finding gold, and the ranch he temporarily owned was lost to creditors; he left civilization for the woods of the Sierras, surviving with some help from local Miwok Indians. He adopted a pair of bear cubs, and one of them, which he named Benjamin Franklin, saved him from an attack from another bear in 1855. After later working for P. T. Barnum's circus, Adams died from side effects from the head injuries he had received during that bear attack from which he had never fully recovered.

What does Tomesha mean?

Tomesha was the Indian name for Death Valley. It means "ground afire," appropriately.

What mineral was mined commercially in Death Valley?

Borax is a natural mineral that has many commercial uses, including in laundry detergent, glazes, and cosmetics. While people up north were looking for gold, some miners saw the value of borax in the desert and began digging it out of Death Valley about the same time as the Gold Rush. Sporadic mining continued until 1915. The equipment of the time was just not efficient enough to make it profitable.

When President Herbert Hoover declared Death Valley National Monument in 1933, mining was contraindicated. Mining equipment improved, however, and the 1976 Mining in the Parks Act allowed very limited mining to resume. The last active mine closed in 2005.

Are Joshua trees only found in Joshua Tree National Park?

No, Joshua trees, which are related to the Yucca, as the scientific name *Yucca brevifolia* indicates, can be found around the southern part of California, as well as southern

Joshua Tree National Park features ancient trees and amazing rock formations that are a favorite among rock climbers.

Nevada and western Arizona, but the park has a large concentration of them. Native Americans used the tough leaves of the trees for weaving baskets, and the seeds and flower buds are edible. It was the early Mormon settlers who named the trees, comparing the branches to the upraised arms of the biblical Joshua in prayer.

The range of these trees is somewhat limited, and in recent years—especially with the California drought—there have been fears that many of the trees have been dying. The park, established in 1994, is also known for its stunning rock formations, which are popular with climbers, picnic areas, and camping grounds. Located about 140 miles (225 kilometers) east of Los Angeles, the park has almost 790,000 acres (320,000 hectares) of wide-open space.

Was the mystery of the "sailing stones" ever solved?

At Racetrack Playa in Death Valley, stones seem to move by themselves, leaving paths on the desert floor. The stones move in erratic ways, moving in different directions, sometimes leaving paths that show them making turns at sharp angles. The stones range in sizes, but some are as large as 700 pounds (about 320 kilograms). For years, no one could figure out what was going on, and, indeed, no one ever actually saw the stones moving. Was it an elaborate ruse?

NASA scientist Ralph Lorenz was finally able to solve the mystery in 2013. He figured out that in the winter, under just the right conditions, ice could form on the rock and, with the help of a desert wind, gently push the rocks over the cracked ground.

ZOOS AND AQUARIUMS

What was the first zoo in California?

Griffith Park Zoo in Los Angeles opened in 1912. It was open until 1966 and then incorporated into the current Los Angeles Zoo.

Which zoo has giant pandas?

San Diego Zoo is the only California zoo where you can see the magnificent black-and-white giant pandas.

How many accredited zoos and aquariums are in California?

Accreditation of a zoo or aquarium means that it meets standards that assure the safety and health of the animals kept in the facility. Accredited by the American Association of Zoos and Aquariums, these institutions are also allowed to participate in breeding and animal exchange programs with other accredited zoos. The following are currently accredited in California:

- Aquarium of the Bay (San Francisco)
- Aquarium of the Pacific (Long Beach)
- Birch Aquarium at Scripps (La Jolla)
- Cabrillo Marine Aquarium (San Pedro)
- California Science Center (Los Angeles)
- Charles Paddock Zoo (Atascadero)
- CuriOdyssey (San Mateo)
- Fresno Chaffee Zoo (Fresno)
- Happy Hollow Zoo (San Jose)
- The Living Desert Zoo and Gardens (Palm Desert)
- Los Angeles Zoo (Los Angeles)
- Monterey Bay Aquarium (Monterey)
- Oakland Zoo (Oakland)
- Sacramento Zoo (Sacramento)
- Safari West (Santa Rosa)
- San Diego Zoo (San Diego)
- San Diego Zoo Safari Park (San Diego)
- San Francisco Zoological Gardens (San Francisco)
- Santa Ana Zoo (Santa Ana)
- Santa Barbara Zoological Gardens (Santa Barbara)
- SeaWorld San Diego (San Diego)
- Sequoia Park Zoo (Eureka)
- Steinhart Aquarium (part of California Academy of Sciences in San Francisco)

SOUTHERN CALIFORNIA

LOS ANGELES AREA

Who were the first people in the Los Angeles Basin—or, at least, who were the people who lived there when the Spaniards first arrived?

At the time Europeans began coming to what is now the Los Angeles area, the Indigenous people living there were the Tongva, who also had villages in the Southern Channel Islands. Archeologists believe that the Tongva came to the area about 3,500 years ago, pushing out Hokan-speaking tribes. As with other Native peoples, the Tongva were pretty much wiped out by the European settlers, and by the early 1900s the Tongva language went extinct.

Why did the Indians call the Los Angeles Basin the "Valley of Smoke"?

Even before L.A. became inundated with people and smog-belching traffic, the area was noted for its hazy skies. Smoke from cooking fires lingered in the basin because it was surrounded by mountains. Ocean breezes blowing in from the west further trapped any air particles. The Spanish, too, recognized this and called San Pedro Bay by Long Beach the "Bay of Smoke." Meteorologists call the effect a "temperature inversion." Warm air above the valley—combined with cool air from the ocean—works like a trap to keep any pollutants from escaping. The problem in modern L.A. became so bad that by the 1970s there was something called "smog alerts," when the local government would declare the air quality so bad that it was unsafe to do much physical activity out of doors. Children playing by their homes would complain of burning lungs and difficulty breathing, and asthma was common. While car emission standards have eased the problem somewhat, the air quality is still bad, and the lack of regular rainfall to clear the skies just makes matters worse.

When was Los Angeles first settled by Europeans?

The first people to arrive in what is now Los Angeles was a group of forty-four settlers (half of them children) from Mexico. They arrived here on September 4, 1781, and established a humble pueblo that had quite a long name: El Pueblo de Nuestra Señora Reina de los Angeles (fortunately, the name was shortened, or instead of calling it L.A., we'd be calling the city P.N.S.R.L.A.!). For over half a century, it remained a rough-and-tumble Old West kind of town under Mexican rule, never really gaining a large population until after California was annexed by the United States in 1846.

Is Olvera Street the original place where the first Mexican settlers made their home?

Almost. The very first settlement was a little southeast of present-day Olvera Street, but the marketplace in the heart of Los Angeles is the oldest preserved street in the city. It's really one of the most authentic and fun experiences to have outside of Mexico itself. Part of the El Pueblo de los Angeles Historic Monument, Olvera Street includes some of the city's oldest-preserved structures, including the Pelanconi House, the city's oldest brick house dating to the 1850s and containing Olvera Street's oldest restaurant, La Golondrina, and the oldest residence still standing in L.A., 1818's Avila Adobe.

Olvera Street was conceived in its present form back in 1930, when the city saw an opportunity to preserve and display an authentic part of Old California. Here, one may

L.A.'s Olvera Street is a historic part of the city that recaptures some of the feeling of the early days of California.

find Mexican restaurants, beautiful architecture, shops featuring hand-crafted items, strolling mariachi bands, and live dances with performers in traditional costumes. Open seven days a week, the best time to go is during a Mexican holiday, such as Dia de los Muertos (Day of the Dead), Mexican Independence Day, or the Day of the Virgin of Guadalupe. A super experience for friends and family.

What, then, is the El Pueblo de los Angeles Historic Monument?

Olvera Street is part of the larger El Pueblo de los Angeles Historic Monument, or Los Angeles Historic Plaza District, a forty-four-acre section of downtown L.A. that was the heart of the city through the nineteenth century. It includes the Plaza, Merced Theatre, Masonic Hall, two historic trails, and other historic structures.

What was "California on Wheels"?

Inspired by the first shipment of oranges that left Los Angeles for the East Coast in 1889, "California on Wheels" was the brainchild of marketing mastermind Frank Wiggins of Los Angeles. It was a traveling exhibit of California-grown produce that was taken to fairs around the country. Many cities around the state initially participated, but when it began to get expensive many cities dropped out, and it became largely a Los Angeles affair that lasted from 1893 to 1909.

Which Los Angeles entertainment venue is well known for its band shell?

Built within what was a natural formation known as the "Daisy Shell" in Bolton Canyon below the Hollywood sign, the Hollywood Bowl is recognized by many at first glance because of its familiar shell. Currently the summer home of the Los Angeles Philhar-

The famous Hollywood Bowl has been, in one form or another, a venue for concerts since the 1920s.

monic, it was first opened on July 11, 1922, when it was little more than a stage and some seating placed by a hill that reflected sound rather well.

The shell over the stage would go through several iterations: a cover with bad acoustics was first built in 1926. The next year, architect Lloyd Wright (1890–1978), the son of Frank Lloyd Wright, built an avant-garde, pyramid-shaped shell with superior acoustics, but people didn't like the look of it, tore it down, and built yet another one in 1928 (these were wooden structures, so they were not too difficult to replace). Finally, in 1929, a more permanent structure was completed, and this is the one that lasted until 2003. This band shell became well known to concertgoers for decades, and preservationists opposed the idea of replacing it. However, musicians and audiences alike were demanding something that provided better sound, and, too, the old structure was showing wear. The latest version debuted for the 2005 season and combined elements of all the earlier band shells, including some of the modern lines of Lloyd Wright's design.

The new Hollywood Bowl seats 17,500 and is owned by Los Angeles County. The Hollywood Bowl Orchestra is its home orchestra. Formed of freelance musicians who often play for film studios, the HBO was founded in 1927 by conductor Eugene Goossens (1893–1962). In addition to the two orchestras it usually hosts, many other concerts by rock musicians (the Beatles and the Doors have both performed there) have taken place there.

Which Beverly Hills street is probably the most chi-chi in the West?

Rodeo Drive (pronounced Roh-DAY-oh) is a two-mile stretch between Sunset Boulevard and Beverwil Drive, but it is the three-block section between Wilshire Boulevard and Little Santa Monica that is famous for its high-end stores, including Giorgio Armani, Cartier, Celine, and Hammacher Schlemmer. The posh stores on Rodeo first began opening in the late 1960s with stores like Giorgio Beverly Hills, Gucci, and Van Cleef and Arpels. Between the expansion of the Beverly Wilshire Hotel in 1971 and the opening of the Rodeo Collection mall in 1983, Rodeo Drive solidified its reputation as the spot for buying luxury items. Rodeo Drive was renovated in 2003 at a cost of $18 million, and the Rodeo Drive Walk of Style, which is similar to the Hollywood Walk of Fame except that it honors fashion icons, was also introduced.

LANDMARKS

How did the Hollywoodland sign become the Hollywood sign?

Many people know that the original landmark sign that sits on top of Mount Lee included the -land ending, so what happened to those letters? Well, the sign, which stands 45 feet (13.7 meters) high, was initially installed in 1923 to advertise a new housing development. As the houses sold, though, it began to outlive its usefulness and fall into disrepair. The local chamber of commerce wished to preserve it without spending too much money, so they decided to restore the Hollywood and demolish the rest. The restoration was completed in 1943 and has remained Hollywood ever since.

Recognized the world over, the Hollywood sign was originally built to promote the Hollywoodland development.

What is the best way to view the Hollywood sign?

The sign itself is surrounded by fencing, and it is illegal to trespass there and get up next to the sign (see the story about Peg Entwhistle below for one reason why), but there are a number of ways for people to get a better look than just the usual view from the city. The three most ideal places to gander at the sign are:

- Griffith Observatory, which sits at a high elevation so you don't have to look up so much, and it also has free parking. While there, you might as well visit the wonderful observatory and science center, too.

- The already scenic Mulholland Drive includes the Hollywood Bowl Scenic Overlook, which, as the name indicates, has a great view of the amphitheater, as well as downtown L.A. and the Hollywood sign.

- Go to the corner of Hollywood Boulevard and Highland Avenue for the best ground-floor view and a great opportunity to take a photo of the sign as a backdrop to the glamorous downtown Hollywood.

Can I help preserve the Hollywood sign?

Yes, you can donate money to the nonprofit Hollywood Sign Trust by going to http://hollywoodsign.org/donate/.

Where can I go to honor departed celebrities?

There is one place that is a must-see for anyone wanting to reflect and remember actors, musicians, and other entertainment royalty, and that's the Hollywood Forever Cemetery at 6000 Sunset Boulevard in Los Angeles. Here, you can see everything from elaborate statues to more modest grave markers from Rudolph Valentino to Mickey Rooney. There

123

Why did Peg Entwhistle jump off the Hollywood sign?

Poor Peg Entwhistle (1908–1932) was a fairly successful Broadway actress, but when she came to Hollywood to make it big in the new movie industry, she could not find work, although she did have a part in the 1932 David O. Selznick movie *Thirteen Women*, starring Myrna Loy. After Entwhistle's body was discovered, a suicide note was also found that said, "I am afraid, I am a coward. I am sorry for everything. If I had done this a long time ago, it would have saved a lot of pain." It's a sad tale of depression that was also translated into a British musical, *Goodnight September*, in 2014.

are also special sections for various religions that are worth a look, including the Jewish section and the Buddhist and Hindu section that contains very exotic and elaborate Asian monuments.

Among some of the more fascinating monuments are the statue of Johnny Ramone (1948–2004) at his prime, playing a guitar; a replica of Toto from *The Wizard of Oz*, huge monuments to Harry Houdini and Howard Hughes, and a life-size stone piano for Pete Stanley (1939–2010). Don't know who Pete Stanley is? You're not alone. He was very wealthy–he spent half a million dollars on the grave marker, proclaiming himself to be "The Piano Man." There is a beautiful, long reflecting pool marking the burial site of Douglas Fairbanks Sr. and Jr., a marker for Don Adams (of *Get Smart* fame) holding his trademark "shoe phone" to his ear, and many other unique sights. The Hollywood Forever Cemetery, founded in 1899, is the resting place for hundreds of famous and wealthy men and women from the Industry, as well as unknown people who just wanted to be buried there. Sitting on a mere forty acres, space has become a premium, and so several multi-story mausoleums are being built to accommodate those who wish to rest there eternally.

Isn't there another memorial park where there are a lot of famous celebrities buried?

Yes, in Westwood the Pierce Brothers Westwood Village Memorial Park is also a resting place for many celebrities, including Marilyn Monroe, George C. Scott, Burt Lancaster, Natalie Wood, Truman Capote, Roy Orbison, Peggy Lee, Eddie Albert, Don Knotts, Walter Matthau, Dean Martin, Donna Reed, Eve Arden, Jack Lemmon, Eva Gabor, and the popular Iranian singer Hayedah.

Which highly visible work of art in Watts was built by an immigrant from Italy?

For many years, local politicians wanted it bulldozed and thought it was an eyesore, but now Watts Towers has been named a Los Angeles Historic-Cultural Monument, a California Historical Landmark, and a U.S. National Historic Landmark, as well as being on the Register of Historic Places. Also known as the Towers of Simon Rodia or Nuestro Pueblo, the Watts Towers were built by Sabato "Simon" Rodia (1879–1965) from 1921 to 1954. Rodia was born in Ribottoli, Italy. They are made out of rebar and some concrete and covered in bits of "found art," such as pieces of ceramic tile, glass, seashells, pottery, and other things he found or that were brought to him. He saw his work as a community piece, which is why he himself called it Nuestro Pueblo, meaning "Our Town," because he "wanted to do something big," as a short biography explains on the wattstowers.us website. Rodia used no power tools or heavy equipment for his huge masterwork—just hand tools. There are seventeen bit towers, with the tallest being 30 feet (9.14 meters) tall.

After Rodia decided to retire to live with his sister in Martinez, California, in 1955, his home caught fire and was slated to be bulldozed. But actor Nicholas King and film editor William Cartwright, fearing the towers would be destroyed, worked successfully to preserve it. Today, Watts Towers is overseen by the City of Los Angeles Cultural Affairs Department. Except for Mondays and Tuesdays, tours are available for a small fee through the Watts Towers Arts Center.

Other than its artistic value, have the Watts Towers been important for anything else?

Interestingly, the towers are also a study in structural stability. When it was first being determined (after Rodia's departure) whether they were safe, a crane was used to give the towers a stress test. They withstood ten thousand pounds of force and might have taken more had the crane not malfunctioned. Since then, the towers have been written

Now a Los Angeles Historic-Cultural Monument, Watts Towers were constructed on private land by Italian immigrant Simon Rodia.

about in architectural books, and their design has influenced the way some buildings are constructed today to improve stability and endurance.

Where is this other Bunker Hill that's not in Massachusetts?

Bunker Hill, as the name suggests, is a hill by Los Angeles's downtown. In the late-nineteenth century, it was a bare hill, free of buildings because it had no water or streets, but a Canadian immigrant named Prudent Beaudry bought the hill for $51 in 1867 and spent $95,000 developing it. It soon became a place known for Victorian-style mansions for the wealthy whose homes had a magnificent view of the city. Years went by, and the area fell into decline; people complained it had become a slum, and by the time Angels Flight was constructed in 1901 (see below), the area was no longer the fashionable place it once was. The city passed the Bunker Hill Urban Renewal Project in 1959, and by 1969 the old neighborhood had been bulldozed and redeveloped.

Older buildings were again demolished to make way for glass and steel skyscrapers in the 1980s, but by the 1990s there was a problem with a high rate of unoccupied office space (in 1999 the office space was only seventy-four percent full, the lowest in the country). An Adaptive Reuse Ordinance was passed by the city council in 2000 that allowed office space to be converted to fashionable residential lofts, and the area began to spring back economically. Today, Bunker Hill is once more fashionable and even artsy. It is home to the Museum of Contemporary Art, the Walt Disney Concert Hall, and the Cathedral of Our Lady of the Angels.

Who designed the Walt Disney Concert Hall?

Canadian-American architect Frank Gehry (1928–) is responsible for the design of this concert hall. A University of Southern California graduate, the famous architect is also currently involved in a huge project to redesign and restore the Los Angeles River.

Does Angels Flight still exist? I thought it was torn down.

It was, and then it was relocated. The original Los Angeles Incline Railway, known as Angels Flight, connected the corner of Hill Street and Third at the bottom with Olive Street at the top. It was supposedly the shortest incorporated railway in the nation. Built in 1901 on a thirty-three-percent incline that ran for two blocks, the rail gave passengers the choice of one of two funicular cars, which were named Sinai and Olivet. At each end of the short rail was a beautiful, red archway.

Although Los Angeles declared it a historical monument in 1962, just seven years later it was leveled as part of a controversial redevelopment project for the Bunker Hill area. The railroad was reopened a short distance away in 1996. Using the same cars, it connected Hill Street and California Plaza. However, while the original Angels Flight only had one accident in its history, the new track had more safety issues. A fatal accident in 2001 saw the new Angels Flight close for nine years, and then two more shorter closures after accidents in 2011 and 2013, and it has not reopened since then.

Is the Crystal Cathedral really constructed primarily out of glass in an earthquake zone?

Yes. In fact, it is the largest glass building in the world and has over 12,000 glass panes in the twelve-story structure. The result of Dr. Robert Schuller's (1926–2015) vision, the Crystal Cathedral in Garden Grove was completed in 1980 and can seat nearly three thousand worshippers. Schuler founded the Reformed Church of America and was well known for his *Hour of Power* television broadcasts. The church fell into financial troubles, however, and the cathedral was closed in 2012. It was later purchased by the Catholic Church, and there are plans to reopen the building in 2017.

What scientific center is a major tourist draw in L.A.?

Griffith Observatory is a science and educational center that has been open for free to the public since 1935. The beautiful Art Deco building is on the south side of Mount Hollywood facing the city. It was a gift to L.A. from Colonel Griffith J. Griffith (1850–1919) in 1935. Griffith had made his fortune not digging gold but as a mining expert who worked for various mining syndicates (although he called himself a colonel, he had only served in the reserves and was never on active duty; people never objected to his self-proclaimed title because he doled out so much money). According to the GriffithObservatory.org website,

Any kid growing up in the L.A. area probably went to Griffith Observatory for a school trip. It is a wonderful center for education and fun.

Colonel Griffith was quite a philanthropist, but didn't he also shoot his wife?

Although Griffith J. Griffith (1850–1919) was quite a philanthropist, he definitely has this dark spot on his record. Suffering from paranoid delusions and desperately trying to hide that he had a drinking problem, he shot his wife, Mary, in the face at the Arcadia Hotel in Santa Monica in 1903. Mrs. Griffith didn't die, but she lost an eye and was permanently disfigured. She divorced her husband and got custody of their son, and Colonel Griffith spent two years in prison for assault with a deadly weapon. The rather light sentence was the result of his defense successfully arguing that Griffith suffered from "alcoholic insanity."

after looking through the Mt. Wilson observatory telescope, he said, "If all mankind could look through that telescope, it would change the world!" Part of Griffith Observatory is the Zeiss telescope, which the public can peek through to see the wonders of the cosmos; and, in fact, more people have used Zeiss than any other telescope in the world.

The observatory is home to much more than that, though. There are lectures and shows regularly; the Samuel Oschin Planetarium, a theater with state-of-the-art projection and laser displays; a solar telescope (coelostat) for observing the sun safely; a monthly "public star" party in which volunteer astronomers explain to the public what they are viewing through a variety of telescopes; a giant Foucault pendulum that demonstrates how the earth is rotating; two large exhibit halls; and more. A $93 million renovation from 2002 to 2006 has refreshed the look and modernized the exhibits further to make Griffith Observatory a true gem of southern California.

What is Griffith Park like?

Griffith Park, which, of course, was also donated by Colonel Griffith, is where Griffith Observatory is situated. Covering over 4,300 acres, the park also offers other attractions, including the Greek Theater, a merry-go-round, the Griffith Park & Southern Railroad (a miniature train ride), the Los Angeles Life Steamers Railroad Museum (includes model trains and public train rides), the Travel Town Museum (more trains! so if you like trains, this is the place to be!), pony rides, bicycle railroads, and, if that weren't enough, the Los Angeles Zoo (see the chapter "Natural Wonders" for more on the L.A. Zoo).

AMUSEMENT PARKS

What are some of the popular amusement parks in the Los Angeles area?

There are several very popular parks in the Los Angeles area, including, of course, Disneyland in Anaheim, Universal Studios in Universal City, Knott's Berry Farm in Buena Park, and Six Flags Magic Mountain in Valencia.

Why did Walt Disney, who was known for making movies and animated features, decide to build an amusement park?

When Walt Disney (1901–1966) came up with the idea for Disneyland, he was already quite famous for his movie studio from which sprang the character of Mickey Mouse and the world's first full-length animated features. Disney movie and television shows were so popular by the late 1940s and early 1950s that many fans were requesting studio tours; kids wanted to see their favorite characters, too. Having so many visitors to the studio lot would be problematic, however, so Disney came up with a plan for a park where all of this could be done in a place removed from the business of making movies and television shows.

The original plan was to use an eight-acre lot in Burbank, but this soon switched to a 160-acre site in Anaheim. At the time, there was little there but fruit orchards, but it was near a freeway and not far outside Los Angeles, so Disney saw the spacious area as perfect. He had a vision of creating several themed "lands" in the park: Adventureland, Fantasyland, Frontierland, and Tomorrowland (largely replaced by "Star Wars" attractions after Disney purchased the franchise). There were boat rides, a train ride, and rides featuring amazing "animatronic" robot animals and people, such as the Jungle Cruise: eighteen attractions were featured, and the park cost $17.5 million.

When Disneyland was completed, it was still out in the middle of nowhere, surrounded by fruit orchards.

What Disneyland ride actually debuted in New York?

The "It's a Small World" ride was built by Walt Disney Studios, but it debuted at the 1964 New York World's Fair. After the fair was over, it was taken down, shipped, and reassembled in Disneyland.

No one had ever seen an amusement park like Disneyland before, and when it first opened on July 17, 1955, in Anaheim, the place was flooded with over half a million eager visitors. Since then, many rides have been added, and attendance has grown. A second park, Disney California Adventure Park, was added in 2001, and between the two parks is a complex of more shops and restaurants.

What was the first amusement park in the United States?

While Disneyland is no doubt the most famous amusement park in California, the honor of the first such park goes to Knott's Berry Farm. As the name suggests, it first began as a simple farm, which was particularly famous for its boysenberries. Founded by Walter Knott (1889–1981) and his wife, Cordelia, in Buena Park, the farm was opened in 1920 to visitors to sell the produce and pies, and Knott had the idea to create an Old West ghost town replica for his guests. The town, which was built in 1940, was created in honor of Knotts' grandparents, who arrived in California in 1868.

The growing park was designed to sell food, primarily, but it became so big that the Knotts were compelled to start charging admission in 1968. Later, in 1983, they also added costumed characters based on the Charles Schultz comic strip, "Peanuts," opening Camp Snoopy. Today, the park stands on about 360 acres and attracts over three and a half million visitors annually. The children of Walter and Cordelia sold it to the Cedar Fair Entertainment Company in the 1990s.

Does Magic Mountain have a special claim to fame?

Now part of the Six Flags chain of amusement parks, Magic Mountain might not be the biggest or most famous amusement park in the country, but if you are a fan of roller coasters, you will get more for your buck here than anywhere else. Located in Valencia, the park opened in 1971 and now has nineteen coasters. It was also the first amusement park to have a steel loop roller coaster—the Great American Revolution—that does a complete, 360-degree vertical loop; the park completely renovated this ride in 2016, too, to celebrate its fortieth anniversary. In addition to the many thrill rides, there are also calmer rides for small children, live entertainment, and, of course, lots of food.

How did the Universal Studios Theme Park come about?

Unlike other amusement parks such as Disneyland and Six Flags Magic Mountain, Universal Studios Hollywood (as it is now called) grew out of the original backlot tours of the famous Los Angeles movie studio. Universal founder Carl Laemmle (1867–1939) started giving public tours for twenty-five cents (you could purchase a lunch for five cents extra) in 1915. By 1930, when sound started to be used regularly in films, the tours stopped because they interfered with production. The tours resumed in 1961, however (soundproofing was much more effective by then, making interference from tourists outside less likely), beginning with bus tours, then this evolved into tram tours in 1964. By then, the tours cost $2.50, but the studio made most of its money by dropping guests off at the commissary for lunch.

The next development came when the tours started asking guests to participate in reenactments from various films. As the tours became more popular and concerns arose again about interference with movie and TV productions, the route of the trams was moved away from the sound stages. This would have been very dull, had Universal not then started adding permanent attractions along the route. In 1968, a mock "flash flood" recreated a scene from *The Ten Commandments*; a hugely popular attraction was added in 1976 in which a fake shark attacked the tourists in honor of the movie *Jaws*. Earthquakes with foam boulders, a giant King Kong, the Jurassic Park River Adventure, and, in 2016, a *Walking Dead* experienced based on the zombie TV show, and *The Wizarding World of Harry Potter,* based on the J.K. Rowling books and movies, have more recently been added.

OTHER FAMOUS L.A. ATTRACTIONS

What popular attraction in L.A.'s Hancock Park involves the discovery of Pleistocene animals?

The La Brea Tar Pits marks a spot that is possibly the best site ever discovered for the remains of numerous species of Pleistocene mammals and birds that lived between ten thousand and forty thousand years ago. It has been surmised that the bones ended up there because prey animals would get stuck in the tar (actually, asphalt), and then predators would come to eat them and get stuck as well. The tar pits have been known to people since the days of the Chumash and Tongva peoples, who actually used the tar to seal boats they used for fishing and for sailing to the Channel Islands. The over one hundred pits at the site were also found by the Portolá expedition, which recorded their existence in 1769. White settlers who came to California in the 1820s also found the tar useful for sealing the roofs of their settlement homes.

The realization that there was more in La Brea than tar did not occur until geologist William Warren Orcutt (1869–1942) found fossils while exploring for oil. While Orcutt came to Hancock in 1901, fossils had been collected by people there as early as 1875. But it was Orcutt who realized how important the tar pits were to the scientific community. Orcutt gave his collection to paleontologist John Campbell Merriam (1869–1945), who became famous for his taxonomic work on the species found there,

Both fun and educational, the La Brea Tar Pits have preserved a wide variety of animals from the Pleistocene epoch. Scientists are still making interesting finds there.

which included saber-toothed tigers, mastodons, giant sloths, dire wolves, camels, and bison.

Today, the La Brea Tar Pits are a popular attraction for tourists and school road trips. The La Brea Tar Pits Museum, a branch of the Natural History Museum of Los Angeles County, opened in 1977 to educate and amaze. The museum includes exhibits, a stage show, an atrium, and an active lab, where research still continues.

Are the La Brea Tar Pits the only ones in California?

Actually, there are two other sites in California: the Carpinteria Tar Pits in Santa Barbara County and the McKittrick Tar Pits in Kern County. Similar pits are also found in Texas, Peru, Russia, Poland, Iran, Venezuela, and Trinidad, but the ones in La Brea remain the most interesting for paleontologists.

Is "The Getty" a museum or something else?

"The Getty," or, more officially, the Getty Center in Los Angeles, includes the world-class J. Paul Getty Museum, but the entire facility encompasses a lot more. Housed here are the Getty Research Institute, the Getty Conservation Institute, and the Getty Foundation, all run by the J. Paul Getty Trust, a huge, nonprofit trust dedicated to the advancement of the visual arts.

Any other museums one should check out in L.A.?

Yes. The Los Angeles County Museum of Art is a compound of five buildings showing every kind of antique and contemporary art. It's located on Wilshire Boulevard.

CRIME AND CHAOS IN L.A.

What caused the Zoot Suit Riots of 1943?

In a rather strange example of racial tension, the Zoot Suit Riots were a violent confrontation between white American servicemen and Latinos (but also some blacks, Filipinos, and Italian Americans) in Los Angeles. Latinos especially favored the men's suits, which featured baggy pants, tight cuffs, and long jackets with wide shoulder pads and collars. The white servicemen found the suits offensively extravagant in a time of war, when the government had posed clothing restrictions on civilians. Tensions rose as more servicemen came to the area because of the war effort, but the catalyst that sparked the riots was probably what is known as the Sleepy Lagoon murder case.

On August 2, 1942, the unconscious José Gallardo Díaz was discovered at Sleepy Lagoon, a reservoir next to the Los Angeles River. He was taken to the hospital but died of injuries he had suffered to the head. Although there was no real evidence leading to a perpetrator, the police began rounding up Latino zoot-suiters, especially those belonging to the notorious 38th Street gang. Seventeen were brought to trial; they were not allowed to talk to their lawyers while in court, and they were forced to wear their zoot suits, too, in an effort to put them in a poor light for the jurors. In other words, they were denied due process, which is why the nine who were eventually sent to San Quentin Prison had their sentences all reversed by 1944.

But the spark had been lit. Riots erupted all over the state, from San Jose and Oakland to San Diego. The most violent outbreaks, however, were in Los Angeles. Some of the worst of these were altercations against Navy sailors and Latinos in late May and early June. Although the white servicemen largely instigated the attacks, they had the support of the press and the L.A. City Council, the latter of which approved an ordinance making it a crime just to wear a zoot suit. As the riots slowly eased by mid-June, there were outbreaks in Arizona, Texas, Michigan, New York, and Pennsylvania.

Political reaction to the Zoot Suit Riots ranged from the logical (blaming them on racism) to the absurd (blaming them on everything from the influx of Southerners to a Nazi plot to create discord between the United States and Latin American countries). When First Lady Eleanor Roosevelt pointed out that the problem was a long-standing one of white prejudice against Latinos, she was accused of being a communist in a *Los Angeles Times* editorial. California Senator Jack Tenney (1898–1970), who was on the State Un-American Activities Committee, came up with the Nazi plot idea, which he never proved or even supported with any evidence. While tensions eventually abated and zoot suits became a thing of the past, however, racial prejudice against Hispanics in California has remained a problem.

What event triggered the Watts Riots, and what was the resulting damage?

Watts is a neighborhood in Los Angeles that had a large African American population at the time of the riots on August 11, 1965. The area had long been plagued by poverty, poor schools, and crime, and the residents felt harassed by the nearly all-white LAPD. When police pulled over a driver named Marquette Frye, the young man's mother, Rena, came to her son's defense, and both Fryes were arrested. The crowd of witnesses had enough, and their agitation quickly spread through Watts. Rioting ensued, and by the time the dust settled, thirty-four people were dead, 1,100 wounded, $100 million in property damage had been done, and an incredible four thousand were arrested.

Who shot Bobby Kennedy?

Only five years after his brother John F. Kennedy was assassinated, and minutes after winning the California primary election for president, U.S. Senator Robert F. Kennedy (1925–1968) was shot dead by Sirhan Sirhan (1944–) on June 7, 1968, in front of Los Angeles' Ambassador Hotel. Sirhan was the child of Palestinian parents and was born in Jerusalem when it was still under British occupation. He strongly opposed the state of Israel. Kennedy, however, was a supporter of Israel, including its Six-Day War battles against its neighbors. Sirhan decided assassination was the best way to keep Kennedy from the Oval Office. He was found guilty of murder and sentenced to death, but that decision was commuted to life in prison in 1972. Today, he remains in a San Diego prison.

Why did Charles Manson lead his "Family" followers to murder?

One of the most shocking chapters in American history is how Charles Manson (1934–) led a group of young, impressionable followers to murder several of Los Angeles's elite. Manson used his charismatic personality, sex, and pseudo-religious rituals to convince Charles "Tex" Watson, Susan Atkins, Patricia Krenwinkel, and Leslie Van Houten to commit murder. The first victims met their fates on August 9, 1969, when Atkins, Watson, and Krenwinkel entered the home of actress Sharon Tate in the Benedict Canyon neighborhood of Los Angeles. They killed Tate, who was the wife of director Roman Polanski, as well as successful Hollywood hairdresser

One of the strangest criminal cases in not only California but U.S. history involved Charles Manson, who created a cult of murderers in Los Angeles.

> ## What is the musical connection to the Manson crimes?
>
> **"H**elter Skelter," the term Manson adopted and used for his vision of a coming apocalypse, came from the name of a 1968 song by the Beatles. Manson quoted the lyrics to describe his vision. Manson himself was once a guitarist and songwriter who had connection to Beach Boys founding member Dennis Wilson. He even wrote a number of folk rock songs that have been performed by such groups as Marilyn Manson, White Zombie, and Guns & Roses.

Jay Sebring, coffee heiress Abigail Folger, and Folger's boyfriend, the Polish author Wojciech Frykowski. The next night, the three killers, joined by Van Houten, went to the Los Feliz neighborhood of L.A. and killed the wealthy Leno LaBianca and his wife, Rosemary.

Manson urged his followers to kill these people because they were white and wealthy, and he was hoping to start a race and class war. The horrifyingly bloody murders were quickly discovered, and Manson and his followers were caught, tried, and imprisoned. The prosecutor in the case, Vincent Bugliosi, wrote the book on Manson, 1974's *Helter Skelter*, with coauthor Curt Gentry.

Who are the Bloods and the Crips?

The Bloods and the Crips are the two most notorious gangs to have originated in Los Angeles. Members can be distinguished by colors they wear, with the Bloods donning red and the Crips blue. Both gangs are composed primarily of African Americans. In the rougher neighborhoods of the L.A. area, one can get into serious personal danger by accidentally wearing the wrong color in a neighborhood controlled by one or the other gang.

What infamous incident started the 1992 riots in Los Angeles?

On March 3, 1991, four police officers pulled over Rodney Glen King III (1965–2012) for reckless driving in the Lake View Terrace neighborhood. King reportedly refused to get out of the car when told to by the police, and he then charged them. The officers tazed King, and when that didn't work, three of them clubbed him repeatedly. According to witnesses, about two dozen officers eventually surrounded the scene, and, instead of stopping it, some officers held King down while others did nothing. Much of this was caught on videotape by George Holliday, who lived in a nearby apartment. King suffered several broken bones, as well as bruises and lacerations, and he was taken to a hospital. According to one nurse's testimony, some of the officers bragged and joked about what they had done.

A trial was held the next year for three of the officers, but they were acquitted by a mostly white jury. Anger the community felt at this perceived injustice set off the Los Angeles riots that lasted from April 29 to May 4, 1992. Fifty-three people died and nearly 2,400 were injured in the violence, and there was an estimated one billion dollars in property damage, businesses were looted, and over seven thousand fires were set. Satellite riots on a smaller scale also occurred in Las Vegas, Atlanta, and even Toronto, Canada.

At the urging of President George H. W. Bush, the U.S. Department of Justice launched a federal prosecution, and a grand jury in Los Angeles indicted four officers. Two of them, Stacey Koon and Lawrence Powell, were found guilty of violating King's civil rights and were sentenced to thirty months in prison.

What are the circumstances behind the O. J. Simpson murder trial?

O. J. Simpson (1947–) was a retired football player who had won a Heisman Trophy and had been a running back for the Buffalo Bills and 49ers. In 1994 he was accused of murdering his ex-wife, Nicole Simpson Brown, and her friend Ronald Goldman at Brown's condo in Brentwood. Shortly after the bodies were found with multiple stab wounds, Simpson was a suspect. In a strange twist, on June 17, 1994, he got into a Ford Bronco driven by former teammate Al Cowlings, and a slow-speed chase ensued on L.A. freeways for sixty miles. Simpson cowered in the back seat and appeared to have a gun, possibly threatening to kill himself. When the police finally pulled the Bronco over, they found Simpson with a gun, family photos, a fake mustache, makeup, a passport, and $9,000 in cash.

Arrested, he went on trial in what many called the "trial of the century." With a team of defense lawyers that included F. Lee Bailey and Johnnie Cochran, one of the key pieces of evidence during the trial was a glove left behind, apparently, by the murderer. Cochran told the jury that if "the glove don't fit, you must acquit." Simpson tried it on, and it did not fit. The case was also hurt by police detective Mark Fuhrman, who was caught on tape saying disparaging things about blacks. It was suspected that the police might have planted evidence.

Simpson was found not guilty, but his troubles were not over. He was sued by Goldman's father in a wrongful death civil suit in 1997 and ordered to pay $33.5 million. The former football star, actor, and broadcaster had more troubles in the 2000s, including charges of battery, money laundering, suspected possession of ecstasy, and even piloting a boat too fast in Florida's manatee habitat. In 2007, he was arrested for taking sport memorabilia out of a Las Vegas hotel room, which Simpson asserted had been stolen from him. The case escalated until Simpson was imprisoned in 2008 for armed robbery and kidnapping and was sentenced to thirty-three years in prison. He was granted parole on some charges in 2013 but has to remain incarcerated until 2017.

PASADENA

When was Pasadena founded?

On April 22, 1875, the San Gabriel Orange Grove Association founded Pasadena as an agricultural cooperative. It became a resort destination for Easterners after the Atchison, Topeka and Santa Fe Railway was constructed through the area. Hotels were built to accommodate them, including the Vista del Arroyo Hotel and the Hotel Green. Soon, Pasadena rivaled Los Angeles in size.

What famous brewer created a famous garden here?

Adolphus Busch (1839–1913) of Anheiser-Busch fame made his home in Pasadena, also creating the first Busch Gardens. This was a beautiful garden for the public that also offered samples of beer products (it was a marketing tool, obviously). By the 1930s, animals, such as the Clydesdale horses, but also more exotic creatures and amusement rides, began to be added. The Pasadena garden closed in 1937. Busch Gardens in Van Nuys was open from 1964 to 1979 (see below), and there was one in Houston, Texas, from 1971 to 1973. Today, SeaWorld Entertainment owns Busch Gardens with locations in Tampa, Florida, and Williamsburg, Virginia.

What important institution of higher education is located in Pasadena?

The California Institute of Technology (Caltech for short) is a prestigious, private university in Pasadena. Founded in 1891 by Amos G. Throop (1811–1894) as a vocational and prep school, it was reimagined and renamed in 1921 as a technical school. Although small in size with a student body of about 2,300, it is ranked highest in the nation for students who go on to get a Ph.D.

Caltech works closely with NASA, running the Jet Propulsion Laboratory, as well as with the Howard Hughes Medical Institute. Furthermore, the university is known for its important work in seismology—something very relevant for the area! Thirty-four faculty from Caltech have, to date, been awarded Nobel Prizes, as well as six Turing Award winners and five Fields Medalists.

How long has the Rose Parade been around?

One of the most wonderful traditions of New Year's Day in the United States is the Tournament of Roses Parade, which is held on the streets of Pasadena. Organized by the Valley Hunt Club, the parade began in 1890 as a way to promote California to tourists escaping the cold of the East and North, as well as to showcase the agriculture (especially citrus crops) of the region. Flowers and other plants were draped off carriages and pulled down the street by horses, and there were also a number of athletic competitions held at Tournament Park, including polo matches, tugs-of-war, and foot races. Today, the pa-

What popular television sitcom features scientists who work at Caltech?

The number-one CBS comedy *The Big Bang Theory* is a humorous take on scientists navigating social conventions that are, for them, more befuddling than the fields of physics and astronomy they study. It has been a popular show since 2007.

137

The Rose Parade in Pasadena is famous for its stunning floats, which the rules say must be completely covered in flowers and other organic materials. Here is an example from 2012 called "Enchanted Paradise" by the Downey Rose Float Association.

rade is run by the Pasadena Tournament of Roses Association and is attended by about 700,000 people, as well as being broadcast nationally.

For information about the Rose Bowl, see the "College and Amateur Sports" chapter.

When did the first Goodyear blimp fly above the parade?

That happened in 1955, when the first "blimpcast" was broadcast of the Rose Parade using cameras aboard the Goodyear blimp.

What is the Doo Dah Parade?

The Doo Dah Parade was conceived in 1978 as an alternative to the Rose Parade. Instead of flowers, quirky and idiosyncratic groups are encouraged to dress up in silly outfits and strut their stuff. Audiences can see everything from Klingons and furries to hibachi grill marching teams. The parade inspired others to form around the country, including in Columbus, Ohio; Kalamazoo, Michigan; and Ocean City, New Jersey.

What important discovery in the field of astronomy was made near Pasadena?

At the Mount Wilson Observatory in the San Gabriel Mountains near Pasadena, one of the most important theories was proposed by Dr. Edwin Hubble (1891–1953). After taking

What popular Pasadena tourist destination featured ostriches?

The first ostrich farm ever opened in the United States was the Cawston Ostrich Farm. Established by Edwin Cawston in 1886, it was home to over one hundred African ostriches. Cawston sold ostrich products (mostly feathers for women's clothing) around the world, but he also saw another opportunity. Because it was conveniently located near the Los Angeles Electric Railway, tourists quickly discovered it, and it was a popular attraction featuring ostrich rides (both on the backs of ostriches and also ostrich-drawn carriages) and shopping for ostrich feather boas and other items. The farm closed in 1935.

photographs of the Adromeda Galaxy in 1923, he noticed that the light was being red-shifted. This indicated that the galaxy was moving away from Earth. With more research, Hubble discovered that the farther away a star was from us, the greater the red shift, and this showed that the universe is expanding. From this, it took little thought to reason that if the universe is expanding, at one time, everything in it must have converged together, and this brought about the Big Bang Theory concerning the creation of the universe.

RIVERSIDE COUNTY

Is—or was—the Inland Empire an actual empire?

No, the term was really a way to promote the area, which has no exact borders but roughly includes cities in western Riverside County and southwestern San Bernardino County. Originally called the Orange Empire because of citrus groves there, the Inland Empire got its new name in 1914 when it was called that in an article published in the *Riverside Enterprise* (now the *Press-Enterprise*).

Which famous general is honored with a museum in eastern Riverside County?

Famous for leading troops in Europe during World War II, General George S. Patton (1885–1945) was a native of San Gabriel. The General George S. Patton Memorial Museum, though, is located in Chiriaco Summit in eastern Riverside County. Opened in 1988, the site is at the entrance to the entrance to Camp Young Desert Training Center. Patton was the first general to command the center.

PALM SPRINGS
AND THE COACHELLA VALLEY

Who were the original inhabitants of the Coachella Valley?

Although a desert, there is abundant water in parts of the Coachella Valley, which is on the eastern side of San Jacinto Mountain. It was settled about two thousand years ago by the ancestors of the current Agua Caliente Band of Cahuilla Indians. These people enjoyed the natural springs, including hot mineral water springs where the Spa Resort Casino now stands, and lush vegetation of the oases here, including the largest natural fan palm oasis in America that is located in the Indian Canyons. Here, the Indians prospered for many centuries. The first European they encountered was Juan Bautista de Anza (1736–1788), who was part of the Portolá Expedition (1769–1770). The Spanish mapped out the area and established a wagon trail through the San Gorgonio Pass. Unfortunately, the white settlers brought smallpox with them, and the native peoples had no immunity to the disease, which killed thousands during an 1863 epidemic.

How was Palm Springs founded?

Palm Springs, which is located at the western end of the Coachella Valley, abutting the base of Mt. San Jacinto, began to be settled by white people in the nineteenth century. When the Southern Pacific Railroad was built in the 1870s, the U.S. government gave the railroad company parcels of land, which it then sold to settlers (half the lots went to the Indians, but they were not allowed to sell or profit from the land). The first permanent white settlers were Judge John Guthrie McCallum and his family, who arrived in Palm Springs in 1884. McCallum (whose name now graces a large theater in Palm Desert) built an aqueduct to bring more water to the valley, which would become a thriving agricultural area. The next prominent settler here was Dr. Welwood Murray, who founded the Palm Springs Hotel in 1886.

By the 1920s, Palm Springs was becoming a resort town that attracted stars from Hollywood such as Rudolph Valentino and Fatty Arbuckle. In the 1950s, many entertainers had homes here, including Cary Grant, Frank Sinatra, Gloria Swanson, Liberace, and Rock Hudson. The area also became known for its mid-century modern architecture, which is still preserved today in many of the neighborhoods.

The city incorporated on April 1, 1938, and in 1939 the U.S. Army Air Corps began work on an airstrip that, after the war, became the city's civilian airport. Bedroom communities began to pop up, and by the 1980s, cities, including Indian Wells, Palm Desert, Cathedral City, and Rancho Mirage became incorporated and started to grow with both full- and part-time residents.

What is Sunnylands?

One of the signature estates in the Coachella Valley, Sunnylands in Rancho Mirage was commissioned by Walter and Leonore Annenberg. Walter Annenberg (1908–2002) was

Sunnylands was the expansive estate of Walter and Leonore Annenberg in Rancho Mirage. Many U.S. presidents have visited here over the years, often to meet dignitaries and captains of enterprise.

a wealthy publisher best known for creating *TV Guide,* as well as owning *The Inquirer* and *Philadelphia Daily News*. He would later serve as U.S. ambassador to the United Kingdom in 1969, while his wife, Leonore (1918–2009), was chief of protocol of the United States during the President Ronald Reagan Administration.

Designed by architect Quincy Jones (1913–1979), who was once dean of the School of Architecture at the University of Southern California, the mid-century-modern home is one of the most beautiful and luxurious of its kind. For decades, the Annenbergs played host to U.S. presidents (from Richard Nixon to Bill Clinton), and even after their passing the estate gets White House visitors (President Barack Obama visited several times), and other heads of state from around the world have also come there as guests and for summits.

Sunnylands is surrounded by acres of gardens, and the facility has a center that is open to the public that includes art exhibits, a café, a movie theater featuring the story of the estate, and a gift store. Tours are available and it can be rented for events.

Was there anything controversial about Sunnylands?

There was a minor problem. Mrs. Annenberg decided to have the wall around the estate painted pink, and the residents in the neighborhood were upset by the bold color choice. However, she prevailed, and the residents got used to it; the long stretches of pink wall even have their own charm, in a way.

What famous story about Marilyn Monroe is actually not true?

Although the legend in Palm Springs circles is that the bombshell beauty Marilyn Monroe (1926–1962) was discovered while visiting the famous Racquet Club in Palm Springs.

Springs, in fact, she was discovered while working at a munitions factory in Burbank, California, during World War II. A photographer was taking pictures of women contributing to the war effort when he spotted the beauty. However, it is true that Monroe was first photographed professionally by Bruno Bernard (1912–1987) at the Racquet Club in 1947, and it was also there that she met her first agent, Johnny Hyde (1895–1950).

Monroe quickly became a model and then an actress in films such as *Gentlemen Prefer Blondes* and *The Seven Year Itch*. She died tragically of a drug overdose in her home in Brentwood on August 5, 1962. Many have suspected she was murdered, but no proof has ever been verified on this account.

What are some facts about the Palm Springs Aerial Tram?

The tramway that goes to the top of Mount San Jacinto was the brainchild of an electrical engineer named Francis Crocker (1900–1992). Crocker first came up with the idea of a tram rising above the valley floor through rugged canyons just north of Palm Springs in 1935, but it took decades for his dream to be realized. Just getting the proposal approved by the city was a challenge, then raising the money, and the engineering challenges that proved difficult to overcome. Helipads had to be constructed so that helicopters could bring up materials. It took literally 23,000 helicopter trips over twenty-six months to haul everything up the side of the mountain. Five support towers for the cables were built, and a spacious mountain station at about 8,516 feet (2,596 meters) elevation (the valley station is at an elevation of 2,643 feet [806 meters]) was completed (the peak of the mountain is at 10,834 feet [3,302 meters]).

The first official tram ride occurred on September 12, 1963. New tram cars were installed in 2000 that have the wonderful feature of slowly rotating as the car goes up and down so that everyone on the ride is guaranteed a great view. At the top of the tram, there are observation decks, a cafeteria, and a restaurant. Behind the mountain station one can walk down a short hill and discover miles of forest trails and camp grounds.

What famous music star once served as Palm Springs' mayor?

Songwriter and producer Sonny Bono (1935–1998), who was well known as half of the Sonny & Cher singing team, was mayor of Palm Springs from 1988 to 1992 (he was also a U.S. congressman, representing California's 44th District from

The Palm Springs Aerial Tramway affords spectacular views of the Coachella Valley and Mt. San Jacinto.

1995 to 1998). While mayor, he was notable for creating the Palm Springs International Film Festival, and he also championed the restoration of the Salton Sea.

LONG BEACH

How did the *Queen Mary* end up in Long Beach?

The luxurious passenger liner RMS *Queen Mary* is a British ship that was active from 1936 until 1967, when it made its last docking in Long Beach after a long career. She was retired because of her age, and the cruise line that owned her, Cunard, was losing money. Long Beach was selected so that she could be preserved in the warmer climate and converted into a hotel that includes restaurants and entertainment.

What city was constructed in a way to mimic Venice, Italy?

Logically, it is Venice, California. The area, originally called Ocean Park, was founded in 1905 by developer Abbot Kinney (1850–1920), who wanted to make it a center for art and culture. To add to the attraction of the city, he built a mile-long canal and five smaller canals, complete with gondolas (piloted by gondoliers hired from Italy), about a quarter mile from the beach. Kinney soon discovered that tourists attracted to the beach weren't looking for culture, they were looking for fun. Soon, instead of lecturers and music for the cultured, it became the "Coney Island of the Pacific." There were amusement rides, freak shows, exhibits, and, of course, a miniature steam railroad, Venician-style buildings, and the beach. Kinney renamed the playground Venice in 1911.

The area fell into decline, people lost interest in the canals, and they were closed down and filled in by 1942. For decades, it remained an unsightly area, but in the 1970s,

The RMS *Queen Mary* is retired in Long Beach, where it serves as a hotel, restaurant, and tourist attraction.

a revival took hold. Ironically, the area began to attract artists, art galleries, and elegant restaurants. But there were still problems. While the canals had been closed, there was still water there, and they began to smell badly of rot and algae, almost like rotten eggs. Los Angeles Councilwoman Ruth Galanter (1941–) led an effort to revitalize Venice, obtaining $6 million in taxes to do so in 1993. Today, Venice is again an attractive spot that has shops, restaurants, a thirty-mile sidewalk for rollerbladers and bicyclists, and the famous "Muscle Beach" weight-lifting area. About one hundred thousand visitors come to Venice annually.

SAN DIEGO AND SURROUNDING AREA

Is San Diego the state's oldest city settled by Europeans?

Yes. Governor Don Gaspar de Portolá and Father Junípero Serra established Basilica San Diego de Alcalá on July 16, 1769, which became the center of the new city (see the "Early California: First Peoples to the 1849 Gold Rush" chapter for more).

Who was the first white settler to have a vision for San Diego?

When entrepreneur Alonzo E. Horton (1813–1909) arrived in San Diego in 1867, it was an uninspired little seaport. But Horton saw an opportunity in the town's location and its wonderful climate. He purchased 960 acres and divided it into tracts, which he then began marketing and selling to new settlers to the area. By the time of his death, San Diego had grown to a respectable size. The five-story Horton Plaza shopping mall is named in his honor.

Who is often considered an important founding father of San Diego?

John Diedrich Spreckels (1853–1926) was the son of a wealthy sugar baron who owned the Spreckels Sugar Company in Hawaii. The young Spreckels worked for his father for a time, but after raising $2 million in capital, he decided to set out on his own, founding the trade company J. D. Spreckels and Brothers. As trade grew, he created the Oceanic Steamship Company to trade with lands as far away as Australia and New Zealand.

After visiting San Diego in 1887, Spreckels fell in love with the small harbor town. He began to set up businesses there and buy land, initially in the Coronado area. He ran

Can you see Mexico from the beaches and harbor at San Diego?

Unlike former Alaska governor Sarah Palin's declaration that she could see Russia from her home, you actually can see Mexico from San Diego, yes. Even on less-than-clear days you can see Tijuana and its beaches.

the Coronado Beach Company, the city railroad, a hotel, and local newspapers. By the turn of the century, he was the richest man in San Diego, owning all of Coronado Island, Belmont Park, Mission Beach, the San Diego–Coronado Ferry System, the San Diego & Arizona Railway, the San Diego Electric Railway, and Union-Tribune Publishing, among other ventures and properties. His former mansion can still be seen today and has been converted to the beautiful Glorietta Bay Inn.

What makes the Hotel del Coronado so notable?

Conceived and built by H. L. Story and Elisha Babcock, the Hotel del Coronado is located on Coronado Island in San Diego. It opened in 1888 and was billed by the owners as a seaside resort that would be "the talk of the Western world." The hotel features residential villas ranging from one to three bedrooms and became a quick favorite of presidents and celebrities. Hollywood actors made it a favorite place to stay, and it was visited by such stars as Clark Gable, Charlie Chaplin, Errol Flynn, Mae West, and Douglas Fairbanks. Designated a California Historical Landmark in 1970 and a National Historical Landmark in 1977, the hotel is noted for its beauty, luxury, and idyllic location.

BALBOA PARK

What are the features of the extraordinary Balboa Park in San Diego?

Balboa Park is truly one of the most extraordinary public parks in the world. It includes 1,200 acres on which sit sixteen museums, numerous gardens, the world-famous San Diego Zoo, movie theaters, a golf course, a stadium, a carousel, a train ride, and acres of parkland grounds.

Who created Balboa Park and when?

In 1835, when the area was still in Mexico, 47,000 acres of land were set aside and designated for public use. Nothing much happened for years, until 1868, when the city of San Diego (now part of the United States), officially declared 1,400 acres for what was then called simply City Park.

Who was "The Mother of Balboa Park"?

Botanist, horticulturist, and landscape architect Kate Sessions (1857–1940), a California native born in San Francisco, promised to plant the grounds in exchange for the city giving her thirty-two acres of the park for her commercial nursery. The city did so, and Sessions ended up planting palm trees, birds of paradise, and other shrubs and trees throughout the grounds. Many of these are still alive today, some seventy-five years after her death.

There is a lot to see and do at San Diego's incredible Balboa Park, from beautiful architecture and parks to world-class museums, theaters, and zoos.

What museums can be found here?

Visitors to Balboa Park could easily spend days taking in all the museums. They include the following:

Museum	Year Founded
San Diego Natural History Museum	1874
San Diego Museum of Man (anthropology)	1915
San Diego Museum of Art	1926
San Diego History Center	1928
San Diego Automotive Museum	1935
San Diego Art Institute	1941
San Diego Hall of Champions (sports)	1959
San Diego Air & Space Museum	1963
Timken Museum of Art	1965
Centro Cultural de la Raza (Hispanic culture)	1970
Reuben H. Fleet Science Center	1973
Mingei International Museum (art and culture)	1978
San Diego Model Railroad Museum	1980
Museum of Photographic Arts	1983
George W. Marston House (history museum)	1987
Veterans Museum and Memorial Center	1989

Which two big exhibitions were held in Balboa Park?

The 1915–1916 Panama-California Exposition was held here (also see the "Northern California" chapter), as well as the 1935–1936 California Pacific International Exposition. Both big events left behind buildings that are still in the park today. These buildings are notable for their range of historic styles, ranging from Aztec inspired to Mexican Pueblo to Art Deco. Both expos were designed (successfully) to attract tourists and promote the city.

When was the San Diego Zoo founded, and who founded it?

During the 1915 exposition (so the story goes), a physician named Harry Wegeforth (1882–1941) encountered a lion that was on exhibit and was inspired to found both the San Diego Zoo and the Zoological Society of San Diego. He started the zoo by adopting the animals that were "leftovers" from the exposition. He would serve as the president of the zoo from its founding in 1916 until his death.

Today, the San Diego Zoo is one of the finest wildlife conservation centers and tourist attractions in the country. It includes such rare species as giant pandas, clouded leopards, tigers, gorillas, and bonobos.

What are some other fascinating points about Balboa Park?

The Spreckels Organ Pavilion, constructed during the 1915 exposition, is one of the world's largest outdoor pipe organs. Free outdoor concerts are regularly held here.

Another point of interest is the WorldBeat Cultural Center, which seeks to educate and inform the public about African diaspora and Indigenous cultures. It offers classes in media arts (often hosting international students) and puts on various events.

Is the San Diego Zoo Safari Park separate from the San Diego Zoo?

Yes, although the confusion is understandable. Both the Safari Park (called the Wild Animal Park until 2010, when the name changed) and the zoo are run by the Zoological Society of San Diego. The zoo is in Balboa Park (see above), while the Safari Park is just outside Escondido about 32 miles (51.5 kilometers) away.

The Safari Park has much more to offer than most other zoos. The grounds are huge, comprising 1,800 acres (730 hectares) of land, where animals roam in the closest thing to the actual wild as one can get. The world's largest wild animal veterinary hospital is also on the grounds. There are three hundred species totaling over 2,500 animals on the ground, including giraffes, lions, gorillas, gazelles, lemurs, and all five species of rhino.

Guests can ride caravans into the grounds and come in close contact with the less-dangerous animals, such as giraffes; they can camp overnight on the grounds; take a behind-the-scenes tour; ride a zipline over the wide-open spaces of the park; or spend five hours with a personal tour guide, all at extra fees, of course.

147

How many—and what sorts—of theaters are there?

Balboa Park has the Starlight Bowl, which is home to the Starlight Theatre run by the San Diego Civic Light Opera Association, the Marie Hitchcock Puppet Theater, the Old Globe Theater, and, as mentioned above, the Spreckels Organ Pavilion.

OTHER SAN DIEGO ATTRACTIONS AND EVENTS

What amusement park has a lot of fun, interactive activities for the family?

Legoland, which opened in 1999, is a very popular theme park that attracts tens of millions of visitors every year. As the name indicates, everywhere one looks, there are structures and statues that appear to be made of Lego™ toy blocks. In addition to rides and a water park, many exhibits and games in the park are interactive, encouraging guests to be creative and inventive. Also in this spirit, Legoland hosts the First Lego League Southern California Regional Championships, a competition for young people to build robots to solve unique problems.

Today, Legoland has only increased in popularity, especially after *The Lego Movie*, which came out in 2014. There is also a Legoland in Winter Haven, Florida, which opened in 2011.

Has the America's Cup been hosted in San Diego?

Yes, the San Diego Yacht Club was home of the America's Cup from 1988 to 1995 and hosted three races there in 1988, 1992, and 1995.

NORTHERN CALIFORNIA

SAN FRANCISCO

What was the original name of San Francisco?

San Francisco was originally called Yerba Buena. The name comes from the Spanish language for the plant *Micormeria douglasii,* an herb common to the area. The pueblo, which included a presidio and mission, was established in the early 1790s by the Spanish. On January 30, 1847, the city was renamed San Francisco by a declaration from the city's Chief Magistrate William Bartlett, who declared:

> Whereas, the local name of Yerba Buena, as applied to the settlement or town of San Francisco, is unknown beyond the district; and has been applied from the local name of the cove, on which the town is built; Therefore, to prevent confusion and mistakes in public documents, and that the town may have the advantage of the name given on the public map, IT IS HEREBY ORDAINED, that the name of SAN FRANCISCO shall hereafter be used in all official communications and public documents, or records appertaining to the town.

Who settled the area?

The Costanoan Indians were the original residents of the peninsula jutting into the bay that is now called San Francisco. Actually, "Costanoan" was the family of eight languages spoken by several tribes there; the dominant Costanoan tribe in what is now San Francisco and San Jose was the Ohlone.

The first Europeans to arrive, of course, were the Spanish. Actually, the Mexican-born José Francisco Ortega (1734–1798) was the first to see the bay. He was a sergeant in Gaspar de Portolá's expedition (see "Early California: First Peoples to the 1849 Gold Rush") in 1769 when he spotted it. Despite Ortega's middle name, no, the city is not named in his honor but, rather, after Saint Francis of Assisi.

The Spanish established a fort (presidio) and mission San Francisco de Asís there. Despite its ideal location, Yerba Buena (as it was first called) was not the largest of the cities the Spanish established, but, rather, Monterey was. That is, until the 1849 Gold Rush.

What were the original Seven Hills?

San Francisco is a notoriously hilly city, which makes it great for your cardiovascular health if you like to walk city streets. Almost everything is on a hill or slope. The city has expanded over the years to encompass forty-four hills, but originally there were only seven hills that were named in the much smaller city of the nineteenth century. These were:

- Mount Davidson
- Mount Sutro
- Nob Hill
- Rincon Hill
- Russian Hill
- Telegraph Hill
- Twin Peaks

Mount Davidson is the tallest hill in San Francisco, rising to 928 feet (283 meters), and is situated in roughly the middle of the city. The hill hosts residential neighborhoods and, at the top, Mount Davidson Park. At the very peak is a piece of private land, and on that is a 103-foot (31.4-meter) concrete cross, which replaced an earlier, shorter cross in 1934. On March 24 of that year, President Franklin D. Roosevelt hit a switch in Washington, D.C., that transmitted a signal to light the cross on the hill. Since that time, the cross has been the site of Easter Day prayer services.

Mount Sutro is a forest-covered hill that is 911 feet (278 meters) high. Much of the eucalyptus tree forest is owned by the University of California, San Francisco, and it is a favorite place for locals to go hiking and biking.

Nob Hill (also known as Snob Hill) is home to many of San Francisco's richer residents, as well as private clubs and chi-chi restaurants. It's been that way since the nineteenth century, and even after the devastation of the 1906 earthquake and fire, millionaires and billionaires returned to their old digs with its outstanding views of the city and bay.

Rincon Hill was also once a place for the wealthy to live, but later it became more industrial in the twentieth century. However, in recent years it has transitioned yet again, becoming a place for residential towers, including the sixty-story-tall One Rincon Hill, which was completed in 2008 and has caused some upset in the city for blocking people's views.

Russian Hill is a pleasant mix of residences, quaint shops, and the campus of the San Francisco Art Institute. It was named Russian Hill because it originally had a graveyard where early Russian settlers had been buried. It is also the hill on which the famous Lombard Street—one of the world's crookedest streets—is located (see below).

Telegraph Hill was once a neighborhood where Irish immigrants flocked in the 1840s, and it also was a graveyard for non-Catholic seamen. The name comes from the fact that there was once a semaphore at the top of the hill (a device predating the telegraph that was used for communicating over distances). The top of the hill is now noted for the presence of Coit Tower, a lovely Art Deco structure that is 210 feet (64 meters) tall. It was constructed from money left by Lillian Coit, who wanted part of her bequest used to help beautify the city.

Twin Peaks is, as the name indicates, actually two hills topping off at 922 feet (281 meters). The top of the peak is preserved wild lands and home to numerous bird, plant, and insect species.

Are there only seven hills?

Actually, there are forty-three hills within San Francisco's borders.

What's up with Lombard Street being so incredibly zigzaggy?

The one-way street is that way because Russian Hill is so steep there that a more rapid descent would be dangerous, even for a horse and carriage. Fortunately, going slowly down the hill (doubly necessary because of the amount of tourist traffic) makes it easier to enjoy the beautiful Victorian mansions that line both sides of the street. Other in-

Scenic Lombard Street is a highlight of any trip to San Francisco. It is not, however, the crookedest street in the city!

teresting sights along the way are the house at number 949 that was used for the television show *The Real World,* and at 900 Lombard there is the building that has the apartment used in the Alfred Hitchcock 1958 movie *Vertigo.*

Is Lombard Street the curviest street in San Francisco?

No, the crookedest street is actually Vermont Street in the Portrero Hill neighborhood. While still a lovely drive, it is less scenic than Lombard Street and, therefore, not nearly as famous.

Where are the mosaic steps in San Francisco?

An impressive outdoor art project created by the local community, the 16th Avenue Tiled Steps Project at 16th and Moraga were constructed from 2003 to 2005. With support from the San Francisco Parks Trust and the Golden Gate Heights Neighborhood Asso-

Who was Emperor Norton?

Joshua Abraham Norton (c. 1818–1880) was possibly the most peculiar personality to ever reside in San Francisco, where he named himself Norton I, Emperor of the United States and Protector of Mexico. Although born in London, England, he moved to San Francisco after inheriting a fortune from his father in 1849. Once in California, he started a wholesale grocery business, but when he went bankrupt after investing heavily in the rice market, poor Norton's mental health suffered. He disappeared for a time—no one knew where—and upon his return to San Francisco had given himself a promotion to emperor.

Norton donned a military outfit, complete with plumed hat, issued his own currency, and made proclamations that he had published in the newspaper. Interestingly, some of his proclamations actually made sense, especially his 1869 proposal to build a bridge across the San Francisco Bay, which was not to be built for many decades.

The Emperor was not feared for his madness by the local people, however. Rather, he became beloved. Norton would go about inspecting streetcars and railroads, police officers and other officials, approving or disapproving of their deportment and condition. Merchants even accepted Norton's "currency" as payment because they felt so kindly toward him. Once, he courageously defended Chinese immigrants from attacks by white rioters by standing between the two groups and reciting "The Lord's Prayer" until the crowds calmed down and dispersed.

When Emperor Norton collapsed and died while walking by Old St. Mary's Church on January 8, 1880, the city mourned the loss, and the *San Francisco Chronicle* published the headline "Le Roi est Mort" ("The King Is Dead").

ciation, as well as tile donations from about 220 people, the beautiful mosaic goes up (or down) 163 stairs and is a beautiful enhancement to the area.

How did Chinatown come about?

Chinese immigrants came to California because of the wars and natural disasters in their homeland and promise of a better life during the Gold Rush and railroad boom in the United States (see the "Early California: First Peoples to the 1849 Gold Rush" chapter). Although Chinese also arrived in Los Angeles, Central Coast towns, and even as far as the U.S. East Coast (some even fighting in the U.S. Civil War as a result), the largest concentration was in San Francisco, which, at the time, was the most important and populous city in California. Once there, cultural and language differences made it more comfortable to converge in one area (the area that became Chinatown). Here, they could support each other while forming businesses in the central part of the city, such as laundry, domestic, grocery stores, and other services, including everything from rooming houses and temples to gambling establishments and opium dens. Staying together also formed a buffer against racism from the white community and some consolation from other discrimination, such as the many laws and regulations being passed against them.

Because they were foreigners, they also had the advantage of not being in unions (and pay dues), instead forming guilds such as the Chinese Hand Laundry Alliance. Many saved as much money as they could and sent it home to China, where a few dollars went a long way.

The area was initially called "Little Canton," but by 1853 newspapers were referring to it as Chinatown. The area is roughly between Bush Street in the south, Broadway on the north, Kearney Street to the east, and Powell Street on the west. The famous Dragon's Gate that most people associate with it is at Bush and Grant.

Was there seriously a war about eggs in San Francisco?

Well, the "war" was not in San Francisco but on the Farallon Islands off the coast (see the "Natural Wonders" chapter). The islands, unsurprisingly, have a lot of seabird life on them, and the Pacific Egg Company laid claim to the eggs there. While the Egg Company did much of the collecting, rival companies and freelance collectors raided the islands, too. Even after the federal government took claim of the islands in 1859 because it wanted the property for use of the lighthouse, the war escalated as people continued to gather

These are the unmistakable gates that lead to San Francisco's Chinatown.

eggs. Things came to a head on June 2, 1863, when a group of men led by David Batchelder approached the islands and was fired upon by Egg Company employees. Batchelder and his companions fired back, and one man on each side was shot dead. Four others were wounded. Batchelder was later accused and tried for murder but was acquitted. The Egg Company continued its operations until 1881, when the U.S. government finally decided to deny its claims on the Farallons.

Is sourdough bread from San Francisco the best of its kind?

Many would say so because sourdough bread originated here. How? By accident. It was during the Gold Rush (sometimes it seems like all things uniquely Californian can be traced back to that period, doesn't it?) that bakers were rushing to supply miners with bread. Some of the dough was contaminated by a bacteria (later identified and named *L. sanfranciscensis*) that gave it a unique sour flavor. Rather than throwing it out, the bakers liked the taste and started saving and growing the yeast it came from. Yeast does not travel well, however, so the bread became unique to the San Francisco bakeries. It was only years later that others around the nation began to grow strains of the yeast that would simulate the flavor, yet to this day San Franciscan sourdough can only be found in the Bay area.

How did the 1906 San Francisco earthquake and fire become such a disaster?

The worst tragedy in California history to date is, without a doubt, the 1906 quake and resulting fire that destroyed most of San Francisco. Striking the growing city of four hundred thousand residents on April 18 at a time when building codes certainly aren't what they are today, the quake measured 7.8 on the Richter Scale. After the initial shock, fires started and burned for the next three days. After it was all over, about three thousand people died either as a direct result of the disaster or indirectly. Nearly five square miles were burnt, 225,000 were made homeless, and over 28,000 buildings were leveled (24,671 of these were wooden structures). The total monetary damage was $400 million (in 1906 dollars).

The first pre-shock of the quake occurred at 5:12 A.M., and about half a minute later the main shock came, lasting nearly a minute. To give one an idea of how strong this quake was: it was felt all the way from southern Oregon to south of Los Angeles and east to Nevada. The result of shifting of the San Andreas Fault was that 296 miles (477 kilometers) of earth

---

Where did the name "sourdough" come from?

Miners used to make their bread on site, which meant keeping yeast and ingredients safe. If the yeast got too cold it would die, so the men literally had to snuggle up to their yeast starter kits to protect them. The miners became known as "sourdoughs" (perhaps their demeanors got a bit grumpy from sleeping next to yeast all night), and this term became associated with the San Francisco bread.

along the fault line shifted. At the time, scientists did not understand plate tectonics, and studies were made of the event that greatly helped in the understanding of such quakes. The most important was the Lawson report written by University of California at Berkeley geology chairman Professor Andrew C. Lawson (1861–1952). His 1908 study is considered a landmark in the science of geology and is still taught in colleges today.

Did anything good come out of the San Francisco earthquake?

In a way, yes. Before the quake, the city, which had sprung from a hodgepodge of quickly constructed buildings trying to accommodate the boom of the Gold Rush, was known for being quite ugly. Indeed, at the turn of the twentieth century, a plan was being put in place by former mayor James P. Phelan (1861–1930) and architect Daniel Burnham (1846–1912) to revitalize the city and make it beautiful. However, the 1906 quake put those plans aside. Even so, it did give San Francisco a chance to change its architecture for the better and make it one of America's more scenic cities. (For more on earthquakes in California, see the "Natural Wonders" chapter.)

Where was the fortune cookie invented?

Although the story has been muddled over time to the point where there is more than one claim to the crispy, after-dinner treat, the tale centered on San Francisco declares that

Few events can match the utter devastation of the earthquake and fire that struck an unfortunate San Francisco in 1906.

it was Japanese—not Chinese—immigrant Makoto Hagiwara who came up with it in 1914. Hagiwara was the master gardener who designed the city's Japanese Tea Garden in Golden Gate Park. He was fired by an ungrateful and racist mayor of San Francisco in 1907 (it's not clear whether this was Charles Boxton, who only served a few days before being fired for corruption, or possibly Edward Robeson Taylor, but it seems more like something Boxton would have done) but rehired later. The grateful Hagiwara designed the cookie in a way so that he could put thank-you notes in them and give them to those who stood by him. These were then provided as part of the teas served in the Japanese Tea Garden.

The other story behind the cookie is that it *was* created by a Chinese man—this time it was a businessman living in Los Angeles named David Jung who owned the Hong Kong Noodle Company. Jung supposedly made the cookies in 1918 and gave them to the poor in his neighborhood. The pieces of paper inside contained inspirational Bible verses.

Why was the Panama–Pacific Exposition held in 1915?

The Panama–Pacific Exposition was a celebration held from February to December 1915 to celebrate the opening of the Panama Canal. The canal was anticipated, correctly, to benefit San Francisco sea trade. Over nineteen million people attended the sea-themed expo during its ten-month run, bringing the city considerable attention to the nation. (See also the "Southern California" chapter under San Diego for more about the southern version of this event.)

The expo included exhibits organized in "palaces," including the Palaces of Agriculture, Food Products, Transportation, Manufacturers, Mines and Metallurgy, Machinery, Education, Liberal Arts, and Fine Arts. The featured structure was the 435-foot (132.6-meter) Tower of Jewels, which was covered in one hundred thousand cut glass, colored "gems" that sparkled by day and were illuminated by searchlights at night.

Holding the expo was important for the city, which wanted to show the world that it had recovered from the 1906 earthquake.

Does anything remain of the Panama–Pacific Exposition?

Yes, the Palace of Fine Arts in San Francisco's Marina District is a leftover from the 1915 Panama–Pacific Expo and remains on its original site. Designed by architect Bernard Maybeck (1862–1957), it was created to look like the ruins of an ancient Greek or Roman temple. Currently on the National Register of Historic Places, it had to be rebuilt in 1965, and in 2009 a seismic retrofit was done to protect it from earthquake damage.

The beautiful Palace of Fine Arts is a leftover from the 1915 Panama–Pacific Exposition.

Other structures and exhibits were saved but moved to other locations, including the Japanese Tea House that is now in Belmont (this isn't the same tea house as the one in Golden Gate Park), the San Francisco Civic Auditorium that was built for the expo but was not on the main grounds, which is now called the Bill Graham Civic Auditorium and is at the Civic Center, and the Wisconsin and Virginia buildings were relocated to Marin County.

What are some notable art museums in San Francisco?

There are several, of course, starting with the San Francisco Museum of Modern Art at the Yerba Buena Gardens, which includes works of many masters, including *Osiris and Isis* by Anselm Kiefer and *Femme au Chapeau* by Henri Matisse. For a bit more of an exotic flavor, stop by the Asian Art Museum housed at a former public library that still has its original Beaux-Ar façade. Many consider its Far and Near East collections to be among the best in the world.

In addition, there are the Fine Arts Museums of San Francisco, which includes the M. H. de Young Memorial Museum at Golden Gate Park (see below) and the California Palace of the Legion of Honor, which includes art by such renowned painters and sculptors as Henri Matisse, El Greco, Edgar Degas, Claude Monet, and Auguste Rodin, including one of Rodin's casts of *The Thinker*.

What distinguished art school is in San Francisco?

The San Francisco Art Institute was founded in 1871, making it the oldest such institution west of the Mississippi.

FAMOUS NEIGHBORHOODS AND TOURIST SPOTS

Why is the Haight-Ashbury neighborhood so iconic?

The neighborhood, which is also called the Haight or the Upper Haight, is best remembered as the center of the hippie movement and the 1967 Summer of Love (see the chapter "The State of California: 1850 to the Present" for more on the hippie culture in San Francisco). Although the 1960s are over, the area is still popular for its stores and beautiful Victorian homes. There is also a large annual street fair that is held on the second Sunday of June that draws thousands of tourists.

What is North Beach famous for?

It is best known for scrumptious Italian food and its European atmosphere—as well as for fooling people into thinking there is a beach there. There is *no* beach at North Beach, so let's get that clear. Centered near Washington Square and running along Grant and Columbus Avenues, the area features European-style cafés, shops, galleries, and the Church of Saints Peter and Paul, which is definitely worth a look. Finally, if you enjoy focaccia, you must stop at the Liguria Bakery at 1700 Stockton Street, which not only specializes in this bread, but it's the only thing they sell! (For more about North Beach and the 1960s, see the chapter "The State of California: 1850 to the Present.")

Why is the Castro District well known?

The Castro District has a high population of homosexuals. This development occurred during World War II and after, when men fighting in the Pacific Theater were dishonorably discharged for being gay. Many of them ended up in the San Francisco area. By the 1960s, the area was being completely changed. The first gay bar, the Missouri Mule, opened in 1963, and soon Castro became a focal point for LGBT activisim during the counterculture movement.

What draws so many tourists to Fisherman's Wharf?

Almost anyone who is planning a trip to San Francisco should include Fisherman's Wharf as a highlight. Take the F-line streetcar to the wharf and enjoy a day of restaurants, shops, and watching sea lions, which can be found at Pier 39's K Dock. The wharf is famous for good seafood restaurants—a treat being clam chowder served in a sourdough bread bowl. Street musicians and performers are all around, lending a festive atmosphere, and there is also a 3-D movie theater.

Should tourists make a stop at Ghirardelli Square, too?

Located in the Fisherman's Wharf area, Ghirardelli Square dates back to 1893, when Domingo Ghirardelli (1817–1894) purchased a city block to be the base for his choco-

Fisherman's Wharf is a fun place to shop and get some of the best seafood in the country. Try the clam chowder in a sourdough bread bowl!

Have sea lions always been at Pier 39?

Interestingly, no. They first showed up in 1990 just after the 1989 Loma Prieta earthquake and have never left. Scientists cannot explain to this day why they showed up and why they never returned from whence they came, but they are a delight to tourists (who don't mind the smell of the sea lions' fish breath).

---

late company's headquarters. After the company was bought out in 1960, shipping executive William M. Roth (1916–2014) and his mother, Lurline (1890–1985), bought the land and hired landscape architect Lawrence Halprin (1916–2009) to make it beautiful. Now on the National Register of Historic Places, the square preserves nineteenth-century architectural elements surrounding shops, restaurants, fountains, and statues, making it a great place to relax.

How did cable cars (streetcars) come to San Francisco?

As with many events in nineteenth-century California, the cable car's invention can be traced back to the Gold Rush. Andrew Smith Hallidie (1836–1900) was working as a gold miner, blacksmith, and surveyor when he came up with the idea for wire rope. He was helping to build a mine flume in 1856, when he devised the metal rope to replace regular ropes, which were wearing out too quickly as they pulled carts full of rocks. Founding a company to make the wire ropes in San Francisco in 1857, the new product was used in bridge building, and ten years later, he invented the patented Hallidie ropeway, a cable system for transporting ores across mountainous areas.

It wasn't too far of a leap from the ropeway to cable cars. How exactly this happened has been the subject of some speculation, but one story is that Hallidie felt sympathy toward the horses he saw pulling heavy carts up San Francisco's steeply graded streets. Another version says that cable cars were actually the idea of attorney Benjamin Brooks, who won a contract from the city to build the line. Brooks' work as an attorney meant he didn't have enough time to devote to the cable car, so he sold it to Hallidie.

What are some other hotspots that no tourist to the area should miss?

Some worthwhile stops for any visitor to the city (other than those already mentioned above) include:

- The Embarcadero, including the Ferry Building, is where ferry boats come and go to travel across the bay. In addition to that, though, there is a wonderful variety of food vendors. It is a great place to go to get a diverse sampling of San Francisco cuisine. The building is easy to spot as it features a 245-foot (75-meter) clock tower.

- The Exploratorium: the city's museum of science and art. It was founded by Frank Oppenheimer (1912–1985), the younger brother of physicist Robert J. Oppenheimer;

they both worked on the Manhattan Project to develop the nuclear bomb. Frank Oppenheimer was a particle physicist and professor who wanted to engage students of all ages in the sciences, so he founded the Exploratorium in 1969. It contains hundreds of interactive exhibits. Originally located at the Palace of Fine Arts, it was moved in 2013 to Piers 15 and 17 on the Embarcadero.

- Union Square: the heart of old town San Francisco has shopping, theaters, and hotels galore.

Both fun and practical, cable cars are a great way to travel around the city.

When did cable cars debut?

The first test run of a cable car was on August 2, 1873, and Hallidie was at the controls as it followed the rails along Clay Street between Jackson and Kearny. Regular service for the public began on September 1. It was not only a first for California but for the world.

Did cable cars change the city of San Francisco?

Yes. They made it much easier for people to build on hills and live in homes in otherwise-difficult-to-reach areas of the city.

Has cable car service gone uninterrupted since 1873?

It's impressive that it did from 1873 until 1982, when a major overhaul of the system was finally done, taking two years and $60 million to complete.

What is the Market Street Railway?

Actually, it is two things: originally, it was a commercially operated streetcar company that ran from 1893 to 1944; currently, it is a nonprofit that has no legal association with its predecessor. The current Market Street Railway works to preserve historic streetcars from not only San Francisco but all over the world. It runs the F Line (Market and Wharves), which runs along Market Street from the Ferry Building to the Castro District.

Who is BART?

BART isn't a "who," it's a "what." It stands for Bay Area Rapid Transit and is a system of trains around the San Francisco area that carries about 425,000 riders on weekdays and around 150,000 passengers on Sundays. The BART system debuted on September 16, 1974, nearly thirty years after the idea was first proposed after World War II by "Borax King" Francis Marion Smith (1846–1931), who made his fortune in mining and developing railway systems. The current electric train system travels 104 miles (167 kilometers) and has forty-four stations. The trains can travel up to 80 miles (129 kilometers) per hour. Currently, the system's trains are being upgraded to include quieter, more comfortable cars.

Is San Francisco biking friendly?

You have to be in good health to bicycle up and down all the hills, but yes, San Francisco is very bike friendly, and there are, actually, flat places in parks and elsewhere. This is the result of a concerted effort by city government to improve life by being friendly to pedestrians, mass transit, and bikers as outlined in the 2009 Bicycle Plan. For the bicyclists, this means that the local government has installed more bike parking (places to easily lock up bikes), improve access to transit and bridges, and promote safety. Thanks to the friendly atmosphere, there has been a proliferation of bicycle clubs, parties, parades, festivals, and even a Bicycle Film Festival that features, of course, movies with bike themes.

The Transamerica Building has become iconic for the city.

What exactly is inside the pyramid-shaped building downtown?

The Transamerica Pyramid located at 600 Montgomery Street has certainly become part of the distinctive San Franciscan skyline. Completed in 1972, it stands 853 feet (260 meters) high, including forty-eight floors. It was the headquarters for the insurance company Transamerica and was designed by architect William Pereira (1909–1985).

GOLDEN GATE BRIDGE AND PARK

Why was the Golden Gate Bridge built?

The bridge was built to better connect the city of San Francisco with Marin County across the 5,000-foot- (1,600-meter-) wide Golden Gate strait. It was designed by Joseph Strauss (1870–1938) and cost $35 million in labor and materials.

Why is the Golden Gate Bridge orange?

It was determined that orange would be the most visible color, considering the foggy weather that regularly shadows the area. Maintaining the color is a constant chore, literally. Painters coat the metal structure from one end to the other, and when they finish, they begin again, using five to ten thousand gallons of paint each year.

How long did it take to construct the Golden Gate Bridge?

The Golden Gate Bridge took four years to build and is almost two miles long.

Groundbreaking for the landmark bridge began on February 26, 1933, and was completed on May 28, 1937. The final length is 1.7 miles (2.74 kilometers). The two support towers stand 746 feet (227 meters) tall, and the main part of the bridge between the towers is 4,200 feet (1,280 meters) long.

It took 600,000 rivets to secure the metal in each tower, and 80,000 miles (128,748 kilometers) of wire were used in the two main cables holding up the bridge. The bridge weighs a total of 887,000 tons (804,673 metric tons). About 120,000 vehicles cross it every day, on average.

When was Golden Gate Park created?

Originally known as the Great Sand Park because it was nothing but sand dunes, Golden Gate Park was authorized for construction by the city of San Francisco on April 4, 1870. It was an ambitious project that would include museums, a conservatory, and sport facilities, as well as gardens ranging from the exotic to the more recreational. Horticulturist Dr. John Hays McLaren (1846–1943), assistant to the park superintendent, was responsible for most of the planning and is now remembered as the "Father of Golden Gate Park."

What are some of the features of Golden Gate Park?

- Japanese Tea Garden—the tea garden's origins go back to the 1894 California Midwinter International Exposition. Instead of destroying the garden created for the expo, it was Japanese immigrant Makoto Hagiwara (1854–1925) who asked the parks horticulturist, Dr. John McLaren, to expand it into a permanent traditional garden. Hagiwara was put in charge, and the garden now includes a tea house, pagoda, rock garden, and many other beautiful features.

- San Francisco Botanical Garden—formerly the Strybing Arboretum, it was made possible by Helene Strybing (1845–1926), who left a large bequest for the project. The arboretum is fifty-five acres in size and includes a wide variety of plants from all over the world.

- Conservatory of Flowers—built in 1879, it is the oldest building in Golden Gate Park. It includes a greenhouse and garden with rare and exotic flowers. The spectacular, Victorian-style greenhouse stands sixty feet (eighteen meters) tall.

What infamous statistic about the bridge has been a black mark on its history?

Sadly, the Golden Gate Bridge has set the record as the place where more people commit suicide than anywhere else in the world. Over 1,500 people have thrown themselves over the side (a little over thirty survived). The first person to do this was H. B. Wobber, who killed himself in August 1937, casually announcing, "This is where I get off," before he leaped. A plan is in the works to build a net under the bridge to prevent such tragedies, and there are special suicide prevention lines just for the bridge.

- California Academy of Sciences—the Academy is a natural history museum that was founded in 1853. One of the largest museums of its kind, it was completely re-built in 2008 and includes an aquarium and rainforest exhibit within its 400,000 square feet (37,000 square meters).

- M. H. de Young Memorial Museum—this is the fine arts museum within Golden Gate Park. Like the Japanese Tea Garden, it originated with the 1894 exposition. Today, about 1.5 million visitors come annually to view its extensive collection that is ranked sixth in the nation.

- Kezar Stadium—opened on May 2, 1925, the stadium was home to the 49ers from 1946 to 1970; the Oakland Raiders also played there in 1960. Santa Clara University, St. Mary's College at Moraga, and the University of San Francisco's football teams have all played there in the past. The original 59,000 seat was torn down in 1989 and replaced with a smaller—but more modern—ten thousand-seater that is now home to the San Francisco Freedom cricket team and is where the San Francisco City Championship football game (the "Turkey Bowl") is played annually.

Is Golden Gate National Recreation Area the same thing as Golden Gate Park?

Nope. Golden Gate Park is within the city of San Francisco, while Golden Gate National Recreation Area is on the north side of the Golden Gate Bridge. Formerly belonging to the U.S. Army and now run by the National Park Service, it comprises 80,002 acres (32,376 hectares) of beautiful, wooded land overlooking the bay and ocean.

Fort Mason is situated here, too. Once the most important military ports for the Pacific campaign during World War II, it was originally built in 1912 on property owned by the explorer and politician John C. Frémont (see the "Early California: First Peoples to the 1849 Gold Rush" chapter). The fort includes forty-nine buildings, some of which are still used by the army, while others have been leased out for public use, including a youth hostel and several buildings used by the Fort Mason Center for Arts & Culture.

What were the Sutro Baths?

Located within the Golden Gate National Recreation Area, the Sutro Baths were the largest indoor pool establishment when it opened on March 14, 1896. Built by millionaire Adolph Sutro (1830–1898), who was also mayor of San Francisco from 1894 to 1896, the baths could accommodate twenty-five thousand people. The facilities included five saltwater and one freshwater pool that were all enclosed in glass and nearly 1.7 million gallons (6.4 million liters) of water. For added fun, there were slides, a trapeze, and a diving platform that could hold 1,600 divers! If you were tired of swimming, a visitor could dine at one of three restaurants, stroll through a sculpture gallery, or view a natural history exhibit. All of this cost only five cents for admission. It was easy to get to, as well, by taking the Ferries and Cliff House Railroad from a station at what is now Presidio Avenue and California Street.

The baths remained open until 1937, when it was converted to an ice-skating rink by Sutro's grandson. In 1964 the property was sold to high-rise apartment developers, and in 1966 a fire destroyed the abandoned structures.

Is the Presidio still a military post?

As you know from reading the second chapter of this book, "presidio" means fort, and for a long time this spot on the tip of the San Francisco Peninsula was a military post manned by the Spanish, beginning in 1776. It continued in this function under Mexican rule and, again, under U.S. rule until October 1, 1994, when the Base Realignment and Closure initiative took effect. Two years later, the U.S. Congress created the Presidio Trust, which manages eighty percent of the Presidio, and the U.S. National Park Service manages the twenty percent along the coastal areas.

Although it was still a military installation, the Presidio was made a California Historical Landmark in 1933 because of its unique natural beauty, and it was named a National Historic Landmark in 1962. Today, it is a popular place for hiking and enjoying the natural landscape and views of the Golden Gate Bridge from the Golden Gate Pavilion that was completed in 2012. Tourists can also learn some military history by visiting Fort Point, a fortification dating back to 1861, and Battery Chamberlin, a seacoast defense museum. In addition, the Gulf of the Farallones National Marine Sanctuary Visitor Center has a hands-on marine exhibit, and the Crissy Field Center educates guests about urban environmentalism.

Why are so many eucalyptus trees planted in the area?

The aromatic tree can now be found all over the state, but it first gained popularity in the Bay Area because (you guessed it) of the Gold Rush. The influx of miners devastated local forests that were being chopped down for construction and firewood. Enter the idea of bringing in eucalyptus trees from Australia. These trees have the advantage of growing very rapidly, and it was known that the Australian lumber was good for construction. With the passing of the California Tree Culture Act of 1868, which offered incentives for people to replant trees that had been lost, eucalyptus farms sprang up all over from Oakland down to Santa Barbara. Favored was the bluegum eucalyptus, which can grow to be over twelve feet (four meters) in just two years.

There was just one problem: after harvesting some of these trees for lumber it was discovered that eucalyptus wood splintered and cracked so readily that it wasn't even suitable for fencing, let alone a building. The wood that had come from Australian trees was, indeed, hard enough, but it had been harvested from eucalyptus that was seventy-five years old or older. The get-rich schemes of some one hundred companies that had been established to grow the trees crumbled. Companies shut their doors, but by this time the trees had gained a foothold and are now considered an invasive species (the climate in California is similar to that in its native Australia, and so the plant thrived).

Today, there are some benefits to the eucalyptus, which can be used to help prevent erosion, as wind breaks, and as ornamental trees. The oil is used for everything from food and toothpaste flavoring to perfumes, menthol cigarettes, and even industrial solvents.

In what way was Mark Twain associated with San Francisco?

Samuel Langhorne Clemens (1835–1910) moved out west after his favorite job as a Mississippi River steamboat pilot was put to an end by the advent of the Civil War. He decided to search for gold in Nevada after a brief stint fighting for the Confederacy, but he had no success trying to dig silver from the Comstock Lode, not to mention he didn't favor the hard work involved. With a suitcase full of Comstock mine stock certificates he headed to San Francisco. But the stocks lost value and Clemens realized he needed to get a job, which he did with the city's *Morning Call,* and he contributed to the *Territorial Enterprise.* It was while working as a journalist in San Francisco that he came up with the pen name Mark Twain.

But Twain's predilection for embellishing the facts eventually got him into trouble with the editor at the *Call* and was fired in 1865. His friend and fellow writer Bret Harte asked Clemens to contribute to his weekly, *The Californian,* and it was while there that he published his famous story "Jim Smiley and His Jumping Frog" (later retitled "The

---

Do Californians still celebrate jumping frogs in Twain's honor?

Every year the Calaveras County Fair and Jumping Frog Jubilee is held near Angels Camp. It is one of the state's oldest fairs, dating to 1893, when it was first held in the town of Copperopolis. The mid-May fair includes the usual fun rides, food, games, and exhibits, as well as the jumping frog competition to see which amphibian can leap the farthest. The winner gets a trophy and $900. Anyone beating the world record holder, however, could get $5,000. This record (as of 2015) is held by Rosie the Ribiter (owned by Lee Guidici), who in 1986 jumped 21 feet, 5.75 inches (6.5 meters).

Celebrated Jumping Frog of Calaveras County"). San Francisco, then, was the place where Clemens finally became the literary Mark Twain.

How did Alcatraz Island become a prison?

Alcatraz Island was discovered by Spanish explorer Juan Manuel de Ayala in 1775. He named it "La Isla de los Alcatraces," which means "Pelican Island," because pelicans were numerous there. Ninety years later, the U.S. Army decided to construct a fort on the island but later decided to convert it into a military prison. In 1934, it was converted from a military to a civilian prison. It was the height of the mob era, and criminals like Al Capone, Alvin Karpis, Arthur "Doc" Barker, and George "Machine Gun" Kelly spent time behind Alcatraz's walls. The prison closed for good in 1963.

Has anyone ever escaped from Alcatraz?

Sometime during the night of June 11–12, 1962, three inmates—Frank Morris, John Anglin, and Clarence Anglin—managed to open ventilator grills in their cells to make their way through an unused utility corridor to the shore, where they deployed a makeshift blow-up raft to escape the island. The fugitives were never found, and many speculated that they drowned. The famous escape was immortalized in the 1979 Clint Eastwood movie, *Escape from Alcatraz*.

Why was Alcatraz Island occupied by Native Americans from 1969 to 1971?

A group called the Indians of All Tribes took the island over on November 20, 1996, claiming it was promised to them by the 1868 Treaty of Fort Laramie between the Sioux and the U.S. government, which said that the Indians could have land that had been abandoned by the government. Since there were no longer any military, immigration, or prison facilities on the island, the Indigenous peoples felt it was within their rights

Once the most infamous prison in the country, Alcatraz is now a bird sanctuary and tourist attraction.

to claim it. The group issued the "Alcatraz Proclamation," which correctly noted all the times the federal government had broken treaties and mistreated Native Americans, including by the Bureau of Indian Affairs, which had issued the Termination and Relocation program. This was a thinly veiled attempt to get Indians off reservation lands so that the government could take that land from them.

The Native people got support from some of the locals, too, as well as some famous people. On shore, people helped to send supplies to the island; the daughter of athlete Jim Thorpe, Grace Thorpe, contacted celebrities to visit the island and give the cause publicity. Credence Clearwater Revival donated a boat to help with transportation of supplies, and actors Marlon Brando, Jane Fonda, Dick Gregory, Jonathan Winters, Anthony Quinn, and Buffy Sainte-Maries visited.

The hopeful mood on Alcatraz turned sour, though, when a little girl accidentally fell to her death. Her parents, grief-stricken, went home, and after that many of the younger people who were college students returned to school. Meanwhile, the government cut off electric and water to the island. By June, only fifteen Indians remained, and they were forcibly removed by government officers.

While this might seem like a failure in the end, the occupation actually inspired hundreds of protests by Native people across the United States and is credited with starting the modern Native American Civil Rights movement.

What is Un-Thanksgiving Day?

Un-Thanksgiving Day jointly celebrates the occupation of Alcatraz Island and also marks a day of mourning as an antithesis to the day most Americans celebrate concerning the Pilgrims having a feast with Natives. It was first held in 1975 and coincides with the National Day of Mourning held in Massachusetts.

Are there any other islands in San Francisco Bay?

Yes, the other islands you should know about are Angel Island and Alameda Island. Discovered in 1775 by Juan de Ayala (1745–1797), under American rule it became a military outpost and home to Fort Reynolds. From 1910 to 1940, it served as a center for processing immigrants from Asia. About one million Asians entered the United States through Angel Island, earning it the nickname of the "Ellis Island of the West." The island was declared a National Historic Landmark in 1964 and is now part of the California State Park system.

Alameda Island has nearly seventy-five thousand residents and is separated from the city of Oakland by the Oakland Estuary. It is connected to the mainland by not only four bridges but also the underwater Posey and Webster Street Tubes.

What's the name of the other big bridge that crosses San Francisco Bay?

Commonly known as the Bay Bridge, the San Francisco–Oakland Bay Bridge was open for traffic on November 12, 1936. It connected the increasingly populated cities of Oakland and Berkeley with San Francisco via a 4.5-mile (7.25-kilometer) expanse.

One of the most prestigious universities in the country is Stanford University, which was founded in 1891.

What university near San Francisco is the United States' most prestigious learning institutions?

Leland Stanford Junior University (better known as Stanford University) in Stanford, California, was ranked as the number-one university in the country in 2015, based on surveys from *Business Insider, Money, Forbes,* the Council for Aid to Education, and others. However, a 2016 ranking by Academic Ranking of World Universities and *Forbes* took it down to number two. Nevertheless, Stanford of the twenty-first century is considered by many to have surpassed Harvard as the nation's leading institution of higher learning.

The school's namesake was Leland Stanford Jr., the son of Governor Leland Stanford. The boy had died at the age of fifteen, and his father dedicated the university to him. The cornerstone was laid on May 14, 1887, and it opened its doors to 555 students on October 1, 1891. Today, it is a leading research and educational center in such areas as physics, biology, and technology.

When was San Francisco State University founded?

Originally called San Francisco Normal School when it opened on May 22, 1899, it was renamed San Francisco State University in 1921.

CRIME

Was the identity of the Zodiac Killer ever uncovered?

Although his first victim was an eighteen-year-old woman named Cheri Jones Bates, whom he murdered on October 30, 1966, in Riverside, the mysterious Zodiac Killer is more often associated with the string of homicides he perpetrated in northern California from 1968 to 1969. All told, some say he killed thirty-seven people, using both guns and knives, but the police only consider seven of those to be directly associated to the Zodiac.

The Zodiac never explained why he called himself that, but he (or she) was notorious for sending letters to newspapers and sometimes private citizens; four of the letters included cryptograms that the Zodiac claimed, if solved, would reveal his identity. Only one of them was solved, but it didn't give a helpful clue. The letters continued as late as 1978, though the last murder likely associated with Zodiac was almost ten years earlier.

The identity of the serial killer was never solved; a Calaveras County schoolteacher named Arthur Leigh Allen was investigated after Bates' death, but he was never convicted. Many theories about the Zodiac Killer have filled discussion rooms on the Internet, but the case has gone cold and might never be solved.

How did heiress Patty Hearst become involved in a bank robbery?

Patty Hearst (1954–) is the granddaughter of newspaper tycoon William Randolph Hearst (1863–1951). On February 4, 1974, she was kidnapped from her Berkeley apartment by members of the Symbionese Liberation Army (SLA), a left-wing revolutionary group that was really just a criminal organization. The reason behind the kidnapping, not surprisingly, was Hearst's money and influence. The SLA had two of its members in prison for the murder of Marcus Foster, who was the first black superintendent of the city of Oakland. When their release was refused, the SLA demanded that Hearst give $70 to every poor person in California (about $400 million). Hearst responded by donating $2 million to Bay Area residents, but the distribution of the money was botched, and the SLA refused to release Patty.

Meanwhile, as Patty Hearst would later report, she was being raped and confined to a closet. But a strange thing happened that psychologists call Stockholm Syndrome:

Who was one of the most notorious highway bandits of post-Civil War California?

The criminal career of Charles Earl Bowles (1829–?), also known as "Black Bart," was the stuff of Western movies. He was a stagecoach robber, targeting over two dozen Wells Fargo coaches in northern California between 1875 and 1883. Well, not *exactly* the stuff of movies, since Black Bart was always on foot during the robberies because he, ironically, was scared of horses. A gentlemanly robber, he dressed well and used polite language, and although he wielded a rifle, he never shot anyone. Arrested in 1883, he served four years in San Quentin before being released on good behavior in 1888. After that, he disappeared, never to be seen by anyone, including his wife.

she eventually became sympathetic to her captors—brainwashed, in a way—as she participated in political discussions with her captors. This, along with the stress of being a captive, led her to be persuaded to participate in the robbery at Hibernia Bank in San Francisco on April 15, 1974. Armed with a machine gun, she was caught on camera at the bank. She continued to be involved in criminal activities with the SLA until she was caught by the FBI in San Francisco on April 15, 1974. After a long trial, in which she was defended by F. Lee Bailey, Hearst was found guilty of robbery and using a firearm during a felony in 1976. She was sentenced to seven years in prison, but President Jimmy Carter had this commuted to less than two years. Later, President Bill Clinton issued a full pardon in 2001. Both presidents felt that Hearst had been brainwashed and was not fully responsible for her crimes.

OTHER BAY AREA CITIES

Where is the East Bay?

The East Bay area is considered to be composed of the towns and cities within Alameda and Contra Costa counties to the east of San Francisco and San Pablo bays. This includes the cities of Oakland, Berkeley, Concord, Fremont, and Hayward.

What are some important facts to know about Oakland?

Though it often plays second fiddle to San Francisco, Oakland is actually an important and vibrant town that is the eighth-largest city in California (estimated 2014 population of 413,775). It is home to major sports teams (see the "Professional Sports" chapter), has the largest port in the northern part of the state, and also is home to the headquarters of large corporations Dreyer's (mmmm, ice cream), health-care consortium Kaiser Permanente, and the Clorox Corporation.

Oakland's star began to ascend in the 1870s, after the Transcontinental Railroad was completed, with Oakland marking the western terminus. People and goods arrived in Oakland, and if they wished to continue to San Francisco, they had to take a ferry (until the Golden Gate Bridge was completed). It was also a port for the U.S. Army, as well as a Navy supply depot. For these reasons, thousands of people, including many minorities, settled in Oakland, making it one of the most diverse cities in the nation.

Are there fun things to see and do in Oakland?

Certainly. For example, if you are a fan of Jack London's books, take a look at Jack London Square. This is where the author's actual Klondike cabin was relocated for tourists to view. Also right there is the U.S.S. *Potomac*, the presidential yacht known as "the floating White House" used by President Franklin D. Roosevelt until 1945. Originally a U.S. Coast Guard vessel, it was converted for presidential use in 1936. A $5 million, twelve-year restoration had the ship reopen for public use in 1995, and you can visit or even take a short cruise on it today. Jack London Square also has a restored, Western-style saloon, restaurants, stores, and hotels.

Another tourist attraction is the Chabot Space and Science Center, which includes hands-on exhibits, telescopes, a theater, and a planetarium. For those who like the outdoors, there's Lake Merritt (see the "Natural Wonders" chapter) and plenty of parks to enjoy. Oakland even has its own Chinatown.

Anything else notable about Oakland?

A little-known fact is that Oakland is an environmental leader in the nation. The Natural Resources Defense Council and the Mother Nature Network ranked the city fourth among U.S. cities for its efforts in keeping the city green and using sustainable energy sources.

Berkeley is well known for its university and its influence on the hippie and other counterculture movements (see the "The State of California: 1850 to the Present" chapter), but what else is there of note about the town?

Really, it is for the university, as well as being a center for arts and culture, that Berkeley has built an international reputation (see the "State of California: 1950 to the Present" for more about the counterculture movement). The city is very supportive of artists and sponsors programs and grants to encourage artists to beautify the area with original works.

The Oakland Museum of California is noted for its architecture and unique methods of organizing exhibits.

Why is the Oakland Museum of California considered to be one of the more innovative in America?

This museum is dedicated to educating the public about the art, history, and nature of California with an interdisciplinary approach. The 300,000-square-foot (27,871-square-meter) museum contains nearly two million objects ranging from natural and historical artifacts to paintings and photographs. The curators attempt to create "environments" instead of static exhibits, combining outdoor landscapes and indoor displays on each of its three levels. First opened in 1969, as of 2016 the museum is still undergoing a $62.2 million renovation in phases, with most of the museum remaining open to the public.

When was San Jose founded?

Initially a Spanish pueblo, the town was established on January 18, 1777, at the south end of San Francisco Bay. It didn't begin to really grow until the Gold Rush, when it fed off the success of nearby San Francisco. San Jose incorporated as a city in 1850, remaining a modest size until the aftermath of World War II, when it grew to about one hundred thousand. It is now the tenth-largest U.S. city with just over one million residents.

What are some notable places in San Jose?

There are two missions close to one another in the area: Mission San José and Mission Santa Clara de Asís in next door Santa Clara. A number of museums are of interest, such as the Rosicrucian Egyptian Museum, the Tech Museum of Innovation, the San Jose Museum of Art, the Children's Discovery Museum, and even the Museum of Quilts and Textiles. The Winchester Mystery House (discussed in "Quirky California") is here, too, as well as a large water park (Raging Waters) and amusement park (California's Great America).

Where, exactly, is Silicon Valley?

There is no actual geographical place called Silicon Valley, but it is, rather, the region around the south side of the Bay Area where a lot of high-tech companies got started. The first of these businesses sprang up in the Santa Clara Valley, which is why the "Valley" remains in the name, but now it includes everything from San Mateo, Palo Alto, and Mountain View to San José and Milpitas (for more on this, please see the "California Means Business" chapter).

SACRAMENTO

How was Sacramento founded?

The area was first settled by John Sutter (see the "Early California" chapter) in 1839 and boomed in the 1850s because of the Gold Rush. The city incorporated in 1850 and chartered in 1920. Sacramento's history is also important as it was a Pony Express terminus and, in 1856, served as the first railroad stop in the state.

When did Sacramento become the state capital?

Competition for the honor was intense between California cities that wanted the prestige and economic benefit of becoming the seat of government. For a few years, this debate went on until 1854, when Sacramento was settled upon. The government didn't fully move to the location until 1860, and the Capitol Building was completed in 1874 (see the "Politics and the Law" chapter for more).

Were people then satisfied with this choice for the state capital?

Amusingly, not really. People tried repeatedly to move the government to their own cities, including efforts to move it to Oakland (1858), San Jose (1875–1878, 1893, and 1903), Berkeley (1907), and back to old Monterey (1933–1941). All failed, of course. Interestingly, no move has been put forward for a southern California capital, even though the majority of the population is now in the Los Angeles metropolitan area.

What are some interesting facts about the State Capitol?

The State Capitol building took thirteen years (1861–1874) to complete. The design follows the neoclassical style reminiscent of the U.S. Capitol and was created by architect M. Frederic Butler. It's located at 10th and L Streets in Sacramento, and the dome at the top is 210 feet (64 meters) high and is topped with a finial covered in gold leaf. On one side of the building is the Senate chamber, and on the other side is the California Assembly chamber. The building was added to the National Register of Historic Places in 1973 and was named a California Historical Landmark in 1974.

Tours are available, and the building also includes a museum located in the West Wing and East Annex of the building. It includes numerous paintings, statues, murals, and antique furniture in both permanent and on-loan exhibits.

How many people live in Sacramento?

Sacramento now has an estimated population (as of 2014) of 485,000, and including the surrounding metropolitan area boosts the number to 2.4 million.

When did the Pony Express arrive in Sacramento for the first time?

On April 16, 1860, the first mail on horseback arrived in Sacramento a mere ten days after leaving St. Joseph, Missouri, a 1,966-mile (3,164-kilometer) trip. The route was broken into 100-mile (161-kilometer) legs, and the last leg was taken on this day by a young man named Johnny Fry, who brought about twenty pounds of mail with him.

The days of the Pony Express were short-lived, however, because the first transcontinental telegraph was completed in 1861, and the Transcontinental Railroad linked the country by 1867.

What is "Constitution Wall"?

A special work of art at the California Museum in Sacramento, Constitution Wall is a six-story-tall wall into which are sculpted key words from the state constitution. The words are varying states of relief so that, at different times of the day and depending on the angle of the sun, some words are more highlighted and prominent than others. In addition to this light effect, the wall incorporates the greens, blues, and tans of California's forests, lakes, and deserts, and different types of metal oxides are embedded into the wall. Over time, these chemicals will change as they oxidize more. The idea is that, just as the state

Old Sacramento is the original downtown area, which has been restored and is now a big draw for tourism in the city.

constitution can change with time, so will the wall. Constitution Wall is the work of three artists: Mike Mandel, Paul Kos, and Larry Sultan.

Is Old Sacramento a historic tourist attraction?

Yes, and one that is worth seeing. Covering twenty-eight acres of riverfront, the old town gives one the feeling of stepping back into the 1870s. It was here that the Pony Express made its final stop and where trains ended their long journey to stock up on California produce or drop off passengers. The area was neglected during the first half of the twentieth century, but restoration efforts were made in the mid-1960s. Today, there are shops, restaurants, and several museums. You can also spend the night on the *Delta Queen,* a riverboat turned into a hotel and restaurant. The museums are definitely worth a look and include the California State Railroad Museum (you can even ride a train during the months of April through September), the California Automobile Museum, the Wells Fargo History Museum, the Sacramento History Museum, the Old Sacramento Schoolhouse Museum, and Huntington & Hopkins Hardware (a museum that recreates the feel of a nineteenth-century hardware store).

What is there north of Sacramento?

The northern third of the state contains a lot of wilderness and a number of small towns. The largest city up there is Redding. The seat of Shasta County, it has about ninety thousand residents and is located on the Sacramento River just south of the Whiskeytown–Shasta–Trinity National Recreation Area. Traditionally a timber town, logging and environmental restrictions have changed the city so that employment is mostly in the service and health-care industries today. A notable symbol of the town is the now-iconic Sundial Bridge at Turtle Bay, which was completed in 2004. As the name indicates, the cantilever-spar cable-stayed bridge was made to look like a sundial; it cost $23.5 million and is restricted to bicycle and pedestrian traffic alone. It is 700 feet (210 meters) long and built in a complex filled with art, history, and environmental exhibits. Turtle Bay Exploration Park has the McConnell Arboretum and Gardens and a thirty-five mile (fifty-six kilometer) trail for hikers and bikers. There's also fishing nearby, with the river providing salmon, rainbow trout, and steelhead.

In addition to Whiskeytown–Shasta–Trinity National Recreation Area, there is also Lassen Volcanic National Park (see the "Natural Wonders" chapter), Redwood National Park, Mount Shasta (14,162-foot peak [4,316 meters]), and beautiful coastlines and redwood forests.

Is Weed, California, a place to buy and smoke marijuana?

Located between Redding and the Oregon border, Weed isn't a mecca for pot imbibers. The town just happens to be called Weed. However, when college students and other tourists started taking their pictures by the town's welcome sign, the city managers had light bulbs turn on over their heads. They have a gift store with lots of items making fun of the name, such as coffee mugs with "I Heart Weed" on them, signs that say "Weed, Next Exit," or you can purchase a "Weed Police" shirt. Besides this profitable joke, the town does afford a sensational view of nearby Mount Shasta.

Why is there a giant statue of Paul Bunyan and Babe the Blue Ox in Redwood National Park?

Visitors will see these iconic statues right before arriving at the Trees of Mystery in Klamath, California. Paul Bunyan stands 49 feet (15 meters) tall and weighs 30,000 pounds (13,610 kilograms), according to the *Trees of Mystery* website. Babe weighs the same but is more horizontal with the tips of the horns reaching up 35 feet (10.7 meters).

Once past these friendly guardians, visitors can walk a 0.8-mile (1.28-kilometer) trail and see stunning examples of some of the world's largest and most interesting redwoods. There is also the Sky Trail, a sky-high gondola ride through the treetops, a museum, restaurant, and hotel, all of which are family oriented.

CENTRAL CALIFORNIA AND AGRICULTURE

AGRICULTURE IN THE LAND OF FRUITS AND NUTS

Which government department is responsible for overseeing food production?

In this state, it is the California Department of Food and Agriculture that is responsible.

Why is agriculture so important in California?

When most Americans think of agriculture, they think of the "American Heartland"; that is, the Midwest and Central Plains states. In truth, California is the country's leader. Agriculture, including vegetables, fruit, meat, eggs, and dairy, is the second-biggest industry in the state after high-tech companies. California is blessed with the Central Valley, which has been dedicated almost exclusively to agriculture and makes the state the most agriculturally productive in the United States. According to the U.S. Department of Agriculture, in 2014 the state had over $54 billion in agriculture receipts (out of $421.5 billion for the entire country), with the runner-up, Iowa, being a rather distant second with $30.65 billion.

Which U.S. state has the most food-processing plants?

Of course, it's California, once again. There are 3,219 food-processing plants and 1,295 beverage plants in the state for a total of 4,514 plants. That's twice as many as the runner-up, New York, with 2,186, according to USDA data from 2010, the most recent available.

How much of the nation's agriculture occurs in California?

While most Americans think the country's breadbasket is in the Central Plains states and Midwest, in reality, California produces more food for the nation than any other state. According to the California Department of Food and Agriculture, in 2014 (the latest report available as of January 2016), there were 76,400 operating farms, and they had an output worth $54 billion. Half of the fruits, nuts, and vegetables consumed in the United States come from California. Most of this is produced in the Central Valley.

Where is the world's largest agricultural exhibition held?

Every February, the International Agri-Center in Tulare holds the World AG Expo. About 1,500 exhibitors display their products in the 2.6-million-square-foot exposition center.

What was COPIA?

COPIA, the American Center for Wine, Food, and the Arts, was a short-lived educational center in Napa that was open from 2001 to 2008, when the venture went bankrupt. It was conceived by vintner Robert Mondavi (1913–2008), who wanted to promote the art of wine tasting and appreciation to the public, which led to also educating people about the food to serve with wine, which then expanded to exhibits on photography, music, sculpture, and more. The exhibits and concept were never as popular to tourists as Mondavi hoped, and revenue projections were never met. After its closure, the building has been used for meetings, and there are other proposed uses that, as of this writing, have not come to fruition.

Almond trees are beautiful in the spring and produce a healthy, profitable nut for farmers, but the trees use a lot of water and have become controversial during drought years.

What are the major products created by California farms?

The top products for the state are dairy, almonds, and grapes/wines. The following table lists major food production.

Top 10 Agricultural Commodities (2014)*

Food	Value
Milk	$9.4 billion
Almonds	$5.9 billion
Grapes	$5.2 billion
Cattle and Calves	$3.7 billion

Food	Value
Strawberries	$2.5 billion
Lettuce	$2.0 billion
Walnuts	$1.8 billion
Tomatoes	$1.6 billion
Pistachios	$1.6 billion
Hay	$1.3 billion

*Source: https://www.cdfa.ca.gov/statistics/.

How did California end up with super rice profits in the 1990s?

In 1993 a devastatingly bad crop of rice in Japan spelled opportunity for the Golden State. Japan had long banned imports of rice, but the crop failure forced them to accept rice from California, and this profited rice growers in the state, which saw about $100 million in sales exports. By 2014, California was second in the nation in rice production ($1.15 billion) behind Arkansas.

While Japan has recovered since then, rice is still an important crop in the state, where about five billion pounds (2.27 billion kilograms) are grown annually, according to the California Rice Commission. Ninety-seven percent of the rice in California is grown in the Sacramento Valley.

Rice fields also benefit wildlife, providing food and a resting place for about 230 species of animals, including shorebirds and seven to ten million geese and ducks.

Is there a controversy about almond orchards?

Yes. While almonds have been extremely profitable for farmers (99% of the country's almonds are grown in California), the problem is that they consume a lot of water to grow properly. It takes about a gallon of water (3.8 liters) to grow one almond to maturity. In a state that has been subjected to drought since 2011, this has not sat well with some people. It's worth noting, however, that other crops consume a lot of water, as well. To grow one tomato takes 3.3 gallons (12.5 liters) of water; a head of lettuce drinks up 3.5 gallons (13.25 liters); a single walnut uses up 4.9 gallons (18.5 liters); and a head of broccoli sucks up 5.4 gallons (20.4 liters; we can hear readers saying now: "Cut the broccoli!").

The Almond Board of California has protested attacks against the crops, stating on its website (www.almonds.com) that almond orchards take up 13% of farmland but consume only 9% of the water, so the trees actually use less proportionately than other crops. The organization also asserts that improved farming techniques have lowered water usage by 33%.

Olives aren't native California plants, so how did they get here?

Spanish missionaries are responsible for bringing olives to the state. Today, California grows 95% of the country's olives. There are four types grown: Mission (the most popular), Manzanillo, Sevillano, and Ascolano. The olives are grown on 27,000 acres of land, picked by hand, and canned in one of two plants: one in Lafayette and one in Tracy.

Are California avocados different from Mexican avocados?

No, not at all. The avocados in California descend from trees first brought to Santa Barbara in 1871 by Judge R. B. Ord.

Which city calls itself the "Garlic Capital of the World"?

California is by far the country's leading producer of garlic (that's why we have no vampires). In 2014, nearly $256 million in garlic was grown here, which was 98.8% of the entire U.S. crop.

Gilroy, outside of San Francisco, is known for its garlic. If you drive through the town with your windows down, you can even smell it (much like smelling chocolate in

Gilroy has declared itself the garlic capital of the world and holds an annual garlic festival. Visitors can indulge in everything from savory main courses to garlic ice cream for dessert.

Hershey, Pennsylvania). To celebrate the abundant crops, the town holds a Gilroy Garlic Festival annually. At the festival, you can purchase foods made with garlic, including garlic ice cream, and learn about the health benefits of the relative of the onion. Garlic can also be used as a natural, nontoxic pesticide.

And how about garlic's relative, the onion?

California farms are number one there, too, growing over $275 million worth of the crop in 2014 (or 29.5% of U.S. production), which is over twice that of runner-up, Washington state.

Which state is the sole producer of artichokes in the United States?

You guessed it, it's California. The farmers here grew $55,517,000 worth of the thistle-related vegetable in 2014. Eighty percent of this is grown in Monterey County, and the city of Castroville calls itself the "Artichoke Capital of the World." This isn't really a valid declaration, however, since the United States is not the world's top producer; Italy, Egypt, Spain, Peru, and Argentina produce far more artichokes.

What other crops do we get a lot of from California?

As of 2014, the Golden State is the country's number-one producer of vegetables and melons overall ($8.28 billion; far above second-place Florida with $1.29 billion), asparagus (producing 53.4% of the crop), cabbage ($177.7 million), green lima beans ($21.3 million); second in sweet potatoes ($148.4 million); third in broccoli ($74 million); fifth in food grains ($1.3 billion) and sunflower seeds ($17 million).

Which nonedible crop is important to California's economy?

With California being best known for its citrus and other produce, people don't think about flowers much, except during the Rose Parade, but the state actually grows about seventy-five percent of all domestically grown and sold flowers, according to the California Cut Flower Commission. Sales of the flowers brought in $330 million to California's economy in 2007, with fifty percent of these sales being international. The most popular flowers were roses (173 million sold in 2006), gerbera (77 million), irises (72 million), lilies (66 million), and tulips (59 million).

More recent statistics from the USDA affirm California is tops when it comes to floriculture, as well. With $1.13 billion in dollars in sales in 2014, the state beat out Florida ($890 million) and Michigan ($405.6 million). This represents 26.6% of total U.S. flowers for wholesale and 78.2% of cut flower sales ($327 million).

According to the California Department of Food and Agriculture website (http://plantingseedsblog.cdfa.ca.gov/), "The top cut flowers in California are lilies, daisies, roses, chrysanthemums, and snapdragons. The top potted flowers are orchids, roses, poinsettias, spring bulbs, and chrysanthemums. The top garden plants are vegetable varieties, pansies/violas, petunias, impatiens, and marigolds."

What is the California Orchid Trail?

The region between the Santa Ynex Mountains and the coast, which includes cities such as Santa Barbara and Carpinteria and has a pleasant, Mediterranean-type climate that is perfect for these flowers, has become a mecca for orchid growers and nurseries. This all began in the early years of the twentieth century, when wealthy families with large estates became hobbyists in growing a diverse assortment of orchid species. Some of these evolved into businesses, such as the Dos Pueblos Orchid Company in Gaviota north of Santa Barbara. Owned by Samuel Barlow Mosher (1892–1970), the founder of Signal Oil who was also a major benefactor to UC Santa Barbara, the orchid nursery was one of the largest in the world and certainly the biggest in the United States in the 1950s and 1960s (it still exists today). Other large orchid growers are Westerly Orchids, Gallup & Stribling, and the Santa Barbara Orchid Estate. If you love orchids, the California Orchid Trail is the place for you. You can learn more at http://www.californiaorchidtrail.com/.

RANCHING IN THE CENTRAL VALLEY AND THE STATE

How did ranching get started in California?

As with many things in the state, it began with the Spanish missions in the eighteenth century. At the height of mission ranching in the 1830s, about four hundred thousand cattle were being raised, and the Gold Rush brought in more people and more ranchers. Since then, California families have largely managed to keep their ranches privately owned, and about thirty-eight million acres of the state are used to raise cattle. The state ranks fourth in the nation (as of 2014) in the number of cattle with 5.2 million head (behind Texas, Nebraska, and Kansas).

Why is cattle ranching controversial?

Because of the drought that has been continuing since 2011, some people are protesting that cattle being raised for meat and dairy products use a lot of water (even more than almonds, the other controversial agricultural product in the state; see above).

Ranchers, however, would argue that they are careful stewards of the land because it is in their interest to be so. Cattle companies practice such strategies as grazing rotation, elimination of invasive weeds, and forming a vegetable management plan. Sometimes they work with environmental groups such as the California Audubon Society to achieve their goals. The National Cattlemen's Beef Association issues an annual Environmental Stewardship Award to the ranch that has done the most to preserve a healthy environment on the lands where it raises cattle.

This dairy farm in central California is one of many creating milk, cheese, ice cream, and other foods in the state's biggest agricultural industry.

How much milk and cheese comes from California dairy farms?

There are 1,750 dairy farms here and 1.79 million dairy cows. About 20% of the milk and 45% of the cheese consumed in the United States comes from California, according to the California Milk Advisory Board, making the Golden State the country's number-one producer of dairy products. The board reported that the state produced 42.3 billion pounds (dairy producers measure output in pounds, not gallons), which is about 4.8 to 5 billion gallons.

Cheese production is about 2.4 billion pounds annually, which makes California the second-biggest producer in the country (as you might guess, Wisconsin is in first place). The favorite types of cheese produced here are mozzarella (59% of production), cheddar (15.4%), and Monterey Jack (11.1%).

Who cares about milk and cheese? I'm curious how much ice cream California makes!

California is also number one in ice cream! Dairies produce 133 million gallons annually in the state. The average American eats 48 pints (6 gallons) a year, so the Golden State ships out enough ice cream for over 22 million Americans each year.

Why is dairy important to California?

The California dairy industry employs over 443,000 people and contributes $63 billion to the economy each year.

183

> ## Is Monterey Jack cheese named after the city in California?
>
> Yes. The name comes from the city and the man who created this unique cheese, David Jacks (1822–1909). It is the one and only cheese variety that originated in California.

How does the state rank in egg production?

The American Egg Board ranks states according to the number of hens producing at the time. By this measure, California is seventh with 11.82 million hens. The USDA ranked the state ninth, producing over $419 million in eggs for 2014.

What recent law enacted in California threatens to raise egg prices?

In 2008 voters in the state passed a law about egg production that went into effect January 1, 2015. Simply put, the law says egg-laying hens can no longer be tightly confined in cages with numerous other hens but must be put in larger or less-populated cages so they have room to move around freely. Because this would mean not as many hens could fit in a facility, not as many eggs will be produced, which will send prices up ten to forty percent, according to some analysts. The National Association of Egg Farmers also protested that it would make injuries such as broken wings more likely, thus giving the argument that it is "more humane" less credence.

What about pork, chicken, turkey, and sheep in the state? Are they as important as beef and milk?

The dairy industry is far and away the biggest moneymaker among the livestock-related farming in California. But the state does well in other areas, too. For example, California is fourth in the nation in wool production (sales of $3.9 million in 2014). Chicken and turkeys combined bring in $2.5 billion annually. As for pork, it's not one of the state's biggest products. California ranks twenty-eighth in the nation, producing 47.7 million pounds (21.6 million kilograms) of pork products in 2014.

Are wild pigs a problem in the state?

Feral pigs are becoming a problem nationwide, including in California. The problem has been increasing since Europeans first brought in the animals; inevitably, some escaped, bred, and became wild. Until the 1950s, hunting of pigs was unregulated; hunters could shoot as many as they wanted. In 1957, they were designated as game mammals with limits on kills, and in 1992 it became state law that hunters needed a license specifically for wild pigs in order to hunt them.

Pigs have become nuisance animals, digging up farmlands for vegetables, befouling water systems with wallowing and feces, eating small animals (some of them threatened or endangered), spreading weeds and disease, and they can be dangerous to people; they *can* become aggressive, and they are very strong and have tusks. Feral pigs can be found in almost every county in the state; the good news for hunters is that they are actually very tasty if cooked correctly.

ORGANICS

How many organic farms are in California?

According to the Organic Farming Research Foundation, in 2014 there were 2,805 organic farms in the state, more than any other state in the United States.

Which organization was the first in the United States to be allowed by the USDA to certify organic foods?

The California Certified Organic Farmers (CCOF) trade association was the first in the nation to be allowed to certify organics by the U.S. Department of Agriculture. Founded in 1973 and based in Santa Cruz, the CCOF consists of three separate entities: CCOF, Inc., which is a trade association geared toward public education, political lobbying, and professional training and development; the CCOF Foundation, which is a nonprofit fundraising group; and CCOF Certification Services, LLC, which has the main function of certifying organic farms and crops. There are currently thirteen chapters of the CCOF around the state.

What does the California Organic Food Act (COFA) of 1979 entail?

COFA legally defined what were to be considered proper organic practices in order for farms to be certified. However, the law provided no money or other support to actually enforce these standards. Therefore, whenever someone or some organization wished to challenge a farm's claim about organics, the issue had to be taken to court.

Have there been other laws governing organics since 1979?

Yes. More recently, there has been the Organic Foods Production Act of 1990 (a federal law) and, on the state level, the California Organic Products Act of 2003. The former authorized the creation of the National Organic Program to certify organic farming practices to be overseen by state or other local groups (in the case of California, by the CCOF). Actual enforcement of the law falls under the aegis of the California Department of Public Health. The California Organic Products Act makes it a crime to sell, advertise, or otherwise represent a product as organic unless it meets federal guidelines and has been certified.

VINEYARDS AND THE WINE INDUSTRY

How did viticulture and winemaking come to California?

Grapes were first grown in the state in the 1770s by mission fathers (guided by Father Junipéro Serra) and made wine for sacramental and personal use. The most productive of the mission wineries was near Los Angeles in San Gabriel, which produced hundreds of barrels annually until the early 1800s.

Did the wine industry emerge in Sonoma and the Napa Valley after the decline of the missions?

Well, vineyards did reach as far as Sonoma by 1823, and the first commercial wines debuted there in 1824 from a vintner named Joseph Chapman (little else is known about him). Another name that is often forgotten in the history of winemaking, however, is Jean-Louis Vignes (1780–1862), the man who brought a fresh stock of European grapes—*Vitis vinifera*—to Los Angeles in 1833. Known to his Mexican friends as Don Luis del Aliso because he named his property El Aliso, Vignes purchased land between the old Los Angeles pueblo and the Los Angeles River, and he began importing French grapes from Bordeaux by the mid-1830s. In the 1840s, he started shipping his wines throughout California. Vignes is also responsible for planting the first orange groves in the Los Angeles area.

Who is considered to have established the first Californian vineyards?

One might think it was Vignes, but in the winery world, the person considered the "Father of California Viticulture" is Ágoston Haraszthy (1812–1869). Born to a noble Hungarian family, Haraszthy's father ran an estate on the Danube, which included a vineyard, which is what inspired his son's interest in wine. Becoming a travel writer, Haraszthy became enchanted by America and decided to move there. He first went to Wisconsin, then started a small vineyard in San Diego, and finally brought grape vine cuttings to San Francisco and also Crystal Springs. He established the first large commercial winery in Sonoma in 1857, importing vines from Europe, which thrived in the California soil at his Buena Vista estate (the Buena Vista winery still exists today, in fact).

Were many of the grape growers from Italy and Germany, then?

Yes, but there were also Americans and, down south, some influential Irishmen, including Andrew Boyle (1818–1871) and Matthew Keller (1810–1881). Boyle was the first to grow vineyards east of the L.A. River; he mostly produced Zinfandel wines under the Paredon Blanco label. Keller had a vineyard of over 13,300 acres near Santa Monica that he called the Rising Sun Vineyard.

Who was William Wolfskill?

One of the most influential and richest figures of early agriculture in California, William Wolfskill (1798–1866) was originally a fur trapper in New Mexico. A naturalized Mexican citizen in the 1920s, the money he earned from furs was invested in land in Los Angeles. Here, he established the largest winery in southern California. He also is largely responsible for the establishment of the citrus fruit industry in the state, first making large profits by selling overpriced lemons and oranges to miners during the Gold Rush. He was also the person who hybridized the Valencia orange, which became the most popular variety for making orange juice.

So who is credited with starting vineyards in Napa Valley?

A trapper named George C. Yount (1794–1865) got a land grant from General Vallejo in 1831 in Napa Valley, and he began growing grape vines there and making wine (Yountville is named after him). However, this wasn't a commercial endeavor. It was Charles Krug (1825–1892), who had learned the art from Haraszthy, who started the first commercial vineyard in Napa in 1858.

William Wolfskill established the largest southern California winery and also was a giant figure in the early citrus fruit industry.

When did the Los Angeles Vineyard Society form?

On February 24, 1857, the Los Angeles Vineyard Society first met, perhaps ironically, in San Francisco before moving back to L.A. The Society was founded by German winemakers from Los Angeles. They came up with a plan to sell stocks that would allow them to buy land in Los Angeles, dividing it into twenty-acre parcels, and each parcel would have eight acres devoted to grapevines. The stockholders paid for the land to be prepared for farming and then moved there when all was in readiness.

The first big property purchase was by the Santa Ana River and was given the name "Anaheim," meaning "Home of the Santa Ana River."

But Napa still wasn't winemaking central in the mid-1800s. When did that change and how?

Anaheim and Los Angeles remained the wine capital of the state from the late 1850s to 1880. The villain (or savior) responsible for the shift was a plant louse called *Phylloxera vitifoliae*, which ruined many of the grape crops ("Mission grapes" were the main variety at the time, still). Many of the vineyards in southern California were destroyed by 1880. That was the bad news. The good news is that the louse managed to bump off the

What was "vine fever"?

By the 1850s, the idea of getting rich was shifting from gold to winemaking (yes, yet another connection between the Gold Rush and things Californian!) Gold was getting harder to find, and now all the people who had rushed to the state to make money needed another way to do so, or else leave. Grapes and wine seemed to fit the bill, and between 1856 and 1858, the number of vines planted grew from 1.5 to 4 million. The Los Angeles area alone had over one hundred vineyards producing over 57,000 gallons of wine annually in the late 1850s, and by 1869 there were forty-three vineyards producing four million gallons of fermented grapes.

more inferior wineries, while those who invested in more diverse and better varieties survived, which actually ended up improving California wines. Another nice result is that many farmers switched to growing oranges, which resulted in the thriving citrus business. Finally, another effect was the shift from the south to the north, which led to the great wineries in Sonoma and Napa Valley. It wasn't that the northern grapes weren't affected by the pest, but it was here that native varieties of grapes that were resistant to it were discovered and cultivated, saving the industry. Even so, it wasn't until the 1890s that the vineyards were able to fully recover from the agricultural disaster.

When did California wines first surpass French and other European vintages?

For many years, California wines were looked down upon by oenophiles, but that all changed for good in 1973, when a competition judged by French wine experts declared a Napa Valley Chardonnay and a Cabernet Sauvignon the best white and red wines, respectively.

How did Prohibition affect the wine industry in California?

Naturally, when the 1919 Eighteenth Amendment was passed by the U.S. Congress prohibiting the sale and drinking of alcohol, this spelled trouble for California's winemakers. At the time, there were over seven hundred wineries in the state, and all but a handful were out of business by 1933, when the Twenty-first Amendment repealed the Eighteenth. Some wine was still produced during this period because the law under Prohibition allowed two hundred gallons a year per person to be produced for personal use, and there was also a loophole that allowed alcohol for medicinal purposes. Illegal "speakeasies" (hidden bars, essentially) cropped up, and booze cruises were organized in which people boarded ships that sailed on international waters so they could drink. There was also the interesting strategy of selling wine to Catholic churches as sacramental wine. Millions of gallons of wine were sold in this manner, until finally federal agents became suspicious and pulled the licenses of some wineries. But, for the most part, Prohibition made a shambles of a thriving industry.

The famous Napa Valley in northern California produces some of the best wines in the world.

What is the state of California vineyards today?

While Napa Valley is still famous, there are vineyards all over the state. They produce not only table wines but sparkling wines, port, and sherry. According to the California Association of Wine Growers, there are currently 5,900 wine growers in the state, employing 330,000 full-time workers and contributing $61.5 billion to the California economy.

California is the fourth leading producer of wine, behind France, Italy, and Spain. The wineries grow 110 varieties of grapes, with the top-selling white being Chardonnay and the top-selling red being Cabernet Sauvignon.

How has the drought affected wine yields?

Drought (at least for a few years) actually improves the quality of wine because grape vines are resistant to drought and enjoy sun and dry weather—to a point—producing a tastier, more flavorful grape. Wine producers are saying that 2014 vintages could be outstanding. If the drought lasts too long, however, water can become a problem for the growers.

What 2014 event damaged the Napa Valley wineries?

A 6.0 earthquake struck the Napa-Sonoma area on August 24, 2014, causing about $80.3 million in damages. However, because the harvest had just begun, the losses were less than they might have been.

LABOR TROUBLES

Why did rioting break out in Yuba County in 1913?

The history of farm labor in California is marked by several ugly bumps in the road. Farm workers often felt underpaid and abused by land owners who were growing in power as the agriculture industry in the state thrived. One of these farm owners was Ralph Durst (1865–1938), who was a leading producer of hops in the Central Valley. Trouble began when Durst put out a want ad for 2,700 workers but only had positions for 1,500, and those that he did want to hire were faced with the prospect of not being provided any housing, very few bathroom facilities, and no pay. A union called the Industrial Workers of the World approached Durst with demands for better conditions, and when he refused the Wheatland Hops-Field Riots broke out on August 13, 1913. And it was indeed a violent riot, resulting in the death of the Yuba County district attorney and his deputy, as well as two of the rioters. The local sheriff was also beaten and hospitalized.

Protests continued into the next year, including a march on the state capital. The farm laborers finally began to feel as if their voices were being heard when Governor Hiram Johnson established the Commission on Immigration and Housing. The report the commission issued was the first step in the gradual enactment of legal processes for workers to have their lives improved. The riot and rise in labor protests also led to the later work of Cesar Chavez and his United Farm Workers union.

What is a *bracero*?

A *bracero* (from the Spanish meaning "manual laborer") is an immigrant worker who only comes to the farms during harvest season.

What was the Bracero Program?

The Bracero Program refers to a national set of laws that permitted laborers to come to the United States legally from Mexico to work for farmers. The first Bracero Program between the United States and Mexico lasted from 1917 to 1921, but Mexico pulled out of it after too many of its citizens complained about rampant discrimination. In 1942, when there was not much available labor due to World War II, California farmers cried out for help and to renew the program. Workers were to be guaranteed a minimum wage (thirty cents an hour at the time) and decent living conditions while they har-

---

What's a "wetback"?

"Wetback" is a derogatory term referring to Mexicans who have crossed the border illegally. The name originates in Texas and refers to the fact that many illegals there swam across the Rio Grande River.

vested crops. The Bracero Program allowed them to circumvent normal immigration laws so they could work in America, and it applied to anyone south of the border, not just Mexicans. Most of the laborers were from that country, however.

Sounds like a good plan, but the problem was that U.S. employers started to like the cheap labor from Mexico too much, and they began hiring people outside the system—that is, illegal immigrants. By 1949 about twenty thousand legal *braceros* from Mexico arrived in the United States, while an additional 87,000 arrived illegally, according to author Philip Martin in his 2003 book, *Promise Unfulfilled: Unions, Immigration, and Farm Workers*. The U.S. Congress passed laws in 1951 and 1952 to punish employers who knowingly hired illegals, but a loophole allowed most to get out of any legal ramifications.

Today, many labor historians trace today's current problems with immigration (in California and elsewhere) to the Bracero Program.

How did the Immigration Act of 1924 affect immigration from Latin American countries?

A rather odd piece of U.S. legislation, this act restricted immigrants from eastern and southern European countries, as well as those from Africa and the Middle East, by placing a 2% cap on annual immigrants. This is to say that two percent of the total of immigrants already in this country could be new arrivals. For example, if there were ten thousand Bulgarians in the United States, only two hundred more would be allowed to immigrate here in a particular year.

An exception was made for those coming from south of the border: no restrictions at all were placed on the number of immigrants from Mexico and Central and South America or from the Caribbean.

What did César Chávez accomplish for agricultural laborers?

As the cofounder of the National Farm Workers Association, labor leader and civil rights activist César Chávez (1927–1993) championed fair pay and labor practices for migrant farm workers, most of them Latinos. The son of migrant workers himself, Chávez quit school in the seventh grade and two years later, in 1944, joined

César Chávez was perhaps the greatest farm worker labor leader the United States has ever seen. He fought for economic justice for migrant workers in California.

the navy. After the war, he went back to work as a migrant farmer in California and became involved with the Community Service Organization, a civil rights group for Latinos. He rose to the post of national director of the CSO before organizing the NFWA with Dolores Huerta (1930–) in 1962.

Chávez opposed the Bracero Program because he felt it was unfair to American workers and also exploited migrant workers. Pressure from the NFWA helped end it in 1964. In 1965, Chávez and Huerta led the historic Delano grape strike in which they managed to encourage people nationwide to stop buying grapes to support the ill-treated laborers. Several companies in the California grape industry bowed to the pressure and, in 1970, signed a collective bargaining agreement with the union.

In 1975, Chávez led a successful strike against the E & J Gallo Winery in Modesto, and he was key in pressuring Governor Jerry Brown to sign the California Agriculture Labor Relations Act of 1975, which permanently established collective bargaining powers for farm workers.

For his lifetime of leadership, which also helped improve conditions for farm laborers in Texas, Florida, Colorado, Arizona, and elsewhere, Chávez has received many honors. Sadly, the most prestigious of these came posthumously, including a Presidential Medal of Freedom in 1994 and induction into the California Hall of Fame in 2006. In California, March 31 is celebrated as César Chávez Day.

CENTRAL VALLEY CITIES

What is the biggest city in the Central Valley?

Bakersfield, which is located in Kern County at the southern end of the valley, is California's ninth-largest city, with a population of about 369,000 as of 2014. It is the county seat of government.

When was Bakersfield founded?

Unlike many cities being established in the mid-nineteenth century, Bakersfield wasn't settled by gold or silver prospectors. Rather, the first people to come over the Tejon Pass and settle what is now that city were simply looking for a nice place to live. They were led by Colonel Thomas Baker, and the plot of land they decided upon in 1863 was promptly called "Baker's Field."

What was Colonel Baker's grand plan for the city?

Baker had a plan to create a navigable river from Kern Lake all the way to San Francisco Bay. That plan, of course, was not very practical, plus it was made irrelevant by the arrival of the railway system in the 1870s.

How did Bakersfield thrive as a city?

In addition to being a center for shipping of the diverse crops of the Great Central Valley, Bakersfield went through a couple of booms. Oil was discovered in the 1860s, and exploration continued robustly through the 1890s. Also, in 1885, gold was discovered in Kern River Canyon.

What disaster hit Bakersfield in 1952?

On July 21 of that year, the Kern County earthquake registered 7.7 on the Richter scale. It killed twelve people and caused $60 million in damages.

Some Californians mock places like Bakersfield (and Barstow) as being dull places to live. Are there some points of interest to the city?

To some it is a surprise that Bakersfield actually has a rich history in music and entertainment. The "Bakersfield Sound" originated here (see the chapter "Movies, Television, and Other Entertainment"), which brought such stars as Buck Owens and Merle Haggard fame. It is also home of the annual Bakersfield Jazz Festival, which has been going on since 1986.

The historic Fox Theater is definitely worth a visit, as well. One of the last theaters built during the Gilded Age of movie houses, it was designed by Los Angeles architect S. Charles Lee (1899–1990), one of the most famous in the field of theater construction.

What's an interesting factoid about farming in Bakersfield?

The largest carrot farm in the world, Grimmway Farms, has its home in Bakersfield. It is certified in organic and kosher products.

Which city is known as the "Raisin Capital of the World"?

Fresno has sometimes called itself that, but Selma, which is in Fresno County, has asserted itself more strongly with that label, while Fresno now prefers "Gateway to Yosemite." Interestingly, Selma was originally "Home of the Peach," another major crop.

When and how was Fresno founded?

The very definition of a railroad town, Fresno was founded in 1872 by the Central Pacific Railroad Company. Now the fifth-largest city in the state, and the largest in the Central Valley, it has a population of about 516,000 people as of 2014.

What is Fresno's slogan?

The city bills itself as "The Gateway to Yosemite," since it's the largest city near the beautiful Yosemite Valley. If you arrive in Fresno by airplane, note the huge display of artificial redwood tree trunks at Fresno Yosemite National Airport.

Is Fresno an international community?

That would be fair to say, as it has drawn people of about eighty nationalities to the region. The reason for this was the availability of jobs in the railroad and farming industries and the excellent residential planning strategy established there. Fresno was the model for creating "colonies" of housing subdivisions. The first of these was the Central California Colony, which created twenty- to forty-acre parcels of land, irrigation, landscaping, and roads in 1875. By the early 1900s, there were about fifty of these colonies, and they were very conducive to small farms and homes. Consequently, immigrants from Scandinavia, Armenia, Russia, Germany, Japan, China, and Mexico flocked there.

What is notable about higher education in Fresno?

Fresno is home to Fresno City College, which was established in 1910 and is the oldest city college in the state.

Who built the Underground Gardens of Fresno, and why did he do it?

Baldassare Forestiere (1879–1946), an immigrant from Sicily, spent forty years building these unique gardens that include about ten acres of underground passages, courtyards, grottos, and rooms that was his home. As the name implies, there are many plants throughout, including shrubs, flowers, and fruit-bearing trees. Forestiere was an uneducated farmer who had come to California to farm. The land he owned, however, proved unsuitable for farming, and his plan, inspired by ancient Roman architecture and his desire to escape Fresno's summer heat, was to create a profitable, unique resort. He began digging it out in 1906, using only hand tools, such as shovels and hoes. There was no master design for the underground labyrinth, either; he just dug and built as his fancy suited him. Sadly, Forestiere died at age sixty-seven before the plan was realized. The gardens remain a popular tourist attraction today.

How did the town of Delano get its name?

Some people think that the city took its name from the middle name of U.S. President Franklin Delano Roosevelt, but the city was founded long before FDR was in office. In

---

What fun roadside stops featuring food and games first opened not far south of Fresno?

Bravo Farms is a chain of four attractions in the Central Valley, including in Tulare, Visalia, Traver, and Kettleman City. Traver, south of Fresno, was the first to open, greeting customers in 1995. It features a series of stores and restaurants in an Old West look, as well as a petting zoo and miniature golf. You can watch cheese being made and taste some wine while the kids play in a treehouse.

1869, when the Southern Pacific Railroad was passing through the area, it gave rise to the new town, which took its name from U.S. Secretary of the Interior Columbus Delano (1809–1896). Delano became a prosperous agricultural town.

What else is interesting about Delano?

Delano is home to the Filipino Agricultural Workers Organizing Committee and is where the Delano Grape Strike occurred (see above). It has been a hotspot for farm worker labor unions predominantly populated by Hispanics and Filipinos.

Is Visalia in the Central Valley where those sweet oranges come from?

Well, Visalia is in the Central Valley, and they are known for their oranges, but you're actually thinking of Valencia oranges, a hybridized, sweet orange developed by William Wolfskill (see "Vineyards and the Wine Industry" above), which lent its name to the city that sprouted just north of Los Angeles.

CENTRAL COAST CITIES

Other than the important history behind Monterey, what are some facts of note about this old California city?

As discussed in the "Early California" chapter, Monterey served as a seat of government back to the Alta California days of Spanish rule. It is the site of the state's first public building, public library, public school, and newspaper. It was also the home of author

Monterey Bay Aquarium is both a center for education and research. The facility also includes a hospital to rescue and treat sick and injured sea otters.

John Steinbeck (see "Notable Californians") and the Monterey Pop Festival (see "The State of California" chapter).

What makes the Monterey Bay Aquarium quite special?

The aquarium at Monterey has the usual ocean life exhibits, but it also has a couple other special things going for it. One is that the facility is set up to rescue and nurse back to health sea otters that have been found in the area. A natural-looking outdoor exhibit allows guests to view the otters that are almost ready to be released back into the wild. Monterey Bay Aquarium also has the Monterey Accelerated Research System, an underwater observatory on the bottom of the Pacific Ocean 32 miles (52 kilometers) from Monterey that scientists can use to observe ocean life in a natural habitat without human interference. As for other things to see, the jellyfish exhibit is stunning, and there are fascinating, little-seen cephalopods such as the mimic octopus, chambered nautilus, and giant Pacific octopus.

Where is Monterey Canyon?

It might be hard to find if you didn't know it was underwater. The Monterey Submarine Canyon is a deep trench off the coast near Monterey and is about 95 miles (153 kilometers) long and a mile (1.6 kilometers) deep in places, which makes it comparable to the Grand Canyon in Arizona. Rich in life, part of the canyon (called the Soquel Canyon State Marine Conservation Area) is protected from fishing.

What special place in California attracted bohemian writers and their followers?

Big Sur is not a city, country, or unincorporated town, but it is a region on the Pacific Coast near the north end of the Los Padres National Forest. Its peaceful location has made it a mecca for writers and artists over the years (see "The State of California: 1850 to the Present").

Was Carmel-by-the-Sea founded by artists?

Usually referred to simply as Carmel, this town north of Monterey has drawn artistic types for years and once had actor-director Clint Eastwood (1930–; see the "California Notables" chapter) as a mayor. Like many California towns, its history goes back to the Indigenous people and Spanish missions and settlers.

Things began to get interesting, though, in 1905, when the Carmel Arts and Crafts Club was established with the goal of supporting the arts. It was fortuitous timing because when the San Francisco earthquake struck the next year, the arts community that had been in the Bay Area was looking for somewhere to reestablish itself. Carmel and the art club seemed the ideal place, and a flood of writers, poets, painters, and actors settled there, including such names as poets Mary Austin and Nora May French, poet and playwright George Sterling, novelists Upton Sinclair and Sinclair Lewis, painters such as William Frederic Ritschel, Anne Bremer, and E. Charlton Fortune, and photographer Arnold Genthe.

The town built one of the first open-air theaters west of the Rockies, the Forest Theater, in 1910. Much later, in 1952, the Golden Bough Playhouse also opened and now hosts the annual Carmel Shakespeare Festival run by the Pacific Repertory Theatre.

What amazing building can be found in San Simeon?

One of the biggest tourist attractions on the Central Coast is Hearst Castle in San Simeon. It was the private home of publishing magnate William Randolph Hearst (1863–1951; see the "California Notables" chapter), who started construction in 1919. Hearst had grown up on the hills overlooking the Pacific Ocean. After becoming wealthy for his newspapers and motion picture company, he returned to his home to build his impressive mansion. The building and its décor are all inspired by his boyhood trip to Italy. Hearst hired a woman architect, Julia Morgan (1872–1957; see "California Notables), to design it.

Built by publishing magnate William Randolph Hearst, Hearst Castle near San Simeon is now owned and operated by the state and is a huge tourist draw.

Construction continued until 1947, and even after that, modifications and adjustments were being made until Hearst's death. The end result can only be described as extremely lavish. Expensive art, including paintings, sculptures, and tapestries, fill the rooms. Wooden features from churches were used, such as pews, to serve as seating along walls. There is a huge, outdoor pool (the Neptune Pool) and an even more impressive indoor, Roman-style pool complete with a diving platform one story up.

Hearst Castle is really a complex of buildings, including four main buildings (Casa Grande, Casa Del Mar, Casa Del Monte, and Casa Del Sol, which have a total of fifty-eight bedrooms and sixty bathrooms) and several guest houses. A grand dining room, libraries, billiard room, and movie theater are also found in Casa Grande, and on the grounds, in addition to the pools, are tennis courts, orchards, an airfield, horseback riding trails, and the world's largest private zoo (at one time; most of the animals are now gone). Hearst used his home, which he adored, as a place for social gatherings, inviting European and Hollywood royalty for extended stays, parties, and outdoor activities.

Hearst Castle is a historic landmark and is now operated by the California State Park System. Tours are, of course, available to the public.

What bizarre kidnapping occurred in Madera County in 1976?

On July 15, 1976, three men kidnapped twenty-six Dairyland Elementary School children from a school bus near Chowchilla in Madera County. Their motive was to hold the children for ransom. Driving the kids to a quarry in Livermore, they hid them in a buried van. With their prisoners buried, the three men left, but the bus driver, Ed Ray, managed to dig them out with a the help of some of the older children. Ray alerted police, and the men were tracked down fairly quickly; one of the kidnappers, Frederick Woods IV, was the son of the man who owned the quarry. Interestingly, investigators discovered that Woods and his accomplices got their idea for the kidnapping from reading a 1969 copy of Alfred Hitchcock's *Daring Detectives* that was available at the Chowchilla Public Library. Today, Woods is still in prison, while the other two criminals, Richard and James Schoenfeld, have been released. Ray received a California School Employees Association citation for outstanding community service.

What's the story behind Santa Cruz?

While not getting the same amount of attention as its more northern neighbor, Berkeley, Santa Cruz is certainly a very liberal college town. Located on the northern end of Monterey Bay, and with a population of around 63,000 in 2014, it was first settled in 1791 with the construction of the Spanish mission there. The arrival of the Spanish spelled the end for the native Ohlone people, and the memory of their existence is all but gone, except for the names of three Santa Cruz County towns that use Ohlone words in their names: Aptos (meaning "The People"), Soquel (referring to the nearby creek), and Zayante (named after one of the Ohlone tribes).

Santa Cruz (meaning "Holy Cross") is home to the University of California, Santa Cruz. It was incorporated in 1866, just after the Civil War, and was once the home of California Powder Words, which made explosives for mining and gunpowder. Today, the main employers are the university and local government. It is also home to audio communications company Plantronics.

Liberal and progressive activism have been part of the city culture for decades. Santa Cruz is home of The Resource Center for Nonviolence, founded in 1776, and the Wo/Man's Alliance for Medical Marijuana and Santa Cruz Cannabis Buyers Club. There is a strong pro-women's rights movement in the town, as well as antinuclear sentiments and a chapter of the Occupy movement (the political movement for economic equality in America).

But Santa Cruz is also a place of beauty, isn't it?

Indeed, there are coastal redwood forests, Natural Bridges State Beach, and a large marine reserve. It's easy to go on hikes or bike rides near the city and enjoy nature everywhere.

What's special about the Santa Cruz boardwalk?

A fun place to visit for shops and food, the boardwalk is also home to California's oldest roller coaster, the Giant Dipper. Built in 1924, it is the fifth-oldest coaster in the country. You can also take a ride on the Charles I. D. Loof Carousel, which dates to 1911. It's named after the famous carousel builder who hand-crafted his amusement rides.

Why is Morro Bay such a notable seaside town?

Although now primarily a tourist town, it dates to 1870, when it became an active port for many of California's agricultural products. Morro Rock, which formed about twenty-three million years ago as a result of activity, is a curiosity that still attracts visitors (see the "Natural Wonders" chapter). The rock was once completely surrounded by water, but some of it was mined and turned into a causeway that now connects it to the mainland. The breakwater created a nice haven for boats, and so the town is a popular place for fishing and recreational boating. On the west side of Morro Rock is a very nice beach, and there is lots of shopping and quality restaurants, especially if one enjoys seafood. Another landmark of the town is the Dynegy Power Plant, which was an important producer of electricity to the central coast for many years, especially during the 2000 power crisis. However, it was decommissioned in 2014 because needed upgrades proved too expensive, neither has it been torn down because that would be prohibitively expensive as well. For now, the three smokestacks, known as "The Three Fingers" to locals, will remain as they are indefinitely.

Which city calls itself "the American Riviera"?

Because of its wonderful, Mediterranean climate and resort-town experience (lots of golf and water sports), Santa Barbara has been described by its local leaders as comparable

Morro Rock in the middle of Morro Bay cannot be missed. The result of volcanic activity, it has long been a point of interest and also includes a very nice beach on its western shore.

What is a Santa Maria-style barbeque?

There's nothing more Californian than barbequing a beef tri-tip (a cut of beef from the bottom sirloin) seasoned with salt, pepper, and garlic over a fire of burning coals made of native red oak wood. The meal is accompanied, traditionally, with salsa, pinquito beans, tortillas, and salad. It has its origins in Mexican cattle ranches but didn't become a popular dish in California until the 1960s.

to life on the coast of Marseilles, France. With plenty of wine being grown in nearby Santa Maria, it certainly can feel that way. In addition to the rich resort life of the area, there is a lot of history, including the Spanish mission and presidio, a past that is celebrated with a popular annual Old Spanish Days Fiesta (watch out for people smashing confetti-filled eggs on your head). And that's not the only festival held there. On Bastille Day, the city also holds the Santa Barbara French Festival, the Santa Barbara International Film Festival, an annual music festival held at the historic Arlington Theater, and an arts and crafts festival. Stearns Wharf, which is full of shops and restaurants, is popular among tourists, and those who like wildlife will enjoy the Santa Barbara Zoo or a trip to the Channel Islands National Park just a short boat ride away, and the sea there is full of dolphins, whales, sea lions, and other marine life, which is why it is also a marine sanctuary.

What else does Santa Barbara have to crow about?

Some other notable facts about the city include:

- It is where the first Earth Day celebration began. A huge oil spill in 1969 off the Santa Barbara coast inspired the residents to start an environmental movement in 1970 that has spread across the world.
- It is the home of the Coronado Butterfly Preserve, one of the country's largest roosting places for monarch butterflies.
- It is home to the largest bay fig tree (called the Moreton Bay Fig Tree) in the United States, which spreads its branches over 160 feet (48.8 meters) wide.
- It is the home of singer Katy Perry (1984–), who attended Dos Pueblos High School.

CALIFORNIA MEANS BUSINESS

What are the top industries in California?

The most profitable businesses in the state are: 1) high tech, 2) agriculture, 3) aerospace, 4) service industry (this includes tourism), and 5) motion pictures and television productions. In this book, see "Central Valley and Agriculture" for more on agriculture and "Movies, Television, and Entertainment" for more on that business.

What does a snapshot of California workers look like?

According to the 2010 U.S. Census, there were 20.8 million working people in the state at the time. Of this number, the workforce population included:

44.9% white
33.5% Hispanic
5.3% African American
16.3% Asian and other groups

SILICON VALLEY AND
MORE HIGH TECH

What the heck is a klystron tube?

Invented in 1937 at Stanford University by brothers Russell (1898–1959) and Sigurd Varian (1901–1961), a klystron tube is a linear-beam vacuum tube that amplifies signals using an electron beam. The technology was useful for satellite, telephone, and television transmissions. Also importantly, it made possible the radar system currently used by today's aircraft and is used in missile guidance systems.

When did a certain computer rodent debut in California?

A prototype mouse was part of an input console demonstrated by Douglas C. Engelbart (1925–2013) on December 9, 1968, at the Fall Joint Computer Conference in San Francisco. Popularized in 1984 by the Macintosh from Apple Computer, the mouse was the result of fifteen years devoted to exploring ways to make communicating with computers simpler and more

The first computer mouse debuted at a conference in San Francisco.

flexible. The physical appearance of the small box with the dangling, tail-like wire suggested the name of "mouse." Engelbart received the Turing Award in 1997 and the National Medal of Technology and Innovation in 2000, and he was inducted into the National Inventors Hall of Fame in 1998 for his invention of the computer mouse.

What is the importance of Apple Computer?

Apple Computer, which was founded by Steve Jobs (1955–2011), Steve Wozniak (1950–), and Ronald Wayne (1934–), was founded in1976 in Jobs' parents' garage in Los Altos. After developing the circuit board that was really the only component of the Apple I, they made the Apple II, which is considered the first personal computer. The company incorporated in 1977 (Wayne bowed out, leaving Jobs, Wozniak, and investor Mike Markkula).

Apple went public in 1980 and raised impressive amounts of money to start its public line of personal computers. Now headquartered in Cupertino, the company's success is rivaled only by Microsoft. It has expanded beyond computers, creating the iPod, iPhone, Apple Watch, Apple TV, and now voyaging into electronic vehicles.

Where do many of the world's computer microchips come from?

The Intel Corporation was founded in Santa Clara by Robert Noyce, Gordon Moore (1929–), and Andrew Grove (1936–). Noyce, who is also known as the "Mayor of Silicon Valley," helped Nobel Prize winner Jack Kilby (1923–2005) invent the integrated circuit (microchip). Taking this invention to the next level, Noyce and his partners founded Intel in 1968. The company came out with the 4004 and 8008 microprocessors, which could perform sixty thousand operations a second, by the early 1970s. Next came the 286 and 486 processors in the 1980s, and the Pentium processors came out by the 1990s. Continuing to improve the microchip over the decades has made Intel one of the most successful high-tech companies in the world.

What's the story behind Atari?

Anyone who grew up in the 1970s playing arcade games is familiar with the brand Atari. Founded in 1972 by Nolan Bushnell (1943–) and Ted Dabney, the Sunnyvale Corporation went out of business in 1984. Atari is responsible for creating the first popular video game, *Pong*, which was basically a table tennis game played with two paddles (rectangles) and a ball (a dot) on the screen. Atari also made some of the first home computers, and you could play *Pong* either by plugging them into your television or by playing at an arcade. Some other Atari games of note were *Millipede, Asteroids, Sprint,* and *Tank.* As arcades declined in popularity in the 1980s, Atari faced other challenges, such as problems with its home computer division, internal corporate strife, and the disastrous failure of its game based on the movie *E.T.: The Extraterrestrial,* a game so poorly executed that Atari buried seven hundred thousand game cartridges in the desert.

How did eBay become so huge?

The Bay in eBay refers to the San Francisco Bay, since the company was founded in San Jose. When it was founded by Pierre Omidyar (1967–) in 1995, the computer programmer was just trying to figure out a way to sell some items he wanted to get rid of. He was stunned to sell a broken laser pointer to a buyer who actually collected broken laser pointers. Realizing that if he could connect buyers and sellers on a searchable site he'd really have something, eBay began to take off. Omidyar brought in Canadian computer entrepreneur Jeffrey Skroll (1965–), who became the company's first president, and Meg Whitman (1956–), who is now the CEO of Hewlett Packard.

The eBay experience was like going to an online garage sale or flea market and looking for bargains and hard-to-find or discontinued items. The company made money by charging buyers and sellers small transaction fees. It originally started just for the San Francisco area but soon became not only national but international in scope because it was a model that turned out to be much in demand: exactly the thing that shoppers in the then-new World Wide Web market were seeking. When eBay went public in 1998, Omidyar and Skroll earned millions.

The company bought PayPal (the online money transfer service) and iBazar (an online flea market like eBay) in 2002 and Skype (the Internet videophone service) in 2009. PayPal was separated as a publicly traded company in 2014.

It's interesting that two of the Internet's largest search engines—Google and Yahoo!—are also based in California.

Yes, the state, especially the Bay Area, certainly is a mecca for the technology of the new era. Google is headquartered in Menlo Park, and Yahoo! is in Sunnyvale. The founders of Google, which is now probably the most popular search engine available, are Larry Page (1973–) and Russian-American Sergey Brin (1973–). They met at Stanford University as graduate students after Page had completed a B.S. at the University of Michigan. They began by experimenting with a program called BackRub that was hosted on the Stanford servers in 1996, renaming it Google the next year (the name is a variation of the word googol, a term that refers to the huge number 1^{100}, which meant that there was a huge amount of information to search on).

The Google headquarters building in Mountain View, California.

In 1998 they found an investor in Sun Microsystems founder Andy Bechtolsheim (1955–), who wrote Google a check for $100,000 to improve the program. Google began getting noticed for its ability to search a vast amount of Web information and come up with relevant matches that were ranked by usefulness in a search. In 2004 the company launched its free email service, Gmail, and also acquired the photo organizing online site Picasa. Google Maps was introduced the following year, as well as Google Analytics, a program to help marketers measure and improve business website performance. Other apps followed, such as Google Finance, and in 2006 the company made perhaps its most important acquisition when it bought YouTube, the video-sharing website that is now the most popular in the world.

Innovations have continued, including Google Wallet for a better shopping experience using phones, voice-recognition software, the Android phone, and, most recently, an initiative to invent a self-driving automobile. With all of this, there is little doubt that Google is one of the most inventive companies in the United States, and it is also rated one of the best places to work for, according to a *Fortune* survey.

So, what about Yahoo!? Where does it fall in?

Yahoo! is right up there with Google, although not at the very top of the list. In surveys, the search engine tends to rank third after Google and Microsoft's Bing but right above

Ask.com. Yahoo! also has a popular email service and online map, as well as the Tumblr (microblogging) and Flickr (photo sharing) services that are in wide use, too.

Founded by Jerry Yang (1968–) and David Filo (1966–), Yahoo! was started at Stanford University, just like Google was, interestingly enough. Yang and Filo were both studying electrical engineering and decided, for fun, to start a directory called Jerry's Guide to the World Wide Web. They renamed it Yahoo in 1995, not as a fun kind of exclamation, but rather as an acronym meaning Yet Another Hierarchical Officious Oracle. The company went public in 1996, selling 2.6 million shares for $13 a share. When the dot-com bubble burst in 2001, stocks fell to a little over $8 a share. Yahoo! managed to survive, however, and grow. It briefly overtook Google in 2013 as the leading search engine and has a revenue of over $5 billion a year, employing over 13,000 people.

Do Yahoo!, Google, and Microsoft work together? Do they own each other? It's very confusing.

Indeed, this has become a tangled web over the last ten or fifteen years. Google and Yahoo! partnered with each other from 2000 to 2004, during which time Google let Yahoo! use its search engine until Yahoo! came up with its own. Yahoo! and Bing (the Microsoft search engine) also had a deal in which they teamed up resources to provide search results to customers and Yahoo! agreed to run Bing ads; the deal was recently renewed, but Yahoo! only has to run Bing ads 51% of the time. In the meantime, Google has wanted to renew its partnership with Yahoo!, but the two companies face the legal issue of antitrust laws both in the United States and internationally.

Which San Jose company set off the desktop publishing revolution?

Adobe Systems, Inc., created software products such as Photoshop and Acrobat that were largely responsible from transitioning the publishing world from mechanical typesetting to electronic typesetting. The company was founded in 1982 by two defectors from Xerox: John Warnock (1940–) and Chuck Geschke (1939–). Their first major software product was PostScript, a computer language that allowed for the design of vector graphics (graphics determined by mathematical formulas rather than pixels). Other

---

Is the verb "Google" now in the Oxford English Dictionary?

Yes, it was added to the OED in 2006, as well as to the Merriam-Webster Dictionary that year. It means, of course, to use the Google search engine to find facts about things or people on the Internet. A variant is also "Googleable" or "Googlable," meaning something that one can locate on the Internet. Probably "Yahoo" as a verb didn't work because "Google" is just so much more fun to say. Why would you "Yahoo Madonna" when you can Google her?

software programs would follow in rapid succession, including Adobe Type Manager, Photoshop, PageMaker, After Effects (for motion files), InDesign (for typesetting), Dreamweaver (websites), and much more.

OTHER TECHNOLOGY AND MEDICINE

What was "Experiment Number Twelve"?

On September 7, 1927, inventor Philo T. Farnsworth (1906–1971) and his team at a lab on Green Street in San Francisco successfully created the first transmission of a moving object onto a screen: the first television image. It was the twelfth version of the experiment that worked: hence the name the event is now remembered as. Two vacuum tubes were used: one to transmit and a second to receive the image; wires connected the tubes and an amplifier boosted the image, which was of a simple triangle. By today's standards, the result was unimpressive—a moving line on the receiving screen—but the experiment laid the groundwork for the fundamental way in which the first televisions operated.

What are some important contributions to medicine by researchers at the University of California at Berkeley?

UC Berkeley biologists Herbert Evans (1882–1971) and Choh Hao Li were able to extract growth hormone from cattle in the 1940s, but it wasn't until 1971 that they and colleagues synthesized human growth hormone using genetic engineering. Human GH can be used for the treatment of everything from dwarfism to treating AIDS patients whose muscles and bones are atrophying as a result of the disease.

What are some other contributions to science developed at UC Berkeley?

In 1954, scientists at UC Berkeley fired up the Bevatron, which, at the time, was the world's largest cyclotron, or particle accelerator. The university had been building cyclotrons since the 1930s, and the smaller ones could create radioisotopes that could be used in the field of medicine to treat tumors and for diagnostics, as well as for the creation of uranium-235 for use as nuclear power plant fuel and bombs.

Philo T. Farnsworth is credited as being the scientist who figured out how to transmit images of moving objects: the television.

The Bevatron could accelerate particles to six billion electron volts, which was useful to theoretical physicists and nuclear medicine.

The next year, UC Berkeley scientists discovered the first antiproton. An antiproton is like a proton, except it has a negative instead of a positive charge. Antimatter could potentially be a great source of energy: collide antimatter with matter, and energy is released in enormous amounts. The problem is that it is difficult to create antimatter, and there is not enough to make such a process practical.

Have many elements been discovered at UC Berkeley?

Indeed, yes. The Lawrence Berkeley Lab has been responsible for the discovery of the following elements:

Element	Year Discovered	Element on Periodic Chart
Technetium	1936	43
Astatine	1940	85
Neptunium	1940	85
Plutonium	1940	94
Americium	1944	95
Curium	1944	96
Berkelium	1949	97
Californium	1950	98
Einsteinium	1952	99
Fermium	1952	100
Mendelevium	1955	101
Nobelium	1958	102
Lawrencium	1961	103
Hahnium	1970	105
Seaborgium	1974	106

FOOD INDUSTRY

What are the two biggest fruit companies in California?

Dole Food Company, Inc., and Sunkist Growers, Inc., are both based in California. Dole is headquartered in Westlake Village, with branches in Fresno, Salinas, and Ontario, while Sunkist is a cooperative of about six thousand growers.

Dole's roots go back to 1851 and the Castle & Cook company founded by Spanish missionaries. This company merged in 1932 with the Hawaiian Pineapple Company, which was founded by James Dole (1877–1958) in 1901, and with the Standard Fruit Company about thirty years later. The new company was called Dole Food Company, Inc. (Interestingly, Castle & Cook later became a separate real estate company in 1991, breaking off from Dole.) After selling its interest in packaged foods to a Japanese company in 2012, Dole has refocused its mission on fresh fruits and vegetables, including pineapples, berries, bananas, and whole and cut vegetables—over two hundred products in all being sold to ninety countries. In 2013, Dole was made a private company by CEO David Murdock (1923–). It reported gross revenues of $4.8 billion in 2014.

The Sunkist Cooperative began in 1893 as the Southern California Fruit Exchange (the name changed in 1954). With $1.1 billion in revenue in 2014, the company was founded by "the Father of the California Citrus Industry," Edward L. Dreher (1877–1964) in Claremont (the company moved to Valencia in 2014). Sunkist is unique because it *is* a cooperative. Growers in California and Arizona remain autonomous but worked together within the company for their mutual, economic benefit. Selling not only oranges but also strawberries, lemons, limes, grapefruit, and tangerines, Sunkist had about $1 billion in sales in 2014; it is the largest shipper of fresh produce in the United States.

I love jelly bellies! Tell me about the Jelly Belly® Factory!

The Jelly Belly® has been around a long time, but they've become even more popular in recent decades when President Ronald Reagan declared jelly beans his favorite candy. In his honor, the company made a new blue Jelly Belly® and served over three tons of them at his first inauguration in 1981. Jelly bellies were even taken on board the space shuttle *Challenger* in 1983.

The company's real name is the Herman Goelitz Candy Company, and it is headquartered in Fairfield near San Francisco Bay. Founded in 1898, it now has sales worldwide, producing sweet beans in fifty flavors, as well as some specialty flavors. You can have regular flavors ranging from root beer and cappuccino to tutti fruitti and watermelon, and you can even go bizarre with flavors like pancakes and syrup, champagne, or beer, and more disgusting flavors like booger (actually peach), stinky socks (really tutti-fruitti), and moldy cheese (caramel corn). Obviously, such names are meant to appeal to little kids' funny bones.

Are there other fun candy shops?

This is California—of *course* there is. For example, anyone who likes Pez dispensers has to go to the Museum of Pez in Burlingame. There are two rooms to the museum. The first is a store, where you can also see the world's largest Pez dispenser (it's 7' 10" tall) that actually works. It looks like a snowman and can dispense 6,480 candies in one tilt of the head. For a $3 admission, you can enter the museum room, which has the full story about how Pez candies were invented in 1927 by the Austrian Eduard Haas III (1897–1989); the dispensers came out in 1950, and two years later the company modified the dispensers with heads of various cartoon characters.

Some other unique candy stores include the Columbia Candy Kitchen in Columbia and Sugarfina in Beverly Hills. The former dates back to the Gold Rush era, when a Danish candy maker moved to Columbia to start his shop. The store still has that old-fashioned feel. You can even watch the candy being made in copper kettles and then cooled,

---

Where does the word "Pez" come from?

The word is a shortening of the German name for peppermint, *pfefferminz*), which was the first Pez flavor.

---

mixed, and cut on the original marble slabs. A bit more chi-chi than the Columbia store is Sugarfina, which is known for confections flavored like alcohol, such as rum and champagne. Private clients can hire their own candy concierge to make special treats for them to be catered at parties.

What upscale grocery chain is based in the state?

Bristol Farms (also known as Lazy Acres Market in Long Beach and Santa Barbara) is headquartered in Carson and opened its first store in Rolling Hills Estates in Los Angeles County in 1982. It was owned briefly by other chains until becoming independent again in 2010. Combining a kind of farmers market ideal with the flashiness of Herrod's department store, Bristol Farms also offers special events such as wine tasting, and even a cooking school and café.

MICROBREWERIES

Are there a lot of breweries in California?

Yes, there has been a "Craft Beer Boom" in the state that began in San Francisco and has spread south all the way to San Diego, which is now regarded by many as craft beer heaven. The state currently has 570 small breweries ((2014's are the latest figures from the California Craft Beer Association), and 240 more are in the planning stages. The industry contributed $2.4 billion to the state's economy in 2014 (growing 18% from 2013). California ranks third (behind Colorado and Pennsylvania) for total beer production (1.3 million barrels) and first in the nation for craft beer production.

Which city has become well known for its craft beer?

San Diego has made a name for itself as "The Craft Beer Capital of America." The city boasts over a hundred breweries, microbreweries, and pubs. The craft beers that are noted for their signature San Diego flare are high-alcohol, hopsy pale ales, especially Double IPA (India Pale Ale), which has a bitterness to it that is three times tangier than the average beer. Bitter doesn't mean "bad," it just has a distinctive flavor that might be an acquired taste for some while others will love it. Of course, there are many alternatives to IPA for those with other preferences.

Probably the oldest brewery in the city is the San Diego Brewing Company, which was established in 1896. Other notable companies include Mission Brewery and the Aztec Brewing Company.

The Mission Brewery is one of many fine, independent beer breweries in the San Diego area.

What's the best way to get a good taste of San Diego beers?

Take the Scavengers Beer Adventure, starting in either Carlsbad or San Diego. The tour takes you to three breweries, a meal at Phil's BBQ, a behind-the-scenes tour of one of the breweries, free samples, and a complimentary tasting glass. You can visit http://www.brewerytoursandiego.com to make a reservation and find out more. Or, if you are in San Diego in early November, you can attend San Diego Beer Week, which is a street fair with lots of booths, entertainment, food, and, of course, beer.

Are there any other cities notable for their beers?

San Luis Obispo, south of Morro Bay, is also quite the hotspot for breweries. It's home to the Creekside Brewing Company and Tap It Brewing.

RESTAURANTS

Where was the first McDonald's opened?

Now the number-one name in fast food in the world, McDonald's had its first restaurant in San Bernardino, California. Brothers Richard "Dick" (1909–1998) and Maurice "Mac" McDonald (1902–1971) opened it on May 15, 1948, at 1398 North E. Street. Early success came with the business model of providing food quickly and inexpensively; the catch was that only hamburgers, fries, milkshakes, and drinks were on the menu, and customers could not make any substitutions to the toppings.

The slowly growing chain was purchased by Ray Kroc (1902–1984), who at the time was a milkshake machine salesman. He began opening restaurants across the country, stressing uniformity of service, prices, and quality of food. While "fast food" was not a McDonald's innovation, this uniformity was. A customer could go to a McDonald's anywhere in the nation and know what he or she would be getting. Today, there are over thirty-five thousand McDonald's in 118 countries.

The oldest still-operating McDonald's is in Downey, California, and still maintains much of its 1950s-era charm.

What other famous burger place opened around the same time as McDonald's?

Founded in Baldwin Park in 1948 by Harry (1913–1976) and Esther Snyder (1920–2006), In-N-Out is not well known outside the West because all the restaurants are in California, Arizona, Nevada, Utah, Oregon, and Texas. Unlike McDonald's, In-N-Out has kept the menu simple. You can order burgers, fries, drinks, and shakes, and that's about it. Also, the owners have not gone public and have refused to expand too quickly for fear of sacrificing quality. Now headquartered in Irvine, the company refuses to freeze the meat and other ingredients it uses, keeping the food fresher than many fast-food places.

A fun, not-so-secret secret is that there's a lot of stuff you can get at In-N-Out that isn't on the menu. You can ask for burgers with three patties, without buns (for the gluten-sensitive), with grilled (instead of raw) onions, chili peppers, or with fried buns. You can order a grilled cheese sandwich or a veggie burger, too, as well as cheese fries. And you can get a Neapolitan milkshake or root beer float instead of chocolate. The most famous option is to ask for your burger or fries (or both) "animal style." When you ask for that, you get extra grilled onions, a dousing of special sauce, and mustard added. Animal-style burgers and fries have become a California favorite.

But what burger place from California is the best?

That honor, according to a 2014 *Consumer Reports* survey, belongs to The Habit Burger Grill, which just edged out In-N-Out (McDonald's ranked last). The Habit was founded in Santa Barbara (now headquartered in Irvine) in 1969. With its signature "charburger" heading the menu, the chain boasts fresh meat in its burgers and also has an albacore tuna filet, chicken club, veggie burger, tri-tip steak, and pastrami sandwich. Salads, fries, onion rings, tempura green beans, and shakes and malts round out the menu. The com-

Is there really a secret message underneath the cups at In-N-Out?

Yes, and not only on the cups. The Snyder family are Christians, and they have printed biblical notations on some of the packaging for their food. On the bottom of the drink cups it has "John 3:16" printed along the inside lip; milkshake cups have Proverbs 3:5; burger wrappers include Revelation 3:30 (or Nahum 1:7 for the double-double burger); and the French fries container has Proverbs 24:16 on it.

pany was bought out by a private equity firm in 2007 and has been rapidly expanding since then.

How did the "Big Boy" hamburger get its name?

Now well known all over the United States, the Big Boy restaurants are famous for their signature hamburger, the Big Boy. The name was inspired by a fan of founder Bob Wian's (1914–1992) double-decker burger. Bob had started his business in 1936 in Glendale, California, where the restaurant was called Bob's Pantry, and he invented his double-decker burger the next year. One of his customers who became very fond of the treat was a six-year-old, chubby boy who wore saggy overalls, and it was this boy who inspired the burger's name, which then became the name of the restaurant, *and* the boy himself inspired the chain's mascot.

What pizza joint for kids almost feels like a trip to Disneyland?

If you are an American, chances are sometime during your childhood your family took you to a birthday party at Chuck E. Cheese's. The combination restaurant and amusement park includes all kinds of games and shows that feature animatronic characters just like at Disney World or Disneyland.

The concept for Chuck E. Cheese's originated with Nolan Bushnell (1943–), who founded Atari, Inc. He created the restaurant in 1977 at least, in part, to market Atari games, such as Pong. It is based in San Jose.

Which restaurant boasts some of the best split pea soup in the world?

Although it was founded way back in 1924 by Danish immigrant Anton Andersen and his French wife, Juliette, Split Pea Andersen's still only has two restaurants: one in the original Buellton location, north of Santa Barbara, and the other in Santa Nella, south of Stockton in the Central Valley. The restaurant became famous for the split pea soup recipe made by Juliette. Then, in the 1930s, their son, Robert, was inspired by a silly cartoon he saw of two men actually splitting peas one at a time using a hammer and chisel. He held a contest after World War II to name the two characters, and the names Hap-Pea (the corpulent guy with the hammer) and Pea-Wee (the smaller, nervous guy holding the chisel)

The Andersen's restaurant sign in Buellton offers a photo opportunity for guests.

were chosen. For those who can't make it to one of the California restaurants, the company sells its trademark soup in cans at many grocery stores around the country.

What Dutch-themed restaurant and bakery became a Los Angeles institution?

The Van de Kamp's Dutch Bakery was founded by Theodore Van de Kamp and Lawrence Frank in Los Angeles in 1915. It started with potato chips and grew into a bakery with a Dutch theme. Employees wore Dutch outfits, and each of the stores that were built, beginning in the 1920s, looked like a windmill with blades that actually moved. These little places grew into larger bakeries and coffee shops, and then Van de Kamps sold packaged food in grocery stores, all with packaging including the trademark windmill. Van de Kamp's was bought by Pillsbury, and in 1995 Pillsbury sold Van de Kamp's seafood and frozen foods divisions to Dartford Partnership in San Francisco.

The windmills are, sadly, gone from any foods still under the Van de Kamp's label, as are the restaurants with the charming Dutch structure—except for one. In Arcadia, just east of Pasadena, one last Van de Kamp's building remains, including the windmill, but the sign on the outside says Denny's. The googie architecture (a futuristic style) and   **213** the fact that it is the last of its kind led to the building being put on the Los Angeles Conservancy's list of historic places.

CLOTHING AND FASHION

How are Levi jeans connected to the gold and silver mining business?

It was German immigrant Levi Strauss (1829–1902) who noticed that prospectors in the San Francisco area needed tougher pants to hold up to their rough life in the mountains and streams of northern California. He came up with a design that was made of denim and reinforced with copper rivets at the points where the pants were most likely to tear. Working with tailor Jacob Davis (1831–1908), he debuted his creation—now known as jeans—in 1873.

What was the inspiration behind Banana Republic?

As one might guess, it was clothing with a safari theme. Founded in Mill Valley by Mel and Patricia Ziegler in 1978, the Zieglers were going for a touristy, fun flare, but after their company was bought by Gap, Inc., in 1983, the clothing emphasis was more on luxury items.

Which big clothing company filed for bankruptcy in 2015?

American Apparel, a company founded in Los Angeles in 1989 by Canadian artist and entrepreneur Dov Charney (1969–). Initially, the clothing chain was a huge success story, becoming the largest company in the United States that actually made clothes in this country and not in overseas sweatshops. Sadly, corporate culture turned unhealthy, and there were several allegations by employees about sexual harassment, as well as a strange lawsuit filed by film director Woody Allen, who objected to American Apparel's use of an image from his movie *Annie Hall* in its advertising. Financial troubles that ensued found Charney kicked out the door in 2014.

TRANSPORTATION

RAILROADS, STREETCARS, AND TROLLEYS

What was the Pacific Electric (Red Car) system?

One development in the history of Los Angeles that was very significant for its development into the metropolis it currently is was the establishment of the Pacific Electric Railway system. Nicknamed the Red Car system for reasons you may easily guess, it was the brainchild of railroad tycoon Henry Huntington (1850–1927), after whom Huntington Beach is named. Huntington was heir to a fortune made by his uncle Collis, who helped build the Southern Pacific Railroad; he served as the company's vice president. The younger Huntington had trolley railways installed from Los Angeles to many of the surrounding, smaller cities from 1901 to 1908, including Riverside, Santa Ana, San Bernardino, Santa Monica, Redlands, La Habra, Pasadena, the San Fernando Valley, and Newport, Hermosa, Redondo, Manhattan, and Long beaches. Making travel much simpler and cost effective for a wide variety of people helped united the region into what became the Greater Los Angeles area.

A partnership with fellow railroad baron Edward Henry Harriman (1848–1909) and mergers with other companies led to a "New" Pacific Electric, which emerged in 1911 and included the Los Angeles Inter-Urban Railway and the Los Angeles Pacific Railway. At its height, the Red Cars ran on about 1,100 miles (1,770 kilometers) of track. But trolley use declined as suburban and outer cities became more populated and people started taking cars because there weren't enough Red Car stations. During World War II, there was a brief resurgence of use because of transportation needs for the war effort, but by the 1950s the increase in the number of people with cars and the construction of freeways doomed the Red Car for good. Car and tire companies worked together to make sure that Red Car ended its run, which it did in 1961.

What was the Yellow Car system?

Yellow Cars were the colloquial name for the Los Angeles Railway, which was part of the streetcar transportation landscape from 1901 until 1963. Yellow Cars actually carried more passengers than the Red Cars did; 1,250 funicular cars traveled along twenty routes in Los

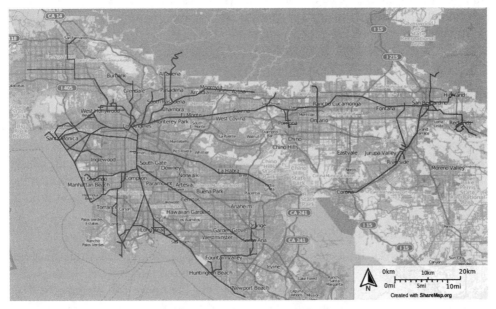

The Red Car system (routes are shown in dark gray on this map) connected much of the Los Angeles area by the 1940s and 1950s.

In what unlikely movie does a scheme to destroy the Red Car system become part of the plot?

In the cartoon/live action movie *Who Framed Roger Rabbit* (1988), it's revealed toward the end of the film that the villain Doom wishes to destroy Toon Town so that he can build a freeway system through it and eliminate trains, including the Red Car.

Angeles and nearby neighboring neighborhoods and cities. But as automobiles began to become the favored form of transportation after World War II, the line went into decline and was eventually absorbed into the Los Angeles Metropolitan Transit Authority.

What about the famous San Francisco streetcars?

A brief history of these iconic streetcars is provided in the "Northern California" chapter under the San Francisco heading.

Why was the Pasadena & Los Angeles Electric Railway important?

Formed on April 11, 1894, the Pasadena & Los Angeles Electric Railway helped consolidate all the smaller, independent horse- and cable-car systems that were in operation in the Los Angeles Basin. Connecting Los Angeles with Pasadena, this new, efficient transportation system created by Eli P. Clark (1847–1931) spurred growth in the area and caused land values to skyrocket in value as it eventually connected Riverside, San Bernardino, Orange, and Los Angeles counties.

When was Los Angeles's Union Station opened?

Designed by architects John and Donald Parkinson, Union Station opened on May 7, 1939, toward the end of railroad travel's heydays and is considered the last of the great railway stations. The station is, indeed, beautiful, combining Spanish, Mission, Moorish, and Aztec styles. By the 1950s, trains were being used much less by passengers, and the station fell into decline over the decades. However, Los Angeles has been adding subway and light rail routes, which are becoming increasingly popular, and Union Station has been making a comeback. It was added to the National Register of Historic Places in 1972.

Does California have a high-speed rail system?

The United States is behind many other countries in terms of high-speed rail (most notably, Japan). The only such system of note in the country, currently, is the Acela Express, which connects Boston, New York, Philadelphia, Baltimore, and Washington, D.C.

California's government began exploring the potential for high-speed way back in the 1980s, but a serious plan was not put into effect until decades later. Traffic congestion, both on land and in the air, was becoming a nearly insurmountable problem. Traffic jams on freeways occurred daily, and navigating Los Angeles International Airport (LAX) was enough to drive anyone's blood pressure sky high. So it was with the help of the federal 1994 High-Speed Rail Development Act during the Clinton Administration that money was made available to make high-speed rail a reality in California.

The construction, which began in 2015, will be implemented in two phases, eventually connecting San Francisco, Sacramento, Fresno, Bakersfield, Los Angeles, San Diego, and many points in between. The total length of track will be over 800 miles (1,300 kilometers), and the top speed of the train should be 220 miles per hour (350 kilometers per hour). If all goes as planned, a passenger will be able to ride the rail from L.A. to San Francisco in about two hours and forty minutes. This would be a six-and-a-half-hour drive by car—er, if you live in an alternate California with absolutely no traffic jams. A flight between the two cities (with no stops) takes about an hour and fifteen minutes, not counting time spent in the airport.

The route and train stations will either use old routes and buildings that will be revamped, or completely new ones will be built. In Phase 1 of the plan, Los Angeles will be connected to San Francisco, and in Phase 2 the tracks will be extended to include Sacramento in the north and San Diego in the south. The entire project is scheduled to be completed around 2029. However, segments of the track will open years before then.

FREEWAYS, HIGHWAYS, AND STATE ROUTES

When did California get its first freeway?

While much of the country waited until the Eisenhower Administration to see freeways running through states in the mid- to late-1950s, the first California freeway was completed in 1940. The Arroyo Seco Parkway, as it is now called, was originally named the Pasadena Freeway because, well, it led to Pasadena. Now SR 110, it is a little over 8 miles (11 kilometers) in length.

Has there been any controversy involving construction plans for the high-speed train?

Indeed, there has. From budget wonks who believe it to be a giant boondoggle that wastes taxpayers' money to farmers resenting having to move some of their buildings or operations or, even, complaining that the train will disturb livestock, the new train has irked many Californians. Legal challenges were filed in 2011 based on the premise that the state was not following the laws in acquiring and developing land, as well as environmental concerns. Such notions were categorically dismissed by the federal Surface Transportation Board in 2014, but some court cases are still pending as of this writing.

What was the earliest paved highway in California?

El Camino Real ("The Royal Road" or "The King's Highway") was constructed by the Spanish to link the missions in the region. It ran from San Diego to San Francisco. Today, much of the original route is still in use as part of Highway 101.

Is historic Route 66 still in use in the state?

The original Route 66 ran from Chicago to the West Coast, with the California section connecting Santa Monica on the coast to Needles near the border with Arizona. The road is still used, but it has been broken up, and more modern freeways (I-15, I-40, and SR 66) circumvent the original route.

With the American lifestyle of traveling the roads, the idea of motels seems a natural development, but who first designed one?

Motels got a bit of a hesitant start in 1925, when hotel developer James Vail hired architect Arthur S. Heineman (1878–1974) to build the Milestone Mo-Tel in San Luis Obispo. Vail had already developed "autocamps" in the 1910s and was working on municipal campgrounds when he came up with the motel (a portmanteau of "motor" and "hotel"). The Milestone, which opened to travelers on December 12, 1925, was the first of what was intended to be eighteen motels, each about a day's drive apart from the next one. However, a few years later, the Great Depression hit, and the other motels were never built.

The first motel in the world, the Milestone Mo-Tel in San Luis Obispo, still exists today. It no longer serves as a motel but is an office for The Apple Farm hotel next to it.

Why do Californians use the article "the" when they talk about freeway and highway numbers?

This habit among Californians sometimes annoys out-of-staters. Why do they say "I took the I-5" and not just "I took I-5"? As the saying goes, old habits die hard. When freeways were first debuting in the state, they were given proper names such as the Pasadena Freeway, the San Diego Freeway, the San Bernardino Freeway, and so on. Many people still refer to them in this manner, but as the freeways started to be assigned numbers, the articles remained, such as "the San Bernardino Freeway" became "the I-10."

The concept of the motel didn't die, however. And when times became better, motels started springing up all over the country. Because Heineman was unable to patent the word "motel," we now have that word applied to all such overnight rest stops.

Where is "The Grapevine"?

The Grapevine is a portion of Interstate 5 that runs the 40-mile (64-kilometer) stretch from Los Angeles to Kern County and the community of Grapevine. Running through mountainous passes, the highway zigzags and looks a bit like a grapevine, too. But the name not only refers to the town of Grapevine and the way the road looks, but, according to legend, it is a reference to the fact that early settlers in the area had to clear a lot of Cimarron grapevines in order to travel through the area.

Which highway is one of the most scenic (and dangerous) in the state?

The Pacific Coast Highway (State Route 1) runs from Orange County in the south to Mendocino County in the north—a distance of 656 miles (1,055 kilometers), much of which is along the coastline. The construction was a massive undertaking that was completed in 1934, but it had been pieced together in various sections that were not all consolidated and placed under the SR 1 name until 1964. Much of the drive—such as in the Big Sur and Monterey portions—afford beautiful views of the Pacific Ocean. It's best to travel along this highway during the dry months of summer. Rain has frequently triggered landslides that pose a danger to motorists and often end up closing portions of the highway. With the onset of El Niño in the winter of 2016, fears of such landslides have escalated.

WATER, AIR, AND AEROSPACE

Why is Matson, Inc., important to the history of California and Hawaii?

Matson, Inc., was founded in 1882 by Captain William Matson (1849–1917) and incorporated in 1901 as the Matson Navigation Company, providing regular shipping services **219** to Hawaii. In 1908, the shipping company offered services to passengers, too, and it was this fact that is credited with the onset of mass tourism to the Hawaiian Islands. The influx of tourists led to the opening of the Royal Hawaiian Hotel in Waikiki, which opened in 1927. Passenger service continued into 1970, but since then Matson has been exclusively a cargo carrier.

What is the best way to get to Catalina Island?

You can take the Catalina Express from Long Beach, Dana Point, or San Pedro, or the Catalina Flyer departs from Newport Beach. If you have deeper pockets, you can charter a private boat, and there are also helicopter and seaplane options.

What kind of cruise ship trips are available?

Cruise lines from Los Angeles typically travel to Mexico and San Francisco, and some also go to Hawaii, Canada, and Alaska.

Did the first glider flight really take off from California?

Yes! On August 28, 1883, engineer, physicist, and Santa Clara College professor John Montgomery (1858–1911) and his brother James successfully launched a glider off of Otay Mesa, south of San Diego. On its maiden voyage, the glider traveled 600 feet (183 meters).

Where was *The Spirit of St. Louis* built?

The famous airplane that Charles Lindbergh piloted from Long Island, New York, to Paris, France, in 1927 was built by the Ryan Airline Company in San Diego.

Made almost entirely of wood, the "Spruce Goose" designed by Howard Hughes proved to be an impractical form of air transportation.

Why would millionaire Howard Hughes build an airplane so large it was impractical to fly?

Howard Hughes (1905–1976) was a movie producer and pilot who founded the Hughes Aircraft Corporation in Glendale in 1932. During World War II, the U.S. government hired Hughes's company to build a large transport aircraft. After spending about $23 million on its design and construction, Hughes still hadn't delivered the plane to the government when the war ended in 1945.

Aggravated by the wasted money, the government threatened a lawsuit. To defend himself, Hughes made an unannounced test of the craft on November 2, 1947. The plane was huge, with a wingspan of 320 feet (97.5 meters) and weighing in at 300,000 pounds (136,100 kilograms), which theoretically could carry seven hundred soldiers. Because steel was scarce during the war, Hughes built the plane out of birch and spruce wood, covered it in fabric, painted it a light gray, and powered it by eight large propellers. Although most of the wood was birch, the H-4 seaplane was nicknamed the "Spruce Goose."

In the test flight, Hughes piloted the plane for about a mile near Long Beach Harbor, raising it about 70 feet (21 meters) above the surface of the water. It was never flown again and was still considered impractical. Nevertheless, Hughes stored the Spruce Goose in ready-to-fly condition for the rest of his life at a cost of a million dollars a year. It is currently on display at the Evergreen Aviation Museum in McMinnville, Oregon.

Was the Douglas Aircraft Company based in California?

Although it merged with McDonnell Douglas in the 1960s, and that company, in turn, became part of Boeing, the Douglas Aircraft Company had headquarters in Santa Monica and Long Beach, originally. They were an important player in early commercial planes and warplanes during World War II. One of the early, major contributions to aviation by Douglas was the DC-3 (DC stood for Douglas Commercial). The DC-3 was one of the most reliable and safe aircraft ever built. It debuted in 1935 and is credited with popularizing air travel for ordinary citizens. The aircraft could carry twenty-one passengers across the continental United States in less than a day. It featured several innovations that are now standard in commercial craft, including wing flaps and retractable landing gear. It was not only used for passenger flights but also during wartime, including World War II, the Korean War, and Vietnam. The DC-3 was also instrumental in providing supplies to West Berlin during the airlift of 1948, when that part of Berlin was under threat of falling to the Communists. By the late 1940s, DC-3s made up about ninety percent of the world's commercial airplanes. Even as of 2014, a few hundred are estimated to still be in use internationally.

What impressive records were made at Edwards Air Force Base?

It was at Edwards Air Force Base (formerly Murdoc Field) that pilots flew jets at Mach 1 and then Mach 2 (the speed of sound [340 miles/547 kilometers per second] and twice

Can people still view the space shuttle *Endeavor*?

Yes, the *Endeavor* is retired at the California Science Center in Los Angeles. After flying twenty-five successful missions from 1992 to 2011, the fifth and last space shuttle to be built was retired here.

the speed of sound), breaking the sound barrier. The first milestone came on October 14, 1947, when Captain Chuck Yeager (1923–) piloted the Bell X-1 experimental craft.

On November 20, 1953, Captain Albert Scott Crossfield more than doubled that speed when he flew a Douglas-558-II Skyrocket above Edwards, shooting across the sky at 1,291 miles (2,078 kilometers) per hour. Crossfield also achieved an elevation record of 83,235 feet (25,730 meters).

Were the space shuttles built in California?

Modern supply and assembly practices are a lot more complex than they used to be. Parts for the space shuttles were produced all over the globe, but the final assembly of the craft occurred in Palmdale, California, at the U.S. Air Force Plant 42 near Edwards Air Force Base. Maintenance and other work on the ships was moved to Florida by 2002, however.

Which company is responsible for the first private spaceship?

Since the days of the Space Race between the Soviet Union and United States, space flight has been the domain of governments only, but that changed in 2004, when the first commercial spaceship debuted, *SpaceShipOne*, a reusable craft built by Scaled Composites, a Mojave-based company, and run by Virgin Galactic in Las Cruces, New Mexico. It made its maiden voyage on June 21, 2004, initially riding on the back of an airplane before firing rockets and obtaining a height of 62.5 miles (100 kilometers) above sea level. The first fourteen flights saw the spaceship get very high but not quite into outer space proper. That came with the fifteenth flight, piloted by Michael Melvill. After two more flights, one by Melvill and the last by Brian Binne, during which the ship reached 70 miles (112 kilometers), *SpaceShipOne* was then retired and is now housed at the National Air and Space Museum in Washington, D.C.

SpaceShipTwo and future spacecraft for Virgin Galactic are to be built by the Spaceship Company (part of the Virgin Group of companies) in Mojave, California. Virgin is owned by billionaire Richard Branson, who believes that space is too important a frontier for humanity to ignore. *SpaceShipTwo* will be carried up to an elevation of 50,000 feet (15,240 meters) attached to a duel-fuselage, custom-built plane called the WhiteKnightTwo, which then releases *SpaceShipTwo* so it can continue its way out of the atmosphere.

TOYS

What toy brought Mattel such great success?

Mattel, Inc., which is headquartered in El Segundo, was founded in 1945 by Ruth and Elliot Handler and Harold Matson (the company name comes from a combination of Matson and Elliot's names) in a garage. After Matson sold his share, the Handlers took full control. It was Ruth who conceived of the iconic Barbie doll in 1959. Barbie became the best-selling doll not just in the United States but around the world. Barbie's boyfriend, Ken, debuted in 1961, and other dolls were added, including Skipper, Tutti, and Scooter. Barbie fans can buy their dolls sports cars, houses, clothing, and other accessories.

Today, it is estimated that over one billion Barbies have been sold in 150 countries and that three of the dolls are sold every second. Even so, sales have been down from 2008 to 2015, so Mattel is launching a new line of Barbies they feel will be more appealing because they are more realistic in appearance. They vary in height, hair color, ethnicity, and there are even going to be Barbies who are not skinny. No longer are customers looking for an idealized young woman; they want dolls that look more like them.

What is the Wham-O company known for?

Now based in Woodland Hills, Wham-O became a big hitter in the toy industry with such fun playthings as the Frisbee, Hula-Hoop, and SuperBall. The company was the brainchild of two University of Southern California students, Richard Knerr (1925–2008) and Arthur "Spud" Melin (1925–2002), who, reminiscent of Apple, began the business in Knerr's garage. After finding some success with a slingshot toy, they moved to Alhambra and then San Gabriel. Their first big hit, though, was the Frisbee, which was originally called the Pluto Platter. Coincidentally, according to Knerr, the name Frisbee just happened to be similar to the pie tins made by the Frisbie Pie Company that Yale students had been playing with on campus. The Hula-Hoop came out the next year and the SuperBall in the 1960s. Other popular Wham-O products include Silly String, the Boogie Board, Slip 'N Slide, and the Hacky Sack.

BIG MONEY

How did Wells Fargo, a delivery service company, become one of the largest banks in the United States?

Well, Fargo and Company opened in San Francisco and Sacramento in 1852 as a delivery and passenger service, one of many businesses that came into existence thanks to the Gold Rush era. Originally founded by Henry Wells (1805–1878) and William G. Fargo (1818–1881), who together also founded American Express, the company also provided banking services to its customers. Isaias W. Hellman (1842–1920) bought the company

What musical features a song about the Wells Fargo wagon?

In the movie musical *The Music Man* (1962, based on the 1957 play), the western town citizens are so excited about a delivery from Wells Fargo that they break into song about it: "The Wells Fargo Wagon."

from Wells and Fargo in 1892. In 1905, Hellman separated the banking and express parts of the company and merged the banking side with Nevada National Bank. When the United States entered World War I in 1918, the express franchise was taken over by the federal government, leaving only the banking side of it to Hellman. Since then, through mergers and other growth, Wells Fargo has grown into the fourth-largest bank in the United States.

What is the connection between the first commercial bank in the West and the death of a popular millionaire?

The Bank of California opened in San Francisco on July 4, 1864, by William Chapman Ralston (1826–1875). Ralston profited off the silver mines in the area, and for the next decade, he built his bank into a financial powerhouse. However, Ralston had a weakness for living the rich life. He bought a huge mansion and hosted huge parties. Worse, he made some shaky investments and was caught using bank funds to finance personal ventures. This, and the aftereffects of the Panic of 1873, led to the failure of the Bank of California, which shut its doors on August 26, 1875. The next day, Ralston's lifeless body was pulled out of San Francisco Bay. There were indications of a stroke, but many speculated his death was a suicide. Many were saddened by the popular man's death, and fifty thousand people attended the funeral procession.

MOVIES, TELEVISION, AND OTHER ENTERTAINMENT

Why is California considered the heart of the entertainment industry?

Since the establishment of the film and, later, television industry in Hollywood and Los Angeles in general, southern California was the place to be if you were in entertainment. Although one can make a strong case for New York City, which is certainly the heart of stage production with its Broadway shows and also has a lot of television being produced, Hollywood has been it since the 1910s. It is the home of the Golden Era of movies and of television. Today, the motion picture industry employs about 2.4 million people in the state, making it one of the top five industries here. But that doesn't mean California can rest on its laurels; it all might change soon.

I've heard that there has been a big shift, though, and production companies are increasingly filming in other states and countries.

That's true. Over the last few years, there has been a lot of anxiety for California's government and supporting businesses that Hollywood is rapidly changing. Other states and countries are starting to give tax breaks and incentives to film and television producers to make their shows outside of Hollywood. Just for a couple of examples, the spooky TV show *The X-Files* was mostly filmed in Canada, and even a movie that was supposed to be set in Los Angeles, *San Andreas,* which is about a huge earthquake in southern California, only shot there for ten days; most of the rest of the production was done in Australia. *Rock of Ages,* set on the Sunset Strip, was filmed in Hollywood—Hollywood, Florida, that is. *Battle: Los Angeles*? Filmed in Baton Rouge, Louisiana. And the list goes on.

Some good news is that, while not Los Angeles, some new production activity is occurring in San Francisco, which is, at least, in California. The reason for this is incentives. The city approved a program that provides film companies with $600,000 in incentives to cover expenses such as rental fees, payroll taxes, police services, street closures, and so on.

Incentives on the local and state level have been implemented elsewhere, too. Among these are sales tax exemptions for the purchase of production equipment, waiver of fees for using a number of city- or county-owned sites (L.A.'s City Hall, for example, is free to use, which is useful for crime dramas, for example), and production incentive programs such as the one in Santa Barbara that helps not only filmmakers and commercial producers but also photographers.

It remains to be seen how much such programs will help, and even if they do, it's likely that the industry will continue to be more national and international in scope in the future. However, Hollywood and Los Angeles will probably always play a big role in movies, television, and also music.

HOLLYWOOD AND THE MOVIE AND TELEVISION INDUSTRY

How did Hollywood get its start?

The town of Hollywood was first conceived by Kansas businessman Harvey Wilcox (1832–1891) as a residential community in 1887. The name was suggested by his wife, Daeida. The town was centered on the main street of Prospect Avenue, and a streetcar connected it to Los Angeles—a two-hour trip at the time. When a new track was completed in 1904, Prospect Avenue was renamed Hollywood Boulevard. The town was annexed by Los Angeles in 1910.

What was the first movie theater to open?

Tally's Electric Theater opened in Los Angeles on April 2, 1902. It was the brainchild of Thomas Lincoln Tally (1861–1945), who also founded First National Pictures with James Dixon Williams (1877–1934). Of course, at the time the idea of moving pictures was novel, and Tally had a hard time attracting an audience until he came upon the idea of putting peepholes in the walls to entice potential ticket buyers. Allowing people a look for free sparked their interest and lured them into the theater.

Businessman Harvey Wilcox's original 1887 concept for what became Hollywood was a simple residential community.

Who invented moving pictures?

As you might have suspected, most people say it was Thomas Alva Edison (1847–1931). Actually, the idea for moving pictures was the brainchild of a British photographer, Eadward Muybridge (1830–1904), who was trying to show that a running horse sometimes had all of its legs off the ground. As for who further developed this idea into a movie camera into reality, that was Edison's Scottish employee, William Dickson (1860–1835); the camera was called a kinetoscope and was completed in 1892. As with many of the inventions to come out of the Edison laboratory, including the incandescent light bulb, Edison would take credit.

Why wasn't the first theater in Hollywood?

Interestingly, the city banned movie theaters in the early 1900s. When films first started being shown in the United States, there was a large backlash from Protestant and other groups that said they were immoral. People were shocked in 1896, when Thomas Edison released the short film *The Kiss,* for example.

When did movies start getting made in Hollywood?

The spark that lit the flame was Edison. Oh, not because the great American inventor told moviemakers that Hollywood would be a great place to produce movies, but, rather, because moviemakers were fleeing Edison. Edison invented the motion picture camera and, therefore, had the patent on it, which meant he could charge people for making movies with his camera. A development that made this possible was that the nascent film industry was changing from one that actually sold films to those who would view them to renting them through a growing new distribution business. Edison charged these distributors royalties for using his patent. This was a shrewd move, and the goal was to drive smaller companies out of business and control the larger companies that could afford the fees, giving Edison effective control over the new movie industry. Edison started partnering with the larger companies, as well as George Eastman (founder of Eastman Kodak), to create the Motion Picture Patents Company in New Jersey.

Filmmakers, tired of being sued by Edison or of having other legal action force them to stop making movies, came up with the idea of taking their production companies to California—in particular, Los Angeles—because it was close to the Mexican border (and in the early 1900s, it wasn't possible for Edison to take quick action on a company thousands of miles away). This way, if word got out that Edison was sending agents out to serve legal papers, the production crews would gather up their equipment and run over to Mexico until the heat cooled off.

One of the first filmmakers to employ this strategy was William Selig, who, in 1909, made the first feature film in Los Angeles: *The Count of Monte Cristo.* Rather

227

quickly, word got out about this plan, and other producers and directors headed to the Golden State.

There were other advantages to southern California, however. One was, of course, the weather. It rained so infrequently that it was much easier to shoot movies outdoors than it was in the Midwest or East Coast. Filmmakers were also able to find cheaper labor here, and the land (at the time, certainly not today) was considerably cheaper than back East. Some historians actually feel it was these three other factors that were much more important to the rise of Hollywood than the problems with the Motion Picture Patents Company.

Despite being able to get a foothold in California, it might seem that the movie industry in Hollywood would not be able to avoid trouble with Edison forever. Thanks to the U.S. Supreme Court, however, the reign of the Motion Picture Patents Company would come to an end by 1915, when the Court ruled it to be an illegal monopoly. With the stake driven into the heart of Edison's plan, Hollywood was now free to grow on its own.

Despite Hollywood being a true mecca, what city claims it had the first studio that made movies?

Sorry, Hollywood, but the first movie studio to start filming silent flicks was the American Film Manufacturing Company (also known as Flying "A" Studios because of its winged-letter logo), which was based in Santa Barbara. Flying A's first releases came in 1912, and it was a productive maker of silent movies until 1921 after losing a major distributor and some of its best acting talent.

When did the first movie studio open in California?

Although it was not located in Hollywood proper, Selig Polyscope Company was founded in 1909 in Edendale, which is just northwest of downtown Los Angeles. The company was created by William Selig (1864–1948) in Chicago, actually, but its California studio was the first in that state. Selig Polyscope will be remembered for releasing films by such early stars as Fatty Arbuckle, Harold Lloyd, Tom Mix, and Colleen Moore.

The first studio to actually be run within Hollywood's city limits was the Nestor Film Company, which moved into the humble-looking Blondeau Tavern in 1911. The first movie stage was built be-

William Selig founded Selig Polyscope Company in Chicago, and he opened the first permanent film studio in California in Edendale near L.A.

hind the tavern. The company found some early success in the silent era with their "Mutt and Jeff" comedy shorts produced by Al Christie (1881–1951). Operating as Christie-Nestor Studios by 1913, the film studio later merged with the Universal Film Company.

THE SILENT ERA

What was Hollywood like during the Silent Movie Era?

Hollywood became an epicenter in the 1910s, with filmmakers flocking to the city, and by the 1920s people readily acknowledged it as the film capital of the world. Virtually all movies shown in the United States were produced in Hollywood, and it was Hollywood that provided about eighty percent of short and feature films to Europe. Movie directors, actors, and actresses from across the nation and Europe were drawn to Southern California, which is how Americans became familiar with Greta Garbo (Sweden), Heddy Lamarr (Austria), Rudolph Valentino (Italy), Peter Lorre (Slovakia), and Bela Lugosi (Romania), and directors such as Fritz Lang (Austria) and Ernst Lubitsch (Germany).

Who was Adolph Zukor?

Adolph Zukor (1873–1976) was the founder of Paramount Pictures. Born to Jewish parents in Hungary, he immigrated to the United States in 1889. He found success as a fur-rier and became wealthy as owner of the Novelty Fur Company. Then, in 1912, he started the Famous Players Film Company with the goal of taking established stage actors and putting them in films. Merging efforts with the Lasky Feature Play Company owned by Jesse Lasky (1880–1958), Famous Players–Lasky became Paramount Pictures in 1914. It was Lasky who hired director Cecil B. De Mille (1881–1959). They soon signed contracts to such immortal actors and actresses as Clara Bow, Mary Pickford, Rudolph Valentino, and Douglas Fairbanks. Zukor was president of Paramount until 1936 and chairman of the board until retirement as chair emeritus in 1959.

What is the significance of D. W. Griffith's film *The Birth of a Nation*?

Debuting on February 8, 1915, at Clune's Auditorium in Los Angeles, *The Birth of a Nation* broke ground for its artistic direction, faithfulness to historic costuming,

D. W. Griffith's *Birth of a Nation* is viewed today as a disturbingly racist movie that portrays the KKK as heroic.

229

and outdoor settings. While it was a silent movie, it was accompanied by original music scores, the first feature movie to do so. That said, the movie about the Civil War and Reconstruction eras was, and is, very controversial for its portrayal of blacks as savage beasts and the KKK as an heroic organization.

Why is the movie *In Old Arizona* an important landmark?

Directed by Irving Cummings and based on an O. Henry story, *In Old Arizona* (1928; also known as *The Cisco Kid*) is a Western that was the first film to be shot entirely outdoors. Locations included Bryce Canyon and Zion National Park. The movie also featured a singing cowboy (Warner Baxter as the Cisco Kid) and was the first Western with sound.

THE GOLDEN AGE AND CLASSIC HOLLYWOOD

Who created United Artists?

That was a partnership between D. W. Griffith, Charlie Chaplin, Mary Pickford, and Douglas Fairbanks Sr., who formed the movie production company in 1919.

When was Metro-Goldwyn-Mayer Pictures formed?

MGM Pictures was formed in 1924 when three other studios—Metro Pictures, Goldwyn Pictures, and the Louis B. Mayer Company—merged.

What were some other prominent studios that became powerful in the early decades?

Other big studios that had an influence on Hollywood were 20th Century Fox, Paramount Pictures, and Warner Brothers. Together with MGM and RKO, these were the "Big Five" (RKO was actually based in New York, however). The "Little Three" included United Artists, Columbia Pictures, and Universal Pictures.

How did the advent of sound in motion pictures change the industry?

Audiences loved them, but it spelled doom for a number of actors, some of whom had a hard time remembering lines or had, well, funny-sounding voices. In silent films, too, a different style of acting was used than in "talkies." For example, slapstick was more effective without sound (Harold Lloyd's career came crashing down, for example), and in drama, one would gesticulate wildly and exaggerate facial expressions to get the point across, but when people could hear dialogue such techniques came off as ludicrous.

Which film had the first sound?

It was not actually *The Jazz Singer* (1927), as most people think. A few shorts with sound and music were released the previous year, and, also in 1926, the feature film *Don Juan* had music. However, *The Jazz Singer* with Al Jolson (1886–1950) was the first with actual talking. A funny fact is that the filmmakers weren't looking for talking in the movie.

They just wanted Jolson to sing, but they couldn't keep him from talking before his numbers and left it in the movie.

Silent films were still made for a few years, but by 1933 the era was at an end.

What was Vitaphone?

In early sound films, the sound was not imprinted onto the film itself. Rather, the sound-track came on separate phonographs that would sync with the film. This system was used from 1926 to 1931.

What was meant by "the studio system"?

The "studio system" was a rigged way of doing business that had two effects: it made moviemaking profitable and helped to establish the film industry and the Golden Age of Hollywood, and it really took advantage of actors, directors, other movie staff, and movie theaters that were not franchised by the studios.

Big Five studios (see above) would force movie theaters to purchase blocks of movies they produced (usually about twenty movies over a year's time). One of these movies would be a top-quality "A" list that the theaters actually wanted to show, and then there would be a mix of lesser-quality films they would have to also run. This "block booking" gave the studios exposure, and sometimes there would be unexpected hits. Usually, however, it simply allowed the studios to make a lot of cheap movies that still made a profit. In the meantime, the studios also purchased their own movie theaters, and at these they would only show the best films, thus out-competing the independents.

The other part of this was the almost slavelike contract system. Actors and actresses who wanted to make it big at a studio would sign contracts that stipulated they must make a certain number of movies, even if they didn't want to make some of them because they didn't like the plots or the writing. This is why there are older movies out there with big-name stars that are simply awful. These days, actors sign contracts on a per-movie basis and, when they are successful and in demand, can pick and choose their projects.

When was the Screen Actors Guild established?

The Screen Actors Guild is a labor union founded in Hollywood in 1933 to help defend the rights of actors. It merged with the American Federation of Television and Radio Artists in 2012.

Why were so many musicals made in early Hollywood films?

Everyone was enamored with the advent of sound in movies, and singing about it just seemed natural! Hollywood was making hundreds of them each year, and they were hugely popular. One of the big early hits was 1929's *The Broadway Melody,* which won an Academy Award for best picture.

Who was the movie director who came up with his trademark dance numbers featuring lots of costumed women and kaleidoscopic effects?

Busby Berkeley (1895–1976) musicals of the 1930s and 1940s became famous for their glitzy showgirl numbers in which the women would form geometric patterns that would shift and morph as they moved their arms, legs, and torsos in creative maneuvers that would remind audiences of looking through old-fashioned kaleidoscopes. "Buzz," who was born in Los Angeles, was the son of entertainers and got his start working for song and dance man Eddie Cantor, became a director and choreographer who cheered Depression-era Americans with his cheerful, fluffy films that showed great creativity in their camera work. Among some of his more memorable work is 1933's *42nd Street,* his

Busby Berkeley musicals (shown here ia a scene from 1933's *Dames*) were famous for their glitzy scenes of dancers creating kaleidoscopic formations.

choreography work for the "I Got Rhythm" number for the 1943 Judy Garland movie *Girl Crazy,* and the unforgettable "Lady in the Tutti-Frutti Hat" performed by Carmen Miranda in 1943's *The Gang's All Here.*

Why was producer and lyricist Arthur Freed influential to American musicals?

It was Arthur Freed (1894–1973) who had a tremendous influence in the 1940s and 1950s, transforming musicals from a rather repetitive formula into movies with stronger plots and songs that actually added to the story rather than just being plopped in for the sake of a song and dance. He is responsible for getting Fred Astaire to move from RKO to MGB and make talents like Gene Kelly and Judy Garland household names. He is best remembered for producing the Academy Award-winning *An American in Paris* (1951) and *Gigi* (1958), as well as the landmark musical *Singin' in the Rain* (1952).

Who is sometimes credited with inventing the "Western" movie?

The first Westerns were a series of movies featuring "Broncho Billy," played by Gilbert M. Anderson (1880–1971). While the production company that made them was based in Chicago, the movies were made all over the country and many of these in or near Niles, just southeast of San Francisco, because it was a good spot for train tracks (the Western Pacific Railroad ran through there).

What was the Hays Code?

Named after former president of the Motion Picture Producers and Distributors of America, Will H. Hays (1879–1954), the Hays Code's official name was the Motion Picture Production Code. This was a set of "moral guidelines" imposed upon the movie studios from 1934 to 1968. In other words, it was a way to censor movies from including material that the MPPDA found potentially offensive. "Offensive" was defined in many ways, including everything from swearing, sexuality (especially homosexuality, bestiality, depictions of STDs, and so on), portraying religion in a negative way, depicting the sanctity of marriage in a negative way, and drug use. All of this was possible because of a U.S. Supreme Court decision in 1915 that asserted that movies were not entitled to First Amendment protection. This started to change in the 1950s with Supreme Court decisions that had to admit that the influx of European movies were not subject to the Code, and, therefore, this should be extended to all movies. The code was dropped and replaced by the movie ratings system.

Who were some important figures in Westerns?

The Western genre was one of the most popular in both film and television through the 1970s. Actors such as John Wayne, Gary Cooper, Glen Ford, Henry Fonda, and Jimmy Stewart and directors like John Ford and Sergio Leone dominated the big screen. TV shows such as *Gunsmoke, Bonanza, Wagon Train, The Rifleman, The Virginian,* and *Rawhide* were among the most popular series in the 1950s through the 1970s. Many of these were shot in California deserts close to Hollywood (a notable exception being the "Spaghetti Westerns" of Leone, who was famous for making Clint Eastwood movies in Spain).

How did horror movies get produced despite Hollywood censorship?

Because of the Hays Code (see sidebar), the largest studios were not able to get away with the scary flicks akin to those already being made in Germany and France. However, smaller studios such as Universal Pictures and United Artists could. This is why the early silent horror movies such as *The Hunchback of Notre Dame* (1923) and *The Phantom of the Opera* (1925), both starring makeup acting wizard Lon Chaney Sr. (1883–1930), were produced by Universal. *Dracula* (1931), starring Hungarian actor Bela Lugosi (1882–1956), was similarly produced by Universal.

The genre was popular for years, but after a while it began to become a satire of itself with movies such as *Frankenstein Meets the Wolfman* (1943) and *Abbott and Costello Meet Frankenstein* (1948). It would not be seriously revived until the 1970s, when "scary" got a new definition with the movie *The Exorcist* (1973) and *The Shining* (1980). By then, the Hays Code was a distant memory.

Buster Crabbe, who was born in Oakland, California, by the way, played Flash Gordon in the old movie serials. In this still from 1940s *Flash Gordon Conquers the Universe,* pictured are (left to right) actors Frank Shannon, Buster Crabbe, Carol Hughes, and Roland Drew.

How did science fiction movies get their start?

As with Westerns, science fiction in the movie theaters started with serials such as the "Buck Rogers" and "Flash Gordon" series of the 1930s. *Buck Rogers* was inspired by a novella by Philip Francis Nolan (1888–1940) and *Flash Gordon* by a comic strip by Alex Raymond (1909–1956). Pulp fiction books, however, really inspired many of the 1950s-era science fiction. These usually were outrageous tales of alien monsters battling humans, either on Earth or on other planets. A few, such as *The Day the Earth Stood Still* (1951), were more cerebral, but the best sci-fi written by the likes of Isaac Asimov, Robert Heinlein, Robert Silverberg, and their like remained in print novels.

The genre saw a decline in the 1960s and early 1970s until it was revived by George Lucas's (1944–) breakthrough *Star Wars* (1977) and Steven Spielberg's (1946–) *Close Encounters of the Third Kind* (1977). Lucas's special-effects company, Industrial Light and Magic, sparked a special-effects revolution that has culminated in advanced CGI evident in such modern films as *Avatar* (2009).

Why did the Golden Age of Hollywood come to an end?

The beginning of the end came with an antitrust case in 1938 concerning block booking, but World War II took attention away from enforcing the decision making the practice against the law. The nail in the coffin came in 1948 with the Supreme Court case *United States v. Paramount Pictures*. With this decision, big studios could no longer force theaters to buy movies in bulk, nor could the studios own their own theater franchises. The result was it permitted smaller studios and independents more freedom to sell their movies. With more competition, the quality of the movies went up, too, while quantity of production went down. This, in turn, also ended the period where actors were overworked making numerous films each year.

Who were the "Hollywood Ten"?

The "Hollywood Ten" were a group of screenwriters (and two directors) who were members of the American Communist Party and accused of being leftist sympathizers in 1947. There were actually more than ten people accused, but several of them never appeared before the House Un-American Activities Committee because they were sick or had scheduling conflicts. Those who did face the witch-hunt got short prison terms (six months to a year), and their Hollywood careers were ruined. They included:

- Alvah Bessie (1904–1985): a journalist, novelist, and screenwriter who was a veteran of the Spanish Civil War, had joined the American Communist Party, and wrote for the left-wing *New Masses* magazine.

- Howard Biberman (1900–1971): a screenwriter and director.

- Lester Cole (1904–1985): a screenwriter.

- Edward Dmytryk (1908–1999): a director best known for his Oscar-nominated-*Crossfire* (1947).

- Ring Lardner Jr. (1915–2000): a journalist and screenwriter who had to write under a pseudonym after going to prison for a year; he later gained fame for writing the 1970 movie *M*A*S*H*.

- John Henry Lawson (1894–1977): a founder of the Screen Writers Guild and first president of the Writers Guild of America, he moved to Mexico after his prison term; he notably wrote a screen adaptation of Alan Paton's *Cry, the Beloved Country*.

- Albert Maltz (1908–1985): after being blacklisted, the screenwriter did not regain his footing until his 1970 movie *Two Mules for Sister Sarah,* which starred Clint Eastwood and Shirley MacLaine.

- Samuel Ornitz (1890–1957): a screenwriter and fiction writer known for his 1951 bestselling novel *Bride of the Sabbath*.

- Adrian Scott: a writer and also a film producer, after the blacklisting, he managed to find work by writing for the television series *The Adventures of Robin Hood* using a pseudonym.

- Dalton Trumbo (1905–1976): possibly one of the most famous writers to be blacklisted, Trumbo was responsible for such notable movie scripts as *Exodus, Spartacus, Roman Holiday,* and *Thirty Seconds over Tokyo*. His credits on those films were stricken until 1960, and this reversal is sometimes seen to mark the end of the blacklisting period in Hollywood.

Does everyone add a handprint or footprint in the cement at the Chinese Theatre?

No, some signers have been unique with their imprints. For example, Jimmy Durante, who was famous for his large proboscis, stuck his nose in the wet cement. The horses of Roy Rogers, Tom Mix, and Gene Autry left footprints. Groucho Marx used his cigar, Betty Grable left an impression with her legs, Daniel Radcliffe of Harry Potter fame squished his wand into the patio, and Herbie the Volkswagen left tire impressions. But the most visited of all the cement squares remains that of Marilyn Monroe.

LANDMARKS OF HOLLYWOOD

What are some facts about Hollywood's iconic Chinese Theatre?

At the time of its opening on May 18, 1927, Grauman's Chinese Theatre (renamed Mann's Chinese Theatre in 1973 and the TCL Chinese Theatre in 2013) on Hollywood Boulevard was the most expensive movie house ever built. As the name indicates, it was designed by Sid Grauman to resemble a Chinese pagoda. Grauman had earlier built the Egyptian Theatre, and he liked his movie houses to have flair. It was his idea to add the famous foot- and handprints to the entrance area, which now has nearly two hundred such autographs. The first of these was by actress Norma Talmadge, which she added for the theater's opening.

Since TCL Corporation bought the building, it has added the country's largest IMAX theater to the screens offered to visitors. The interior of the building remains stunning, and it was named a Los Angeles Historical Landmark in 1968.

How did the Hollywood Walk of Fame get started?

Everyone who visits Hollywood must spend at least a little time studying the stars that cover about fifteen blocks of Hollywood Boulevard and three blocks of Vine Street. As of early 2016, there are about 2,500 stars, each star made of brass encased in terrazzo tile. In addition to the

Now the TCL Chinese Theatre, the iconic movie house is famous for its architecture and for the foot- and handprints from stars at its entrance.

name on the star (or name of a group—for example, the Supremes; the Munchkins from the movie *The Wizard of Oz* were the largest group, at 134, to get a star), there is a symbol that indicates whether the recognition is for work in movies, television, radio, music, or stage theater.

The Walk of Fame idea dates to 1953, when E. M. Stuart, who was the volunteer president of the Hollywood Chamber of Commerce at the time, proposed it. No one is sure how Stuart came up with the idea, but one notion is that he got it from looking at the ceiling of the Hollywood Hotel, which had stars painted on it, and each star had the name of a celebrity.

After much planning and delays, the first star debuted on February 8, 1960. Whose name was on the first star? Stanley Kramer, a director and producer of such notable films as *The Defiant Ones* and *The Caine Mutiny*.

The initial cost of the walk came to $1.25 million, but it has been worth it to Hollywood tourism, which sees about ten million people annually visiting the streets and the Walk of Fame. About two dozen new stars are added every year. To get a star, a person needs to be nominated, submit an application, pay a $30,000 fee, and be present at the ceremony revealing the star (Barbara Streisand was the only person to fail this last requirement and still get a star).

What was the last great movie house built in Los Angeles?

Another creation of Sid Grauman is the Hollywood Pantages Theater, which, like the Egyptian and Chinese theatres is also still to be found on Hollywood Boulevard. Com-

---

What was the Brown Derby?

The Brown Derby was a chain of restaurants popular with many Hollywood actors during the Golden Age of Hollywood. The most famous of the restaurants was the one on Wilshire Boulevard, which opened in 1926 and actually looked like its namesake, but there were also locations in Hollywood on North Vine Street and the Los Feliz location. Despite its funky appearance, it was actually a high-end restaurant that required patrons to wear formal attire, and it became quite the place to be seen.

The restaurant was also the site of filming for episodes of some TV shows and movies. For example, the comedy series *I Love Lucy* filmed a scene there. Another claim to fame is that the Cobb Salad was invented at the Hollywood restaurant, supposedly by owner Bob Cobb, who needed to whip up something quick for hungry theater owner Sid Grauman.

All the L.A. restaurants are now closed, though you can still see part of the Wilshire Boulevard hat, which was incorporated into the architecture of the Brown Derby Plaza shopping center.

pleted on June 4, 1930, when it was called the RKO Pantages Theatre, it is the largest and most decoratively elaborate of the theaters, and from 1949 to 1959, it hosted the Academy Award ceremonies. By the late 1970s, it had been converted to mostly showing live theater, and it is now operated by the Detroit-based Nederlander Organization.

Where did the early Hollywood studios get wild animals for their motion pictures?

There were a couple of lion farms in the early part of the twentieth century that Hollywood accessed for large, wild animals. Gay's Lion Farm was in El Monte and operated from 1925 to 1942. Another place for exotics started off as Goebel's Lion Farm in 1926 and later became much more than that. It was located where the Thousand Oaks Civic Plaza now stands, becoming Jungleland as it grew to 170 acres. Both a zoo and a place that supplied Hollywood with exotic animals such as elephants and lions for film appearances, it became a popular Thousand Oaks attraction. As a supplier of animals, Jungleland was the home of the talking horse Mr. Ed, Getta the chimpanzee, who appeared in Tarzan films, and two lions who were filmed to be the MGM logo lions. Jungleland also supplied animals to circuses and became famous for tiger-taming shows performed by Mabel Stark (1880–1968), who spent the final years of her illustrious career there. By the 1960s, though, Jungleland was in trouble. As an attraction for tourists, it couldn't compete with Disneyland and Knotts Berry Farm. Bad publicity from an incident in which a lion mauled the son of actress Jayne Mansfield was a huge blow, too, and it closed in 1969.

Today, there are several professional companies that train and prepare animals such as tigers and bears for films. There is, however, a growing use of CGI for such movie needs that may soon replace the use of real animals. In the movie *Life of Pi* (2012), for example, about half of the footage showing a tiger is computer animation.

Do any theaters in Los Angeles still show silent movies?

Yes, and appropriately enough, it's called the Silent Movie Theater. Located on Fairfax Avenue just south of Melrose, it was opened in 1942 by John Hampton and his wife, Dorothy. It was a strange business decision because "talkies" had been the norm for some time, yet the Hamptons found an audience who still enjoyed the silent features. After closing the theater about thirty years later, it was purchased by Laurence Austin in 1991. Austin was shot dead six years later by a hit man and again the movie house closed, but it reopened a couple of years later. Today, in addition to still showing silents, the theater shows art, underground, and independent films and is a venue for weddings and other celebrations and special events.

UNIQUE MOVIE LOCATIONS

Where are those unique rock formations seen in a lot of Westerns and some science-fiction movies and television shows located?

Vasquez Rocks in the Sierra Pelona Mountains has been used numerous times for a couple reasons: the rock formations are visually interesting, and the park is located just

If you've seen a lot of Westerns and sci-fi movies and TV shows, chances are you recognize this rock. Vasquez Rocks have served as the backdrop for many Hollywood productions.

north of Los Angeles, so it's convenient for on-location shots. Vasquez Rocks served as the backdrop for many TV episodes of *The Big Valley,* for example, and *Star Trek* fans will likely recall the episode "Arena" in which Captain Kirk fights the Gorn there. More recently, they were featured in the Michael Jackson music video "Black or White," *Power Rangers* episodes, and an episode of the sitcom *The Big Bang Theory.*

What other location was frequently used for early Western movies and is still used today by moviemakers?

Although it's not very well known, the Alabama Hills near the town of Lone Pine in the Eastern Sierra Nevada Mountains was one of the most frequently used locations for Western movies featuring such stars as the Cisco Kid, Tom Mix, Hopalong Cassidy, Will Rogers, Gene Autry, Roy Rogers, and John Wayne. It all started in 1920 with the movie *The Roundup* and has remained a popular locale ever since. In the early days, gangster movies were also popularly made in the Alabama Hills, and memorabilia from them can be seen along with an extensive Western film collection at the Museum of Western Film History in Lone Pine. If you are ever driving through this rustic town, the museum is definitely worth a stop. Old movie posters, saddles and other riding gear, wagons and coaches, guns, and more can be seen here. Of particular note is the fully restored 1937 Cord Model 812 Supercharged Phaeton, which is the car that Tom Mix died in. There is also memorabilia from more recent movies, including *The Transformers, Iron Man,* and *Django Unchained.*

Where are George Lucas's ILM and the Skywalker Ranch located?

Lucas, of course, is known for his *Star Wars* film series, which he sold to Disney in 2012 along with his company LucasFilm. Industrial Light and Magic (ILM), his special-effects

239

Were the Tarzan films shot at the L.A. Arboretum?

Yes, some of the Tarzan pictures did have some footage taken at the arboretum. Many native Angelinos know this, but not as many know that parts of the *Wonder Woman* television series starring Linda Blair were also shot at the L.A. Arboretum.

company, is still going strong. It was founded in 1975, and the headquarters are in San Francisco. As for his private ranch, it is located in Marin County near Nicasio and is not open to the public.

Where do movie, TV, and commercial directors often shoot footage set inside airplanes?

There's one place in Los Angeles where people go to shoot such scenes, and that's Air Hollywood. The L.A. facility has all the props, both historical and modern, and well as fuselages complete with either passenger seating or the pilot's cabin. Air Hollywood was established in 1998 and can reproduce the look and feel of commercial and passenger aircraft, as well as small or jumbo planes. Not a Hollywood filmmaker? No problem. Air Hollywood will also rent out some of its props for dinners and other special events. The most popular of these is a reproduction of a Pan Am passenger plane from the golden era of air travel.

RADIO AND TELEVISION

What was the first radio station to broadcast in California?

KCBS (AM) in San Jose was the first radio station. It began broadcasting as early as 1909, using an experimental license, as KQW until 1921, when it gained a commercial license and, in 1949, became KCBS. The first Los Angeles station was KHJ, which began broadcasting in 1920. And the first twenty-four-hour radio station was KGFJ Los Angeles, which began its all-night programming in 1927.

What was another important early station in Los Angeles?

KFI-AM (640 AM) began broadcasting on April 16, 1922, from a garage owned by Earle C. Anthony (1880–1961), who made his money establishing a Packard dealership with his father and creating the first two gas stations in the state and founding what would later become the Pacific Greyhound company. KFI would become an NBC affiliate and from 1960 to 1972 was home to Dodgers radio. It was also an early home of disc jockey radio personality Gary Owens (1934–2015) and, during the 1970s and '80s, *The Lohman and Barkley Show,* a groundbreaking, humorous morning show featuring Al Lohman (1933–2002) and Roger Barkley (1936–1997). Today, KFI is operated by iHeartMedia.

Who started "progressive radio" in California?

Disc jockey Tom "Big Daddy" Donahue (1928–1975) was working for KMPX-FM in San Francisco when he introduced "progressive radio" on April 7, 1967, a mix of modern rock and liberal talk and commentary. The next year, he and his staff moved to KSAN-FM and continued their progressive format there. Sadly, Donahue died of a heart attack just seven years after innovating modern radio formats forever.

How did the "The Dr. Demento Show" come about?

One of the most wonderfully silly radio shows to ever come out of California is the brainchild of broadcaster Barry Hansen (1941–). It all started in 1970, when he was working at KPPC-FM in Los Angeles. Hansen was called "demented" for playing the song "Transfusion" by Nervous Novus on his rock music show, and that gave him the idea not only for his alter ego's name but also for a show featuring novelty songs. It has featured songs by the likes of Tom Lehrer, Spike Jones, Weird Al Yankovic, Stan Freberg, and many more.

"The Dr. Demento Show" ran for years, moving to KMET from 1972 to 1983, then to KLSX and KSCA. Eventually, the program went off the radio airwaves, but in 2010 Hansen made it available online, where you can find it today at drdemento.com.

The Doctor is also working on a movie about his life to be called *Under the Smogberry Trees: The True Story of Dr. Demento and Mr. Hansen.*

Second only to the Oscars, the Emmy Awards for television achievements have been held in the L.A. area since 1949.

Why are there two Emmy Award ceremonies, one for prime time and one for daytime shows?

In 1977 the Television Academy experienced a rift, and the National Academy of Television Arts and Sciences was formed in New York City. The Academy in Los Angeles runs the prime-time Emmys, which are for programs airing between 7:00 and 11:00 P.M., and the National Academy has a ceremony for daytime, news, sports, documentaries, international shows, and local programs.

How were the Emmy Awards started?

The first Emmy Awards were presented by the Television Academy (now the Television Academy of Arts and Sciences) on January 25, 1949, at the Hollywood Athletic Club; at the time, only one million TVs existed in the country. Only TV shows produced in Los Angeles were eligible for the awards, a restriction that was later eliminated.

How did the Emmys get their name?

The name "Emmy" is a feminization of the name first proposed by Television Academy president Harry Lubcke: Immy. An "immy" is a nickname for the image-orthicon camera tube, the cathode ray tube used in early television sets.

MUSIC

THE BAKERSFIELD SOUND

What, exactly, is the "Bakersfield Sound"?

It's a form of country music that sprang up in the 1950s in Bakersfield and is epitomized in the stylings of such artists as Merle Haggard, Buck Owens, Dallas Frazier, Roy Nichols, Bill Woods, Billy Mize, Susan Raye, Freddie Hart, Jean Shepard, Wynn Steward, and Dennis Payne. The sound, distinct from what was popular back in Nashville, was once described by Jeff Nickell, assistant director of the Kern County Museum, this way: "[T]he Bakersfield Sound was marked by the sharp, loud, high-end sound of the electric and steel guitars, fiddles, and lead and harmony vocals influenced by rock and roll and rockabilly as well as traditional country."

The Bakersfield Sound has its roots in the 1930s and 1940s, when people called Okies from the Central Plains fled the Dust Bowl for California. The ones who ended up in Bakersfield found the area ripe for music, which was a popular place for honky tonks. "Fancy music" wasn't the style there, and the immigrants from the heartland found a great deal of camaraderie by sharing their music.

Who is considered the "Father of the Bakersfield Sound"?

Well, it's not Owens or Haggard; it's Bill Woods (1924–2000). Woods came to Bakersfield from Texas with his family in 1940, and ten years later he was bandleader at the Blackboard Café. He remained there for the next fourteen years, laying the foundation of his brand of music with such artists as Tommy Collins (1930–2000) and Ferlin Husky (1925–2011). Woods was also mentor to Buck Owens and other country stars. In his later career, he worked with Capitol Records to help launch the national careers of many of the musicians from Bakersfield.

What are some details about Bakersfield star Merle Haggard?

Merle Haggard (1937–2016) was born in Oildale. A guitarist, fiddle player, and singer, he is both one of the originators of the Bakersfield Sound and also falls into the category of "outlaw country" singers who included the likes of Johnny Cash, Hank Williams Jr., and Willie Nelson. Song such as "Okie from Muskogee," "Mama Tried," "Think I'll Just Stay Here and Drink," "Bigger Side of Me," and "The Fightin' Side of Me" appealed to working-class people who often thought of themselves as the "silent majority." His career slowed down some in the 1980s and 1990s but picked up since then. Haggard was inducted into the Country Music Hall of Fame in 1994 and the Oklahoma Music Hall of Fame in 1997. He passed away on April 6, 2016, from complications due to double pneumonia.

Is the Buck Owens Crystal House a museum or a music hall?

It's both. Located, of course, in Bakersfield, it was built by Buck Owens (1929–2006) and opened in 1996. Though born in Texas, Owens was another star associated with the Bakersfield Sound. He formed the group the Buckaroos that was active in the 1960s and had fifteen number-one country songs. Owens was also famous for hosting the television variety show *Hee Haw* with Roy Clark from 1969 to 1974. When his best friend died in 1974, Owens fell into a depression and slipped out of the public eye until 1988, when he began performing again, this time with Dwight Yoakam. He was inducted into the Country Music Hall of Fame in 1996.

That year he performed at his newly opened Crystal House, which now has a

Merle Haggard was one of the early Bakersfield Sound artists whose music appealed to the working class.

243

museum dedicated to his career. Country music is still performed there. There is also a restaurant and a gift store.

THE CALIFORNIA SOUND

Where did that surf music sound originate?

It could be said that the beginning of Surf Music, or the California Sound, could be traced back to the night of December 29, 1961, when Dick Dale (1937–) and the Del-Tones headlined at the Rendezvous Ballroom in Balboa Beach. They were joined by the Challengers and the Surfaris, as well as a very new group called the Beach Boys, who were relegated to playing during intermissions when headliner Dale was taking a break.

Surf music was purely instrumental, and it would influence such guitarists as Jimi Hendrix and Eddie Van Halen. Later, with the addition of harmonious vocals by the Beach Boys and others, it would evolve into what might be called Surf Rock or the California Sound.

When did the Beach Boys make their first public appearance?

Just two days after playing at the Rendezvous with Dick Dale, the Beach Boys played a New Year's Eve concert at the Long Beach Memorial Auditorium in 1961. The original

The Beach Boys, shown here in 1964, are credited with making the "California Sound" or "Surf Music" popular in the 1960s. Pictured are (left to right) Al Jardine, Mike Love, Dennis Wilson, Brian Wilson, and Carl Wilson.

> ## Arabic music was an important influence on Surf Music—really?
>
> **Y**es! Dick Dale had an uncle who was Lebanese, and he listened to a lot of music from that region of the world. It was the rapid, alternate-string-picking style of Arabic music that helped give Surf Music its distinctive sound.

members of the group were brothers Brian (1942–), Dennis (1944–1983), and Carl Wilson (1946–1998), their cousin Mike Love (1941–), and friend Al Jardine (1942–). Brian Wilson was the genius behind their unique sound.

Why is the Beach Boys' music still important?

The Beach Boys' sound epitomized the surfing and beach lifestyle of the era. Many of the songs were about surfing, enjoying the beach, driving cars, and just hanging out and enjoying life in songs such as "Surfin' Safari," "409," "Good Vibrations," "Fun Fun Fun," "California Girls," "I Get Around," "Wouldn't It Be Nice," and many others. Their distinct, signature sound remains memorable decades after they were at their height in the 1960s.

Over time, members of the original group dropped out or, sadly, passed away. Dennis Wilson drowned in 1983, and Carl Wilson died of lung cancer in 1998. Their last big hit was 1988's "Kokomo," the same year the group was inducted into the Rock and Roll Hall of Fame, but by the late 1990s, the only original member left was Mike Love. The reimagined group still performs their old hits around the country today.

Did Brian Wilson have serious mental or emotional problems?

Brian Wilson, often called the most brilliant of the Beach Boys, had a breakdown while working on a project called *Smile* in 1966 and had to leave the group as its primary writer and producer. He retreated more and more into his Bel Air mansion and, for a short time, ran a health-food business. Wilson still worked off and on, however, and returned to his old group in 1983. Suffering through the deaths of his brothers and a lawsuit brought against him by Mike Love (which was eventually settled), Wilson actually was doing better, creatively, by 2000, and that year he was inducted into the Songwriters' Hall of Fame. In 2004 he finally completed his long-awaited album *SMiLE*.

Were there other bands like the Beach Boys?

Perhaps the most famous musicians to rival the Beach Boys were Jan and Dean. William Jan Berry (1941–2004) and Dean Ormsby Torrence (1940–) produced such hits as "Baby Talk," "The Little Old Lady from Pasadena," "Dead Man's Curve," and "Surf City," the last of these actually written by Brian Wilson. Their career hit a big bump when Jan was in a car accident in 1966 that left him partially paralyzed and with some brain damage. He

Is Dead Man's Curve an actual place?

Yes. Actually, a couple road turns have this designation in California (as well as other states). Located by Lebec, California, one such hazardous road is a cliff-side loop around a hill on the 1915 Ridge Route that is now closed because other highways (the 99 and the 5) opened up. There is also a bend on State Route 76 in San Diego County that is infamous for motorcyclists' deaths. However, the curve referred to in the Jan and Dean song is on Sunset Boulevard, where Jan had his car accident.

spent two years slowly recuperating and began to sing again by the 1970s. They continued to work and perform until March 26, 2004, when Jan suffered a severe seizure and passed away.

ROCK HISTORY

Why was Laurel Canyon a mecca for musicians in the 1960s?

Laurel Canyon is a hilly, rustic area just north of West Hollywood, which was discovered as a cozy retreat for creative counterculture types at a time when the houses were still very inexpensive. It became second only to the Haight-Ashbury district of San Francisco for Hippies at the time. People such as Graham Nash, Joni Mitchell, Frank Zappa, Carole King, Jim Morrison, and the Mamas and the Papas lived and composed their songs there. Mitchell's "Ladies of the Canyon" is about Laurel Canyon, and she wrote "Clouds" there, too. The Psychedelic Rock Movement was centered around Frank Zappa's cabin on Lookout Mountain.

As with Haight-Ashbury, it was the proliferation of illicit drugs that brought this halcyon period low. Police raids became common, and the problem culminated with four murders on Wonderland Avenue in 1981. Porn star John Holmes was initially a prime suspect, but it was later blamed on the owner of a strip club—who was also later acquitted.

Later in the 1980s, property values started going up again as the hills near Los Angeles became valuable to a much richer class of people. Homes that once sold for tens of thousands of dollars were soon worth hundreds of thousands and the character of the neighborhood was forever changed.

Is the Capitol Records building supposed to look like a stack of records?

Designed by a young architect named Lou Naidorf, who, at the time, was still in graduate school, the erection is the first circular office building and was completed in 1956. Supposedly, the resemblance to a stack of records on a turntable is only a coincidence, but most who view it can't help but think it was on purpose. Another interesting fact is that the red light at the top of Capitol Records Tower blinks a Morse code that spells H-O-L-L-Y-W-O-O-D.

How is the Fillmore in San Francisco significant as a music venue?

Founded way back in 1910 by Emma Gates Butler, the Fillmore on the corner of Fillmore Street and Geary Boulevard in San Francisco originally started as a dance hall and dancing academy called the Majestic Hall and Majestic Academy of Dancing. Over the years, it morphed into a place for masquerade balls, dance socials, and, in the 1940s, a roller-skating rink, changing names along the way. Finally, in 1952, it became the Fillmore under the management of Charles Sullivan, who booked African American musicians to play blues, soul, and rock, including performers ranging from James Brown to Tina Turner.

While supposedly not intentional, the design of the Capitol Records building on Hollywood Boulevard looks a lot like a stack of LPs.

Beat poets and folk performers worked there in the 1950s, too, and the Fillmore became known for its Bohemian flair. Later, from about 1966 to the summer of 1968, there was a golden period at the Fillmore in which the careers of several now-famous performers and groups were launched, including the Grateful Dead, Santana, Jefferson Airplane, the Butterfield Blues Band, Jimi Hendrix, Cream, Muddy Waters, Otis Redding, and The Who.

During the 1970s the Fillmore was a private club, and in the 1980s it was renamed the Elite Club. Acts such as the Dead Kennedys, Flipper, and Public Image Ltd. performed there during the decade. By the late 1980s it was the Fillmore again. As the years passed, a string of greats played at the Fillmore, including the Smashing Pumpkins, Chris Isaak, Primus, Gin Blossoms, Huey Lewis and the News, Tom Petty and the Heartbreakers, The Cure, Prince, and on and on. It remains one of the most storied venues in California and rock history to this day.

What made the nightclub Whiskey a Go Go so famous?

Located at 8901 Sunset Boulevard in West Hollywood, Whiskey a Go Go was established in 1964. It became a hub for musical acts that are now hugely famous figures and bands in rock and roll, including Johnny Rivers (1942–), who was the first musical act hosted there, Alice Cooper (1948–), Frank Zappa (1940–1993), Mötley Crüe The Byrds, Van Halen, the Mothers of Invention, and The Doors.

Whiskey a Go Go really epitomized the mood of the 1960s with its shows that featured go-go dancers performing in cages suspended from the ceiling. In fact, Smokey Robinson and the Miracles made the place immortal with their 1966 song "Goin' to a Go Go." The next year, Arthur Lee also sang about the venue in "Maybe the People Would Be the Times or Between Clark and Hilldale."

After a fire in 1971, the Whiskey sprang back in the late 1970s, hosting hard rock, then punk and grunge acts such as The Melvins, Soundgarden, and Fitz. Closing again in 1982, it reopened in 1986 and remains so today, although primarily as rented space.

MOTOWN TO RAP

Why was Motown moved from its original home in Detroit to Los Angeles?

Motown had produced amazing music in Detroit from 1959 to 1967, but when rioting broke out in that city, producer Berry Gordy (1929–) decided it was time to go. In addition, many of the acts that made Motown great were either moving on to other labels or their popularity was on the wane (with the exception of some groups, such as the Jackson 5). While Gordy continued to have some success in Los Angeles with the talents of such artists as Rick James and Lionel Ritchie, by 1988 he decided to sell his record label to MCA.

What is West Coast hip hop?

A subgenre of rap music, West Coast hip hop refers to the music, naturally, that originates on that coast, but most specifically to rap that comes from California. The movement originates around the period of the 1965 Watts Riots (see the "Southern California" chapter) and includes not just music but also breakdancing, graffiti art, MCing, DJing, and beatboxing. Artists such as Ice-T, Eazy E, and 2Pac represent the genre.

Did gangsta rap originate in California?

The popular 2015 movie *Straight Outta Compton* reminded rap lovers of the first blockbuster album of the genre, the 1988 collection by the group N.W.A., which was, indeed, founded in Compton, a Los Angeles neighborhood. However, the originators of gangsta rap were people like Ice-T and Schoolly D, who were from the East Coast. So, while we can't say that gangsta rap originated in Los Angeles, it did get its legs there.

What are some influential record labels when it comes to rap and hip-hop music?

A couple important influences in the genre have been Death Row Records in Los Ange-

Dr. Dre is a rapper who also founded the influential Death Row Records in Los Angeles.

les and Top Dawg Entertainment in Carson. Death Row was founded in 1991 by Dr. Dre (Andre Romelle Young), Suge Knight, and The D.O.C. and produced such acts as Snoop Dog, 2Pac (Tupac Amaru Shakur), M.C. Hammer, Danny Boy, and Jewell, but after the death of 2Pac, many of the performers left the label, and a company that was once making $100 million annually had to file for bankruptcy in 1996. Death Row was bought by WIDEawake Entertainment Group in 2009 and continues to operate under that parent company today.

Top Dawg was founded in 2004 by Anthony Tiffith, producing such acts as Juvenile and The Game; the company can also take credit for discovering Kendrick Lamar and Ab-Soul and has also produced songs by the likes of Lil Wayne, Jay Rock, SZA, and Isaiah Rashad.

OPERA AND ORCHESTRAS

Does California have any opera companies? Where do they perform?

Yes, there are quite a few opera companies, as shown in the table below.

City	Opera Company
Berkeley	West Edge Opera
Casnoga Park	Center Stage Opera
Fairfield	North Bay Opera
Fremont	Fremont Opera
Livermore	Livermore Valley Opera
Long Beach	Long Beach Opera
Los Angeles	Los Angeles Opera
Los Angeles	Lyric Opera of Los Angeles
Martinez	Martinez Opera Contra Costa
Modesto	Townsend Opera Players
Oakland	Oakland Opera Theater
Palo Alto	West Bay Opera
Pomona	Repertory Opera Company
Sacramento	Capitol Opera Sacramento/Davis
Sacramento	Sacramento Opera
San Diego	San Diego Opera
San Francisco	Lamplighters Music Theatre
San Francisco	Pocket Opera
San Francisco	San Francisco Lyric Opera
San Francisco	San Francisco Opera
San Jose	Opera San Jose
San Luis Obispo	Opera San Luis Obispo
Santa Barbara	Opera Santa Barbara
Santa Monica	Los Angeles Metropolitan Opera
Sausalito	Golden Gate Opera
South Pasadena	Celestial Opera Company
Stockton	Stockton Opera
Vallejo (touring)	Verismo Opera
Walnut Creek	Festival Opera

How did orchestras relate to the movie industry?

Orchestras in California got their start with movie theaters that needed music to accompany movies in the 1920s. When sound was added to film, studios created their own orchestras to record soundtracks for their movies. Probably the most successful of these is the MGM Studio Orchestra. The Hollywood Studio Symphony and the Hollywood Symphony Orchestra both record soundtracks for movies and television. The latter also performs live at venues such as Royce Hall at UCLA.

Which orchestras are based in the L.A. area?

The Los Angeles Philharmonic was founded in 1919 and is the oldest. The group performs at the Walt Disney Concert Hall and at the Hollywood Bowl, as well as touring the world. There is also the Los Angeles Chamber Orchestra, which performs at UCLA's Royce Hall and the Alex Theatre in Glendale, and the Golden State Pops Orchestra is noted for performing movie and TV scores at the Warner Grand Theatre.

Why did the San Francisco orchestra have such a rocky start?

It was shortly after the devastating 1906 earthquake that the city's leaders came up with the idea to found an orchestra as a way of boosting the morale of the residents. After some years of effort, the San Francisco Symphony Orchestra gave its first performance in 1911, making it the oldest such orchestra in the state. That community spirit has continued to this day, with the organization providing free educational programs. These days they perform at Davies Symphony Hall and the Flint Center.

Which music group has tried to inspire children to love the classics?

The San Francisco Chamber Orchestra designs concerts specifically with children in mind, and it also offers free concerts at a variety of Bay Area venues.

Which city offers some very off-the-wall concert experiences for orchestra lovers?

San Diego has two groups that enjoy being untraditional. Orchestra Nova is noted for being quite experimental. This group, which has also been noted for its renditions of "Handel's Messiah" at local churches, treated audiences to "The Legend of Zelda 25th Anniversary Symphony" in 2011—music from a popular video game. Meanwhile, the Heliotrope Ragtime Orchestra, which is also in San Diego, gives concerts featuring Scott Joplin.

ART MOVEMENTS

Are there many art movements that have their origins in California?

Yes, the Sunshine State does have its own flair for the visual arts, perhaps inspired by the unique cultural atmosphere here.

What is the California Art Club?

The California Art Club is a nonprofit based in Pasadena devoted to educating people and supporting traditional- and contemporary-style artists. Founded in 1909, it is considered to be one of the largest such organizations in the country.

How did Northern California Tonalism and California Plein-Air Painting relate to American Impressionism?

While American Impressionism was popular in the late-eighteenth and early twentieth centuries, California artists formed their own twist that was inspired, in turn, by the Barbizon School in France. Plein-Air Painting involved the artists going out into nature (*plein-air* refers to the outdoors) and being inspired directly from what they saw there rather than working in studios indoors. William Wendt (1865–1946), known as "the Dean of Southern California Landscape Painters," was a leader of this movement.

Northern California Tonalism was also interested in natural landscapes, rejecting photographic detail in its attempt to capture colors, emotions, and textures of the natural world. William Keith (1838–1911), "the Dean of Northern California Painters," was a leader in this school of art popular in the 1890s.

What is the Bay Area Figurative Movement?

This was a movement reacting to Abstract Expressionism in favor of a return to paintings featuring perceivable figures (objects, people). It was at its height in the 1950s and 1960s by artists in the Bay Area.

Did the American Clay Revolution begin in California?

Yes, which is why it is often called the California Clay Movement. The idea was that the craft of working in clay could be artistic, not just functional. Peter Voulkos (1924–2002) was the leader of this movement in the 1950s, establishing the Ceramic Center at the Los Angeles County Art Institute.

Which art movement was strongly influenced by jazz music in the 1950s?

The Funk Art movement originated in the Bay Area, especially in Marin County,

Peter Voulkos spearheaded the California Clay Movement.

Berkeley, Big Sur, and North Beach, and saw its peak in the 1960s and 1970s. This style of art was playful, distorting forms in quirky, passionate, sometimes sensuous ways and experimenting with color.

How did pulp comics, underground art, and hot rods inspire a school of art?

Also called "pop surrealism," "lowbrow" art originated in 1970s Los Angeles and was indeed inspired by what some might consider the seedier side of modern culture. Underground cartoonists ranging from Robert Williams (1943–) and R. Crumb (1963–) to Art Spiegelman (1948–), who published in such comic books as *Zap Comix* and *Juxtapoz,* can be considered part of the school, although it was a label more imposed on them than something these artists were trying to deliberately create. It was given the label as a reaction to "highbrow" art that was accepted at museums and galleries, whereas these artists' works were not.

Did the Chicano art movement originate in California?

No, the movement, also called the "Chicano Renaissance," is prevalent in the American Midwest and Northwest, as well. However, it has a significant presence in California, especially the barrios of the Los Angeles area. Chicano art cannot be narrowly defined, as it has a range of styles from the more realistic work of Diego Rivera (1886–1957) to graffiti art and even such cultural oddities as lowrider cars. All of this is tied together by cultural pride and, often, themes of economic activism and social injustice in America.

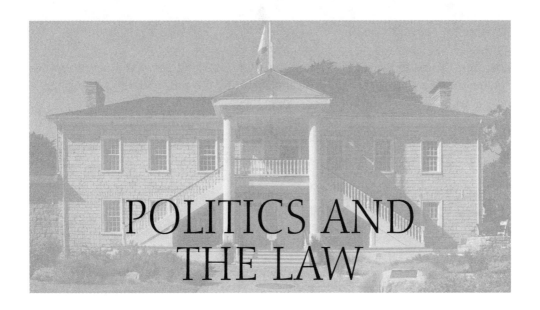

POLITICS AND THE LAW

ESTABLISHING A STATE

Where was the California Constitutional Convention held?

It was held in Monterey in 1849 and attended by forty-eight delegates. All of the delegates were men, and except for eight Hispanics, they were all whites with roots back East. Robert Semple (1806–1854) served as the convention's president. Semple, a journalist originally from Kentucky who was co-publisher of the *Californian,* was a hero of the Bear Flag Revolt.

What were some early issues decided at the convention that were unique to U.S. states at the time?

The delegates decided that all California laws should be published in both English and Spanish. They also declared that, contrary to English common law, married women would be allowed to keep ownership of all property they had before and during their marriages, rather than those rights being taken over by the husbands.

How were the state borders decided upon?

The north and south borders of California were not difficult to figure out. The southern border was already determined by the Treaty of Guadalupe-Hidalgo. For the north, the delegates quickly settled on the 42nd parallel. It was the eastern border that was a headache.

Some of the delegates were completely unrealistic, wanting to make a huge land grab of parts of Arizona, Utah, and Nevada (no one from these areas had been invited to attend the convention—not a minor point). Others felt that anything east of the Sierras was basically desert and not worth having, so it would make more sense to draw the line there. These delegates also noted that the U.S. Congress would never approve boundaries for a state that would basically gobble up the entire Southwest. A compromise eventually settled the borders to where they stand today.

How many counties does California have?

There are fifty-eight counties in California, as follows:

County Name	City Seat	Founded
Alameda	Oakland	1853
Alpine	Markleeville	1864
Amador	Jackson	1854
Butte	Oroville	1850
Calaveras	San Andreas	1850
Colusa	Colusa	1850
Contra Costa	Martinez	1850
Del Norte	Crescent City	1857
El Dorado	Placerville	1850
Fresno	Fresno	1856
Glenn	Willows	1891
Humboldt	Eureka	1853
Imperial	El Centro	1907
Inyo	Independence	1866
Kern	Bakersfield	1866
Kings	Hanford	1893
Lake	Lakeport	1861
Lassen	Susanville	1864
Los Angeles	Los Angeles	1850
Madera	Madera	1893
Marin	San Rafael	1850
Mariposa	Mariposa	1850
Mendocino	Ukiah	1850
Merced	Merced	1855
Modoc	Alturas	1874
Mono	Bridgeport	1861
Monterey	Salinas	1850
Napa	Napa	1850
Nevada	Nevada City	1851
Orange	Santa Ana	1889
Placer	Auburn	1851
Plumas	Quincy	1854
Riverside	Riverside	1893
Sacramento	Sacramento	1850
San Benito	Hollister	1874
San Bernardino	San Bernardino	1853
San Diego	San Diego	1850
San Francisco	San Francisco	1850
San Joaquin	Stockton	1850

County Name	City Seat	Founded
San Luis Obispo	San Luis Obispo	1850
San Mateo	Redwood City	1856
Santa Barbara	Santa Barbara	1850
Santa Clara	San Jose	1850
Santa Cruz	Santa Cruz	1850
Shasta	Redding	1850
Sierra	Downieville	1852
Siskiyou	Yreka	1852
Solano	Fairfield	1850
Sonoma	Santa Rosa	1850
Stanislaus	Modesto	1854
Sutter	Yuba City	1850
Tehama	Red Bluff	1856
Trinity	Weaverville	1850
Tulare	Visalia	1852
Tuolumne	Sonora	1850
Ventura	Ventura	1872
Yolo	Woodland	1850
Yuba	Marysville	1850

CALIFORNIA'S CONSTITUTION

When was the state constitution signed?

The first constitution was signed and ratified in 1849, and then it was presented before the U.S. Congress on September 9, 1850. Since then, the original document was superseded just once, in 1879, the state's official second constitution. From 1966 to 1974, it underwent a number of revisions but not to the point of becoming a new constitution.

Why has the California Constitution been criticized?

While it has managed to remain the law of the land for over 130 years, the state constitution has been criticized for being overly long and unnecessarily detailed. At a length of eight times that of the U.S. Constitution, California's legal document has 512 amendments.

A big reason why the second California Constitution is so long is that legislators tried to address many economic and social reforms due to the problems of the times that began with the Panic of 1873 and that were still going on as a major depression in 1878.

Modifications continued, and by 1930 the constitution was over sixty-five thousand words long. On several occasions, it was proposed to have a new Constitutional Convention to rewrite it from scratch, but each time, circumstances thwarted the effort, such as the Great Depression, World War II, and, often, simple disinterest on the part of the voters to approve ballot proposals for a convention.

Now a museum run by the state, Colton Hall in Monterey is where the 1849 California Constitution was signed.

By the end of the twentieth century, the government had become bloated with thousands of agencies. It had become so inefficient that many predicted the state would collapse should a major crisis happen, to which it would be unable to react appropriately because it was bogged down by bureaucracy. This prediction almost came true with the housing crisis and resulting recession in 2008. The state quickly found itself over $20 billion in debt and with an unemployment rate of over 11%. It was only Governor Jerry Brown's actions of raising taxes and cutting the budget that kept the state from going bankrupt.

How is the government organized?

The California State Legislature is a bicameral (two-house) system. There is the California State Assembly, which has eighty members, and the California State Senate, with forty. The term in the Assembly is two years, and it is four years for the Senate.

Are senators and assembly people term limited?

Yes. In 1990 Proposition 140 was passed. It limited senators to two four-year terms and assembly people to three two-year terms. It also set limits to staff salaries and expenditures and prevented legislators from earning retirement benefits. Proposition 28, which passed in 2012, modified this somewhat. It permitted legislators to serve in the Assembly or Senate for up to twelve years. Legislators can serve all twelve years in one or the other chamber, or a combination of both, but they cannot serve more than twelve years total.

How much did the first state legislature accomplish?

Quite a bit, actually. In the first two years of statehood, the state's leaders drew county lines, organized the state militia, set up elections and the basics of government organization, established the state library and archives, and set up printing operations for government documents. On the negative end, it passed a law that discriminated against foreign miners by imposing a heavy tax on them. It also failed to establish a state public schools system.

What changed with the 1879 constitution?

The 1879 constitution set the number of senators at forty and the number of assemblymen at eighty. The 1849 constitution had been much looser; the number of total assemblymen could be anywhere between thirty and eighty, and the number of senators would be half of whatever size the Assembly was.

Which two major parties ran candidates in the first non-Mexican election?

The two parties were the Republicans, who ran Peter Burnett for the office of Judge of the Superior Court, and the People's Party, which ran Horace Hawes against him. There were also openings for prefect, subprefect, first alcalde, second alcalde, town council (*ayuntamiento*, as it was listed in Spanish), delegates to the convention, and supernumeraries.

Who were some of the first politicians chosen to lead the new state?

Peter Burnett (1807–1895) was elected the first governor of American California, and his lieutenant was John McDougal (1818–1866), who would become the state's second gov-

Why do counties in northern California tend to be smaller and have fewer people than in southern California?

When the legislators were drawing county lines in the early 1850s, the northern part of the state was much more heavily populated than the south. But when Los Angeles began to blossom, as well as surrounding cities, the result was that Los Angeles County (9,818,605 people in 2010) and others in the south had millions of people in them, while smaller ones to the north, such as Alpine County (population 1,175 in 2010), had just a few thousand. It's led to a significant imbalance as to how Californians are represented.

ernor after Burnett. George Washington Wright (1816–1885) and Edward Gilbert (1819–1852) were elected the first two congressmen to represent California in the U.S. House of Representatives, and William Gwin (1805–1885) and military hero John C. Frémont (1813–1890) were named senators.

Why was the first session of the new state government called "the Legislature of a Thousand Drinks"?

That name makes it sound as if California's first American politicians were all bombed on alcohol. Actually, it just proved they had a little sense of humor. One of the delegates, Thomas Jefferson Green, liked to invite everyone to have a thousand drinks after their work was done, and the joke stuck.

Green was actually a distinguished politician, having served in public office in North Carolina, Florida, and the Republic of Texas before moving to California during the Gold Rush. He was instrumental in helping to establish the University of California system.

The first governor of California under United States rule was Peter Burnett.

Which city was chosen as the first California state capital?

San Jose (then known as Pueblo de San Jose), near San Francisco, was the original choice of the California Constitutional Convention in 1849, but the state's seat of government moved a couple of times. It was moved to Vallejo in 1851, then to Benicia (both towns are just northeast of San Francisco), where it would be housed at the city hall from 1853 to 1854. Finally, in 1854, with plans for the construction of a new capitol building, the state's leaders chose Sacramento as their new home. Interestingly, in the mid-nineteenth century, most Californians—about ninety-five percent of them—lived in the northern part of the state (Los Angeles was still very modest in size at the time). Sacramento was, therefore, not too far from most residents. Today, of course, there is more of a balance between North and South, but with improved transportation the exact location of the capitol is not as big of a concern.

What are some of the features of the state capitol?

The state capitol building was constructed between 1860 and 1874 and designed by architects M. F. Butler and Reuben Clark, who used a neoclassical style reminiscent of buildings in Washington, D.C. It includes granite archways and Corinthian columns. A forty-acre garden surrounds the building and includes a Civil War Memorial Grove, as well as memorials to those who fought in other wars. The capitol building is listed on the National Register of U.S. Historic Places.

Why was Harvey Milk murdered?

On May 21, 1979, Milk and San Francisco mayor George Mascone (1929–1979) were both murdered by Dan White (1946–1985). White was a disgruntled conservative member of the San Francisco Board of Supervisors who had resigned his post be-

Harvey Milk with his sister-in-law Audrey during his 1973 campaign.

cause he didn't like working with liberals, especially the gay Milk. He changed his mind, though, and asked Mascone to allow him to return to the board. The mayor refused, and this angered White so much that he marched into the city hall and fired a gun, killing Milk and Mascone.

White was sent to Soledad State Prison, but in 1984 he was paroled. In 1985, he committed suicide by running his car in the garage and dying from the carbon monoxide.

How did Tom Bradley become the first black mayor of Los Angeles?

Thomas Bradley (1917–1998) was the son of Texas sharecroppers who is definitely an American success story. Moving to Los Angeles in 1923, when his father found work as a train porter, he attended Los Angeles Polytechnic High School, where he was a track and football star, and then the University of California, Los Angeles, where he won a scholarship.

After school, he joined the Los Angeles Police Department, one of only a hundred or so black officers at the time (0.25% of the entire force). Bradley rose to the rank of lieutenant, studied law at night, and left the force in 1961. Two years later, he was elected to the Los Angeles City Council. After an unsuccessful bid in 1969, he was elected mayor in 1973 and was in office until 1993 (he ran twice, and lost, for governor).

Bradley's accomplishments as mayor included fighting racial discrimination in the police department, passing the city's first homosexual antidiscrimination rights bill in 1979, and forming the Christopher Commission to investigate the Rodney King beatings. He helped improve the business environment in the city, expanded Los Angeles International Airport, and led the city's organization of the 1984 Olympics.

Does California hold primary elections or caucuses?

Like most U.S. states, California is a primary state in which people cast secret ballots for their choice of candidate in their political party of choice. This is in contrast to a cau-

Can California be considered a Democrat Party state?

Some might be surprised to learn that since becoming a state California has gone with Republican presidents twenty-three times and Democrats seventeen times. However, since 1992 Democrats have carried the state.

cus, in which registered members of a party gather at local meetings to cast their votes, often in association with the state's convention.

How many electoral votes does California carry in presidential elections?

California currently has 55 electoral votes.

Does this mean that more and more people are voting Democrat in California since the 1990s?

Actually, the number of registered Democrats has decreased from 58% of voters in 1950 to only 43% in 2006. On the other hand, the percentage of those registered to vote Republican has remained fairly steady at around 35%. What has changed is that there has been a slight increase in those voting for third parties (1% in 1950 versus 4% in 2006) and a dramatic increase in those voting either independent or refusing to state in surveys which party they favor. So, currently, Democrats maintain an edge, but that could change in coming elections.

Do whites vote more than minorities in general elections in California?

Yes. Although, as stated in the "California Basics" chapter, there are as many or more Hispanic Americans in the state as whites, they are a much smaller percentage of the voting public. In 2000, this is how voting broke down:

Ethnicity	Percentage of Total Voters
White	71%
Hispanic	14%
Black	7%
Asian	6%
Other	2%

What is California's 2016–2017 budget, and where does the money come from?

The state anticipates a budget of about $125 billion for that year. The source of that money comes from the following, according to the governor's proposed budget:

Source	Amount (in millions of dollars)
Personal income tax	$83,841
Sales & use tax	$25,942
Corporate tax	$10,956
Insurance tax	$2,549
Alcohol tax	$373
Cigarette tax	$81
Pooled money interest	$89
Other	$1,247

Source: www.ebudget.ca.gov.

And where does the money go?

The following table explains the 2016–2017 expected expenditures for the state:

State Agency	Amount (in millions of dollars)
Health and Human Services	$52,546
K–12 Education	$51,442
Higher Education	$14,903
Corrections and Rehabilitation	$13,305
Transportation	$12,237
General Government	$7,342
Legislative, Judicial, and Executive	$6,819
Natural Resources	$5,442
Environmental Protection	$3,356
Business, Consumer Services, Housing	$1,417
Government Operations	$1,020
Labor and Workforce Development	$896

Source: www.ebudget.ca.gov.

PUBLIC EDUCATION

What is the state's main system of higher education institutions?

The University of California was founded in 1868, with its first campus being built in Berkeley near San Francisco. As of 2016, the university system has a student body approaching 240,000 students, employs 430,000 staff, has five medical centers and three national laboratories, and contributes over $46 billion to the state's economy. Sixty-one Nobel laureates have graduated from one of its colleges. The UC library system is one of the largest collections of published knowledge in the world, including about thirty-four million items.

The University of California, Berkeley, is the oldest and most storied of colleges in the UC system.

How many campuses does the UC system currently have?

There are ten campuses, which were founded in the following order:

Campus	Year Founded
Berkeley	1868
San Francisco	1873
Santa Barbara	1891
Los Angeles	1919
Riverside	1954
Davis	1959
San Diego	1960
Irvine	1965
Santa Cruz	1965
Merced	2005

Why is the University of California system run by the government as a separate agency?

The California Constitution of 1879 established that the University of California would operate as a separate constitutional agency. This means that the university system is exempt from laws that apply to the state government.

What about the California State University system? What is it like?

In addition to the University of California system, the state also has the California State University system, which has twenty-three campuses, 460,000 students, and 47,000 faculty and staff members.

The CSU system morphed from the California State Normal Schools that date back to 1870. The normal schools became the California State College system and then, in 1960, the California Master Plan for Higher Education transformed them into the CSU system.

What are the CSU campuses?

As of 2016, the campuses include:

Campus	Year Founded
San Jose State University	1857
California State University, Chico	1887
San Diego State University	1897
San Francisco State University	1899
California Polytechnic State University, San Luis Obispo	1901
California State University, Fresno	1911
Humboldt State University	1913
California State University Maritime Academy	1929
California State Polytechnic University, Pomona	1938
California State University, Los Angeles	1947
California State University, Sacramento	1947
California State University, Long Beach	1949
California State University, East Bay	1957
California State University, Fullerton	1957
California State University, Stanislaus	1957
California State University, Northridge	1958
California State University, Dominguez Hills	1960
Sonoma State University	1960
California State University, Bakersfield	1965
California State University, San Bernardino	1965
California State University San Marcos	1988
California State University, Monterey Bay	1994
California State University Channel Islands	2002

Is the CSU system noted for anything in particular?

While obviously offering degrees in all the major academic disciplines, CSU is particularly notable for its programs on public policy issues and politics. The Center for California Studies at the Sacramento campus teaches a multidisciplinary approach to understanding policy issues in California (which is why it has a front-row seat at the state capitol) and has many alumni who are now state and federal legislators. The California African American Political and Economic Institute at Dominguez Hills has programs specifically designed to train future leaders in the African American community. San Francisco State University, furthermore, has a noted law school.

What are some of the state's best private colleges and universities?

California has nearly four hundred public and private institutions of higher learning, which is more than any other state (New York has 307). Of the many excellent private colleges and universities in the state, here are just ten that are considered among the best:

Insitution	Location	Established	Student Body (2015)
University of San Francisco	San Francisco	1855	10,689
University of Southern California	Los Angeles	1880	42,453
Stanford University	Stanford	1885	16,963
Pomona College	Claremont	1887	1,650
California Institute of Technology	Pasadena	1891	2,209
San Francisco State University	San Francisco	1899	29,465
Pepperdine University	Malibu	1937	7,417
Claremont McKenna College	Claremont	1946	1,324
University of San Diego	San Diego	1949	8,349
Harvey Mudd College	Claremont	1955	804

What are some notable facts about community colleges in the state?

The state legislature created the California Community Colleges System in 1967. It currently consists of 113 colleges overseen by a seventeen-member board of governors that is appointed by the state's governor. About 2.4 million students attend the colleges in this system.

How do California's kindergarten through high school students fare compared to the rest of the country?

While the state has some of the country's (and the world's) best colleges, and while the state spends a huge chunk of its annual budget on education, the K-12 schools do not do well. According to a report issued by the nonprofit Editorial Projects in Education's *Education Week* in January 2015, the state ranks forty-second in the nation with a D grade (C was the average for the country). Some of the factors contributing to this poor performance, according to the report, were the number of students from low-income homes and from homes where English is not spoken at home or is not the primary language at home (California was second to last in this category).

UTOPIAN (OR NEAR-UTOPIAN) SOCIETIES

What is a utopian society?

A utopian society consists of any group of people who remove themselves from general society to establish a new community that follows ideals of a new social pattern—often one outlined in a book or philosophy founded by a dynamic individual.

What is a commune?

A commune is a community in which all the members share responsibility for work and also share the possessions and assets of the community. While many people think of communes as rising in popularity in the 1960s, in California they actually have roots back to the nineteenth century.

Have there been many utopian societies established in California?

About a dozen efforts to establish utopian communities have been tried over the last couple centuries. Among these are the Kaweah Colony, Altruria, Druid Heights, and Halcyon.

Why did the Kaweah Colony not succeed?

The Kaweah Colony, which lasted from 1886 to 1892, was a group of people, led by James J. Martin and journalist Burnette G. Haskell, following the socialist ideas of attorney

---

What was the idea that founded the town of Allensworth?

Allensworth was a short-lived, all-black community located in Tulare County. It was the brainchild of Lieutenant Colonel Allen Allensworth (1842–1914), a Baptist minister and the first black chaplain to serve in the U.S. military, which he did during the Civil War for the all-black 24th Infantry. Incorporating the town in 1908, the idea was to have a community completely run by African Americans and, consequently, free from the disruptions of prejudice from the white community. Initially, the town prospered. It became a railroad transfer point and flourished with the farm trade. But there was a dramatic, two-punch reversal of fortunes in 1914: Allensworth was killed when a motorcycle struck him accidentally, and the Santa Fe Railroad moved its stop from Allensworth to Alpaugh, effectively killing easy trade in the town. Residents were forced to look for work elsewhere, and the 1930s Depression and World War II contributed to the drain on residents. The town of Allensworth still exists today (population 471, as of 2010), however, and its founder is commemorated at the Colonel Allensworth State Historic Park there.

and activist Laurence Gronlund (1846–1899), the utopian novel *Looking Backward, 2000–1899* by Edward Bellamy (1850–1898), and the communist philosophy of the International Workers Association labor union. Workers all earned the same income, no matter the occupation, as long as they put in comparable hours of labor. They lived in the redwood forests of Tulare County in the Sierras, where Haskell and Martin hoped they could earn an income for the colony by logging the redwoods. But when the area was turned into Sequoia National Park in 1890, their days were numbered.

ACTORS IN POLITICS

How did the star of *Bedtime for Bonzo* evolve into the governor of California?

Perhaps it isn't fair to mock Ronald Reagan (1911–2004) for a few bad movies like *Bonzo* (1951), which was a comedy about a psychology professor working with a chimpanzee. Reagan also starred in some solid movies, such as *Knute Rockne, All American* (1940) and *Kings Row* (1942), and he later hosted television episodes of *General Electric Theater*.

He started getting involved in politics when he became a secret FBI informant during the McCarthy era, testifying before the House Un-American Activities Committee against people accused of being communist sympathizers during the 1940s. Later, he became active in the Screen Actors Guild, rising to the office of president, in which capacity he served from 1947 to 1952, and again in 1959.

A registered Democrat at first, Reagan became involved in various political committees and proved himself an effective political speaker. Interestingly, he opposed the Republican right-to-work position, as well as nuclear proliferation and the idea of mutually assured destruction as a deterrent to war (when president, his support of a strong military was credited for helping take down the Soviet Union).

By the 1960s, Reagan's positions were shifting. He joined the National Rifle Association and opposed the introduction of Medicare in 1961. He got the notice of the Republican Party and in 1965 decided to run for governor of California on the Republican ticket. He defeated Pat Brown in 1967 and served in that office until 1975.

Reagan's time as governor proved a preview of his years as president of the

Newly elected Ronald Reagan with his wife, Nancy, celebrating winning the office of governor of California in 1966.

United States. Just as he would face down the air traffic controllers when he was president, he didn't hesitate to use muscle to put down the People's Park protest in 1969 (see the chapter "The State of California: 1850 to the Present"). Reagan called in the California Highway Patrol and the National Guard; a student was killed and another protestor was blinded during the confrontation. He also supported the public carrying of firearms and signed the 1967 Mulford Act to make it a law, and he wanted to allow capital punishment in California, an effort that the state supreme court nixed. In 1969, he signed the Family Law Act, which allowed for no-fault divorces.

By the time he decided not to run for a third term, Reagan's politics were firmly in place: antilabor, anti-abortion, and pro-military and police.

How did entertainer Sonny Bono become a politician?

Many remember Sonny Bono (1935–1998) as the man who made Cher a singing star and who appeared with her in the *Sonny & Cher Comedy Hour* (1971–1974) TV show and *The Sonny & Cher Show* (1976–1977). Bono wrote many of the duo's songs, including "The Beat Goes On" and "I Got You, Babe." He divorced Cher in 1975, going on to marry again, and he also continued his involvement in music. However, it was while trying to open a business in Palm Springs, California, that he became so frustrated with the political blockades in the city's government that he decided to run for mayor as a Republican.

He won, serving as mayor of Palm Springs from 1988 to 1992. During this time, he tried to improve the business climate, including discouraging some of the overly rowdy partying that was going on downtown. One of his biggest accomplishments was founding the Palm Springs International Film Festival, an annual event that continues today and draws a large crowd of celebrities from Los Angeles.

Bono would go on to serve in the U.S. Senate, representing California's 44th District from 1995 until his untimely death. He championed the restoration of the Salton Sea and cosponsored a bill to extend copyright on original works published before 1978 (this makes sense, given that his popular songs were written in the 1960s and early 1970s). While that law never got voted on, a similar law was passed after his death and nicknamed the Sonny Bono Copyright Term Extension Act of 1998.

Sonny passed away after a skiing accident in Nevada on January 5, 1998. He is buried in Cathedral City, and there is a statue in his honor in downtown Palm Springs.

Which city was actor Clint Eastwood mayor of?

Eastwood (1930–), the actor with a tough-guy reputation for his roles in everything from Spaghetti Westerns to the "Dirty Harry" films, was mayor of Carmel-by-the-Sea from 1986 to 1988. An owner of several business ventures in the scenic, coastal town, as mayor, Eastwood was a strong supporter of small businesses; he also opposed projects that threatened to be environmentally unsound.

Which governor of California was also once called "the Governator"?

Famous bodybuilder-turned-actor-turned-politician Arnold Schwarzenegger (1947–) started his career winning the Mr. Olympia contest seven times (1970–1975, 1980). Knowing he couldn't make a career of bodybuilding last forever, he also wanted to be an actor, winning the title role in the horrendously bad *Hercules in New York* (1970) in which he had hardly any lines, which is just as well because his very thick, Austrian accent and still-limited command of English made it hard to understand what he was saying. Things improved, though, with roles in *Stay Hungry* (1976), for which he won a Golden Globe playing an Austrian bodybuilder (an acting stretch if there ever was one), and *Pumping Iron* (1977) as himself. It was an action hero, however, that he achieved a claim to fame playing, appearing in *Conan the Barbarian* (1982), *The Terminator* (1984), *The Expendables* (2010), and their sequels, as well as other action movies and even comedies.

So how does a bodybuilder and movie star become a politician in California? A Republican since he heard President Richard Nixon give a campaign speech, Schwarzenegger got involved in antidrug and physical fitness initiatives championed by the Reagan Administration in the 1980s. While this got him some political contacts, he had little or no experience when he decided to run for governor. He announced his candidacy in 2003, taking advantage of the recall election of Governor Gray Davis (the first governor to be removed from California's highest office in the state's history). Schwarzenegger ran against Republican State Senator Tom McClintock and Democrat Lieutenant Governor Cruz Bustamante as his chief opponents in a field that included over 130 candidates (many of them celebrities like Schwarzenegger). The Governator, as some would later call him, won 48% of the vote, which was not a majority, but because the other candidates split the remaining vote and Schwarzenegger had over one million votes more than the runner-up, Bustamante, by the state constitution, he won without the need for a recount.

Schwarzenegger ran the state until January 3, 2011. The first couple of years went well for him, and his popularity remained high among voters. But with the economic problems the state faced after the 2008 Great Recession ensued, compounded by a soaring budget deficit for California, voters turned their backs on him, and his approval rating was around 25% by the time he left office. His tenure was marked by several deeds, accomplishments, and drawbacks: he made it a requirement for the state to have a "rainy day fund" set up during good economic

A former professional bodybuilder and action movie star, Arnold Schwarzenneger was elected governor of California in 2002 and served two terms.

times (usually, governments simply spend surpluses), he established an open primary election system (voters were not required to declare party loyalty to vote in a primary), he believed in environmental efforts to stem climate change both in his state and at the federal level, and although he successfully opposed state initiatives to legalize gay marriage, when Proposition 8 was reversed by a federal judge, allowing gay people to marry, Schwarzenegger did nothing to try to reverse it.

After he left office, there were rumors Schwarzenegger would run for president. However, the U.S. Constitution prohibits someone who is not a natural-born U.S. citizen to do so. Since he was born in Austria to Austrian parents, he is ineligible for the nation's highest office.

IMPORTANT STATE LEGISLATION

What is the importance of Proposition 13?

Passed on June 6, 1978, Prop 13 (also known as the People's Initiative to Limit Property Taxation) was a permanent amendment to the state constitution that reduced the property tax burden of California homeowners. It was championed by state senator Howard Jarvis (1903–1986), who had earlier founded the Howard Jarvis Taxpayers Association.

The new law lowered taxes in several ways:

- Property values were immediately reduced to 1975–1976 levels—that is, they were cut fifty-seven percent.

- The property tax rate was capped at one percent of total assessed real estate value.

- Property taxes could not be raised by more than two percent annually.

- Both legislative houses could only pass increases in state tax rates if there was a two-thirds majority vote.

- A two-thirds majority was also required for most local governments to raise special taxes.

While voters loved these laws, it had the effect of reducing state revenue by over sixty billion dollars. The result was that local governments were forced to take on more services that the state could no longer afford.

Is assisted suicide legal in California?

Yes. Governor Jerry Brown signed a measure in October 2015 that makes assisted suicide legal. For this to be done, the patient must be of sound mind and must be diagnosed with a terminal illness that will lead to death within six months. Should this be the case, doctors may prescribe drugs that will end the person's life. The formal process is, however, fairly involved. The ill person must make not one but two formal, written requests to a doctor, and they must be written at least fifteen days apart from each other. The requests must be signed by two witnesses, no more than one of whom can be a family member. The doctor must thoroughly assess the patient's mental competence, and this determination must be verified by a second physician. Two days before the patient takes the drugs, he or she must be formally asked again whether he or she still wishes to die. Finally, the patient must take the drugs him/herself, without any assistance, because euthanasia is specifically prohibited in the state's law.

When was gay marriage made legal?

The issue of same-sex marriage in the state was one that went back and forth a few times in the 2000s. In May 2008, the state Supreme Court ruled that gay marriages were legal. But in November of that year, Proposition 8, which amended the state constitution to ban such marriages, passed with fifty-two percent of the vote. Prop 8 was the law of the land for a couple years, but in 2012 the U.S. State Court of Appeals for the Ninth Circuit overturned the ban, and the next year it was upheld in another appeals case. So, in short, LGBT marriages were legal, except for a short period from 2008 to 2012. That is all moot now, since the U.S. Supreme Court finally put the issue to rest once and for all, making all marriages between hetero- and homosexual couples legal.

Why did voters pass Prop 187?

There has long been tension in the state concerning immigration, especially from Mexico. Proposition 187 was passed by voters in 1994. It stated that illegal immigrants were only entitled to emergency medical care but not nonemergency care. Also, children of illegal immigrants could not go to public schools, and their families could not collect any welfare benefits. The federal courts declared the law unconstitutional, however, and a 1999 appeals challenge was dropped because, at the time, tensions had lessened and the economy was doing well.

TRAFFIC AND VEHICLE RULES

What do the signs mean when they say a lane is for HOV only?

The abbreviation HOV means High Occupancy Vehicle, which in California means two or more people must be inside a car that is in the "diamond lane," a lane on the left (inside) of a freeway. In northern California, this rule only applies during high-traffic commuting hours on the weekdays, but in southern California it is in effect seven days a week, twenty-four hours a day. Furthermore, in the south, the diamond lanes are often separated by barriers or double lines, and you are not supposed to cross into the double lane unless there is a break in the double lines. Some of these rules can vary somewhat from city to city, so it is important for drivers unfamiliar with the local laws to observe HOV street signs.

The idea behind diamond lanes is to encourage carpooling and gas conservation (the lanes usually move along faster than other lanes during high-congestion periods). Motorcycles and mass-transit vehicles are also permitted to use the lanes.

What are some unusual California traffic laws?

There are a few that are rather silly. For example, in Hermosa Beach it is illegal to spill a margarita on the street. In Chico, it is forbidden to plant rutabagas on any roadway. You can't sleep on a road in Eureka. And in Glendale they found it necessary, for some reason, to tell people they can't jump from a car traveling 65 miles (105 kilometers) per hour or more (is 64 okay, then?)

Why do I see motorcycles riding between lanes? Is that legal?

In California, lane-splitting, as it's called, *is* legal for motorcycles (it's not illegal *per se* in a lot of other states, but only California specifically states that it is permitted). However, it is still controversial, and many people believe it to be an unsafe practice.

How often are smog inspections required in order to renew one's car registration?

A car must pass a smog inspection every two years in California for the driver to renew his or her registration.

Why are many catalytic converters illegal to buy or use in California?

California has the strictest smog-control laws in the nation, and one thing that this affects is the installation of catalytic converters, a device that is attached to car exhaust systems to filter out or convert harmful pollutants to more benign emissions. To meet the stringent pollution guidelines in the state, one needs to install a three-way catalytic converter, not the cheaper two-way catcons.

Since when have illegal immigrants in California been allowed to obtain driver's licenses?

Actually, for many years undocumented workers in the state were allowed to have a driver's license. This changed in 1993, when Governor Pete Wilson (1933–) signed a law that said people had to provide a social security number to get a license. Then, in 2013, the state legislature passed Assembly Bill 60, which came into effect at the beginning of 2015. It allowed undocumented aliens to obtain a special license (not a regular California license) to drive if they are sixteen years old or older and pass the driving test. The license specifically states that it is for driving only and cannot be used for any other identification purposes.

The advantages of the law are several: it will force these drivers to get auto insurance, it will require them to take driving education and pass a test (making roads a bit safer for others), and, of course, it will permit agricultural workers, especially, to more easily run errands, take their children to school, and so on. However, because the driver's license is different from a regular California license, there is a risk that police of-

What is a "California stop"?

Sometimes called a "Hollywood stop," it is the act of slowing down but not stopping fully at a stop sign, red light, or any other place where you should stop fully, such as at the end of a row of cars in a parking lot. Whether or not this practice actually started in the Land of Fruits and Nuts is open for debate, and you do see people performing rolling stops elsewhere in the country, but it does seem to be more prevalent here. That doesn't mean it is legal, however; a California police officer can certainly still ticket you for doing a California stop.

ficers stopping such drivers will report them to Immigration, even though the law stipulates that the Department of Motor Vehicles does not have to provide information on a person's legal status.

Did Californians invent the practice of turning right on a red light?

It is legal in California to turn right after coming to a complete stop at a red light, so long as there is no oncoming traffic and there are no signs indicating that at a specific stop it is not allowed. Also, if there is a dedicated right arrow light controlling turns, that always takes precedence. California was, indeed, the first state to allow this rule, making it a law way back in 1947. It was not until 1978 that the other states all caught up. Even so, New York City prohibits a right turn on red, *except* when a sign specifically indicates it is okay.

THE DEBATE TO DIVIDE THE STATE

Why are there some people who want to break up California into smaller states?

There are a couple reasons why this is. A big one is the resource of water. Many in the northern part of the state resent that the water that falls there or that is collected from mountain runoff is sent down to the state's largest city, Los Angeles, in the south. Farmers also dislike how water prices have skyrocketed because of urban needs or that sometimes they are even denied watering some crops and have to leave them fallow because of statewide water shortages.

Another reason is differences in the population. In metropolitan and coastal areas such as the Bay Area and greater Los Angeles, more people tend to have liberal politics and voting tends toward the Democrat Party, while in rural farming areas and the more conservative inland areas, the tendency is toward conservative politics. The culture of southern California is also quite different from northern California, and the region of the state north of San Francisco is practically a different world altogether. The more sparsely populated Central Valley and points east and north of the coastal populations therefore feel like they don't get a say in what goes on in the state.

How many times during the 1850s were proposals made to divide the state?

Sometimes it's amazing that California is still in one piece when one considers that just in the 1850s there were three attempts to break it up. The first effort was in 1850, when it was put forward to make the northern part of the state "the Territory of Colorado," and the south would be called "Southern California." In 1854, the state legislature heard arguments to divide it into three: Shasta in the north, Colorado in the middle, and California in the south. Then, in 1859, there was yet another attempt to create a Colorado and California. (People must have loved the name "Colorado," and, blessedly, the name was finally taken in 1876 by another state.)

Has the issue been brought up again?

Yes. The issue arose again in 1881, when the *Los Angeles Herald* suggested that San Bernardino, Los Angeles, and San Diego counties should be annexed by Arizona to become Calizonia, a name that sounds more like a meaty Italian pastry than a state.

But it didn't end there. Indeed, over the years there have been over 220 proposals to divide California up. It's almost become a political hobby to the point of being ridiculous.

What are some of the more recent efforts to divide California into smaller states?

In 1993, the California State Assembly put the measure on the ballot again, but the proposal died in the State Senate. More efforts were put forth in 2003, 2009, 2011, and two in 2013, usually with the idea of two or three states. In 2015, however, a six-state model was proposed by venture capitalist Tim Draper (1958–). Draper proposed the creation of the states of Jefferson (in the north), North California (just south of Jefferson), Silicon Valley (San Francisco and down the Central Coast), Central California (encompassing most of the Central Valley), West California (the L.A. area and halfway up the coast, encompassing much of the richest parts of the state), and South California (San Diego and the southeast corner of the state, which is mostly desert). Draper argued that this model would be much more efficient to govern, and he spent about $5 million to get it on the 2016 ballot, but he failed to do so. Opponents believe that Draper's proposal was a move to separate right and poor parts of the state, shifting the influence of Democrat and Republican parties.

If so many people have tried to split the state, why haven't any attempts been successful?

A big reason that California has never been divided up is that even if many of the residents passed a resolution to do so, the final decision is up to the U.S. Congress, which has to approve it by a two-thirds majority. Such a process is not unheard of, of course, and has been used five times in the past: Kentucky and West Virginia were sliced off of Virginia, Tennessee was part of North Carolina, Maine was part of Massachusetts, and Vermont was once in New York.

273

Have some people gone even further when it comes to running the state of California?

There is a growing movement in California for the state to become its own country. According to the website YesCalifornia.org, the state was taken over by the United States against its will and through military force (see the "Early California" chapter to see why this really isn't true). It does make the valid point, however, that as its own nation California would command the world's seventh-largest economy that would be diversely invested in everything from agriculture to high technology.

The movement is the brainchild of Louis Marinelli (1986–), an English teacher at Alliance International University and, as of 2016, a candidate for California's 80th Assembly District. He argues that federal taxes from Californians are misspent, that the government illegally spies on citizens, that the president of the United States and the U.S. Supreme Court have repeatedly violated the law at the expense of the country's citizens, and that it is an imperialistic power that is itself indulging in terrorist acts.

Political activist Louis Marinelli runs the YesCalifornia movement that favors making the state an independent nation.

As an independent nation, according to YesCalifornia, more money could be directed toward education, helping the poor, and other social programs. The state would have more control over important policies, such as immigration, distribution of water, funding public parks, and so on. Of course, defense of the new country could be problematic without the U.S. military. To this end, the organizers are trying to get a referendum on the 2020 ballot that would recognize California as a sovereign nation yet still have strong economic, military, and political ties to the rest of the nation; this would be akin to Scotland or Wales within the United Kingdom.

PROFESSIONAL SPORTS

Which major sports teams call California home?

In baseball, the major league teams are the Los Angeles Angels of Anaheim (West division of the American League), the Los Angeles Dodgers (West division of the National League), the San Diego Padres (West division of National League), the Oakland Athletics, or A's (West division of the American League), and the San Francisco Giants (West division of National League).

In football, the teams include the Oakland Raiders, the San Francisco 49ers, and the San Diego Chargers. As of this writing, the St. Louis Rams (who were once based in Los Angeles) have been talking about moving back to their former home. The Chargers are also considering moving to Los Angeles. L.A. also had an arena football team called the Avengers, but they only lasted from 2000 to 2008.

Californians are well represented in the NBA with the Los Angeles Clippers and Lakers, the Golden State Warriors, and the Sacramento Kings; on the WNBA side of the net, there is also the Los Angeles Sparks. For hockey, it's the Los Angeles Kings, the Anaheim Ducks, and the San Jose Sharks. And California has two professional soccer teams: the L.A. Galaxy and the San Jose Earthquakes.

BASEBALL

What marked the beginning of professional baseball in California?

The first two pro teams formed were the Pacifics and the Eagles, and they played their first game in San Francisco on February 22, 1860.

275

What were the first professional baseball leagues in California?

The California League was formed in the 1880s and was the first pro baseball league in California (not to be confused with the current minor league California League that was founded in 1941). It was replaced in 1903 by the Pacific Coast League, which then folded in 1958.

Why did the Dodgers and Giants move from New York to Los Angeles?

The Brooklyn Dodgers and New York Giants both abandoned the East Coast in 1957, much to the sadness of their fans, who at least got to keep the Yankees and, beginning in 1962, the Mets. Both teams, moved to California, which, at the time, had no major league baseball teams, for financial reasons. While the Dodgers were making money in the 1950s, owner Walter O'Malley wasn't happy with Ebbets Field in Brooklyn, the home of the team since 1913. He also didn't like the neighborhood, which was becoming increasingly black (oh, yes, racism definitely was a factor here). O'Malley wanted the taxpayers to buy him a new six million dollar stadium, but the city wouldn't approve it, and that was the nail in the coffin for Brooklyn fans.

The Giants played a variation of that game. Unlike the Dodgers, though, their finances were not doing so well, even though they had won National League pennants and three World Series in the years between 1900 and 1925. The Polo Grounds in Upper Manhattan were the problem. Baseball fans preferred going to games in the Bronx (Yankees) and Brooklyn, and so the Polo Grounds, which seated fifty-five thousand, was not filling up. The Giants owners therefore decided to try San Francisco out.

DODGERS

Which league are the Dodgers in?

The team is part of the National League's Western Division.

When did Dodger Stadium debut?

Groundbreaking for Dodger Stadium was on September 17, 1959. Between 1957, when they left Brooklyn, and the opening of the new stadium, they played at the Coliseum.

Why are they called the "Dodgers"?

The name is a leftover from the team's Brooklyn days. The team had gone through a number of name changes, including Trolley Dodgers from 1911 to 1912, which referred to the fact that there were a lot of trolley tracks around the stadium and one had to dodge all the trolleys to get there. After a couple more name changes, including the Robins from 1914 to 1931, they reclaimed the Dodgers name in 1932, and it has stuck ever since.

Dodger Stadium in Los Angeles has been the team's home since 1962.

Their first game in Los Angeles was against the San Francisco Giants on April 18, 1958, and they won 6–5. Their first season was a bit disappointing, with a seventh-place standing. The new stadium was completed in 1962, and the team moved there.

How many world series have the Dodgers won?

Not counting 1955, when they were in Brooklyn, the Dodgers have won five World Series in 1959, 1963, 1965, 1981, and 1988.

How did they win that first national title in 1959?

The Dodgers had some great players at the time (although the legendary Jackie Robinson had retired before they got to L.A.), including pitcher Don Drysdale (1936–1993), first baseman Gil Hodges (1924–1972), and center fielder Duke Snider (1926–2011), among others. They got past Milwaukee for the National League title and then faced off against the White Sox. After an embarrassing Game 1 at Comiskey Park in which they lost 11–0, the Dodgers came back to win the next three games. They lost Game 5 at home, and then walloped the Chicago team at their stadium 9–3.

How was pitcher Sandy Koufax key to the Dodgers' success in the early 1960s?

There was no better pitcher in the game in the 1960s than Sanford "Sandy" Koufax (1935–). What's interesting is that the pitcher was actually pretty mediocre when he was with the team from 1955 to 1960 and was seriously thinking of quitting the game for good. Instead, he decided to try one more season and during the winter focused on working his body, and he also changed his pitching technique. In addition, the move to Dodger Stadium in 1962 proved to be a better venue for the pitcher. All of these things

277

combined saw him lower his ERA from 4.28 to 1.75. The next year, he had a 1.88 ERA and chalked up 306 strikeouts.

From 1963 to 1966, Koufax was on fire; he was ERA leader from 1962 to 1966, strikeout leader in 1961, 1963, 1965, and 1966, World Series MVP in 1963 and 1965, and Triple Crown and Cy Young Award winner in 1963, 1965, and 1966. He led his team to win the 1963 and 1965 World Series, beating the Yankees in 1963 and the Giants in 1965. The Giants series was particularly exciting, going into seven games. In Game 7, he only allowed three hits and no runs.

Injuries to his pitching arm plagued Koufax in 1965 and 1966, and he retired on advice of his doctor and the risk that continuing to pitch might actually cause him to lose function in that arm.

Who helped the Dodgers get out of a slump in the 1970s?

The late 1960s and early 1970s were unremarkable for the team, but they perked up in 1974 after acquiring first baseman Steve Garvey (1948–) and winning the National League pennant against the Pittsburgh Pirates three games to one. Facing the Oakland A's in the World Series, though, they only won Game 2 and lost the series in five.

Another factor in the 1970s was the coaching. Manager Walter Alston retired in 1976 while the season was ongoing and was replaced by someone who would become a fan favorite for the next twenty years, the inimitable Tommy Lasorda (1927–).

What were some of Tommy Lasorda's accomplishments with the Dodgers?

Lasorda, who actually played a year with the team back in Brooklyn in the 1955–1956 season, led the Dodgers to four National League championships (1977, 1978, 1981, 1988) and two World Series (1981, 1988), being named Manager of the Year both times (he was also the AP and UPI Manager of the Year in 1977). His sixteen games won in National League play was the most of any coach at the time, and he was inducted into the Baseball Hall of Fame in 1997, the year after he retired. Afterward, he was the manager of the U.S. baseball team at the 2000 Sydney Olympics, and his team won the gold!

What record feat did Dodger pitcher Fernando Valenzuela achieve in 1986?

Fernando Valenzuela (1960–) was a Mexican-born pitcher who played for the Dodgers from 1980 to 1990. He was the first

Shown here in 2011 after his retirement, former Dodgers manager Tommy Lasorda was a favorite of fans as he led them to two World Series.

Who is known as "the Voice of the Dodgers"?

A remarkable broadcaster by the name of Vin Scully (1927–) began as a play-by-play announcer for the Brooklyn Dodgers in 1950, and as of this writing (2016), he is still giving fans a lively description of the game on radio and television. He was inducted into the American Sportscasters Hall of Fame in 1992, the National Radio Hall of Fame in 1995, and the National Association of Broadcasters Hall of Fame in 2009, among many other awards and honors.

rookie to win the Cy Young Award (1981), the same year he was Rookie of the Year and the Dodgers won the World Series. Valenzuela had a namesake pitch, the "Fernando Fade-away," that was a variation of the screwball over which he displayed remarkable control.

Who were some notable Dodgers in the 1990s who were all Rookies of the Year?

Some of the standouts of the time were catcher Mike Piazza (1968–), who was with the team from 1992 to 1998 after being drafted in 1988. He was named Rookie of the Year with a batting average of .318, 35 home runs, and 112 RBIs; in 1997, his best year, he batted .362 with 40 home runs and 122 RBIs.

The 1994 Dodger of note was outfielder Raúl Mondesí (1971–; Dodgers 1993–1999), who was Rookie of the Year with a .306 batting average, 56 RBIs, and 16 homers. Pitcher Hideo "The Tornado" Nomo was the next Rookie of the Year, throwing 236 strikeouts in 1995.

What happened when Rupert Murdoch bought the team?

Dodger fans weren't too happy with media mogul Rupert Murdoch (1931–) buying the Dodgers and proceeding to trade some favorite players such as Mike Piazza. However, he did get outfielder Gary Sheffield (1968–), who had outstanding seasons in 2000 and 2001.

How well did the Dodgers do in the new century?

They've won several Western Division titles (2004, 2008, 2009, 2013, 2014, 2015) but haven't moved beyond that point.

What unique distinction did the Dodgers share with the Arizona Diamondbacks in 2014?

They were the first American teams to play a major league baseball game in Australia—the Sydney Cricket Grounds, specifically.

ANGELS

In which league are the Angels?

The team is in the American League, Western Division. The team has the honor of being the first expansion team in the league in about sixty years when they were formed in 1961.

How well did the expansion team do the first few years?

No one expects a new team to make the playoffs at first, but the Angels did okay. They shared Dodger Stadium for the first few years until their own stadium was completed (see below) and had a 71–79 record their first season. The Angels had a pretty decent pitcher, too, named Dean Chance, who was with them until 1966 and had a great ERA (1.65 in 1964). They wouldn't win their division until much later, however, in 1979.

What's the background of the home of the California Angels?

Angel Stadium was opened on April 9, 1966, when it was named Anaheim Stadium after its location near Los Angeles. It originally seated 43,204 fans. The opening game was an exhibition in which the Angels hosted the San Francisco Giants. The stadium would also host the NFL's Rams and Raiders until 1996, when the stadium was renovated with the intention of hosting baseball games exclusively. From 1998 to 2003 it was called the Edison International Field of Anaheim, but it has since been called the Angels Stadium of Anaheim.

Why were they called the California Angels for three decades?

The team officially changed the name to the California Angels from 1966 to 1996 because they wanted to have an identity separated from the Dodgers. They changed it again after that and are now the Anaheim Angels.

Who was the pitcher who gave the team a fighting chance in the 1970s?

That would be Nolan Ryan (1947–), who would be best remembered for his years with the Texas Rangers but who also pitched for the Angels from 1971 to 1979.

What other player finally got the team to a division title?

It wasn't enough to have a strong pitcher in Nolan Ryan without some hitters to back him up. That changed when they acquired Rod Carew (1945–) from the Minnesota Twins in

---

Who was the singing cowboy who first owned the Angels?

Gene Autry (1907–1998) was the original owner and also gave the Angels their name. He named them after the Pacific Coast League team that had played in Los Angeles until 1957.

1979. Don Baylor (1949–), who joined the Angels in 1977, was also a big asset, and the team found themselves in the Western Division playoffs for the first time, beating the Kansas City Royals. At the American League series against the Baltimore Orioles, however, they lost in four games.

Who was an unlikely addition in 1982 that helped the Angels return to the playoffs?

Hall of Famer Reggie Jackson (1946–) left the Yankees in 1982 and would play with the Angels until 1986 (filling a void created when Ryan left in 1980). While he wouldn't take his new team to a World Series, they did win the Western Division again in 1982

Reggie Jackson was one of a couple of big-name players whom the Angels acquired in the late 1970s and early 1980s to help them win titles.

with the pitching arm of Tommy John (1943–) on the mound. They would go on to lose the American League Championship to the Milwaukee Brewers in five games.

And what was their next Western Division appearance?

That came in 1986 when they faced the Red Sox, which had Roger Clemens (1962–) pitching at the time. The Halos gave Boston a run for its money but still ended up losing after seven games.

How did they do in the late 1980s and the 1990s?

The Angels were not very inspiring in these years. Interestingly, however, they became the subject of a Disney movie called *Angels in the Outfield* (1994), a remake of a 1951 movie that had the Angels getting assistance from heavenly, real angels. That was great for the fictional world, but in reality....

Were things improving by the twenty-first century?

Oh, yes, indeed! The years between 2004 and 2014 have been the best in Angels history. The Halos won their division in 2004, 2005, 2007, 2008, 2009, and 2014, but, more importantly before that, they won the World Series in 2002.

How did they get to the 2002 World Series if they didn't win the division that year?

Even though the Angels had a franchise-best 99–63 season, they didn't get to go to the division championship, yet they grabbed the wild card slot. This was appropriate, as the Halos had a kind of comeback vibe going in 2002 in which they would often pull off a win at the last minute. After being down 6–14 at the beginning of the season, they would win the next

What fun, and appropriate, nickname does the team go by?

The logo has a halo over the A in their name, and so it was a natural that the nickname for the Angels is "the Halos."

21 of 24 games, thanks to such performances as shortstop David Eckstein's (1975–) back-to-back grand slam homers during the season. They would go on to beat the Yankees in the division series, and then won the AL title against the Minnesota Twins in five (after losing Game 1). Venezuelan pitcher Francisco Rodríguez (1982–) was a key player.

Who have been some important players in more recent years?

Some of the notable Angels on the roster in recent years have been the following:

Player	Position	Years with Angels	Batting Average or ERA
Garret Anderson (1982–)	left field	1994–2008	.293
Troy Glaus (1976–)	first, third base	1998–2004	.254
Vladimir Guerrero (1975–)	right field	2004–2009	.318
Troy Percival (1969–)	pitcher	1995–2004	3.17
Tim Salmon (1968–)	right field	1992–2006	.282
Mike Trout (1991–)	center field	2011–	.304
Jered Weaver (1982–)	pitcher	2006–	3.40

ATHLETICS

Just who are the Athletics?

The Oakland Athletics (or A's) are one of the most successful and oldest major league teams in the nation. They have won nine World Series titles, which puts them behind only the Yankees (twenty-seven) and the Orioles (eleven) and ahead of the other Bay Area team, the Giants, who have eight as of 2016.

The A's were not always in Oakland, however. They were founded in 1901 in Philadelphia, then Kansas City from 1955 to 1967. They moved to Oakland in 1968 to the Oakland-Alameda County Coliseum, which is now called the O.co Coliseum.

What league do the A's play in?

They are in the Western Division of the American League.

How well did the A's do after moving to Oakland?

Very well, actually. Although it wasn't like they were a new expansion team, they did have some young and inexperienced players, yet they performed admirably. The young

Reggie Jackson (1946–) had thirty-nine home runs in 1969, and the team finished second in its division with a record of 88–74.

How did the A's get on a roll to three World Series from 1972 to 1974?

In their first winning streak since moving to Oakland (and the first since 1930), the Athletics were unstoppable. Even when Reggie Jackson injured his leg playing the Tigers for the 1972 American League title, the team stepped up to the plate. First baseman Gene Tenace (1946–) did especially well against the Cincinnati Reds in the World Series and was named MVP as the A's took Game 7 to win it all.

The next year, Jackson was back with a vengeance. The A's faced Yogi Berra's Mets in the World Series, and the pennant seemed in question when, in Game 2, second baseman Mike Andrews (1943–) made two errors that cost them the game in the twelfth inning, prompting owner Finley to threaten to ban him from the rest of the series. Andrews' teammates came to his defense and said they would quit right there if Finley got his way, so the owner backed down. They came back to win Game 3 but then lost Games 4 and 5. Reggie to the rescue! His performance in the last two games led to another pennant, and he was named MVP. After the big win, however, manager Dick Williams quit the team after disputes with Finley.

The 1974 championship team enjoyed the pitching power of Rollie Fingers (1946–), who was the World Series MVP and was still sporting the handlebar mustache he grew back in 1970, and 1974 Cy Young Award winner Jim "Catfish" Hunter (1946–1999). Of course, Jackson was still on the team, too. It was an all-California series that year with the A's facing the Dodgers, beating them in five. There was a sour taste after the big win, however, when owner Finley was found guilty of backing out of a contract promise with Hunter, who then left the team as a free agent.

Why did the A's fall apart in the mid-1970s?

The A's had done well in 1975, thanks to Jackson and strong pitching from Vida Blue (1949–), and won the Western Division, but things went south after that. Many people

What quirky things did team owner Charles O. Finley try with the team?

Finley (1918–1996) might have tried some unconventional things, but sometimes they worked. He bought the team while they were still in Kansas City, and the move to Oakland seemed to give them a boost. On the other hand, his idea of using yellow bases at the 1970 home opener led to a ban on the color by Major League Baseball. The next year, he instructed all his players to grow mustaches and, if they did, they would get bonuses. The goofy tactic boosted morale, and the A's won 101 games that year and won the Western Division.

283

place the blame on owner Charlie Finley. After Hunter left to be a free agent, he made a deal with the Orioles to take Reggie Jackson for Don Baylor (1949–), then tried to send Vida Blue to the Yankees and Rollie Fingers to the Red Sox, but Commissioner Bowie Kuhn blocked the deals, infuriating Finley. Most of the core players became free agents in 1977, and it was all downhill from there. They were in last place in 1979, and at one game only about 650 fans showed up.

Did bringing in Billy Martin help?

Hiring Martin (1928–1989) from the Yankees in 1980 did revive the A's somewhat. Practicing a style of coaching that was called "Billy Ball," the team went from bottom to winning the West in 1981. But the next year there were a lot of injuries on the team, and then Martin went back to the Yankees in 1983.

Who was the king of stealing bases?

Rickey Henderson (1958–) is still considered to be the best base runner and stealer of his generation, if not all time. He had a complicated career of playing for a number of teams, but was most often with the A's (1979–1984, 1989–1993, 1994–1995, 1998). He led the American League in stolen bases (1980–1986, 1988–1991, and 1998), which includes the MLB record of 130 bases in a single season (1,406 in his career). The A's retired his #24 jersey in 2009.

A's legend Rickey Henderson is shown here in a 1983 game doing what he did best: stealing second.

> ## What devastating event occurred in Game 3 of the 1989 World Series?
>
> Just before Game 3 was going to start on October 17, the Loma Prieta earthquake struck the Bay Area (see the "Natural Wonders" chapter) with a force of 6.9 on the Richter scale. The entire area suffered extensive damage, and the series was postponed for ten days.

And who was the next big name to come to the A's bench?

First baseman Mark "Big Mac" McGwire (1963–) joined the team in 1986 and made his debut in 1987, which would mark the beginning of another streak of happy years for Oakland fans. McGwire, who was with the A's until 1997 and would hit 583 home runs in his career (the last five years with the Cardinals), led the charge to three American League championships in 1988, 1989, and 1990, and a World Series title in 1989.

Who was named MVP of the 1989 World Series?

Playing against the Toronto Blue Jays, the A's won in five games with the help of that year's MVP, pitcher Dave Stewart (1957–). They beat the Giants in a four-game sweep.

Were the A's in trouble in the 1990s?

After winning the American League pennant in 1990 but being swept in the 1990s World Series by the Reds, the Athletics really struggled. Ricky Henderson got his 1,000th stolen base in 1992, but that was the only highlight in the early '90s, especially with Mark McGwire being injured for much of the time. He was well again by 1995, hitting thirty-nine homers that year and following up the next year with fifty-two, but it wasn't enough to pull the entire team forward. The renovation of the Coliseum in 1996 was also disruptive. The A's had to play in a minor league park in Las Vegas temporarily, and when they came back home, the stadium's effort to accommodate football and soccer, too, made it less than ideal for baseball. Big Mac left the team as a free agent in 1997, and although the A's had some good rookie talent with Jason Giambi (1971–) on first base and Rookie of the Year Ben Grieve (1976–), they finished in last place.

What do Billy Beane and the term "money ball" have to do with each other?

With the new 1998 season, the A's got a new general manager in Billy Beane (1962–), who would lead them until 2016. Beane, with the considerable help of assistant manager Paul DePodesta's (1972–) knowledge of sabermetrics, employed a new strategy to improving the A's performance. Instead of working to draft big-name players, he took sabermetrics (the study of statistics in baseball) to a new level. He realized that really solid players who had gifts in certain areas of the game but who went mostly unnoticed because they didn't have splashy statistics could really lift the team out of their hole. In other

285

words, he built a well-rounded team with no big stars and, over the next decade, won six Western Division titles (2000, 2002, 2003, 2006, 2012, 2013). No, he didn't take the team to a World Series, but the rise from bottom rung to strong performances was impressive, especially since a big reason he didn't have big-name players was he wasn't given the budget to hire them.

It was so noteworthy that Beane became the subject of a book by Michael Lewis (1960–) called *Money Ball: The Art of Winning an Unfair Game* (2003), which was then adapted as the 2011 movie *Money Ball,* starring Brad Pitt (1963–) as Beane.

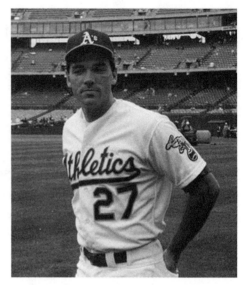

Billy Beane, former manager of the A's, used the science of sabermetrics—baseball statistics and analysis—to win games.

GIANTS

How did the Giants get their start?

California's second-most successful team after the Oakland Athletics, the Giants go back all the way to New York's Polo Grounds in 1883. They were originally named the Gothams, but they moved to San Francisco in 1958 and became the Giants. The team moved into Seals Stadium at first and then, in 1960, to Candlestick Park, which became a storied and favorite ballpark for decades. They left the aging park in 1999 and now play at AT&T Park.

What was their record like in New York?

They had a great record, winning league pennants in 1888, 1889, 1904, 1905, 1911, 1912, 1913, 1917, 1921, 1922, 1923, 1924, 1933, 1936, 1937, 1951, and 1954 and World Series titles in 1905, 1921, 1922, 1933, and 1954.

What famous concert occurred at Candlestick Park?

The Beatles performed their last public concert at Candlestick Park on August 29, 1966. Much later, on August 14, 2014, former Beatle Paul McCartney performed there as a farewell to the park, which was torn down the next year.

Who is the famous Hall of Famer who helped the Giants get to the 1962 World Series?

One of the all-time greats, center fielder Willie Mays (1931–), was on the Giants roster from 1951 to 1972, except for 1952, when he spent a year in the army. Twelve times a Golden Glove Award winner and two dozen times an All Star, Mays was Rookie of the Year

Willie Mays still has many admirers today. In 2009, President Barack Obama (left) took Mays aboard Air Force One.

and National League MVP in 1954 and 1965; he would hit .302 and have 660 home runs (the fifth highest of all time as of this writing). His 600th homer was hit in 1970, while he was still with the Giants, but it was during a season they would finish in third place.

Mays led the team in several offensive categories and helped them tie with the Dodgers for the season. They beat them in the National League playoffs and then met the Yankees at the World Series, taking it to seven games but losing in the end.

How long before they won a pennant in their new home?

Not long at all. They won the National League championship in 1962 by beating the downstate rival Dodgers 2–1.

Besides Willie Mays, who were some other standout players during the 1960s and early 1970s?

The Giants had a great pitcher named Juan Marichal (1937–), who had come to America from the Dominican Republic and would play for San Francisco from 1960 to 1973. In many ways on a par with Dodgers star Sandy Koufax, "the Dominican Dandy," as he was called, often had seasons with twenty or more wins and was the only pitcher besides Koufax to have more than one twenty-five-win season. Although he would play his last two years with the Red Sox and then the Dodgers, most of his career was in San Francisco, and he racked up 2,303 strikeouts with an ERA of 2.89. A Hall of Famer, his number 27 was retired by the Giants in 1975.

Another great player of the era was first baseman Willie McCovey (1938–), who had 521 homers during his Hall of Fame career, most of which (1959–1973) was with the Giants. McCovey had many memorable moments and successes, including hitting .357 in 1959 (Rookie of the Year), being a National League home run leader in 1963, 1968, and 1969, and 1969 National League MVP. Despite all of this, many remember him as the batter who almost but not quite hit the winning run in the Game 7 of the 1962 World Series. The score was 1–0 with the Yankees ahead. Willie Mays was on base in the ninth inning, and McCovey hit a hard line drive. Everyone, even the Yankees players, thought that was the end and the Giants would win, but Yankee Bobby Richardson (1935–) stopped the ball, and the Yankees emerged triumphant.

Juan "the Dominican Dandy" Marichal was one of the greatest pitchers of his day and was sometimes compared to Sandy Koufax.

Cy Young Award winner Mike McCormick (1938–; Giants 1956–1962, 1967– 1970), was also key for his pitching. Although he was a solid pitcher, his time with the Giants would not see the team win a pennant.

How close did San Francisco come to losing the Giants?

In 1975 the Giants were nearly bankrupt, so owner Horace Stoneham tried to sell the team to the Labatt Brewing Company and move the Giants to Toronto, where the Labatt group was based. San Francisco's Mayor George Moscone tried to keep them and got a judge to issue an injunction to stop the sale. The next year, minority owner Bob Lurie managed to buy the Giants for $8 million, while Toronto got an expansion team, the Blue Jays.

What was "The Year of the Fox"?

The year 1971, with manager Charlie Fox (1921–2004) in charge, was given that name because it was really a fun year for Giants fans as they watched Fox manage a team of talented young and experienced older players. They went all the way to the National League playoffs but lost to the Pirates.

How did they do during the rest of the 1970s?

While Willie McCovey continued to deliver for his team, smacking his 500th homer in 1978, the Giants went nowhere during the lackluster decade.

> ## Dominican players made another significant contribution to the Giants. What was that?
>
> In 1963 the Giants sported the first all-brother outfield with the Dominican trio of Felipe Alou (1935–) and his brothers, Jesus (1942–) and Matty (1938–). Because they played for the Giants during different years, though, 1963 was the only season they were all together on the same team.

What racial line was snapped in 1981 by the Giants?

That was the year that Frank Robinson (1935–) became the first African American to manage a National League baseball team. During a twenty-year playing career (1956–1976), Robinson had 586 home runs and nearly three thousand hits. As a manager for the Giants (1981–1984) he had less success, with 1984 being a disappointing 66–96 season.

Who brought the Giants around in the 1980s?

The Giants had some miserable years in the early part of the decade, including their worst ever, 1985, when they had an abysmal record of 62–100. But manager Roger Craig (1930–) joined the team in 1986 and turned that around the first year with an 83–79 record, and then in 1987 they won the Western Division and went to the National League payoffs, where they faced the Cardinals. The Giants gave the St. Louis team a run for their money, but the last two games were played on Cardinals turf, and they lost in Game 7. Even though he was on the losing side, Giants left fielder Jeffrey Leonard (1955–) was named MVP. Given that he had four homers, five RBIs, ten hits, and a .417 batting average during the seven-game series, it was a no-brainer to give him the award.

After a troubled 1988 season in which many players had injuries, the Giants came stomping back like, well, giants in 1989 and took it to the National League pennant series against the Cubs 3–1. First baseman Will Clark (1964–) was MVP. Moving on to the World Series, they played the Oakland A's (see above), losing after four games. Even though the Giants didn't go all the way, it was their first time back since 1962, and that represents a triumph overall.

What happened next that was positive for the Giants?

After a few off years post-World Series, a new spark came to the team in the form of left fielder Barry Bonds (1964–), who left the Pirates for the Giants in 1993 and stayed until 2007. With a batting average of .298, he would chalk up numerous awards, including three Hank Aarons (2001, 2002, 2004), eight Golden Gloves, twelve Silver Sluggers, and a partridge in a pear tree—well, too many others to run through here. But despite being a great player who helped the Giants win a National League pennant in 2002, he would be gone before the team would go to the World Series in 2010.

Another big help was Manager Dusty Baker (1949–). Well known for his years as a Dodger, Baker coached the Giants from 1993 to 2002. Named manager of the year his rookie season, as well as in 1997 and 2000, he rebuilt the team all the way to an NL pennant win.

And how has the twenty-first century been working for the Giants?

Great! The team moved to their new park (Pacific Bell Park, now AT&T Park) in 2000, Barry Bonds hit his 500th homer in 2001, and, as mentioned above, they won the NL pennant in 2002. Attendance was strong at the new park, even when the team wasn't winning. Felipe Alou (see above) returned to his team as manager from 2003–2006 and had a strong 2003, but the next couple years saw a drought in playoff appearances.

There is a statue of Willie Mays near the entrance to the Giants' AT&T Park.

Bruce Bochy (1955–) took on the manager role in 2007, and under his leadership brought about the new dynasty. Bochy hired pitcher Tim Lincecum (1984–), who would take the Cy Young Award in 2008 and 2009. In 2009, they had some other great pitchers, including Matt Cain (1984–), Jonáthan Sanchez (1982–), and future Hall of Famer Randy Johnson (1963–), who spent his last year with the Giants. With the acquisition of first baseman and catcher Buster Posey (1987–), the team was getting set up for an amazing few years.

Are the Giants the dynasty to beat in the 2010s?

With World Series wins in 2010, 2012, and 2014, it certainly has looked that way so far. It's interesting that after a win, the Giants would take a step back for a year before coming back again for another World Series. Below is a summary of how it has panned out.

Year	Series	Opposition	W–L Results
2010	NLDS	Atlanta Braves	3–1
	NLCS	Philadelphia Phillies	4–2
	WS	Texas Rangers	4–1
2012	NLDS	Cincinnati Reds	3–2
	NLCS	St. Louis Cardinals	4–3
	WS	Detroit Tigers	4–0
2014	NLDS	Washington Nationals	3–1

Why did the National League make a rule change in 1997 concerning the playoffs?

The Giants were having a strong year and were just a couple games from the National League Division Series win but had to face the Florida Marlins at home in the first two games of the series, losing both. The league changed the rules after that so that top-seeded teams would not play the first two games away.

Year	Series	Opposition	W-L Results
	NLCS	St. Louis Cardinals	4–1
	WS	Kansas City Royals	4–3

NLDS = National League Division Series; NLCS = National League Championship Series; WS = World Series

Who were the World Series MVPs for those years?

Shortstop Édgar Rentería (1975–) was MVP for 2010, in 2012 it was third baseman Pablo Sandoval (1986–), and in 2014 it was pitcher Madison Bumgarner (1989–).

PADRES

How far back does Padres history go?

Besides the Angels, the San Diego Padres are the only other pro baseball team to have always been in California. They started off as a minor league team in the Pacific Coast League in 1936, and their claim to fame was that they had a very young Ted Williams (1918–2002) on the roster (see the chapter "California Notables").

When did they join the majors?

The Padres were one of four expansion teams in 1969 and are in the National League's West Division.

Where do they play ball?

After playing for many years at Qualcomm Stadium (originally San Diego Stadium), the Padres moved to Petco Park in San Diego's Mission Valley in 2004.

What were the '70s like for the Padres?

Pretty uninspiring. San Diegans weren't too inspired, either, and attendance was pretty low until 1974, when McDonald's owner Ray Kroc (1902–1984) bought the team and had new uniforms made. For some reason, this caused attendance to go up about seventy-five percent. The Padres had their first winning season in 1978, but it was followed by more losing seasons.

Did the team start digging out of a hole by the 1980s?

There was some improvement, yes. In 1980, the team had three leading base stealers in Jerry Mumphrey (1952–), Ozzie Smith (1954–), and Gene Richards (1953–). Then, in 1983, the Padres acquired Steve Garvey (1948–) from the Dodgers, and the next year, with additional help from veteran third baseman Graig Nettles (1944–) and right fielder Tony Gwynn (1960–2014), they won the West Division title for the first time and, beating the Chicago Cubs, the National League pennant. But when they faced off with the Detroit Tigers for the World Series, they were outmatched and lost by Game 5.

What was the big trade in 1991?

The Padres obtained shortstop Tony Fernandez (1962–) and first baseman Fred McGriff (1963–) from the Toronto Blue Jays in exchange for second baseman Roberto Alomar (1968–) and outfielder Joe Carter (1960–) in what is considered one of the biggest pro ball trades of the last few decades. Interestingly, McGriff was traded away just two years later.

How did the Padres turn things around in the late 1990s?

As the 1990s progressed, it seemed like the only thing keeping the Padres from being a complete failure as a team was the ray of sunshine they enjoyed from Tony Gwynn. Then, in 1995, they traded for slugger third baseman Ken Caminiti (1963–2004) and outfielder Steve Finley (1965–), who would be on the Padres roll call for the next three years. Caminiti and Finley (along with Gwynn, of course) helped lead the team to division titles in 1996 and 1998.

Did the Padres have a great 1998?

They had a splendid 1998 with lots to celebrate. Relief pitcher Trevor Hoffman (1967–) tied the National League record with fifty-three saves in fifty-four games pitched, and left

---

Who was known as "Mr. Padre"?

A native of Los Angeles, Tony Gwynn Sr. (1960–2014) spent his entire professional career with the Padres (1982–2001). During those years, he was on fifteen All-Star teams, won five Golden Gloves and seven Silver Sluggers, and was the National League batting champion eight times. Gwynn won the Roberto Clemente Award in 1999, and his number 19 jersey was retired by the Padres.

fielder Greg Vaughn (1965–) had fifty home runs, a Padres record. They sprinted into the National League Championship Series, beating the Atlanta Braves for the pennant, and it was off to the World Series to face the Yankees. Even with Gwynn batting .500, though, the Yankees were just too immensely talented and swept the series.

And how has the twenty-first century treated the Padres so far?

Once again, there were some sour seasons at first. Even in 2005, when they got to first place in their division, they only had an 82–80 record (their competitors were all weak that year). They won the West Division that year and also in 2006.

FOOTBALL

49ERS

What was the All-American Football Conference?

The AAFC was a football league that competed with the National Football League from 1946 to 1949. The San Francisco 49ers joined the AAFC after being rejected by the NFL, debuting at Kezar Stadium in 1946. The team had increasingly better performances over the next couple years, climaxing in 1949 with a championship bid against the Cleveland Browns, which they lost 21–7.

How did the 49ers fare in the 1950s?

With the folding of the AAFC, the 49ers managed to be one of three teams to move to the NFL. They had a rough first year (a 3–9 record) but bounced back the next season (7–4–1). One of their stars was fullback Joe Perry (1927–2011), who was the NFL's rushing champion in 1953 and 1954 with over a thousand yards each year (he was NFL MVP in 1954) and played with the 49ers until 1960.

The 49ers would have a couple of winning seasons in the late 1950s but were not stellar performers at the time. They did, however, make the NFC Championship in 1957,

Which player was a particularly interesting hire for the 49ers in 1947?

When the team selected running back Wally Yonamine to play for it, the Raiders became the first professional American football team to have an Asian American on its roster. He only played one season, however, as Yonamine, who was born in Hawaii, was really more of a baseball player and spent most of his career playing with Japanese teams.

losing to the Detroit Lions in a heartbreak in which they had been ahead before allowing three unanswered touchdowns in the fourth quarter.

What other heartbreak occurred for the team in 1957?

While watching his team play the Chicago Bears on October 27, owner Tony Morabito collapsed and died of a heart attack on the field. The players learned of the sudden loss at halftime and rallied from being behind 7 to 17 to making two touchdowns to beat the Bears.

Who came up with the "Alley-Oop Pass"?

Quarterback Y. A. Tittle (1926–) and wide receiver R. C. Owens (1934–2012) first developed the pass in 1957 for the 49ers. Named after the comic strip character by V. T. Hamlin, the pass was a strategy of throwing the ball high above the head of the receiver in the end zone with the intention that the receiver would have to jump high to catch it.

Trading card for Y. A. Tittle, the 49ers quarterback who developed the Alley-Oop Pass with receiver R. C. Owens.

Who created the "shotgun formation"?

Another innovation in the game that came from the 49ers was the shotgun formation developed by Coach Howard Wayne "Red" Hickey (1917–2006) in 1960. Traditionally up until then, the quarterback always stood immediately behind the center to receive the snap. In the shotgun, he stands five or seven yards back to get a longer snap, usually in preparation for a pass. While this formation offers more maneuverability for the offensive linemen and can help them protect against a blitz, it also usually gives away the plan to pass rather than run.

Who was the leading man in the late 1960s and early '70s?

Quarterback John Brodie (1935–) played with the 49ers from 1957 to 1973. Born in Menlo Park, the California native, who played for Stanford and is in the College Football Hall of Fame, had good and bad seasons as a pro player. He did lead his team into their first really successful NFL seasons, though, winning the NFC West in 1970, 1971, and 1972 to make the playoffs for the first time since 1957.

The arrival of which two people marked a new era for the 49ers?

Undoubtedly, the 1979 addition of quarterback star Joe Montana (1956–) was the beginning of the team's halcyon days. Bill Walsh (1931–2007), a Los Angeles native, was hired away from the Stanford University team that year, too, to become head coach, and the two of them together packed a one-two punch against all opponents through much of the 1980s.

What's Joe Montana's record like?

One of the greatest quarterbacks to play the game, Joe Montana (1956–) was on the team from 1979 to 1992 and led the 49ers

Quarterback Joe Montana (shown here in 2010) was the heart and soul of the 49ers in the 1980s.

to four Super Bowl championships: XVI (1982), XIX (1985), XXIII (1989), and XXIV (1990). He was MVP for all of those games, except for Super Bowl XXIII, when it was wide receiver Jerry Rice. Montana's list of honors is too long to go into here, but among them are being the NFL passing touchdowns leader (1982, 1987), NFL MVP (1989, 1990), Offensive Player of the Year (1989), *Sporting News* Sportsman of the Year (1989), *Sports Illustrated* Sportsman of the Year (1990), and eight times on the Pro Bowl team. After recovering from a spinal disc injury, he was also named *Pro Football Weekly*'s NFL Comeback Player of the Year. Montana was inducted into the Pro Football Hall of Fame in 2000. When he retired in 1995 after a year with the Chiefs during which he took them to their first AFC Championship, the quarterback had thrown over 3,400 completed passes for 40,551 yards and 273 touchdowns. The 49ers retired his jersey (#16) in 1993.

How about Bill Walsh's record?

Walsh coached the Niners from 1979 to 1988. He had an overall record of 102–63–1, was an NFL Coach of the Year twice (1981, 1984), won three Super Bowls—XVI (1982), XIX (1985), and XXIII (1989)—and was inducted into the Pro Football Hall of Fame in 1993.

Who were the players who became stars when Montana left?

Quarterback Steve Young (1961–), who had been sharing the spotlight with Montana, took the steering wheel for the team; linebacker Ken Norton Jr. (1966–) and cornerback Deion Sanders Sr. (1967–) were the standouts and helped take the team to Super Bowl XXIX in 1995. They defeated the San Diego Chargers 49–26.

Who was the first NFL football player to win three consecutive Super Bowl rings?

Ken Norton Jr. will always have this to be proud of about his career. He was in the Super Bowl XXVII and XXVIII Championship Dallas Cowboys teams in 1993 and 1994 and the

Super Bowl XXIX 49ers team. Later, as coach of the Seattle Seahawks, he would get his fourth ring at 2014's Super Bowl XLVIII against the Denver Broncos.

How has the team done since their last Super Bowl win?

As of this writing (early 2016), the team has won five AFC titles (1995, 1997, 2002, 2011, 2012) and has made nine playoff appearances. There were some highlights, such as Steve Young passing for over four thousand yards in 1998, and new quarterback Jeff Garcia (1970–) beating that in 2000 with 4,278 passing yards, but the 49ers still struggled, especially when Jerry Rice left after the 2000–2001 season because of a salary cap.

Jim Harbaugh coached the 49ers for four seasons.

The team had losing records from 2003 to 2010, then they got a light of hope the next year.

Who changed the 49ers' luck when he joined the team in 2011?

Coach Jim Harbaugh (1963–), who had been a pro ball player and had coached both college and pro teams, was hired in 2011 to turn the team around. Under his leadership, they had records of 13–3 (2011), 11–4 (2012), and 12–4 (2013), each year making the playoffs. When the next year ended with a mediocre 8–8 record, Harbaugh and the owners agreed to part ways. He was hired as head coach of the University of Michigan Wolverines in 2015.

When did the 49ers move into their new stadium?

They moved to the newly constructed Levi's Stadium in Santa Clara in 2014.

RAIDERS

How did the Raiders get their start?

Originally, they were going to be a Minnesota team as part of the American Football League, but they couldn't get a deal there and landed in Oakland, playing their first season in 1960 with a 6–8 record at Kezar Stadium in San Francisco. They played another season at Candlestick Park before moving to their Oakland home in 1962 at Frank Youell Field, where they played until 1965. After the NFL and AFL began to merge, the Raiders moved into their new Oakland Alameda County Coliseum.

When did they first reach a Super Bowl?

The Raiders faced off against the Green Bay Packers in Super Bowl II in 1968, losing to the cheeseheads in 33–14.

What was their record like in the late '60s and early '70s?

The team did very well those years, winning AFL Division West championships in 1967, 1968, and 1969, then AFC West championships in 1970, 1972, 1973, 1974, 1975, and 1976. They won the 1967 AFL Championship and Super Bowl XI in 1977, beating the Minnesota Vikings 32–14.

Who was the MVP of Super Bowl XI?

A College Football Hall of Famer (Florida State Seminoles) and (at the time) future Pro Football Hall of Famer, wide receiver Fred Biletnikoff (1943–) gained seventy-nine yards and set up three touchdowns for his team.

Did they win any other Super Bowls?

Yes, the next few years were Oakland's time in the sun. They won Super Bowls XV (1980) and XVIII (1983), defeating the Philadelphia Eagles 27–10 and then Washington Redskins in a 38–9 blowout. Quarterback Jim Plunkett (1947–) was MVP in Super Bowl XV, while running back Marcus Allen (1960–) got the nod in the Redskins game. Allen ran 191 yards and scored two touchdowns.

What famous football announcer once coached the Raiders?

John Madden led the team from 1969 to 1978 (he had been a linebacker coach previously), taking the team to a Super Bowl and several division championships. After leaving the job, he became a familiar face on television, working as a color commentator for ABC, NBC, CBS, and Fox until finally retiring in 2008. His announcing style and enthusiasm were popular with fans, and there is even a football video game series named after him.

The Raiders have a record now of bouncing back and forth between cities. What years did they play where?

The Raiders were in Oakland from 1960 to 1981, Los Angeles from 1982 to 1994, and

Running back Marcus Allen was a key player for the 49ers, including being MVP of Super Bowl XVIII.

Why did the Raiders' logoed apparel become hip to wear in American pop culture?

Jackets, hats, shirts, and other clothing in black and silver with the pirate logo of the Raiders has been popular with African American youth and others into hip hop and rap since the 1990s, when artists and groups such as N.W.A., Dr. Dre, and Eazy-E started wearing it in their videos. The Raiders, being based in Oakland, became associated with the rougher, ghetto neighborhoods of the city; of course, the pirate image also appealed to the rebellious sensibilities of those into gangsta rap.

then back in Oakland. In 2015 the team tried to negotiate a return to Los Angeles again, but they lost that bid to the Rams.

Why did the team play in Los Angeles from 1982 to 1994?

As is often the case, the dispute about a stadium led to the move. Owner Al Davis (1929–2011) wanted luxury boxes and other additions made to the Oakland Coliseum, but the city refused to pay for it. Davis petitioned the NFL in 1980 to allow him to move the team, but he was voted down. Los Angeles, in the meantime, wanted the Raiders because the Rams had left. Davis and the Los Angeles Memorial Coliseum teamed up to file antitrust lawsuits, eventually winning their case.

How well did the Raiders perform in L.A.?

As noted above, they won the Super Bowl in 1983, and they would win the AFC West in 1985 and 1990. It would be fair to say the star of the early 1980s was probably running back Marcus Allen (1960–), who was named NFL MVP and Offensive Player of the Year in 1985.

Why did Marcus Allen spend so much time on the bench in the late 1980s?

In 1986 injuries troubled Allen, and then things got ugly with owner and general manager Al Davis, who claimed Allen was faking being hurt because of a contract dispute. The controversial result was that Davis kept Allen on the bench through 1989. Many felt this was the reason the Raiders underperformed. In 1990, Allen was back full time on the field, and the Raiders had a 12–4 record. He was then back on the bench, and in 1992 Allen became a free agent and signed with the Kansas City Chiefs.

Why did the Raiders go back to Oakland?

The city agreed to overhaul the Oakland Alameda County Coliseum. After a somewhat disappointing stay in L.A., the Raiders seemed glad to return to their old stomping grounds in 1995.

What are some highlights of the years since the team returned to Oakland?

The Raiders won the AFC West in 2000, 2001, and 2002, as well as the AFC championship in 2002, but they have struggled a lot in recent years. There has been a revolving door of coaches (nine since 1995), and even getting some outstanding players such as wide receiver Jerry Rice (1962–) and the promising-but-underperforming quarterback JaMarcus Russell (1985–) didn't result in any runs toward the Super Bowl. When owner Al Davis died in 2011, it was a dent in their morale. Davis's son Mark took over, however, and spurred the Raiders to an emotional win against the Houston Texans the day after Al Davis died.

With their stadium falling into disrepair, the Raiders have once again been looking to move, although it won't be to Los Angeles, as the Rams won the bid to go back to their former home.

Who were some other great Raiders players?

There have been many, including Fred Biletnikoff (see above), but some of the standouts include:

- Gene Upshaw (1945–2008): played center, guard, and tackle for the Raiders from 1967 to 1981. One of the best line anchors in the game, he was on the Super Bowl II and XV teams. He was inducted into the Pro Football Hall of Fame in 1987.
- Willie Brown (1940–): was on the team from 1967 to 1978 as a cornerback. Helped clinch Super Bowl XI by intercepting the ball near the end of the game; Hall of Famer in 1984.
- Ken Stabler (1945–2015): quarterback of the winning Super Bowl XI team, he was inducted into the Pro Football Hall of Fame posthumously in 2016. He was with the Raiders from 1970 to 1979.
- Jim Plunkett (1947–): the team's anchor in Super Bowls and was on the team from 1978 to 1986; he is a Heisman Trophy winner (1970) and in the College Football Hall of Fame.
- Art Shell (1946–): one of the best tackles of his generation. Raiders player from 1968 to 1982, he also was an offensive line coach (1983–1989) and head coach (1989–1994); he was inducted into the Hall of Fame in 1989.
- Howie Long (1960–): a powerful defenseman from 1981 to 1993, he was inducted into the Pro Football Hall of Fame in 2000.
- Ray Guy (1949–): one of the best punters in NFL history, he played for the Raiders from 1973 to 1986 and made the Hall of Fame in 2014.

RAMS

In what city were the Rams originally based?

The Rams played in Cleveland, Ohio, from 1936 to 1945, the year they won the NFL Championship. It was quite a coup, then, for Los Angeles to get such a strong team moving to the West Coast.

How well did the team perform those first years in Los Angeles?

They did very well their first half dozen or so years. They won NFL Western Championships in 1945, 1949, 1950, 1951, and 1955 and another NFL National Championship in 1951.

Who were the "Fearsome Foursome"?

After things slowed down for the Rams in the late 1950s and early 1960s, a new ray of hope came in the shape of four defensive linemen: Rosey Grier (1932–), Deacon Jones (1938–2013), Merlin Olsen (1940–2010), and Lamar Lundy (1935–2007). With this big defense and the coaching of George Allen (1918–1990), the Rams were once again in the running for a title. But although they won the 1967 and 1969 Coastal Division and went to the playoffs, the Rams couldn't go all the way, losing the Western Conference to the Green Bay Packers in 1967 and to the Minnesota Vikings in 1969.

Defensive End Deacon Jones was one of four players who constituted the "Fearsome Foursome," including Merlin Olsen, Lamar Lundy, and Rosey Grier.

What bold move did the Rams make that was a win for civil rights?

The Rams hired wide receiver Woody Strode (1914–1994) and halfback Kenny Washington (1918–1971) to play on the team in 1946. They were the first African Americans to play in the NFL since the league officially banned black players in 1932. It's worth noting here that both Washington and Strode were more than football players. Washington, who had been a star at UCLA, was also a war hero and helped free the Jews from Auschwitz during World War II. Strode also served in World War II, was a decathlete, and was an actor in later life who was nominated for a Golden Globe for his supporting role in *Spartacus*.

Which team proved to be quite the nemesis for the Rams in the 1970s?

The Dallas Cowboys under legendary coach Tom Landry (1924–2000) frustrated the Rams in the division playoffs in 1973 and in the NFC Championship game of 1975.

Who was one of the most notable players of the 1970s and early 1980s?

Former Rams Defensive End Jack Youngblood (1950–) is a Hall of Famer who has won almost more honors than one can count, including All-Rookie (1971), three times a Rams MVP (1975, 1976, and 1979), Defensive Lineman of the Year (1975–), and a Rams Ring of Fame.

Did the Rams ever make it to the Super Bowl while they were in Los Angeles?

Yes, they first went to Super Bowl XIV in 1979, where they went head to head with the mighty Pittsburgh Steelers under another quarterback legend, Terry Bradshaw (1948–), who had taken his Steelers there for the fourth time. It was an exciting game, and the Rams were ahead 19–17 in the fourth quarter before Bradshaw led two touchdown drives to win the game.

How did the team fare in the 1980s?

After moving from the Coliseum to Anaheim Stadium in 1980, the Rams had solid performances in the 1980s, making the playoffs in 1980, 1983–1986, 1988, and

Defensive End Jack Youngblood played for the Rams from 1971 to 1984.

1989. Running back Eric Dickerson (1960–) was with the team until 1987 and pulled off record performances, such as rushing over two thousand yards in 1987.

Why did the Rams leave Los Angeles?

The early 1990s saw game attendance decline, and the team was noticeably absent from any of the playoffs or championships. The team owners approached the NFL and got approval to move to St. Louis in 1995.

How did Los Angeles get an NFL team again?

Pretty much by promising the Rams a new, shiny stadium in Inglewood. They, along with the Chargers and Raiders, were all eyeing L.A., but it was the Rams who will be returning for the 2016–2017 season after twenty years in St. Louis. The other two teams were promised $100 million each toward new stadiums in their current cities. The new stadium will have a seating capacity of 70,000 with the ability to hold another 30,000 for standing-room-only crowds.

CHARGERS

How did the Chargers get their start?

The team was in the American Football League from 1960 to 1969. Their first season was spent at the L.A. Coliseum, then in 1961 they moved to Balboa Stadium in San Diego's Balboa Park, and in 1967 they moved once more—to San Diego Stadium (now Qualcomm Stadium). The team did well in the AFL, going to the playoffs five of those first

301

ten years under the guidance of Coach Sid Gillman (1911–2003). They won the 1963 championship against the Boston Patriots.

Did the Chargers do well once they were in the NFL?

They struggled in the 1970s after the AFL–NFL merger. They spent almost all of the decade trying to find their footing in the league.

Who turned it around for the team?

The credit for that goes to Coach Don Coryell (1924–2010), who led the charge from 1978 to 1986. He also made good use of quarterback Dan Fouts (1951–; Chargers, 1973–1987). Coryell loved the passing game so much that his nickname became "Air Coryell"; Fouts was well used and had a career record of 43,040 passing yards and 254 touchdowns, all with the Chargers. The result was the team winning their AFC West division from 1979 to 1982, though they didn't manage the playoffs.

Did the Chargers ever make it to the Super Bowl?

Yes, with a lot of work and the leadership of Coach Bobby Ross (1936–; Chargers, 1992–1996) after three losing seasons with Coach Dan Henning (1942–; Chargers, 1989–1991) they turned it around with help from quarterback Stan Humphries (1965–), who joined the team in 1992 and stayed for five years. They had an 11–5 record in 1992, followed by a mediocre 1993, but then rejuvenated and had another 11–5 season in 1994, the year Ross was named NFL Coach of the Year. They had the bad luck, however, of facing Joe Montana's still-hot 49ers and lost Super Bowl XXIX 26–49.

What two tragedies struck San Diego the years after the Super Bowl?

In a sad turn of events, the team lost two players to accidents in 1995 and 1996. Linebacker David Griggs (1967–1995) died on a freeway near Fort Lauderdale, Florida, when

---

Who was the 1980s Chargers star with a nickname that sounds like a toy train?

Lionel "Little Train" James (1962–) was a running back for San Diego from 1984 to 1988. At a mere 5' 6" and 171 pounds, he was small, but speedy, and popular with both teammates and fans. In 1985 he set an NFL record with 2,535 all-purpose yards and also a record for receiving yards (1,027). His 1988 performance was not quite as stellar (he was made a punt returner, which was not his forte), and then Coach Dan Henning surprised everyone by cutting James from the team the next year (the suspicion was it was a financial move because the team owners felt James's $300,000 salary was too much). James never returned to the game as a player, coaching at Auburn University and then as a running back coach for the Chiefs.

his car went out of control and hit a sign pole. The next year, running back Rodney Culver (1969–1996) and his wife died when ValuJet Flight 592 crashed into the Everglades shortly after taking off from Miami on May 11.

What the heck happened to the Chargers in 2000?

The team imploded, really, and had its worst season ever with a 1–15 record. Quarterback Ryan Leaf (1976–) was let go after throwing numerous interceptions. Amazingly, Coach Mike Riley (1953–) was allowed one more season (5–11) before he, too, was fired.

How well have the Chargers performed so far in the twenty-first century?

For the most part they performed mediocrely, although they did have some good

Known as the winningest coach never to make it to the Super Bowl, Marty Schottenheimer coached the Chargers from 2002 to 2006.

seasons under Coach Marty Schottenheimer (1943–) with a 12–4 season in 2004 (losing in the Western Conference game) and a 14–2 season in 2006 (losing the division title to the Patriots). Schottenheimer has the dubious distinction of being the winningest NFL coach to never make it to the Super Bowl.

The team also did pretty well under Coach Norv Turner (1952–) with strong seasons in 2007 (11–5) and 2009 (13–3), but, again, they couldn't take it all the way.

A big reason for the successes the Chargers have had since 2004 has been quarterback Philip Rivers (1981–). Rivers, who is still with the Chargers as of this time (2016), is a first-round draft choice out of North Carolina State. His first season as a starter was 2006, when the Chargers had their 14–2 season. He was NFL Passer Rating Leader in 2008 (105.5), Passing Yards Leader in 2010 (4,710), Completion Percentage Leader in 2013, and AFC Passing Yards Leader in 2015 (4,870).

BASKETBALL

LAKERS

Where do the Lakers play?

They find their home at Los Angeles's Staples Center, which they moved into in 2000.

Who were the powerhouse players in the 1960s?

The two future Hall of Fame stars on the team in the 1960s were forward Elgin Baylor (1934–) and guard Jerry West (1938–). Both players would spend their entire careers with the Lakers, with Baylor joining the team back in Minneapolis in 1959, retiring in 1971, and West coming to town in L.A. and staying until 1974. West had over 25,000 points in his career and a points-per-game average of 27. Baylor also had over 23,000 points and a PPA of 27.4.

Which team became the Lakers' big rival, starting in the 1960s?

That would be the Boston Celtics, of course. Actually, the rivalry began back when the Lakers were still in the land of lakes. They first faced Boston in the 1959 NBA championship, losing to them 4–0, and since then they have met the Celtics in the finals more than any other NBA team. The rivalry in the championships continued as follows:

Year	Winner	Win-Loss
1959	Celtics	4–0
1962	Celtics	4–3
1963	Celtics	4–2
1965	Celtics	4–1
1966	Celtics	4–3
1968	Celtics	4–2
1969	Celtics	4–3
1984	Celtics	4–3
1985	Lakers	4–2
1987	Lakers	4–2
2008	Celtics	4–2
2010	Lakers	4–3

Who was Jack Kent Cooke?

Canadian entrepreneur Jack Kent Cooke (1912–1997) was involved in newspaper and magazine publishing, as well as owning radio stations. After succeeding in these ventures, he began buying sports teams, including the Washington Redskins, the Los Angeles Kings, the Los Angeles Wolves (a soccer team in the United Soccer Association),

---

Why is a basketball team based in dry L.A. called the "Lakers"?

Because they were originally based in Minnesota, the "Land of 10,000 Lakes." They were Minneapolis's team from 1947 to 1960. While in the north, they won five championships (1949, 1950, 1952, 1953, 1954).

and the Los Angeles Lakers. Cooke had a flair for managing these teams, hiring coaches and talented executives who helped their teams to win championships.

Cooke bought the Lakers in 1965 and had the good sense not to let his ego get in the way of an already talented team, keeping the leadership and roster about the same. In 1967 Cooke built the Lakers a new stadium, the Forum, to replace their home at the L.A. Memorial Sports Museum.

One of the greatest hoopsters of his generation, Wilt Chamberlain (at right during a 1971 game) was a Laker from 1968 to 1973.

Toward the end of the West–Baylor dynasty, what player joined the Lakers as a new star on the court?

A former Harlem Globetrotter who then played for the Warriors and 76ers, center Wilt "The Stilt" Chamberlain (1936–1999) will always be one of the most memorable Lakers. They got him in a trade in 1968. From then until he retired in 1973, the Lakers won every conference title except in 1971, when they lost to the Milwaukee Bucks, led by Lew Alcindor (Kareem Abdul-Jabbar).

What led the Lakers to their first NBA championship since moving to Los Angeles?

Although Baylor retired the year before because of chronic knee problems, Wilt Chamberlain, along with guards Jerry West and Gail Goodrich (1943–) and forwards Harold "Happy" Hairston (1942–2001) and Jim McMillan (1948–), were an unbeatable combination. In the 1971–1972 season, they won thirty-three games in a row. That is a winning streak that has never been matched by any other American professional sports team. They finished the season with an NBA best of 69–13.

After sweeping the Chicago Bulls for the division title, they took out the previous champion Milwaukee Bucks 4–2. For the finals, the Lakers faced the New York Knicks, taking them out in five games.

Who were the next big stars to enter the fold?

With Jerry West retiring after a dispute with owner Jack Cooke, the Lakers needed some new muscle and traded for former rival Kareem Abdul-Jabbar (1947–) of the Milwaukee Bucks in 1975. It was a brilliant trade, and Kareem—who has too many honors to list here—would be a Lakers center until his 1989 retirement. At that time, he was the NBA leader in points scored (38,387), rebounds (9,394), and blocked shots (3,189), as well as other records.

305

Next, they acquired Earvin "Magic" Johnson (1959–) in 1979 as a point guard right out of college (Michigan State University). Magic would be a Laker for his entire professional career. He retired in 1991 after learning he had HIV but would return to his team briefly to coach in 1994 and even played in 1996 before leaving for good. He would finish his career with 17,707 points (19.5 PPG), 10,141 assists, and 6,559 rebounds.

How well did the Lakers perform in the 1980s?

Incredibly well. They won championships in 1980 (against the Philadelphia 76ers), 1982 (76ers), 1985 (Celtics), 1987 (Celtics), and 1988 (Detroit Pistons).

The incredibly talented Kareem Abdul-Jabbar was on five Lakers NBA Championship teams, plus one championship team with the Milwaukee Bucks.

What was "Showtime" basketball?

This was the name given to the run-and-gun style of play that characterized the Lakers' strategy during the 1980s, when they won five championships and were led by Magic Johnson and Kareem Abdul-Jabbar. Run-and-gun is a kind of fast and loose style of play that relies on fast breaks and increased field goal attempts. Many fans enjoy this more active, less conservative play strategy.

Besides Abdul-Jabbar and Magic Johnson, who was another outstanding player during this era in Lakers history?

One has to at least mention James Worthy (1961–), another Laker who managed to spend his career in Los Angeles (1982–1994). Playing small forward, "Big Game James" was an asset in the clutch. He scored 16,320 points over the course of his career and 4,708 rebounds.

Which Lakers coaches have earned Coach of the Year honors?

Bill Sharman (1926–2013) was the first in 1972, followed by Pat Riley (1945–) in 1990 and Del Harris (1937–) in 1995.

When did the next round of successes occur for the Lakers?

While the 1990s weren't bad years for the team (they won the Pacific Division in 1990 and the Western Conference in 1991 [losing the finals to Chicago]), the next reboot came with the twenty-first century. The team brought on guard Kobe Bryant (1978–)

and center Shaquille O'Neal (1972–) in 1996. Bryant is considered by many to be one of the best shooting guards in the game's history (just behind Chicago's Michael Jordan), and "Shaq" dominated the game by his sheer size—standing at 7'1" tall and weighing 325 pounds (147 kilograms). Once the ball was in Shaq's immense hand, if he was anywhere near the net, he just had to drop it in. By 2000 they got into the groove as a team and won the NBA finals in 2000, 2001, and 2002.

Whom did the Lakers beat, and who was MVP in their 2000–2002 run of the finals?

The Lakers' record for the finals those years was as follows:

Year	Opposing Team	Win–Loss	MVP
2000	Indiana Pacers	4–2	Shaquille O'Neal
2001	Philadelphia 76ers	4–1	Shaquille O'Neal
2002	New Jersey Nets	4–0	Shaquille O'Neal

What beloved announcer passed away shortly after the Lakers' 2002 championship win?

Chick Hearn (1916–2002) was a broadcaster who did play-by-play for the Lakers from 1961 to 2002. A legend in his field, he was credited with inventing such terms as "air ball," "slam dunk," and "no harm, no foul" that are in common use today. He was the recipient of the 1991 Gowdy Award, and he was inducted into the American Sportscaster Hall of Fame in 1995 and the National Sportscasters and Sportswriters Association Hall of Fame in 1997. He passed away on August 5 after a fall caused a severe head injury.

Did Shaq's departure in 2004 have a bad effect on the team?

Shaq was traded to the Miami Heat that year and, yes, 2004 to 2007 were largely rebuilding years for the team, although they still had Bryant as a valuable asset. With Shaq gone, Bryant was the *de facto* lead scorer and would be named MVP when his team won the 2009 and 2010 NBA championships.

Shaquille O'Neal's sheer size made him practically unstoppable on the court.

Which Laker once played a genie in a movie?

Shaquille O'Neal might be a great basketball star, but his attempts at acting have not been so highly praised. He played a five-thousand-year-old genie in the family musical comedy *Kazaam* (1996) that was a complete flop in the box office. He's continued to play with movie parts over the years, including appearances on TV series and other movies. He was the voice of Smooth Smurf in *The Smurfs 2* (2013) and also voiced himself in *The Lego Movie* (2014).

Which teams did the Lakers beat in 2009 and 2010?

They defeated the Orlando Magic 4–1 in 2009 and their Boston rivals in 2010.

Who looks like he could be the next Lakers star?

The team drafted guard D'Angelo Russell (1996–) from Ohio State University in the first round of the 2015 NBA draft. An All-American, Russell was the Big Ten Freshman of the Year. The Lakers have high hopes for him.

What was Kobe Bryant's record when he retired in 2016?

Bryant retired that year with a record of 33,643 points (25 PPG average), 7,047 rebounds, and 6,306 assists. He had been on five NBA championship teams (2000, 2001, 2002, 2009, 2010), eighteen All-Star teams, and was the Lakers' all-time leading scorer. He also was on two Olympic gold-medal teams (2008 and 2012). No doubt, he will be in the Hall of Fame.

CLIPPERS

Where has this team played in the past?

The Clippers began in 1970 as the Buffalo Braves. They moved to California in 1978 but initially played in San Diego before moving to Los Angeles for the 1984 season. Today, they share the Staples Center with the Lakers.

Why the name "Clippers"?

Well, it's not because the athletes enjoy clipping coupons. When the Braves moved to San Diego, the city pushed for a name change, so they became the Clippers, which refers to the type of large sailing ships that once frequented the harbor city.

Do they have any big wins to their credit?

As of the end of the 2015–2016 season, no, they don't. The Clippers have not won an NBA championship or even a division title (they are in the Western Conference, Pacific Divi-

---

Are there any WNBA teams in California?

Yes, the Sparks play in Los Angeles, where they play at the Staples Center. There was also the Monarchs, based in Sacramento's ARCO Arena, but that team folded in 2009. The Monarchs won the WNBA championship in 2005, and the Sparks won championships in 2001 and 2002 in a league that has only been around since 1996; they also won a conference title in 2003. They have appeared in the playoffs fifteen times as of 2015.

---

sion). They have, however, finished as Pacific Division champions in 2013 and 2014. In 2016, they were taken down in the first round of the Western Conference playoffs against the Portland Trail Blazers.

Who was their biggest star to date?

That would probably be Bill Walton (1952–), who played for them in San Diego and Los Angeles from 1979 to 1985 before playing the last two years of his career with the Celtics (he played for the Portland Trail Blazers from 1974 to 1978). Although a talented player, he spent much of his time with the Clippers on the injured list because of foot injuries, and many of his honors (including NBA MVP) would come before and after he was on the team.

What was the "Clippers Triangle"?

The Clippers' first years have been very difficult. A big part of the problem was that they were plagued with player injuries. For example, they were hopeful when they acquired Danny Manning (1966–; played with the team 1988–1994), who led the University of Kansas to a national title, but he got a knee injury his first year. Ron Harper (1964–; with the Clippers 1989–1994) similarly went down with a knee injury in 1989. These and other injuries became so symptomatic of the team that sports journalists dubbed it the "Clipper Triangle," after the Bermuda Triangle where ships and planes have disappeared mysteriously—a suitable play on words, given that the team name refers to a ship.

When did they start turning things around?

Things began improving for the Clippers by the early and mid-1990s. They made playoff appearances in 1992, 1993, and 1997. Ron Harper and Danny Manning had regained their health and were raring to go; they also had a good coach in Larry Brown (1940–), although he'd only be with the Clippers in the 1991–1992 and 1992–1993 seasons. They were knocked out of their chances of advancing in 1992 by the Utah Jazz and in 1993 by the Houston Rockets. There was also a brief bit of sunshine in 1997, when the team made the playoffs with the help of Loy Vaught (1967–; Clippers, 1990–1998).

There wasn't much good news in the early 2000s for the Clippers, was there?

No, they had repeated losing seasons from 2000 to 2005.

Who showed up to play in the 2005–2006 season?

Elton Brand (1979–), who had joined the team in 2001, but it really wasn't until this year that he became a star player to help lead the Clippers to the first playoffs in nine years. They enjoyed an exciting play-off game, with Brand repeatedly swoosh-ing the ball through the hoop for over thirty points a game, but they fell to the Phoenix Sun in Game 6.

Power Forward Blake Griffin has raised the Clippers' hopes for success since he joined the team in 2009.

How did they get to their run of wins in the 2010s?

After the 2006 playoffs, the Clippers lagged behind for a while because of injuries and losing some key players. Two key players would really make the difference in the 2010s, however: Chris Paul (1985–; Clippers, 2011–) and Blake Griffin (1989–; Clippers, 2009–). These two talents became the heart of the team, which made the playoffs each year from 2012 to 2016.

Where did the nickname "Lob City" come from?

During a media conference, Griffin offhandedly said that it would be "lob city" on the court with him and Paul there, tossing alley-oops and making slam dunks.

Who was the Clippers' controversial owner until 2014?

Real estate developer Donald Sterling (1934–) bought the team in 1981. Three years later, he moved them from San Diego to Los Angeles without the NBA's approval and was subsequently fined $25 million; he countersued for $100 million but dropped his suit when the NBA agreed to reduce his fine to $6 million.

Sterling remained a controversial figure; his coaching staff passed through revolving doors, being replaced frequently, and the owner was accused of not paying staff and players on time. The continuing upset with the organization had a noticeable effect on the Clippers, who repeatedly had dismal years, often ranking last and sometimes being called the worst professional sport franchise in America.

It all came to a head in April 2014, when a recording of Sterling talking with his girl-friend was released. In it, he makes a number of racial remarks, including a request that she

---

Were the Clippers the poor stepchild of the Staples Center?

After playing at the L.A. Sports Arena and Anaheim's Arrowhead Pond, the Clippers got to move to the new Staples Center in 1999. Problem was, they had to share it with the Lakers and the Kings (the hockey team, not the basketball team), and when it came to scheduling, the Clippers were always stuck with whatever days the other two teams didn't want, sometimes having a double header with one or the other. This was because the other teams had better game and attendance records (the Clippers had ended the 1998–1999 season, which had been shortened by a lockout, at 9–41).

---

not bring her black friends to his ball games. Everyone from the black Clippers players to the NAACP to President Barack Obama condemned Sterling, and on April 29 NBA commissioner Adam Silver banned Sterling for life from having anything to do with the NBA.

Did they win the Pacific Division in the 2010s?

Yes, in addition to regularly making the playoffs, the Clippers won their division in 2013 and 2014. The 2012–2013 was a strong one for the team and included a seventeen-game winning streak that was the longest in franchise history. They were stopped from heading to the Western Conference title by the Memphis Grizzlies, however.

The 2013–2014 season had the Clippers still playing strong, but the controversy with Donald Sterling (see above), which occurred in the first round of the playoffs against the Warriors, was extremely upsetting to the players, many of whom protested and demanded NBA action against the owner. Moving on, the Clippers faced the Warriors in the first round, going through to Game 7, which ended in a shootout and, finally, a Clippers division victory. They advanced to the conference finals against the Oklahoma City Thunder. It was another rough contest, and in Game 5 a controversial call went against the Clippers when officials said an out-of-bounds play was the result of the ball bouncing off a Clippers player. After the game, video showed it actually hit a Thunder player, but the game had already been called 105 to 104 for the Thunder. The series went to Game 6, and even though they were on home turf, the Clippers would lose 104–98.

What interesting NBA "first" happened in 2015?

When guard Austin Rivers (1992–) was added to the team that was coached by Doc Rivers (1961–), it was the first time in NBA history that a father coached his son in the league.

KINGS

Were the Kings an expansion team for the West?

No, the Kings' history goes back to 1923, when they were the Rochester Seagrams, making them the oldest continually operating professional basketball team in the United

States. They morphed into the Rochester Eber Seagrams (1942–1943), the Rochester Pros (1943–1945), and the Rochester Royals (1945–1957). It was as the Royals that they became part of the NBA. In 1957 they moved to Cincinnati, and in 1972 they made another change, becoming the Kansas City–Omaha Kings and then, in 1975, just the Kansas City Kings. Finally, in 1985, they moved to Sacramento, where they currently play at Sleep Train Arena.

Have they won any titles since moving to Sacramento?

The Kings won Pacific Division titles in 2002 and 2003, and they won the 2002 Western Conference, but have not advanced any further than that as of this writing (2016).

Who are some notable players who were on the Kings' roster?

Hall of Famers who played for the Kings include center Ralph Sampson (1960–; Kings, 1989–1990), guard Mitch Richmond (1965–; Kings, 1991–1998), and forward Sarunas Marciulionis (1964–; Kings, 1995–1996, and also see Warriors below).

The 1990s are often thought of as "the Mitch Richmond Era." What happened of note during that decade?

Other than making the 1996 playoffs, it was a very lackluster time for the Kings, who had losing records every season that decade, with the exception of the 1995–1996 and 1998–1999 seasons. Richmond did well, averaging over twenty points a game, and he was on the NBA All-Star team six times (All-Star MVP in 1995) during his Kings years (he later was on the 2002 championship Lakers team), but the Kings weren't well rounded enough to make a mark that decade, even with the future Hall of Famer.

So, the Kings' heyday was in the early 2000s, yes?

Yes. They were in the playoffs every year from 1999 to 2006 and, as mentioned above, division champs in 2002 and 2003.

What do those years have in common that might explain the success?

Three words answer that question: Coach Rick Adelman (1946–). Adelman, who coached the Warriors two years previously, led the Kings from 1999 to 2006, exactly the same years the team found its greatest success, which can't be a coincidence.

Shooting Guard Mitch Richmond would play for three California teams during his NBA career: the Warriors (1988–1991), the Kings (1991–1998), and the Lakers (2001–2002). He also played for the Wizards.

What happened to promising rookie Ricky Berry?

Ricky Berry (1964–1989) was a top draft pick from San Jose State when he joined the Kings in 1988. He had an amazing rookie season, especially with his three-point shots (over forty percent). During the 1989 break, however, he was discovered dead in his home. He had committed suicide after a fight with his wife.

Why are the 2002 Western Conference Finals considered a great series?

The 2002 Western Conference Finals against the L.A. Lakers is still considered one of the most exciting playoff series in NBA history. Games went back and forth, and it was 2–2 before the Kings led the series 3–2. Then came the controversial Game 6, which had so many fouls called that people questioned whether it was fixed after the Lakers tied up the series. In fact, referee Tim Donaghy (1967–) would, years later, tell the media that the NBA instructed officials to make sure the series went to seven games so they would make more money. Therefore, more fouls were called against the Kings to make sure the Lakers would tie. Game 7 was played on the Kings' home turf. What a battle! The lead changed nineteen times, and the game went into overtime, but the Lakers pulled ahead 112–106 in the end.

How about the 2003 playoffs?

Injuries were once again a problem for the 2002–2003 season, but they still won the Pacific Division with a 59–23 record. They then moved on to defeat the Utah Jazz in the first round, leading them to a face-off with the Dallas Mavericks. Injuries proved too much for them, however, and even though they went the full seven games, they lost to Dallas in the end. Point guard Bobby Jackson (1973–) was named NBA Sixth Man of the Year because of his contributions when coming off the bench.

And how about after Coach Adelman left?

Since Adelman's contract expired in 2006, life for the Kings has been one of decline and then efforts to rebuild. Sometimes, it has been downright ugly, such as the 2008–2009 season, when their record was 17–65, or when Coach Eric Musselman (1964; coach 2006–2007) got arrested for a DUI, or when Ron Artest (1979–) got accused of domestic assault. The Kings have suffered losing seasons since 2007.

Who the heck is Metta World Peace?

Ron Artest changed his name to Metta World Peace legally in 2011. Metta is a word meaning "kindness" or "friendliness" toward all that is used in the Buddhist lexicon. World Peace, which is his full surname now, is simply meant as a name trying to inspire the world to come together.

GOLDEN STATE WARRIORS

Have the Warriors always been in Oakland?

No, like many sports teams, they have moved around. They were originally the Philadelphia Warriors from 1946 to 1962, and then the San Francisco Warriors from 1962 to 1971. At that point, they decided to change their name to remake themselves as the basketball team for *all* of California, becoming the Golden State Warriors in 1971. For purposes of this book about California, we will cover the San Francisco and Oakland years.

Where do the Warriors play today?

They play their home games at Oracle Arena in Oakland.

Which famous Lakers star played earlier for the Warriors?

Wilt Chamberlain (1936–1999) played for the Warriors from 1959 to 1965 (see "Lakers" above).

How did the Warriors end up in San Francisco?

The team was purchased by television and radio producer Franklin Mieuli (1920–2010), who lived in the Bay Area and naturally wanted the team near him. Mieuli was the principal owner of the team from 1962 to 1986.

How did the Warriors do in their first years in San Francisco?

The 1960s were very up-and-down years for the team. Not surprisingly, the 1962–1963 season was a rough debut as they got adjusted to their new location, finishing with a

Oracle Arena in Oakland is the home of the Warriors.

31–49 record. But the next season was quite a turnaround. With the leadership of Wilt Chamberlain and help from other talents such as NBA All-Rookie team member Nate Thurmond (1941–), they won the Western Division against the St. Louis Hawks but lost to the Celtics in the 1964 finals.

The Warriors traded away Chamberlain in January 1965 and suffered the consequences with a dismal 17–63 record in the 1964–1965 season. They brought in Rookie of the Year Rick Barry (1944–), who would later be named one of the "50 Greatest Players" in history by the NBA. Barry would leave the team in 1967 but returned to play with them from 1972 to 1978. With Barry, the team got all the way to the 1967 finals, defeating the Lakers in the Western Conference and the Hawks for the Division title before falling to the Philadelphia 76ers in six games.

With Barry's departure to the ABA's Oakland Oaks, the Warriors leaned on Thurmond, and he delivered. He had a great season and took the Warriors to the Western finals, beating the Hawks again. But they couldn't get past the Lakers in the 1968 Division title. They finished off the decade by losing to the Lakers in the 1969 Western Division championship. Thurmond's injuries the next year led to a losing record in the 1969–1970 season, and they were bumped out of the playoffs early by the Milwaukee Bucks.

Did moving across the bay in 1972 bring about change for the Golden State Warriors?

Not the move so much as probably the fact that Rick Barry was back on the team, renewing their hopes for the playoffs. They did well in the 1973 playoffs, beating the Bucks for the Western title before losing to the Lakers, which now had Wilt Chamberlain. The next year was uninspiring, but the 1974–1975 season would be great!

How did the Warriors win in 1975?

Two words: Rick Barry. The Warriors traded away Nathan Thurmond, and Cazzie Russell, a solid player since 1972, joined the Lakers, which left Barry as the undisputed star and leader of the team. While the Warriors had a good season under Coach Al Attles (1936–) and made the finals, they weren't the favorite to go all the way. Attles' style was to work his players as a team, with everyone playing a

Rick Barry, shown here in a 1976 game, was the star of the Warriors during much of the 1970s.

role. This actually suited Barry, who had become a much more diverse player during his ABA years and assisting in shots as much as making them himself. They walked all over the Seattle Supersonics for the Western title, then trounced the Chicago Bulls to face the Washington Bullets (now the Wizards) in the NBA Finals. The Wizards were the heavy favorite, but in one of the NBA's biggest upsets in history, they won 4–0, and Barry was named MVP.

What are some stats and facts of note about Rick Barry's career?

At the end of his career, he ended up sixth in all-time scoring in the NBA and ABA with 25,279 total points (18,395 in the NBA); he was tenth in career steals (1,104) and had a .900 free-throw percentage, which was the best in NBA history (interestingly, Barry was a rarity in that he took his free-throw shots with an underhand toss). Inducted into the NBA Hall of Fame (1987) and College Basketball Hall of Fame (2006), he went from 1966 Rookie of the Year to having his number 24 jersey retired by the Warriors.

Did the Warriors become a dynasty after the 1975 Finals?

They did well the next year, winning their Division before falling to the Phoenix Suns in the Western Finals in 1976. After that, there was a long quiescent period as experienced players left the team over the next couple years, including Barry in 1978. For years, they couldn't manage to turn it around, but that began to change by the mid-1980s. Coach George Karl (1951–) brought a bit of energy to the team during his 1986 to 1988 stay, and a 1987 Western Finals game against the Lakers and Wilt Chamberlain is still remembered by many fans, but they continued to struggle.

Why did Rick Barry end up in court three times during his career?

The first legal action came when he left the Warriors for the ABA's Oaks in 1967 and was sued over breach of contract, and he ended up not playing the entire 1967–1968 season (he worked as a broadcaster for the Oaks that year). The next year, however, legalities were put aside, and he played for the Oaks and led them to the 1969 ABA Championship title. The next season, the Oaks decided to move the team to Washington, D.C., which Barry didn't like, so he tried to go back to San Francisco and was again sued, forcing him back east. When his team wanted to move again (this time to Virginia), he left for the New York Nets. Finally, the courts decided again to bring Barry's case to litigation, and he was forced to return to the Golden State Warriors in 1972, which actually turned out to be a good move for him and marked a more stable time in his career. His time with the ABA completed a trio of achievements seen by no other basketball player in that Barry would be a leading scorer in the NCAA, the NBA, and the ABA.

What was "Sleepy" Floyd's role in the classic Lakers–Warriors 1987 Semifinals game?

A point guard for the Warriors from 1983 to 1987, Eric Augustus "Sleepy" Floyd (1960–) added some much-needed spark to the team, including scoring fifty-one points against the Lakers to win a game in the semifinals. It was the one rough spot in a Lakers drive to the championship that year.

So, when did things really start to turn around for the team?

The "Sleepy Floyd game" gave the Warriors a boost, and with the help of new coach Don Nelson (1940–; coaching from 1988 to 1995), point guard Tim Hardaway (1966–) and guard Mitch Richmond (1965–), and the continued talents of Chris Mullin (1963–) as small forward/shooting guard (the three players were fondly nicknamed "Run TMC"), the late-1980s through much of the 1990s were good years but not championship years. Injuries plagued many of the players, and they just couldn't get their fortunes together to make a solid playoff run.

What are some awesome stats for the "Run TMC" guys?

Well, all three were on U.S. Olympic gold basketball teams (Richmond in 1996, Mullin in 1984 and 1992, and Hardaway in 2000). Hardaway would finish his career with 15,143 points and 7,095 assists. Richmond had 20,497 points with 3,801 rebounds and 3,398 assists; he finished his career with the Lakers and retired after they won the 2002 championships, and he was inducted into the Hall of Fame. Mullin, also a Hall of Famer, had 17,911 points, 4,034 rebounds, and 3,450 assists; he also won gold at the 1983 Pan-American Games.

Did 1997 mark a new era?

It was a fresh start in many ways. The Golden State Warriors got a new arena, new uniforms and logo, and a series of new coaches over the next few years.

What was the Sprewell choking incident?

Latrell Sprewell (1970–) played for the Warriors from 1992 to 1998. He had already had serious violent confrontations in 1993 and 1995 with teammates (once threatening to bring a gun into an argument), but in 1997 he actually choked Coach P. J. Carlesimo (1949–) for almost ten seconds before people were able to pull him off. The team suspended him, then voided his contract, and the NBA banned him for a year of play. During his suspension, Sprewell was charged with reckless driving that injured two people, as well, for which he spent three months under house arrest. But Sprewell took his case with the Warriors and NBA to court, getting his contract put back in place and the NBA suspension reduced to sixty-eight games.

How did the Warriors do in the new century?

It was a long, hard road for many years. The 2000–2001 season was dismal with a 17–65 ending that was the team's worst ever. By the 2006–2007 season, they held the infamous NBA record of most years (twelve) for a team to have not appeared in the playoffs. Don Curry, who had coached the team from 1988 to 1995, returned in 2006 for another four years to revive the spark some. That year, the Warriors had what fans called the "We Believe" season, and they made the playoffs, finally. Sadly, they lost to the Jazz, but the point was that they were back as contenders.

Stephen Curry, who was drafted as a Warrior in 2009, has become a fan favorite who has teamed up with Klay Thompson to form the "Splash Brothers."

Who are the "Splash Brothers"?

Even more game changing for the Warriors than Coach Curry, however, was the addition of point guard Stephen Curry (1988–) in 2009. Together with shooting guard Klay Thompson (1990–), they formed the "Splash Brothers." Separately or together, these two have proved themselves nearly unstoppable. Curry set NBA records in 2013, 2015, and 2016 for three-pointers (272, 286, and 402 points respectively), and when Thompson is added to the mix, you get a record 525 combined three-pointer points in 2014 and 678 in by the end of the 2015–2016 regular season's play. That year, Curry joined the 50-40-90 Club, which means he scored fifty percent of the time in field goals, forty percent for three-point shots, and ninety percent from the free-throw line for the regular season.

How did the Warriors achieve their greatest victories in 2015 and 2016?

After a rather contentious 2014, during which there seemed to be a lot of infighting with the coaching staff, the Warriors lost the first round of the playoffs against the Clippers (see above). The next year's playoffs were a different story, however. Curry, the first Warrior to be NBA MVP since Wilt Chamberlain in 1960, led his team in the 2014–2015 playoffs. They would cause the New Orleans Pelicans to flounder in round one, hunt down the Memphis Grizzlies in round two, and steal the fuel from the Houston Rockets to win the Western Conference. In their first NBA Finals since 1975, the Warriors were up against the Cleveland Cavaliers.

LeBron James was the man to worry about on the opponents' side, but the Warriors were heavy favorites and had a more well-rounded team. The first two games went into overtime, with each team winning one. The Warriors lost Game 3 in Cleveland, and then Coach Steve Kerr (1965–) put guard Andre Iguodala (1984–) in the starting lineup. It

---

What record set by the Chicago Bulls did the Warriors break in 2016?

The 1995–1996 Bulls had the most wins in a season with seventy-two, which the Warriors surpassed with seventy-three in the 2015–2016 season, which also gave them the highest NBA winning percentage: 89%. That year they also broke the Bulls' record for most home games won (forty-four). The San Antonio Spurs, interestingly, also broke that record in 2016, but they had forty-eight wins to the Warriors' fifty-four.

---

was the right move, with Iguodala scoring twenty-two points to help even the series. Curry sunk a total of thirty-seven points through the hoop to put away Game 5. Back in Cleveland for Game 6, it was the Curry and Iguodala show, as each of them scored twenty-five for the championship. Iguodala was named the MVP.

How far did they get in 2016?

The Warriors won the Western Conference Finals 96–88 against the Oklahoma City Thunder to face the Cleveland Cavaliers. Up 3–1 in the finals, it looked like the Warriors would win it all, but the Cavs made an amazing comeback, winning the next three games to take the NBA championship.

HOCKEY

When did professional hockey come to the Golden State?

The first National Hockey League (NHL) team to come to California was the Los Angeles Kings. The Kings were one of six new teams added to the league in 1967 as part of what was called "the great expansion" when the NHL added the West Division.

What NHL hockey team that was part of the expansion in 1967 no longer exists?

Initially part of the World Hockey League when they were the San Francisco Seals, the California Seals were only around as part of the NHL from 1967 to 1976, when they moved to Cleveland and became the Cleveland Barons before merging with the Minnesota North Stars in 1978.

KINGS

Where is the Kings' home stadium?

The Kings played at the Forum in Inglewood from their founding in 1967 to 1999. That year, the Staples Center opened, and the Kings moved there.

How many Stanley Cups have the Kings earned?

The Kings have won two Cups, as of this writing, in 2012 and 2014. They were also Western Conference champions those years, of course, as well as in 1993.

What major trade benefited the Kings in 1975?

The Kings got Marcel Dionne (1951–) that year and quickly proved to be an asset playing center for the "Triple Crown Line" with Charlie Simmer (1954–) and Dave Taylor (1955–). Dionne scored fifty or more goals in six out of twelve seasons with the Kings.

Which respected 1970s player for the Kings later also coached the team?

Bob Pulford (1936–) initially played for the Toronto Maple Leafs before joining the Kings in 1970, where he was captain. Retiring from active play in 1972, he coached the Kings from then to 1977 and was credited with making them one of the finest defensive units and serious playoff contenders. Pulford won the Jack Adams Award in 1975 and led the Kings to their first playoff appearance in five years in 1974. He was, however, never able to lead the Kings past the second round of the playoffs. After five years with the Kings, he moved on and became coach and general manager of the Chicago Blackhawks. He was eventually promoted to senior vice president and took over the general manager duties again for three stints: 1992–1997, 1999–2000, and 2003–2005. He was inducted into the Hall of Fame in 1991.

What was the "Miracle on Manchester"?

Playing in a best-of-five postseason game against the Edmonton Oilers on April 10, 1982, the Kings stunned the Canadian team, which had had a very strong season. The Oilers were ahead 5–0 in the second period when the Kings made a surprise comeback in the final period, scoring five goals to tie it up. The game went into overtime, and the L.A. players made the final goal to take the game 6–5. The win lifted their spirits, and they ended up winning the series against Edmonton. (Manchester refers to the road where the Forum is located.)

How did the Kings manage to steal Wayne Gretzky from the Oilers?

Kings owner Bruce McNall (1950–) decided to give the aging Marcel Dionne to the New York Rangers in 1987, but the trade meant the team now lacked a major star. McNall therefore put his sights on future Hall of Famer Gretzky (1961–). The deal was to give the Oilers Jimmy Carson and Martin Gelinas, plus $15 million *and* the Kings' first-round picks in 1989, 1991, and 1993. In addition to Gretzky, the Kings also got Mike Krushelnyski and Marty McSorley. One of the most stunning deals in NHL history, fans of the sport simply call it "The Trade," while Edmonton fans wept.

Who was another great addition to the Kings lineup in the 1980s?

Luc Robitaille (1966–) was also a rock star for the Kings, which he joined as part of the 1984 NHL draft, and he played for the Kings through the 1993–1994 season. After playing junior hockey for three seasons, he jumped onto the ice roaring, scoring forty-five goals in the 1986–1987 season and averaging over forty goals for the next six seasons. In the 1992–1993 season, he had sixty-three goals. He was traded to the Penguins the next year.

What was "the McSorley Blunder"?

Kind of stinks to have a gaffe named after you, but that's what happened to Mary Mc-Sorley (1963–) in Game 2 of the 1993 Stanley Cup Finals against the Montréal Canadiens. The Kings were ahead 2–1 in the third period and looked close to leading the series 2–0 when McSorley was called for having an illegal stick (Canadiens coach Jacques Demers noticed it). This resulted in a penalty and a loss of one player for the Kings. Coach Demers pulled his goalie to outmatch the Kings 6–4 on the ice, and this helped Eric Desjardins score a goal on L.A.'s net. Montréal then scored again in overtime and tied up the series. The change in momentum would continue through the finals, and Montréal won the Cup that year.

Left Wing Luc Robitaille started his career with the Kings, giving them a needed boost. He would go on to win a Stanley Cup with the Detroit Red Wings.

How well did the Kings do in the early 2010s?

After making their mark on the league in 2012 by capturing the franchise's first-ever Stanley Cup, the Los Angeles Kings solidified their respected presence in the league by taking home their second Stanley Cup in three years in 2014. Although a tight series in which four games were decided by one goal—three of which were decided in overtime—the Kings, led by all-star goaltender Jonathan Quick, were able to defeat the New York Rangers in five games. Defensemen Alec Martinez put home a rebound off Rangers goalie Henrik Lundqvist 14:43 into the second overtime in front of his home crowd at the Staples Center.

Ducks

Why did the Anaheim team start off being called the Mighty Ducks?

Perhaps the truest hockey team to the fantasy side of La-La Land is the Ducks (formerly the Mighty Ducks) who got their name by virtue of being owned by Disney Corp., which had put out a movie by that name (continuing the apparent fascination with that particular bird species). Excitement in Los Angeles over hockey had grown with the arrival of Wayne Gretzky on the Kings' team, and so the hope was that the metropolis would have enough fans for two teams.

The Mighty Ducks played, naturally, at Arrowhead Pond, beginning with the 1993–1994 season, and although they lost the opening game to the Detroit Red Wings, for an expansion team they didn't do too badly, winning nineteen games on the road and beating the New York Rangers (that year's Cup champions) twice.

Who were the first stars of the Ducks team?

The standout players for the Ducks in the early years were Paul Kariya (1974–) and Teemu Selánne (1970–). Kariya had come from Canada, and Selánne was "The Finnish Flash"; both were wingers. Kariya would lead the team to Cup contention in the 1995–1996 season, and the next year they made the second round of the playoffs. Injury and a contract dispute made Kariya less of a factor in the 1997–1998 season, and for the next couple of years, the Detroit Red Wings were so dominant that it seemed to suck the energy out of other teams. Selánne was traded to New Jersey in 2001 after years of solid performances, often scoring over fifty goals a season.

When did Anaheim first make the Stanley Cup playoffs?

They made it to the playoffs in 2003, and a big reason for the success was goalie Jean-Sébastien Giguère (1977–), who had joined the team in 2000. Giguère had an outstanding 2002–2003 season and would win the Con Smythe Trophy that year for Playoffs MVP, although his team lost to the Devils in Game 7, barely being edged out of a Cup. Kariya left the team the next season, joining the Colorado Avalanche.

Have the Ducks ever won the Stanley Cup?

Yes, and it helped that Selánne returned to the team in 2006. The Ducks had gotten Sergei Fedorov (from the Detroit Red Wings) after Kariya had left, but Fedorov, who had helped the Wings win Cups, was in his waning years and not a great help. The team also added future Hall of Fame defenseman Chris Pronger (1974–), and the rebuilt team played under Captain Scott Niedermyer (1973–), who is also in the Hall of Fame. Together, they won the 2007 series 4–1, with Game 5 going into double overtime on their home ice.

When did the "Mighty" get dropped from the Mighty Ducks?

They dropped the Mighty in 2006 just before winning their first Cup.

Why were the years 2012 to 2015 both very successful and incredibly frustrating for the Ducks?

In the 2012–2013, 2013–2014, and 2014–2015 seasons, the Ducks won first place in their division but lost in the playoffs. In 2013 they lost the quarterfinals to the Red Wings in seven games, then they lost in the semifinals to the Kings in seven games, and they made the finals with the Chicago Blackhawks but also lost in seven games. While not quite raising the Cup over their heads, the Ducks' performance in the 2010s still makes them one of the best teams in the NHL in recent years.

SHARKS

What team replaced the California Golden Seals?

As you guessed by looking at the header above the question, it was the San Jose Sharks filling that gap for the Bay Area. The former owner of the Seals, George Gund III (1937–2013), wanted to move the North Stars to the Bay Area, but the NHL wouldn't let him. Instead, they granted him license to own an expansion team that became the Sharks. Now based at the SAP Center, they actually began their run in 1991 at the Cow Palace (originally a livestock pavilion) in Daly City near San Francisco. They moved to the San Jose Arena in 1993 (now the SAP Center).

When did the Sharks start picking up some speed?

Most new teams start off slowly before getting their footing in the NHL ranks, and that was true of the Sharks, as well. But in the 1993–1994 season, they did remarkably well. They faced the Detroit Red Wings in the first round of the playoffs and upset them in Game 7 to proceed to round two. Here, however, they were faced down by the Toronto Maple Leafs.

They did well the next year, too, making the second around again until Detroit got its revenge and took down the Sharks in four games.

Who were the goalies who gave the Sharks a boost in the 2000s?

One strategy Head Coach Darryl Sutter (1958–) tried during his years with the Sharks was to fortify the front of the net. First he tried with former Detroit Red Wings Con Smythe winner Mike Vernon (1963–) in 1997, and when that didn't pay off, he brought in Evgeni Nabokov (1975–), who is considered one of the top ten goalies to have ever defended the net. But even the Calder Trophy winner could not lead the Sharks to a Cup; he left the team in 2010.

Have the Sharks ever won a Stanley Cup?

As of this writing, no, they haven't. They won their Pacific Division championships, however, in 2002, 2004, 2008, 2009, 2010, and 2011, as well as the President's Trophy (team with most points) in 2009.

Then, in the 2015–2016 season, they got very close. They won the Western Conference by defeating St. Louis 4–2, which took them to the Stanley Cup Finals against the Pittsburgh Penguins. They took it to six games, but in the end the Sharks lost 2–4.

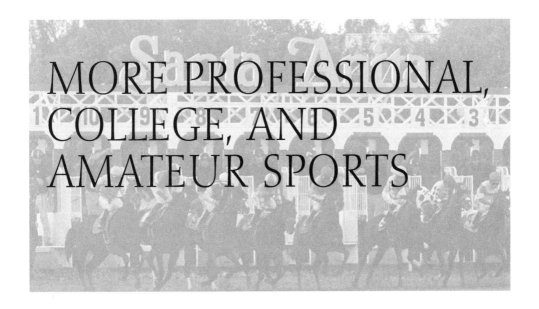

MORE PROFESSIONAL, COLLEGE, AND AMATEUR SPORTS

EARLY CALIFORNIA SPORTS

Before there was professional football, or baseball, or hockey, what kind of sports were being played in California?

Some early sports that made their way to California included tennis and boxing, but when it was still very much a frontier, sports generally involved hunting and fishing. The waters off the coast were rich in fish, one of the most popular of which was bluefin tuna, which would grow to be bigger than most men.

One sad aspect of the popularity of hunting, however, was catching and killing grizzly bears for sport. The *Ursus horribilis* of California could weigh up to 1,200 pounds (544 kilograms) and were considered a threat to farmers and settlers. The Spanish colonists, drawing on their tradition of bullfighting back in Europe, would capture grizzlies and put them in an enclosed area with a bull and then watch the two animals fight to the death. Capturing grizzlies by roping them while on horseback was considered an extremely manly pursuit. To have the bull-bear fights, the bears had to be captured alive, of course. This was not a job for just one man, however manly he might be. Usually, four men on horseback would go after the bear. They would use special, greased lassos after discovering that a bear could grip an ungreased rope and pull a man off a horse to kill him. The Spaniards would rope each paw and then secure the muzzle, then drag it to its fate at the nearest mission or town.

Bull-bear matches were typically scheduled to occur during one of the festivals to celebrate a saint's birthday. Although a healthy bear could often defeat a bull in a ring, the contest was never fair for it. There were plenty of bulls for the Spanish to use, and if the bear killed one or two, more bulls would be brought in until the bear became too exhausted and finally lost.

By the mid-1800s, such battles were deemed uncivilized by a California now in American hands. They fell into disfavor, and the last bull-bear fight on record was in San Diego County in 1880. The end of the bear fights did not mean the grizzly was saved, however. With the Gold Rush and the flood of white settlers, grizzlies were killed right and left by hunters for the supposed safety of the growing population of people. Black bears survived the slaughter, but the California grizzly was doomed. The record shows the last one to be shot was killed in Tulare County in 1922.

How big was sport fishing in nineteenth-century California?

It was pretty darn big, especially when it came to tuna. The Tuna Club on Catalina Island is the oldest sportfishing club in the world (to see more about Catalina Island, go to the "Natural Wonders" chapter and find the section on islands). Some amazing fish were caught by members of the club around the end of the nineteenth century, including a 183-pound (83-kilogram) tuna caught in 1897 and a 251-pound (114-kilogram) tuna snagged by Pasadena fisherman C. P. Morehouse. An even more impressive tuna was reeled in more recently, in 1988, by Jim Bateman of the Tuna Club. His 269-pound (122-kilogram) bluefin was a record in the United States (the largest tuna in the world that has been hauled in weighed 489 pounds [222 kilograms] and was found off the shore of Japan).

Who was the Indigenous athlete who made headlines in 1913 for his running achievement?

Albert Ray, a Pima Indian, made headlines in the April 19, 1913, issue of the *Los Angeles Times* when he won "The Times" Marathon. He ran the 26 miles in 54 minutes, 38.8 seconds, which was 38 seconds faster than the runner-up.

Ray was destined to go to the 1916 Olympics, but fate had other plans. World War I canceled the games; Ray joined the military and was killed in action in 1917.

AUTO RACING

What was so cool about two guys driving a car out of San Francisco in 1903?

It all started with a bet at the University Club of San Francisco, where some of the members were debating the merits of horses versus the newfangled horseless carriages (automobiles). When he was bet $50 that he couldn't successfully drive a car from San Francisco to New York City, former physician Horatio Nelson Jackson (1872–1955; he had quit being a doctor because of a bout with tuberculosis) took that challenge. He purchased a twenty-horsepower Winton touring car, which he nicknamed "Vermont," and hired a young mechanic named Sewall Crocker to accompany him.

They departed San Francisco on May 23, 1903. At the time, there certainly was no paved highway system (only about 150 miles of the 4,500-mile [7,242-kilometer] route they took were paved), or even gas stations, along the way. Jackson took camping equipment and a gun with him and purchased fuel at general stores. In addition to just making it across the nation, Jackson had to do so in ninety days or lose the bet. The car suffered damage from the rough roads, and Jackson had to get parts delivered by stagecoach and hire blacksmiths who served as mechanics, too. A couple times, he had to get horses to pull his car; gas leaks, flat tires, a broken crankshaft, and other problems plagued the intrepid duo. Jackson wasn't alone, either, as a couple other cars were racing him, including drivers in a Packard and one in an Oldsmobile, but the Packard, which was in second place, arrived three weeks after Jackson.

They arrived in Manhattan on July 26, just sixty-three days after leaving the West Coast. Winning the $50 bet was not the point, since the trip ended up costing Jackson $8,000, but it did gain him and Crocker great celebrity. A display recreating the Vermont can be seen at the National Museum of American History in Washington, D.C.

What auto racing courses are located in California?

The table below lists tracks currently available in California for racing events.

Name	Opened	Location	Type
Auto Club Raceway at Pomona	1951	Pomona	Concrete Drag Strip
Auto Club Speedway	1997	Fontana	Road Course
Buttonwillow Raceway Park	1996	Buttonwillow	Road Course
California Speedway	1997	Fontana	Speedway
California State Fairgrounds Race Track	1907	Sacramento	Dirt Oval
Chuckwalla Valley Raceway	2007	Desert Center	Road Course
Irwindale Speedway	1999	Irwindale	Asphalt Oval Track
Mazda Raceway Laguna Seca	1957	Monterey	Road Course
Riverside International Raceway	1957	Riverside	Road Course
Sonoma Raceway	1968	Sonoma	Asphalt Drag Strip and Road Course
Thunderhill Raceway Park	1994	Willows	Road Course
Willow Springs International Motorsports Park	1953	Lancaster	Road Course

Does Santa Monica owe its independence from Los Angeles to car racing?

It would seem so. Back in the early 1900s, when auto racing—and cars, for that matter—were still new ideas, races were held not on tracks but on existing city and country streets. In 1909, Santa Monica decided it could make its mark by holding auto races within the city; if this could bring in enough money, then perhaps they could maintain independence from Los Angeles, which had been busy annexing land all over the area.

Setting up an 8.4-mile (13.5-kilometer) loop through the city (this was considered very short at the time) that would be circled several times, the city created the Santa Monica Road Race, which ran from 1909 to 1919.

In addition to this race, Santa Monica also hosted the Vanderbilt Cup and American Grand Prize races in 1914 and 1916. The strategy of having these races proved successful enough for Santa Monica to maintain its own identity separate from Los Angeles. One race, in 1913, even drew a crowd of one hundred thousand people—which amounted to about twenty percent of the state's population at the time!

What was the importance of the short-lived Los Angeles Motordome?

Although it only existed from 1910 to 1913, the Motordome near Playa del Rey helped spur the sport of racing in California and the nation. Based on velodromes built for bicycle races, the Motordome was a one-mile, circular, wooden track conceived by engineer and Stutz Motor Company president Frederick Moskovics. Automobiles at the time were not owned by many people (they were too expensive until the advent of the Ford's Model T), and racing was seen as a way to promote and sell cars. Early racers were, therefore, quite rich and bore now-familiar surnames such as William K. Vanderbilt II and Louis Chevrolet.

In addition to car races, the Motordome hosted motorcycle races and aircraft shows hosted by the Aero Club of America that were attended by the likes of the Wright Brothers.

Although an August 11, 1913, fire destroyed much of the track, which was never rebuilt, the Motordome inspired other tracks to be built.

Where was the Los Angeles Motor Speedway located?

Despite its name, the Los Angeles Motor Speedway was located at the intersection of Wilshire Boulevard and Rodeo Drive in Beverly Hills. The track was only operated from

A period postcard shows what the Los Angeles Motordome once looked like.

> ## What was Dead Man's Curve?
>
> Not to be confused with another famous *Dead Man's Curve* (see the "Movies, Television, and Entertainment" chapter question about the musical duo Jan and Dean), this was the turn at Wilshire Boulevard and Ocean Avenue that was part of the Santa Monica race. No drivers ever died there; the name was given to the turn to hype the race and generate excitement for the race.

1920 to 1924, pushed aside when the land was considered more useful for other improvements to a quickly growing city.

When did the Ontario Motor Speedway hold races?

On September 6, 1970, the newly completed, $25.5 million track 40 miles east of L.A. held the California 500, emulating the Indy 500 competitions. Despite making a concerted effort to divert some racing dollars its way, the Ontario track never made a profit, and in 1981, it was demolished.

Why did the Altamont Motorsports Park and Ontario Motor Speedway tracks close?

The Altamont Motorsports Park in Tracy had oval and figure-eight tracks; it operated from 1966 to 2008 and hosted the Whelen All-American series; USAC and Grand National championships were hosted at the Ontario Motor Speedway from 1970 to 1980, as well as at Marchands Speedway in Hanford from 1960 to 1980.

Altamont (also the home of a famous concert; see the "The State of California: 1850 to the Present" chapter) closed because the Bay Area track was simply too sun-baked for both drivers and audiences to endure during the season. It had never been an ideal location, and over its history it actually closed six times, but in 2008 it turned off the lights for good.

The Ontario Motor Speedway closed after just ten years because of pressure from land developers to turn it into residential and commercial property for businesses.

Who are a couple of top NASCAR racers from California?

NASCAR is often thought of as being the domain of fans in the southeastern part of the United States, but several accomplished drivers are from the Golden State. Among them is Jimmie Johnson (1975–), who was born in El Cajon. His many wins include the 2006 and 2013 Daytona 500, Spring Cup Series championships in 2006 to 2010 and again in 2013, wins at the Southern 500 in 2004 and 2012, ten Dover International Speedway wins, and Coca-Cola 600 victories from 2003 to 2005.

Another native son is, perhaps, even more recognizable even to non-fans: Jeff Gordon. Gordon was born in Vallejo in 1971. Among his many victories are Daytona 500s in 1997, 1999, and 2005; Southern 500s in 1995–1998, 2002, and 2007; Brickyard 400s in 1994, 1998, 2001, 2004, and 2014; and he won the Winston Cup Series in 1995, 1997, 1998, and 2001.

One might also note that Casey Mears (1978–), the son of legend Rick Mears (not a California native), was born in Bakersfield, but he hasn't quite achieved prominent status in NASCAR as yet.

What's unique about Chuckwalla Valley Raceway?

Chuckwalla Valley Raceway is really not a place for the public to view a professional race for the cost of admission. Located in the rather isolated Desert Center in the Colorado Desert, it is a playground for the rich, who purchase memberships for the privilege of using the high-end facilities to drive their expensive racing and collector cars.

One of the heroes of modern auto racing is Jeff Gordon, a Vallejo, California, native.

BOXING

Who was the first boxer of note to come from California?

That would be Solomon "Solly" Garcia Smith (1871–1933). Born in Los Angeles of Irish and Mexican parents, he made a name for himself in 1897 when he defeated champion fighter George Dixon (1870–1908) for the featherweight title. Smith would lose the title the next year to Dave Sullivan but would continue to box until 1902. He spent the remainder of his life working in the family oil business in Culver City.

If Solly Smith won in the featherweight category, was there a first heavyweight champion from the state?

Yes, but, as of this writing, there has only been one heavyweight champion from California: Jim Jeffries (1875–1953). Nicknamed "The Golden State Boilermaker," Jeffries stood 6'2" (1.87 meters) tall and weighed 225 pounds (102 kilograms) and said that his massive arm strength came from building boilers at the Lacy Manufacturing Company; he had also worked in a mine and as a coal shoveler for the trains on the L.A.-to-San Bernardino route. He trained at the Los Angeles Athletic Club and began working his way up the boxing ranks until he was able to challenge Bob Fitzsimmons to the title in 1899. Jeffries knocked him out in the eleventh round at the Brooklyn rink and took the title. He defended his title repeatedly until retiring in 1905.

What classic low blow ended a pro boxing fight in 1912 that historians still talk about?

In a lightweight fight between Joe Rivers (1892–1957) and Ad Wolgast (1888–1955) at the Vernon Arena just south of downtown L.A., Rivers was challenging Wolgast's lightweight title in a twenty-round match on July 4, 1912. After twelve rounds of brutal fisticuffs, the fighters charged at each other in round thirteen, punching each other simultaneously. Rivers punched Wolgast smack in the middle of his torso, but Wolgast's fist landed in Rivers' groin. The challenger went down with an agonizing scream, and many of the 3,600 spectators booed at what they saw as a rules violation; some audience members even stormed the ring when referee Jack Welsh declared Wolgast the victor. Welsh sneaked out of the arena, and his ruling stood. The event, which went down as boxing's only double knockout, was published in an edition of *Ripley's Believe It or Not.*

What underdog win upset the boxing world in 1933?

Jimmy McLarnin (1907–2004) knocked out Young Corbett III (1905–1993) for the world welterweight title on May 29, 1933, at L.A.'s Wrigley Field. It was an unexpected stunner as McLarnin clocked Corbett with a left hook in the first round.

What boxing match in L.A. marked a beginning for Cassius Clay?

After being banned from the ring for two years because he refused to be drafted into the military because he was a conscientious objector (he believed African Americans were treated like second-class citizens), Cassius Clay (1942–2016) entered the ring against former light heavyweight champion Archie Moore (1916–1998) on November 15, 1962, and took him down in Round 4. This would mark the beginning of Clay's (Muhammad Ali's) rise to dominate boxing for years to come.

What 1950s-era boxer was famous mostly for being simply colorful?

Although he never won a title, "Arrogant" Art Aragon (1927–2008) had a solid 90–20–6 record with sixty-two knockouts. Born in New Mexico, he grew up in East Los Angeles, and his boxing career lasted from 1944 to 1960. He was known for having a smart mouth and became the fighter people loved to hate, sometimes because he beat popular fighters like Enrique Bolanos. Aragon didn't mind being hated, though, because he discovered that the more he became the villain in the ring, the more he got paid. His personal life was colorful, too, including four marriages and numerous affairs, including (possibly romantic) friendships with such Hollywood stars as Marilyn Monroe and Jayne Mansfield. After he retired, he was once asked what he missed about boxing. Aragon replied that he hated everything about it, except for "the broads."

GOLF

Why is golf so popular in California?

The answer must be the climate, especially in southern California, and also the fact that the state has some famous courses by designers such as golf legend Arnold Palmer and Jack Nicklaus. There are outstanding courses in places such as Pebble Beach, Pacific Palisades, and La Quinta. The Professional Golfers Association (PGA) holds many tournaments in the Golden State. Amateur golfers flock to the state, as well, to play on public and private courses. This remains true, even with the drought in the 2010s; many of the courses are watered with recycled "gray water" to help conserve this valuable resource.

Which courses are considered the best in the state?

According to a July 30, 2015, article published in *Golf Digest*, the top ten courses in the state are:

1. Cypress Point Club, Pebble Beach
2. Pebble Beach G. Links (above), Pebble Beach
3. Riviera C.C., Pacific Palisades
4. Los Angeles C.C. (North), Los Angeles
5. The Olympic Club (Lake), San Francisco
6. San Francisco G.C., San Francisco
7. Spyglass Hill G. Cse., Pebble Beach
8. Monterey Peninsula C.C. (Shore), Pebble Beach
9. The Quarry at La Quinta, La Quinta
10. The Valley Club of Montecito, Montecito

Only a couple of the above are open to the public, right? How about a list of the top golf courses that the public can play on?

Sure! Here are fifteen outstanding courses recommended by *Golf Digest* for the general golf-loving public:

1. Pebble Beach G. Links (above), Pebble Beach
2. Spyglass Hill G. Cse., Pebble Beach
3. Pasatiempo G.C., Santa Cruz
4. Torrey Pines G. Cse. (South), La Jolla
5. PGA West (TPC Stadium), La Quinta
6. CordeValle G.C., San Martin
7. The Links at Spanish Bay, Pebble Beach
8. Pelican Hill G.C. (Ocean South), Newport Coast
9. Poppy Hills G. Cse., Pebble Beach

> ## What amazing golfing feat occurred at the
> ## Del Valle Country Club in Saugus, California?
>
> On September 2, 1964, amateur golfer Norman Manley made a hole in one on a 330-yard, par-4 hole, then he made a second hole in one on the next hole (another par 4 at 290 yards). The "double albatross," as it's called, is considered the greatest golf feat in history and has not been repeated as of this writing.

10. Pelican Hill G.C. (Ocean North), Newport Coast

11. Trump National G.C. Los Angeles, Rancho Palos Verdes

12. Maderas G.C., Poway

13. Sandpiper G.C., Santa Barbara

For how long has Tiger Woods been on golf's forefront?

Eldrick Tont "Tiger" Woods was born in Cypress in 1975. He was a golf prodigy, appearing on television at the age of two when he appeared on *The Mike Douglas Show* and showed his putting skills. At three he shot a forty-eight on nine holes, and he was winning junior tournaments by the time he was eight. At fifteen, he became the world's youngest U.S. Junior Amateur champion. Woods entered professional golf in 1996 and that year was named Rookie of the Year on the PGA Tour. Since then, he has won fourteen major championships, the first being the Masters Championship in 1997. He has been inducted into the California Hall of Fame and was named Sportsman of the Year by *Sports Illustrated* twice, the only person to be so named more than once.

HORSE RACING

What are some notable horse-racing tracks in California?

The most famous tracks for horse racing in California are Santa Anita Park in Arcadia, the Los Alamitos Race Course, Hollywood Park in Inglewood, and the Del Mar Racetrack. Those aren't the only tracks for horses, however. Other prominent ones include Cal Expo in Sacramento (where harness racing is the sport) and Golden Gate Fields in Berkeley. Hollywood Park, which opened in 1938, was also a popular track, but it closed in 2013.

How is the history behind Santa Anita tied to the Gold Rush?

The Santa Anita Ranch was used by Lucky Baldwin to race his thoroughbreds (see "Early California"). His daughter Anita later built the track and stands in the 1930s, and the new track premiered on December 25, 1934, to a crowd of almost 31,000 spectators. As with

Santa Anita Park is one of the most famous horse-racing tracks in the country. A place for thoroughbred horses to compete, it hosts the Santa Anita Handicap and Santa Anita Derby and has also hosted the Breeders' Cup.

Del Mar (see below), Hollywood stars gravitated to Santa Anita, including Cary Grant, Spencer Tracy, and Charlie Chaplin.

Why were Japanese Americans made to camp at Santa Anita during World War II?

During the war, many Japanese Americans were forced out of their homes by the federal government and made to live in internment camps. Santa Anita served as a temporary holding place for these people before they were sent to more permanent camps (see "The State of California").

Which famous horse won the Santa Anita Handicap in 1940, even after recently rupturing a ligament?

Seabiscuit was well past his prime at age seven when he won the March 2, 1940, race with Red Pollard (1909–1981) as his jockey. Just the year before, Seabiscuit had ruptured a suspensory ligament, but the horse's spirit had him running again after some recuperation time. He was a 6–5 favorite to win, and he did so by a full length over Kayak II, winning over $1.7 million.

Just ten years later, there was another great horse race at Santa Anita. Which two horses are noted for that 1950 race?

On March 4, 1950, Citation faced Noor in front of 58,730 people in two races that day. In the first, Noor shot around the track in two minutes flat, beating the great Citation by 1.25 lengths. People complained that Citation was carrying twenty-two more pounds than Noor. The horses were pitted against each other a second time with only thirteen pounds difference. It came down to the home stretch and a photo finish that Noor won in what is still regarded as one of the most exciting horse races in history.

Did famous actors really found Del Mar?

Yes, Del Mar Racetrack was the brainchild of singers and actors Bing Crosby, Jimmy Durante, and Pat O'Brien. Other actors got in on the game, including comedian Oliver

Hardy and Joe E. Brown, as well as Gary Cooper. The idea was simply to have a horse track they could enjoy for themselves, but not long after its 1937 opening, it grew in popularity, and they were persuaded to make it public. The track became known for attracting other Hollywood stars, especially during the 1940s and 1950s. It is home to a number of well-known races, including the Bing Cosby Stakes, Del Mar Oaks, and the Pacific Classic Stakes.

SOCCER

What were some early soccer teams in the Golden State?

There were a number of soccer clubs in the state, mostly in the Los Angeles area, such as the California Surf, the Los Angeles Aztecs, and the Los Angeles Salsa. The first professional team was the Los Angeles Kickers, a team founded in 1955. Major League Soccer was not founded until 1993, so before then, there were such leagues as the American Soccer League and the North American Soccer League.

Does California have any teams in Major League Soccer?

Yes. California is home to the L.A. Galaxy and the San Jose Earthquakes. Both teams joined the MLS in 1996. The Galaxy play at StubHub Center, and the Earthquakes (who were originally called the Clash) play at Avaya Stadium.

What is the Supporters' Shield?

The Supporters' Shield is the MLS award for the team with the best regular season record. The Quakes won it in 2005 and 2012, and the Galaxy won the award in 1998, 2002, 2010, and 2011.

THE GALAXY

Tell me about the Galaxy.

They are based in Carson, a suburb of Los Angeles, where they play StubHub Center and are part of the Western Conference. The team has won the MLS Cup five times: 2002, 2005, 2011, 2012, and 2014.

Obviously, the Galaxy has been a successful team. What were their first years like?

They did well, generally, in the late 1990s, beginning with an appearance at the 1996 MLS Cup. There they faced DC United, which kept the Galaxy from grabbing the title. After a mediocre 1997 and a loss to the Dallas Burn in 1997, they sprang back in 1998 to enjoy a 24–8 season and an MLS record 68 points, becoming Western Conference champions. Facing the Chicago Fire this time, the strong regular-season performance didn't pay off, and Chicago swept them in three games.

After changing coaches—Octavio Zambrano (1958–) was replaced with Sigi Schmid (1953–)—another Western Conference championship in 1999 led the Galaxy to go head to head with the Dallas Burn again for the MLS Cup. The pattern of reaching the finals only to lose continued, however, and the Galaxy would once again fail to go the distance. The team brought on Mexican star Luis Hernández (1968–; played for the Galaxy 2000–2002) to help get them past the final yards. Again, they made the finals in 2001, only (sigh) to lose yet again, this time to fellow California team, the San Jose Earthquakes (see below).

How did they finally win an MLS Cup?

Acquiring a "Little Fish" from Guatemala named Carlos "El Pescadito" Ruiz (1979–; played for the Galaxy 2002–2004, 2008) helped the team get that extra spark. Beating the Colorado Rapids for the Western championships, they advanced to the MLS Finals to be pitted against the New England Revolution. It was a difficult situation; the Revolution was on its home turf, and the game went into overtime. In a heart-stopping moment, the Revolution almost had a game-winning goal, but the ball hit the crossbar. That's when Ruiz kicked the ball in such a subtle way that it surprised the other team's goalie. The ball went in, and the 2002 Galaxy finally had a Cup.

How about the second Cup?

The irony of the Galaxy was that they kept getting to the playoffs—the only team to do so from the time they were formed in 1996 until 2005—but only had one Cup. That changed in 2005. Even though they had a modest 13–13–6 record and were on the lowest rung entering the playoffs, they caught fire in the last games of the season. Of great help that year was forward Landon Donovan (1982; played with the Galaxy 2005–2014), a German player who had previously kicked the ball around for Bayer Leverkusen, as well as with the upstate rival Quakes (see below). They stomped the Earthquakes to win the Western Conference and then Donovan scored two goals to put down the Colorado Rapids for the Cup.

Which player for the Galaxy is probably considered one of the greatest contributors to the team in its first decade?

Cobi Jones (1970–) was a Detroit-born midfielder who played for the Galaxy from 1996 to 2007, scoring seventy goals during that time. He was also on the U.S. National Team, participating in the 1994, 1998, and 2002 FIFA World Cups, appearing in 164 games in those tournaments, more than any other U.S. player at the time, and scoring fifteen times. He was named the U.S. Soccer Athlete of the Year in 1998 and is in the National Soccer Hall of Fame.

Who is probably the most recognizable player to be part of the L.A. Galaxy team?

David Beckham (1975–) is a household name, even in the United States, where soccer is not the most popular professional sport. The former Manchester United and Real

Madrid player spent some of the last years of his professional career (2007 to 2012) in Los Angeles. Combining his skills with Donovan would eventually prove profitable for the Galaxy.

How did they get to their more recent run of championships?

After a couple rough seasons, including the loss of general manager Doug Hamilton (1963–2006) to a heart attack and a number of player injuries, the Galaxy got a foothold on the playoffs again in 2009. Despite their star power, though, they would lose the Cup to Real Salt Lake (enjoying their first championship) in a shootout.

Soccer legend David Beckham played for European and British teams, with the exception of the Galaxy from 2007 to 2012.

FC Dallas blocked their path to the finals in 2010, but with the addition of Irish forward Robbie Keane (1980–), they showed up for a fight in 2011. The previous year's championship Real Salt Lake fell to the Galaxy in the conference finals. They then slammed the Houston Dynamo for the Cup in overtime, giving Beckham and Keane their first championships, and Donovan was named MVP.

The Galaxy repeated this performance in 2012, upending the Houston Dynamo, and defender Omar Gonzalez (1988–) was named MVP. This was Beckham's last year with the Galaxy, and in 2013 they failed in their hopes to win three championships in a row.

As for their 2014 win, it would be the last season with Donovan on the payroll. But it would be Keane who would score a winning goal in overtime to put the Revolution down and make the Galaxy the first MLS team with five Cups on their trophy shelf.

THE EARTHQUAKES

Who were the Quakes before they were the Quakes?

The franchise started its history as the San Francisco Bay Blackhawks in 1974. They were in the Western Soccer Alliance, beginning in 1989, and when Major League Soccer was formed the Blackhawks were one of the inaugural teams in the league, changing the name to the Clash from 1996 to 1999, when they were renamed the Earthquakes.

How well did the Clash do?

While they had winning seasons in 1996 and 1999, they didn't make the playoffs while called "the Clash."

And after they became the Earthquakes?

The first couple of years were remarkable. After renaming themselves in 1999, they were dead last in 2000 with a record of 7–17–8. The very next year, they went from bums to heroes to win their first MLS Cup.

What happened that led them to two MLS Cups?

How was this turnaround achieved? Two words will explain most of the credit: Landon Donovan (1982–), who had joined the team in 2001 and would play with them until 2004, when he defected to the Galaxy. Donovan would lead them two victories in 2001 and 2003. In the first one, they met their southern rivals, the Galaxy. In an overtime game, Dwayne De Rosario (1978–) kicked the ball between two Galaxy defenders and the goalie to win it six minutes into overtime. He was consequently named MVP.

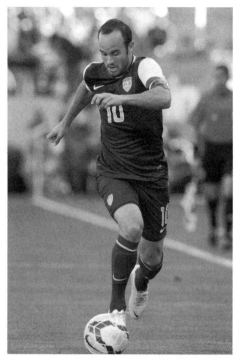

Landon Donovan is shown here playing on the U.S. National Team in 2014. He played for the Earthquakes for three years before moving to the Galaxy in 2004.

The Columbus Crew would set up a blockade in the 2002 playoffs that stymied the Quakes, but they were back in 2003. After walking over the Galaxy and the Kansas City Wizards, they headed into the finals against the Chicago Fire. Donovan and Ronnie Ekelund (1972–) scored a goal each in the first half, and Richard Mulrooney (1976–) did in the second half, making it 3–1. An embarrassing moment came when Quakes goalie Chris Roner (1980–) accidentally tipped the ball into his own net, scoring one for Chicago and making it a 3–2 game (this was the first own goal in MLS history). Roner's overall contribution to the team's win outweighed the faux pas, however. Donovan then scored again and was named MVP of the championship game.

After the 2003 Cup win, the Quakes have struggled, haven't they?

Yes, it's been a rough road over since then. Some things that happened that didn't help the team included losing Coach Frank Yallop (1964–) to the Canadaian National Team, and in 2005 Donovan left for the Galaxy (Yallop did that, too, the same year).

Why did the Earthquakes disappear from the MLS from 2006 to 2008?

The team's owner, Anschutz Entertainment Group, decided they would move the team to Houston, Texas, because the company was upset they could not get a stadium dedi-

---

What was the "other" San Jose Earthquakes team?

The present team should not be confused with the San Jose Earthquakes (or Golden Bay Earthquakes), a team in the North American Soccer League from 1974 to 1984 and then in the Western Soccer Alliance from 1985 to 1988 (both leagues went defunct). When the WSA closed its doors, this Earthquakes team also came to an end. This left the name available for the taking, which is what the Blackhawks did in 1994. Therefore, the current Earthquakes are not, technically, the same franchise as the earlier team.

---

cated to the Quakes' soccer games. The MLS, however, would have none of this; they would allow the owners to create a new soccer team in Houston, but they could not call it the Earthquakes, nor could they transfer the team's records to the new franchise. What happened then was that there was no San Jose team. A new owner, real estate developer Lew Wolff (1935–), agreed to buy the San Jose franchise, and in 2008 the Earthquakes were reborn.

How have the Quakes fared in more recent years?

Not too badly at all. They made it to the playoffs in 2010 and 2012; they lost to the Colorado Rapids in the 2010 semifinals. After a losing year in 2011, they had a banner year in 2012, the best in their franchise's history. Winning their second Supporter's Shield, they had a record of 19–6–9 with 66 points and 72 goals in the regular season. In the playoffs, though, they were knocked out by the Galaxy.

What bit of good news came in 2015?

The Quakes finally got their soccer-specific Avaya Stadium, after playing in a number of other venues over the years. It is the first professional soccer stadium to be built in the Bay Area.

WOMEN'S AND WORLD CUP SOCCER

Are there any professional women's soccer teams in California?

Well, there were, briefly. The Women's Professional Soccer league only existed from 2009 to 2011, shutting its doors in 2012. California had one team in the league: the FC Gold Pride, which was based in Hayward and played at Pioneer Stadium.

What event happened in 1999 involving women's soccer?

In 1999 the U.S. women's team got to play for the World Cup at the Rose Bowl in Pasadena, where they faced the Chinese team. After a scoreless game in regulation play, they ended the game on penalty kicks, and Brandi Chastain (1968–) scored the game winner.

Has Pasadena hosted other World Cup events?

Yes, the Rose Bowl was the site of the 1994 FIFA World Cup, which Brazil won; Italy was the runner-up.

TENNIS

Are any big professional tournaments played in California?

Tennis in California used to be a pretty big deal. There was a pro men's tournament at UCLA until 2012, and there were important women's tournaments at Manhattan Beach, Carlsbad, and Stanford. These have fallen by the wayside, and the only important pro tournaments now being held in the state are the USTA International Spring Championships in Carson (formerly at Manhattan Beach) and the BNB Paribas Tournament in Indian Wells.

What is the state of professional tennis in California?

The Southern California Section of the U.S. Tennis Association was founded back in 1887. It has county chapters in Los Angeles, San Diego, San Bernardino, Orange, Riverside, Santa Barbara, Ventura, Kern, and San Luis Obispo counties, making it one of the smaller USTA sections.

Who built the Indian Wells Tennis Garden?

The tennis garden in the Coachella Valley city of Indian Wells that was built in 2000 was purchased by billionaire Larry Ellison, who made his fortune by cofounding the computer technology company Oracle Corporation in 2009. Ellison has financed huge renovations of the facility, which now includes two large stadiums (one that seats 16,100 and the other that seats 8,000), tennis club facilities that include twenty-nine concrete courts, and several high-end restaurants, including world-famous Japanese restaurant Nobu. A tennis museum is scheduled to open in 2017, and it will be the first such museum in the world that is incorporated within a stadium.

What is the California Tennis Club's claim to fame?

Located in San Francisco, the California Tennis Club is the oldest private tennis club west of the Mississippi. Founded circa 1884 (exact records have been lost), the current facilities have been in use (and renovated) since 1887.

COLLEGE SPORTS

Which universities have Division I sport teams?

The following is a list of California's Division I teams:

College	Team	Conference
California Polytechnic State University	Mustangs*	Big West
CSU Bakersfield	Roadrunners	Western Athletic Conference
CSU Fresno	Bulldogs*	Mountain West
CSU Fullerton	Titans	Big West
CSU Long Beach	49ers	Big West
CSU Northridge	Matadors	Big West
CSU Sacramento	Hornets*	Big Sky
Loyola Marymount University	Lions	West Coast
Pepperdine University	Waves	West Coast
San Diego State University	Aztecs*	Mountain West
San Jose State University	Spartans*	Mountain West
St. Mary's College of California	Gaels	West Coast
Santa Clara University	Broncos	West Coast
Stanford University	Cardinal*	Pac-12
UC Berkeley	Bears*	Pac-12
UC Davis	Aggies*	Big West
UC Irvine	Anteaters	Big West
UCLA	Bruins*	Pac-12
UC Riverside	Highlanders	Big West
UC Santa Barbara	Gauchos	Big West
University of San Diego	Toreros*	West Coast
University of San Francisco	Dons	West Coast
University of Southern California	Trojans*	Pac-12
University of the Pacific	Tigers	West Coast

* Indicates the sport program has a football team.

There are also many California universities and colleges with Division II and Division III teams, as well as those participating in the National Association of Intercollegiate Athletics and the California Community College Athletic Association.

Jackie Robinson is best remembered as a Brooklyn Dodger, but didn't he come from California?

The amazing Jackie Robinson (1919–1972) was, indeed, a Californian in many ways. Although born in Cairo, Georgia, his family moved to Pasadena when he was a year old. He attended John Muir High School and then Pasadena Junior College.

The reason Robinson is listed here at the top of the college sports section is that it is impossible to categorize him. In high school, he lettered in football, basketball, track,

341

and baseball. At Pasadena Junior College, he continued participating in all of those sports, then he transferred to UCLA and was the first athlete at that university to letter in all four of those sports.

COLLEGE FOOTBALL

What's the biggest college football rivalry in the state?

That would probably be the University of California at Los Angeles (UCLA) Bruins versus the University of Southern California (USC) Trojans. From 1929 to 2015, they have faced each other eighty-three times. The win-loss record is USC forty-five wins to UCLA's thirty-one, with the other seven games being ties.

What are some other big college football rivalries?

The University of Southern California seems to have lots of rivals. Not only UCLA but also the University of California Golden Bears and Notre Dame's Fighting Irish have both been counted by college sports aficionados as among the most intense continuing match-ups in the game. In the Notre Dame–USC rivalry, Notre Dame leads 45–36–5 as of 2015.

What is "The Big Game" in California?

"The Big Game" refers to the rivalry football match between the University of California Golden Bears and the Stanford University Cardinal. Stanford leads this series 60–46–11 as of this writing.

USC Trojan fans celebrate a touchdown against UCLA during a 2007 game. The USC/UCLA rivalry is one of the strongest in the state.

What are some memorable moments in California college football?

Some of the most remarkable plays in sports history have involved California college football. For example, in the UCLA vs. USC game of November 18, 1967, people who watched will always recall how USC player O. J. Simpson (1947–) secured a Heisman by catching a pass from quarterback Toby Page and running sixty-four yards for a touchdown and a 20–14 win. The Trojans won the national title.

On November 20, 1982, during a California–Stanford game, there was some sneaky strategy forever known as "The Play." The Golden Bears employed five lateral passes to move the ball fifty-seven yards for a score and a 25–20 win.

More recently, on October 15, 2005, Notre Dame thought they had defeated USC when the referees decided to put seven seconds back on the clock. The Trojans had the ball on the Notre Dame 1-yard line; the ball was hiked to Matt Leinart (1983–) who, with a helpful push from tailback Reggie Bush (1985–; the move is now known as "the Bush Push"), blasted over the goal line for a touchdown and the win.

Why did the first Rose Bowl game result in football being cancelled for the next fourteen years?

The first Rose Bowl game in Pasadena was played on January 1, 1902, between the University of Michigan and Stanford University. The Michigan team defeated Stanford so thoroughly (the score was 49 to zip) that the organizers of the game decided not to hold another football face-off until 1916. Instead, mock chariot races were held after the Rose Parade at Pasadena's Tournament Park. But football returned, and in 1923 the Rose Bowl Stadium was completed. The University of Southern California beat the Nittany Lions of Pennsylvania State by a score of 14 to 3.

Over the years, the seating capacity of the Rose Bowl has increased to 92,542. The game is now a solid tradition of New Year's Day for many Americans.

What record does California currently hold concerning the Heisman Trophy?

More Heisman Trophy winners have come from California than any other state in the country. The winners include:

Athlete	High School	Year Won
Glenn Davis	Bonita HS, La Verne	1946
John Huarte	Mater Dei HS, Santa Ana	1964
Mike Garrett	Roosevelt HS, Los Angeles	1965
Gary Beban	Sequoia HS, Redwood City	1967
O.J. Simpson	Galileo HS, San Francisco	1968
Jim Plunkett	James Lick HS, East San Jose	1970
Charles White	San Fernando HS, San Fernando	1979
Marcus Allen	Abraham Lincoln HS, San Diego	1981
Gino Torretta	Pinole Valley HS, Pinole	1992

Athlete	High School	Year Won
Rashaan Salaam	La Jolla Country Day School, La Jolla	1994
Ricky Williams	Patrick Henry HS, San Diego	1998
Carson Palmer	Santa Margarita Catholic HS, Rancho Santa Margarita	2002
Matt Leinart	Mater Dei HS, Santa Ana	2004
Reggie Bush	Helix HS, La Mesa	2005

COLLEGE BASKETBALL

Why was UCLA the team to beat in the early 1970s?

The UCLA Bruins enjoyed an eighty-eight-game winning streak from 1970 to 1974. Coached by the legendary John Wooden (1910–2010), the Bruins also enjoyed winning twenty Pac-10 championships, ten national championships, thirty-eight NCAA tournament wins, and four perfect seasons. The team featured such now-legendary players as Kareem Abdul-Jabbar (1947–) and Bill Walton (1952–). The streak was finally ended on

January 19, 1974, when UCLA lost to Notre Dame. Even so, they almost won that game except that in the last three minutes of play, the Irish scored twenty-four unanswered points.

Are there any big college basketball rivalries at California universities?

Just as with football, there is a big Stanford–California rivalry, as well, that tends to be overlooked because of the popularity of the gridiron competition.

How about rivalries involving out-of-state foes?

There is quite a hoops rivalry, too, between the UCLA Bruins and the Arizona Wildcats. Both teams have been very competitive in the Pac-12 over the last thirty years or so.

UCLA basketball coach John Wooden was one of the winningest coaches of the sport. The university erected a statue of him in 2012 next to Pauley Pavilion.

OTHER AMATEUR SPORTS
AND OUTDOOR FUN

What was the first athletic club in the United States?

California has the honor of being the home of the first U.S. athletic club, San Francisco's Olympic Club, which opened on May 6, 1860. The idea originated with brothers Arthur and artist Charles Christian Nahl (1818–1878), who were sharing their backyard gym with so many friends that they felt they needed to start something more formal. The new facilities became popular with many prominent San Franciscans, ranging from railroad executive Charles Crocker and publishing magnate William Randolph Hearst to boxer "Gentleman Jim" Corbett.

The original structure burned down in 1906, along with most of the rest of the city, and the club moved into the City Clubhouse and natatorium in 1912. The club hosted all kinds of activities, as well as many amateur teams in sports such as football, baseball, wrestling, swimming, gymnastics, tennis, fencing, boxing, bowling, and billiards. Golf was added in 1918, when the club took over operations of the Lakeside Golf Club.

Most recently, the club building was renovated in 2006. It now features updated swimming pools, basketball courts, a fitness center and circuit training facilities, handball and squash courts, and a cardio solarium, as well as hotel facilities.

Are there really Quidditch teams in California?

Yes! Not just in California but all over the place, there are teams based on the sport invented by author J. K. Rowling (1965–) for her "Harry Potter" fantasy book series. In the stories, Quidditch is played by wizards and witches who can fly around a field on brooms. They throw a ball through a hoop to score points, and there is also a special flying ball called "the snitch" that is incredibly hard to grab. If it is caught, however, the game is over. In real-world Quidditch, players can't fly, but they must run on the field with a broomstick between their legs. The snitch is played by a human being who tries to keep from being caught.

There is, as yet, no professional Quidditch league, but there are university and adult community teams. The following is a list.

Location	Team Name	Type of Team
Alviso	Silicon Valley Skrewts	Adult Community
Berkeley	Cal Quidditch	University
Goleta	Santa Barbara Blacktips	Adult Community
Lomita	The Lost Boys	Adult Community
Long Beach	The Fighting Farmers of America	Adult Community
Los Angeles	University of California Los Angeles	University
Los Angeles	University of Southern California	University
Los Angeles	Wizards of Westwood	Adult Community

Location	Team Name	Type of Team
Mountain View	Silicon Valley Vipers	Adult Community
Newark	Skyfighters Quidditch Club	Adult Community
San Jose	San Jose State University Spartans	University
San Jose	South Bay Blizzards	Adult Community
South Gate	California Dobbys	Adult Community
Stanford	Stanford Quidditch	University
Stockton	Pacific Phoenix Quidditch Club	University
Torrance	Los Angeles Gambits	Adult Community
Westminster	The Long Beach Funky Quaffles	Adult Community

SURFING

How old of a sport is surfing?

Surfing goes as far back as the 1500s, when the royalty of the Sandwich Islands used boards 18 feet (5.5 meters) long and weighing as much as 150 pounds (68 kilograms) to ride the waves. More recently, Captain Cook reported seeing Hawaiians surfing back in 1778, but white settlers to the islands discouraged it as a "heathen" activity. By 1900, it had largely died out, but it was revived on Waikiki Beach around 1905. The sport migrated to California by 1907.

Who is the "Father of Modern Surfing"?

George Freeth (1883–1919) first popularized the sport of surfing in California. Of Hawaiian and Irish parents, he was discovered surfing in Waikiki by industrialist Henry Huntington (see chapter "California Means Business"). Huntington invited Freeth to California, where he was promoted as "the Man Who Walks on Water" at exhibitions in Redondo Beach to help promote the opening of the Redondo–Los Angeles Railroad. After that event, Freeth decided to remain in California, where he taught people to surf. He is also credited with helping to develop modern lifeguard services.

Surfer George Freeth popularized the sport in California.

Which other early surfer is sometimes given the title of "Father of Modern Surfing"?

That would be Duke Kahanamoku (1890–1968). Also called "The Big Kahuna," he gave exhibitions around the world, including in California. His influence in California, though, is less than that of Freeth, and he is more a subject to be mentioned in books about Hawaii.

What contribution did Jack O'Neill make to surfing?

O'Neill introduced wet suits to the sport in 1952, starting with northern California. The wet suits kept surfers warm, allowing them to remain in the ocean longer.

Who was Bob Simmons?

Bob Simmons (1919–1954) was the inventor of the lightweight, modern surfboard. His was a rather tragic tale, however. As a teenager, he had a tumor on his ankle that almost cost him his leg; then, while riding a bicycle to regain his strength, he had an accident that took a lot of time to recover

The Big Kahuna himself, Duke Kahanamoku, did a lot to popularize surfing in California and around the world.

from. It was suggested to him in 1939 that he try surfing as a new form of physical therapy; he tried it at Newport Beach and fell in love with the sport. Studying hydro- and aerodynamics at CalTech, he developed a new surfboard to replace the large, cumbersome ones used until then. His design has influenced surfboard making ever since. Unfortunately, Simmons drowned while surfing at Windansea Beach in San Diego.

Where do surfers compete in California?

There are many surfing competitions held in California all through the year. Many of these are in Huntington Beach, which is kind of where it all started, so that's appropriate. Among the Huntington State Beach surfing competitions are:

- Katin Pro/Am Team Challenge
- Surfing America Prime
- Vans Pro Junior
- NSSA West Coast Championships
- NSSA National Championships
- ASP Prime US Open of Surfing
- US Open Junior Pro

What are some other surfing competitions?

Outside of Huntington Beach, there is also the following:

What is the Surfrider Foundation?

One of the great things to come out of the popularity of surfing is the Surfrider Foundation. Created in 1984 by a group of Malibu surfers, the foundation seeks to preserve beaches from pollution and overdevelopment. The foundation has now grown across the country, and, according to its website at www.surfrider.org, members have helped to preserve about fifty-six percent of the country's coastlines, but they won't stop until all of it is protected.

- Doheny Longboard Surfing Association at San Onofre State Beach (Church)

- Surfing America Prime at Steamer Lane, Lighthouse Field State Beach

- O'Neill Surfing America Prime West at San Onofre State Beach (Upper Trestles)

- WSA West Coast Championships at Church, San Onofre State Beach

- Santa Cruz Longboard Union Memorial Day Contest at Steamer Lane, Lighthouse Field State Beach

- Surfing America USA Championships at Lower Trestles, San Onofre State Beach

- WSA USA Championships Prelim & Finals at Lower Trestles, San Onofre State Beach

- ASP World Tour Hurley Pro at Lower Trestles, San Onofre State Beach

- Malibu Surfing Association MSA Classic Invitational at Surfrider Beach, Malibu Lagoon State Beach

- Doheny Longboard Surfing Association Dale Velzy Surf Classic at Doheny State Beach

- Swami's Surfing Association Return to the Reef Contest at Cardiff State Beach, Cardiff-by-the-Sea, San Diego

SKIING

Where are the best places to ski in California?

When visitors think of California, it's usually about the south and the state's sunny beaches, but there are also some great skiing spots here, especially in the Sierras and near Lake Tahoe. One of the top rated is on Mammoth Mountain near the town of Mammoth Lakes, south of Mono Lake and on the other side of the state from San Francisco. This skier's heaven has 3,500 acres (1,400 hectares) of skiable terrain and twenty-eight ski lifts. Speaking of heaven, there is, not far away, Heavenly Mountain Resort on the California side of Lake Tahoe, on the south end of the lake. It has ninety-seven runs and thirty lifts.

Skiing in California is not limited to the Sierras. There are many places in the southern part of the state, including Big Bear, where you can ski.

Another cool spot by Lake Tahoe is the Squaw Valley–Alpine Meadows ski area. Squaw Valley is where the 1960 Winter Olympics were held (see below). There are 3,600 acres (1,460 hectares) of skiable trails and slopes there. Alpine Meadows has a hundred trails and 2,400 acres (970 hectares).

Kirkwood Mountain and Northstar are two other resorts also near Lake Tahoe that have been ranked high as providing a good skiing and snowboarding experience.

What about skiing that's not near Lake Tahoe or in the Sierras?

One can also go skiing or snowboarding in such areas as Mount Baldy, Big Bear, Mount San Jacinto, or Mount Gorgonio in the southern part of the state.

What is Far West Skiing?

Far West Skiing is a division of the U.S. Skiing Association. Based in Truckee, California, this organization promotes the development of young alpine skiers, offers scholarships, and also promotes ski competitions in the West.

Are there skiing competitions in California?

Most definitely, but there are too many to list here in this book. To find out about skiing competitions, it's best to visit the FWS website at www.fwsskiing.us.

349

THE OLYMPICS

How many Olympics have been held in California?

Two Olympics have been held in California, both in the city of Los Angeles: the Tenth Olympiad in 1932 and the Twenty-third Olympiad in 1984.

1932 GAMES

Why was the 1932 Olympics particularly important for Los Angeles and California?

The Tenth Olympiad was a feather in the cap of a city that was looking to get on the international stage. Few things could do that better than hosting an Olympics. It was also the Great Depression, and the athletic event was something that could raise the spirits of people going through a difficult time.

What facilities were used for the 1932 games?

The Los Angeles Coliseum had been completed in 1923, and this was not by accident. City leaders knew by 1920 that they wanted to host the games in L.A., and they renovated the stadium to seat 105,000 people, which made it the largest sporting arena in the world at that time. Other facilities that were used included the Rose Bowl, athletic fields at UCLA, the Long Beach Marine Stadium, the Riviera Club for equestrian competitions, the shooting range (for gun events) used by the LAPD, and an auditorium on Grand Avenue.

Who was the most amazing athlete to perform at the 1932 games?

Although she was a Texan and this is a book about California, Babe Didrickson (1911–1956), who later married famed wrestler George Zaharias, needs to be noted here as one of the most amazing athletes of her generation. An amazing golfer who would win three U.S. Women's Opens after the Olympics as well as eleven other titles, during the games she shined in track and field, winning gold in the javelin and eighty-meter hurdles and a silver in the high jump. Tragically, she died far too young from cancer.

What Olympian in 1932 also became a Hollywood star?

Clarence Linden "Buster" Crabbe (1908–1983), who was born in Oakland, was a swimmer at the event and won gold in the 400-meter freestyle. He was discovered while competing there and was hired to perform in about 180 movies, most notably starring in the *Flash Gordon* serials. (Interestingly, Johnny Weissmuller, who played Tarzan in the movie serials, had also been a gold-medal swimmer, though at the 1928 Paris Olympics.)

When were the Winter Olympics held in California?

Today, the summer and winter games are held at the same time, but it used to be that the summer games were hosted one year and then the winter games another year in another location. That was the case in 1960, when the Winter Olympics were played in California's Squaw Valley.

1960 WINTER GAMES

The 1960 games were a bit limited. Which competitions were held that year?

Events included speed skating, figure skating, ice hockey, alpine skiing, cross-country skiing, ski jumping, Nordic combined, and the biathlon. Women's speed skating and biathlon debuted that year.

What winter sport was excluded at the 1960 winter games?

For the first and only time in the games, the bobsled was excluded from the Squaw Valley events. This was because the game organizers didn't want to pay for the construction of the expensive bobsled runs. The resort area had been relatively undeveloped at the time, and the organizers had already spent about $80 million in improvements and were unwilling to do more for one sport.

1984 GAMES

What was peculiar about the 1984 L.A. games?

The United States, along with other Western nations, had previously boycotted the 1980 Olympics in Moscow as a way to protest the Soviet Union's invasion of Afghanistan the previous year. For the 1984 Olympics, the games were basically given to the U.S. to compensate the athletes who missed out four years before, but this time Eastern Bloc countries boycotted. Not all communist countries stayed away, however. The Romanian team showed up, and because the competition was limited, they ended up winning fifty-three medals that year.

Who were some standout athletes at the 1984 games?

American gymnast Mary Lou Retton (1968–) became the first Western woman to win the all-around gymnastics medal, and U.S. sprinter Carl Lewis (1961–) earned ten medals in track and field.

Gymnast Mary Lou Retton was a member of the President's Council on Physical Fitness and Sports in 2004.

What interesting story about the 1984 Olympics involves a Moroccan athlete?

Nawal El-Moutawakel (1962–), a female track and field star from Morocco, became the first Moroccan to win an Olympic medal of any kind (a gold in the 400-meter hurdles). She was also the first Islamic woman to win an Olympic event.

Another amazing performer was Greg Louganis (1960–), who competed in the diving events. He won gold in springboard and platform diving (the first to do so since 1928). He would win two more golds in the 1988 Olympics, too.

What were some firsts at the 1984 Olympics?

The 1984 Los Angeles Olympics was the first Olympics in which there was a women's marathon, the first with synchronized swimming as a medal event, and the first to have windsurfing. It was also the first time an Olympics would be in the black, bringing in $200 million.

OTHER NOTABLE CALIFORNIA OLYMPIANS

Who was the famous decathlete from Tulare, California?

Bob Mathias (1930–2006) was a two-time gold winner. In 1948, when he was just out of high school, he qualified for the U.S. team and won the gold in the decathlon in London. That year, too, he was presented with the James E. Sullivan Award for outstanding amateur athlete. Mathias attended Stanford University, where he played football and, in 1950, set a decathlon world record of 7,287 points. He did it again in the 1952 Helsinki Olympics with 7,592 points (an amazing 912 points more than the silver medalist).

Afterward, Mathias served in the U.S. Marines for two and a half years, achieving the rank of captain. He then became an actor, staring in a short-lived TV series called *The Troubleshooters* (1959) and in such movies as *The Bob Mathias Story* (1954), *China Doll* (1958), and *Minotaur, the Wild Beast of Crete* (1960). From 1967 to 1975, he was a Republican congressman representing California, and from 1977 to 1985, he was director of the U.S. Olympic Training Center.

Which athlete from Kingsburg was a decathlete at the Melbourne and Rome Olympics?

Rafer Johnson (1935–) was a former UCLA track star when he made the U.S. Olympics team for the 1956 Melbourne, Australia, games. Johnson won the silver in the decathlon there, and four years later, he was in Rome facing former UCLA teammate C. K. Yang (a.k.a. Yang Chuan-kwang, 1933–2007), who played for China. Their 1960 competition for the 1960 decathlon gold was won of the more intense stories in Olympic history, but Johnson narrowly defeated Yang for the top medal.

After the 1960 games, Johnson vowed to retire from competing. He worked as a sportscaster and was an actor in a number of movies, including two Tarzan movies, a role in *Roots: The Next Generation* (1979), and the James Bond film *License to Kill* (1989). (Interestingly, he almost had a role in 1960's *Spartacus* but had to turn it down or else lose his amateur athlete status.) He also became involved in the Special Olympics and, in 1969, founded the California Special Olympics.

Who was the USC student who superbly won gold for the high jump?

Charlie Dumas (1937–2004) was the first athlete to make it over a bar that was seven feet above the ground. He accomplished the feat while still attending Crompton College on June 29, 1956, at the Olympic trials. Naturally, he got on the U.S. team and competed in Melbourne, Australia, where he won gold, jumping just a half inch under his previous record. But he wasn't done yet. Dumas attended USC and won a 1958 NCAA track and field title. The next year he competed at the Pan American Games in Chicago and took home a gold. He would go on to the 1960 Olympics in Rome, Italy, but unfortunately he suffered a knee injury and didn't medal.

What rock star swimmer from Pasadena went to the 2012 Olympics and has earned an ESPY?

Melissa "Missy" Franklin (1995–) is an amazing swimmer who holds the world record in the 200-meter. She went to the London Summer Olympics, where she obtained the gold not once but four times in the 100-meter, 200-meter, 4 × 100-meter medley, and 4 × 200-meter freestyle, as well as a silver in the 4 × 100-meter freestyle. In world championship competition, she has racked up eleven gold, four silver, and three bronze, and in the Pan Pacific Championships, she has one gold, two silver, and one bronze.

The honors don't end there, as she also has the FINA Swimmer of the Year Award in 2011 and 2012, *Swimming World's* World Swimmer of the Year and American Swimmer of the Year Award in 2012, and the Best Female College Athlete ESPY Award in 2015.

QUIRKY CALIFORNIA

ODD PLACES

Why would people go to see a bunch of gum stuck on a wall?

No one is quite sure how it started—perhaps a goofy rivalry between high schools—but on the 700 block of Higueroa Street in San Luis Obispo that is lined on both sides by tall walls, people have been sticking their used chewing gum for years. It all began some-time in the 1940s or '50s, and by the 1970s it was gaining both fans and protestors, the latter saying it was disgusting and unsanitary. There have been at least three attempts to clean off all the gummy gunk since then, but it has proven a losing battle. The tradi-tion is a solid part of the neighborhood culture and has attracted the attention of na-tional television shows ranging from *The Tonight Show Starring Johnny Carson* to MTV. Poets, artists, and musicians have written about it, too, including in the 1999 song "Wall of Gum" by Those Darn Accordians, Weird Al Yankovic's "Take Me Down" (1978), and artist Matthew Hoffman's "Projectable Gum."

Why was the Bridge to Nowhere built?

Located in the San Gabriel Mountains near Azusa, it was constructed in 1936 as part of a plan to connect the town of Wrightwood to the San Gabriel Valley. When the East Fork Road leading to the bridge was washed out by a flood in 1938, however, the bridge was abandoned and the route never completed. Today, the bridge is part of the Sheep Moun-tain Wilderness and attracts hikers and bungee jumpers (see the chapter "College and Amateur Sports").

Why did Michael Jackson build Neverland?

Located in Los Olivos, Neverland was purchased by the late King of Pop, Michael Jack-son (1958–2009), and was his home from 1987 until 2005, when financial troubles and

Fans paid respect to Michael Jackson at the gates of his Neverland Ranch shortly after he died in 2009. The Disneyland-inspired amusement park, mansion, and zoo was put up for sale.

his trial in which he was accused of child sexual abuse (and acquitted) forced him to put it on the market. Many of the pop star's fans suspect that he put an amusement park and zoo on the ranch in an attempt to reclaim his lost childhood. He invited children to the estate regularly, taking them on train rides and feeding them ice cream. During its heyday, the Neverland zoo, which was clearly inspired by Disneyland, included giraffes, tigers, an elephant, snakes, flamingos, alligators, llamas, orangutans, and chimps, including Jackson's beloved Bubbles. After the ranch's closing, the animals went to sanctuaries, animal parks, and, sometimes, private collectors. PETA investigated the sales, sometimes leading them to find that animals (such as giraffes) had died, and the fate of the Asian elephant, Gypsy, was never tracked down.

In 2015, the ranch, now called Sycamore Valley Ranch, was put on the market for $100 million. The amusement park and zoo are gone, but the twenty-two buildings, including the main 12,000-square-foot mansion, remain.

Why is the Madonna Inn in San Luis Obispo so unique?

Opened on December 24, 1958, and still in operation today, the Madonna Inn is truly a unique experience. The name actually comes from the founders' surname: Alex and Phyllis Madonna, who gave each room a unique feel. There is the Caveman, for example, which is designed as if you were inside a cave; the Tall and Short Room, which has one bed that is 6.5 feet long and one that is 5.5 feet long; a Safari Room with appropriate decor; some rooms with tall ceilings, circular staircases, round beds, geometric designs, and all kinds of variations. Even the bathrooms are quite "different." One has a men's urinal that looks like a waterfall, and another has one that is fashioned after a copper waterwheel. The women's restrooms include one with pink Italian marble decor and another with stall doors padded in red leather. Every room is unique and includes handcrafted furniture and other features by skilled artisans. It is considered a landmark of central California that has become popular for weddings, anniversaries, and Valentine's Day getaways and more.

Is there a "glass beach" north of San Francisco?

Yes, on the coast of Mendocino County north of San Francisco and just west of Fort Bragg there is one. The beach there is covered in colorful, tiny pebbles that, upon closer inspection, are seen to be bits of glass. How did all this glass get there? It's the result of people dumping their trash into the ocean over decades. This was especially true after the 1906 San Francisco earthquake. People had so much rubble to clear away that they decided to throw much of it into the Pacific Ocean, hoping it would wash away. Instead, it washed inland. This made an unsightly mess, at first, but the action of the ocean waves gradually crushed and smoothed out the glass that was there, resulting in a stunning, sparkling beach.

The Madonna Inn in San Luis Obispo is famous for its many uniquely styled guest rooms.

The glass pebbles on Glass Beach should not be confused with what sailors call "mermaid tears." These are natural glass pebbles formed in the sea. The myth behind them is that they form from mermaids weeping after a sailor dies.

What is possibly the weirdest vending machine ever?

Located at the Glaum Egg Ranch in Aptos, near Santa Cruz, is, believe it or not, an egg vending machine. Put in your change, get a tray of eggs. And not only an egg! You also get a little show behind a glass inset stage next to the vending machine. When you buy the eggs, the curtain goes up, and a cast of colorfully clothed chickens clucks out a tune for you.

Are there any weird roadside oddities a tourist might come across while traveling the state?

- Fish Head Rocks: Between Ridgecrest and Trona on Highway 178 in San Bernardino County, there is a pile of rocks that have been painted with eyes and teeth so that they look like fish or, perhaps, moray eels.
- Avenue of Faces: In the town of Tehachapi in Kern County, one can see a series of trees into which whimsical faces have been carved. The residents call them tree spirits.
- Gumby and Pokey Statues: In the town of Norco in Riverside, there are huge statues of Gumby and Pokey, the claymation characters from a popular television show.
- Kenny Irwin Home: On a residential street in Palm Springs, sculptor Kenny Irwin has filled his yard with colorful sculptures created with found objects. You can learn more about Irwin and his art at http://kennyirwinartist.com/.
- Giant Santa Claus: There is an eighteen-foot-high statue of Santa Claus in Oxnard overlooking Highway 101. It was originally on Santa Claus Lane in Carpenteria, but when it began to fall apart, some people got together, rescued it, and moved it to Oxnard.

MUSICAL WONDERS

Where are those musical sounds coming from near San Francisco Bay?

If you are referring to the large, concrete structure located on a jetty just down from the St. Francis Yacht Club in the Marina district, then that's the Wave Organ designed by artist Peter Richards and constructed by George Gonzales. It consists of twenty-five pipes made of PVC and surrounded by concrete. Sounds are made as waves splash against the pipes and water goes in and out. The organ works best at high tide, and the sounds can be rather subtle, so it encourages people to stand and take the time to listen to the waves and the organ, an exercise in not just music appreciation but also in the appreciation of nature and of taking time out of one's day to reflect and take in the world around us.

What unusual auditory event occurs when motorists drive over part of Avenue G in Lancaster?

If you enjoy classical music (or the Lone Ranger), then you'll love this: drivers rolling over the pavement on Avenue G's grooves will cause sounds to be produced that evoke "The William Tell Overture" from the opera by Gioachino Rossini. To hear the music properly, remain in the left lane of the three-lane road and drive the posted speed limit of 55 miles per hour (88.5 kilometers per hour).

What is the unusual instrument to be found near Solvang?

Originally constructed for the 1915 Panama Pacific International Exposition in San Francisco, the towering Aeolian (or wind)

The Wave Organ by the St. Francis Yacht Club in San Francisco Bay uses the action of ocean waves to create natural music.

harp was moved to Solvang. Modeled to resemble the top of the St. Nikolai Church in Copenhagen, the wind harp creates music as wind passes over and through its many threads. The intriguing instrument is somewhat neglected these days, and one can only see it by venturing behind a nursing home located on Atterdag Road.

LOONEY LANDMARKS

Why is there a 28-foot (8.5-meter) dog peeing on a wall in Newport Beach?

The "Bad Dog" sculpture in Newport Beach pees on the wall of the city's art museum. It was created by artist Richard Jackson (1939–) in 2013 and is made of fiberglass. Originally, yellow paint sprayed from the dog's penis, but no more. It was originally going to be only a temporary exhibit, but it has now been standing for three years.

How tall is the world's largest totem pole?

Although there is a totem pole that is taller, the one in McKinleyville is the tallest to be carved out of a single piece of wood. The original log was 500 feet (152 meters) tall, and the resulting artwork is 144 feet, 8 inches (44 meters) tall. Carved from a redwood tree in 1962, it was designed by artist Ernest Pierson. The reason it was erected was to promote McKinleyville Shopping Center.

Why are there oil derricks painted like animals near Coalinga?

There are a number of areas in California from which oil has been pumped, and one of these is in the Central Valley near Coalinga. Motor lodge owner Jean Dakessian Jones decided to do something about the unsightly oil pumps in the hopes of attracting visitors, some of whom might stay at her inn. With permission from Shell Oil Company, she began painting the derricks to look like various wild animals, such as giraffes, zebras, lions, and so on. She painted twenty-three of the derricks and then asked some other artists to help her. Some derricks also had horns, antlers, wings, and other beastly features added to them. A few were turned into human beings, such as a cowboy and a sailor. Sadly, when the oil began to run out and the derricks were disassembled, only a few of the creatures of the Iron Zoo were allowed to remain.

THE SUPERNATURAL, PARANORMAL, AND ALIEN

Is the Winchester House truly haunted?

That's a matter of debate, but the house itself is actually more interesting than the potential spiritual residents. Possibly the oddest house ever seen in the United States, the large mansion built by Winchester rifle heiress Sarah Winchester (1840–1922) in San Jose is a labyrinth of halls, secret passageways, unexpectedly positioned rooms, and weird stairways (one stairway goes down seven steps and then goes up eleven, and another one has forty-four steps, but each step is only two inches high). The design is Victorian inspired, with many traces of the macabre (spider web and other ghoulish designs meant to honor Winchester's belief that the home was haunted by the spirits of those killed by her family's weaponry).

A big reason for the odd construction is that there really was no plan for the home. Winchester hired the first builders in 1884, and construction continued nonstop until her death in 1922. She would simply direct the construction crew to build a room there, add a hall here, and so on without reason. She would have rooms repeatedly remodeled, torn apart, and redone. Some believed that she deliberately made things confusing in order to befuddle possible evil spirits. Although it is estimated that over 500 rooms were built over time, the mansion now has 160 rooms, forty staircases, three elevators, forty-seven fireplaces, and two ballrooms.

After she passed away, the house was deemed unlivable, not only for the peculiar floor plan but also because of earthquake damage. It is, happily, open to the public, and information about tours can be found at www.winchestermysteryhouse.com.

Which house in San Diego is considered by many to be the most haunted in the country?

Located in Old Town San Diego, the Whaley House was the home of Thomas Whaley (1823–1890). New York born, he traveled to San Francisco in 1849 to set up a store and take advantage of the Gold Rush economy. An arsonist burned down his business, however, and he relocated to San Diego in 1851. After marrying Anna Eloise DeLaunay back in New York, the couple returned to San Diego, and Whaley built his house in 1855. They had three children, one of whom died at just eighteen months old; then tragedy again struck as his business was once again the target of an arsonist. Despondent, he moved the family to San Francisco, and he worked for a time in Sitka, Alaska, while his family (including three more children) remained in California. Financial problems saw Whaley moving to New York and then San Francisco again for a time. From 1868 to 1869, the home briefly housed San Diego's first theater (the Tanner Troupe Theatre), and the courthouse rented three rooms for records storage in 1869, too.

Later, his daughters married in the San Diego home, but one of them, Violet, became divorced. Out of humiliation, she shot herself in the heart on August 18, 1885. After this, the family moved to a new house in San Diego, leaving the brick home vacant until 1909, when one of his sons, Francis, restored it. He lived there and gave tours of the home as a historic place. Other family members moved back to the old home, too,

The unusual Winchester Mystery House is strange not only for rumors of it being haunted but even more for its bizarre and confusing floor plan.

and several of them died there of natural causes, including Anna, who died in 1913, Francis, who died in 1914, and Lillian, who passed in 1953. The home again fell into disrepair, but by 1960, it had been restored and was opened to the public.

Even without ghosts, the home is a beautiful example of mid-nineteenth-century Greek revival architecture. Period furnishings decorate the rooms, and docents dressed in period outfits give tours and explain its history (sometimes catching one of these employees out of the corner of one's eye has caused guests to be startled, thinking they had just seen a ghost). Operated by the San Diego Historical Society, this first brick home built in southern California has many tales to tell, as author Brad Steiger wrote in his book *Real Ghosts, Restless Spirits, and Haunted Places:*

> Almost every facet of haunting phenomena has been observed or encountered in this mansion. Footsteps have been heard in the master bedroom and on the stairs. Windows, even when fastened down with three- or four-inch bolts on each side, have opened of their own volition, often in the middle of the night, triggering the burglar alarms.
>
> As they tour the mansion, people have often smelled cooking odors coming from the kitchen, the sweet scent of Anna Whaley's perfume, and the heavy aroma of Thomas Whaley's favorite Havana cigars. Screams have frequently been heard echoing through the upstairs rooms, as well as the sound of girlish giggles and the rattling of doorknobs. Once a large, heavy china closet toppled over by itself. Many people have heard the piano playing in the music room and phantom crowds milling and shuffling about in the courtroom. The ghostly images of Thomas and Anna Whaley have been seen on numerous occasions.
>
> Numerous individuals have sensed or psychically seen the image of a scaffold and a hanging man on the south side of the mansion. According to Mrs. Reading, ten years before Thomas Whaley constructed his home on the site, he witnessed the execution of a renegade sailor named Yankee Jim Robinson. The scaffold had stood on the spot that would later become the arch between the music room and the living room in the mansion.
>
> In the fall of 1966, a group of reporters volunteered to stay in Whaley House to spend the night with Yankee Jim. Special permission was granted to the journalists by the historical society, and the ghost hunters settled in for their overnight stay. The wife of one of the reporters had to be taken home by 9:30 P.M. She was badly shaken and claimed that she had seen something on the upper floor, which she refused to describe. The entire party of journalists left the house before dawn. They, too, refused to discuss the reason for their premature departure, but some people say that they were confronted by the ghost of Yankee Jim, still protesting the horror of his death.
>
> The primary spirits are Thomas and Anna Whaley and Yankee Jim, but Mrs. Reading said that the other ghosts have been seen, including phantoms of a young girl named Washburn, a playmate of the Whaley children; and "Dolly

Varden," the family's favorite dog. Some visitors to the Whaley house have reported seeing a gaudily dressed woman with a painted face lean out of a second-story window. In Mrs. Reading's opinion, that could well be an actress from one of the theatrical troupes that leased the second floor in November 1868.

The Court House Wing of the mansion is generally thought to be the most haunted spot in the Whaley House, due to the violent emotions of legal proceedings there in the early days of San Diego. Many individuals who have visited the old house have heard the sounds of a crowded courtroom in session and the noisy meetings of men in Thomas Whaley's upstairs study. According to many psychic researchers, the fact that this one building served so many facets of city life, in addition to being a family home, almost guarantees several layers of psychic residue permeating the environment.

Are there places that aren't houses that are haunted?

One hotspot for ghosts seems to be Santa Maria, which has a hotel and high school that are haunted. Santa Maria High School is regularly spooked by a young ghost. As the story goes, sometime in the 1920s, a student named Jeanette was about to perform in a production of *Romeo and Juliet,* but depending on the version of the tale, she either died in an accident or killed herself. In the suicide story, Jeanette was upset that she didn't get a big part in the Shakespeare play and hung herself from the catwalk above the stage while the performance was still going. The other version is creepier still. In this one, Jeanette actually won the role of Juliet. Riding her bicycle to the auditorium, she arrived just in time for the opening curtain and performed her role brilliantly. However, after the final bows, she departed quickly. The following day, the school received a call from Jeanette's mother that her daughter had been killed by a car *before she ever made it to the school.* Ever since then, the ghost of Jeanette has been seen on multiple occasions in the auditorium.

The Santa Maria Inn, just across the street from the high school, is also a place for spooks. Built in 1917, it was a resting spot for travelers between L.A. and San Francisco, including a number of VIPs such as Charlie Chaplin, Cecil B. DeMille, Rudolph Valentino, and President Herbert Hoover. It's Valentino's ghost that is said to like to make noise in the room in which he stayed. Another ghost there is the spirit of a sea captain who was supposedly murdered by his mistress while staying at the inn.

Is the Mystery Spot near Santa Cruz really a paranormal phenomenon?

There is a spot in the Santa Cruz Mountains that is about 150 feet (46 meters) in diameter where weird stuff definitely happens. Animals refuse to go there, plants grow in unnatural twists and curls, and compasses go crazy, as if this were part of the Bermuda Triangle. Perhaps the oddest effect reported is that balls will actually roll uphill.

First discovered in 1939 by a group of surveyors, it was made public the next year. Since then, there have been many theories as to what is going on, but none have been proven, and the strange things that go on here have never been explained. Some believe that powerful magnets, or even an alien craft, are buried beneath the spot. Albert Einstein is said to have surmised that a piece of star underneath the earth was responsible. Other theories involve percolating carbon dioxide, ozone layer anomalies, an underground magma vortex, radiesthesia (a force allowing people to do such things as dowsing), and dielectric biocosmic radiation, whatever that is.

What's the next best thing to Hogwarts?

While it's not a place for wizards and witches like in the *Harry Potter* books by J. K. Rowling, the Magic Castle in Hollywood is the next best thing. It houses the Academy of Magical Arts, which is a club exclusively for magicians and those who support and train them. The castle itself houses memorabilia—much of it rare—related to magic acts, and there is a restaurant and magic shows, of course.

The Mystery Spot near Santa Cruz is noted for strange phenomena that might have something to do with magnetic forces in the area.

The castle was first constructed in 1908 by real estate magnate Rollin B. Lane, who wanted to plant orange groves and run a ranch. A drought ended that dream, and he moved out in the 1940s. The building was converted to multifamily living and became rather run down and unsightly. In 1960, Milt Larsen decided to buy it. Milt was the son of William Larsen Sr., a former attorney-turned-magician who made his act a family affair, including his wife and sons, Milt and Bill Jr. Bill Sr. also founded the Academy of Magical Arts and Sciences in 1951.

Bill Sr. died in 1955, and his sons moved on: Milt became a writer for the TV show *Truth or Consequences,* and Bill Jr. was a producer for CBS television. Milt convinced his brother to help with the castle, and they managed to restore it by 1963.

To enter the castle, you must be a member or be invited by a member. There are several types of members, the most prestigious being magicians (professional or amateur, as long as you are approved as a serious artist). Magicians get access to the world-class library there and also can attend lectures. There are also associate, honorary, and, for kids thirteen to twenty, junior memberships.

In a state known for being liberal, it's strange to find that the Museum of Creation and Earth History is located in Santee, California, near San Diego.

Indeed, but perhaps it was built in the "land of the heathen" in an effort to counteract "evolutionary humanism." Founded in 1992 by the Institute for Creation Research (ICR),

Hollywood's Magic Castle is a place for professional and student magicians to learn and share their craft.

which is based in Dallas, Texas, the museum promotes the Bible and creationism in such a way as to argue that it is scientific fact. The museum includes a representation of the Garden of Eden, an exhibit showing how the earth was created in six days, an explanation of how the Grand Canyon was dug out by the biblical flood, models of Noah's Ark and the Tower of Babel, and a Hall of Scholars that includes scientists who believed in the Bible's version of creation. Originally, the museum was free, but it now charges admission. In 2008, the ICR turned operations over to the Life and Light Foundation.

Have there been any UFO sightings in California?

Oh, indeed, there have been several reports of UFOs over and in the Golden State. Perhaps the earliest one came in 1896, when several people riding an Oakland streetcar said they saw cigar-shaped UFOs ranging from a mere twelve feet in length to up to seventy feet (3.5 to 21 meters). This was actually part of a series of sightings all over the country (nineteen states) that happened between November 1896 and May 1897.

Can you see Bigfoot in the forests of northern California?

That's a matter of considerable debate. There have, indeed, been reports of giant Sasquatch in the area, but the mysterious creature is notoriously hard to spot. What you can do, though, is visit the Bigfoot Discovery Museum in Felton, which is in Santa Cruz County. Operated by Michael Rugg, who opened the museum in 2005, the modest-looking building contains a wealth of Bigfoot paraphernalia, including footprint casts, artifacts such as a tooth supposedly belonging to a Bigfoot, Sasquatch droppings (scat), reproductions of skulls and what the creature could look like, a diorama, books, movie clips, and souvenirs for sale.

A TASTE OF THE GROTESQUE

Which bizarre museum has a mission to make visitors "happy to be alive"?

That would be, ironically, the Museum of Death in Hollywood. First opened in a San Diego mortuary in 1995, it later moved to the current location and recently opened a second museum in New Orleans. J. D. Healy and Cathee Shultz opened the exhibit because they felt that American society did not do enough to educate people about a very painful reality that we all must face. The goal is to educate, not to shock, though a number of visitors have fainted upon viewing certain exhibits (the owners note that most of the faint of heart have been men).

The Museum of Death advertises that it houses more artwork by serial killers than you can find anywhere else. Other items include a collection of coffins, autopsy and mortician instruments, replicas of machines and devices designed to execute criminals, photos from Charles Manson and Black Dahlia crime scenes, taxidermy exhibits, and the severed head of Henri Landru (the serial killer known as the Blue Beard of Paris).

What can one see at the California Institute of Abnormal Arts?

Located in North Hollywood, this oddball collection of freakish displays is also a venue for live performances in what is a kind of combination museum/night club/circus. On display are various preserved body parts (as well as a mummified clown in full dress and makeup), curios, circus signage, and various screens showing clips from horror movies.

Is there a place one can go to buy some of this strange stuff?

Need you ask? This is California, so of course there is! It's called Necromance, and it's located just south of Santa Monica Boulevard on Melrose Avenue in Los Angeles. Here, customers can purchase old taxidermy specimens, old-fashioned surgical instruments, preserved bugs and bones, skull-emblazoned collectibles, and more. It's the perfect gift shop for those who enjoy the macabre.

UNCONVENTIONAL RELIGIONS, BELIEFS, AND SOCIETIES

What religion was established in Los Angeles?

Some call it a religion, while others say it is pseudoscience, but there's no denying that Dianetics and Scientology have had an influence on spiritual practices in the United

States. Science fiction author L. Ron Hubbard (1911–1986) established the Church of Scientology in Los Angeles in 1954. This new religion centered on principles drawn from Hubbard's 1950 book, *Dianetics: The Modern Science of Mental Health.* The word "Dianetics" comes from the Greek *dia* ("through") and *nous* ("mind"), and the underlying concept is that there is a metaphysical connection between mind and the body.

Scientology teaches that many of our woes in our current life are caused by negative "engrams," which are unconscious mental images from early childhood and even past lives that prevent us from achieving our full potential. The good news is that going to "auditing" sessions of dianetic counseling can clear the mind and bring peace and happiness—for as much as $1,000 an hour.

Scientology has many critics who have called it everything from a sneaky business scam to a cult, but it does have many adherents, including such movie stars as John Travolta and Tom Cruise.

What is "est"?

Founded in 1971 when Werner Erhard (1935–) first held seminars at the Mark Hopkins Hotel in San Francisco, "est" is short for Erhard Seminars Training (lowercase letters are used in the abbreviation for some reason). A kind of mix between Scientology and Zen Buddhism, est involves taking classes to get people in better touch with their true selves and, in this way, be better able to achieve their life goals. The est movement was fairly popular in California until 1984, when the company that ran the seminars closed its doors. Erhard continued to run other seminars after that through 1991 with his Werner Erhard Foundation and Werner Erhard and Associates.

Was the first UFO society founded in California?

What better place? The Amalgamated Flying Saucer Club of America was established by Gabriel Green in Yucca Valley in 1959 and was the first such organization in the country for people who believe UFOs are real.

COOL AND KOOKY CONVENTIONS

Is San Diego Comic-Con International the biggest comic book convention in the world?

No, it's not, but at about 130,000 attendees, it's certainly crowded. The largest is Comiket in Tokyo, which had a staggering 590,000 attendees in 2015. In the United States, the New York Comic-Con is the biggest at about 150,000 attendees. Comic-Con, however, is still huge and, being fairly close to Los Angeles, is attended by a lot of Hollywood moviemakers, such as the producers, directors, and actors for DC and Marvel films. Founded in 1970, it is also the oldest of the large comic book conventions and has a special place in the hearts of geeks all over the world. The biggest problem with Comic-

Con is that it can be very challenging to get tickets. Only so many are sold, and they go in a blink of an eye when online sales are opened.

Are there alternatives to Comic-Con?

Certainly. Comic book conventions have grown in popularity over the years and can be found all over the world. In California, another large convention is Wondercon, which originally ran in Oakland until 2011, then Anaheim until 2015, and, starting in 2016, now it is held in Los Angeles. It has about half the attendance as Comic-Con.

Other comic book conventions include Long Beach Comic-Con, Silicon Valley Comic-Con (in San Jose), and Wizard World Sacramento.

How about for fans of anime? Where can they go for a fun convention?

Again, yes. Several large anime conventions are held in California, including Anime Expo in Los Angeles, Anime Conji in San Diego, FanimeCon in San Jose, and Bak-Anime in Bakersfield. Anime Expo had over ninety thousand attendees in 2015, making it the largest one in the state.

Can I go to the Electronic Entertainment Expo (E3)?

If you are a professional in the video game industry, you can, but if you are just a fan, sadly, no. E3 is a professional convention meant for manufacturers, merchants, and ad-

A "fursuite parade" at the 2012 Califur convention, which is a convention for fans of anthropomorphic animal characters in fiction and art.

vertisers. It began in Los Angeles in 1995 and has an annual attendance of about fifty thousand.

Did the furry fandom originate in California?

Furries are a unique group of people, indeed. In a way, this fandom is related to sci-fi, fantasy, and animation/comic book fandoms, but with a twist: they enjoy characters in fiction who are anthropomorphized animals. That means animal characters who have human characteristics such as the ability to speak and, often, walk erect. These are the sorts of characters seen in everything from Disney and Warner Brothers cartoons to Japanese anime and underground comic books. Unlike many fandoms, furries often design their own original characters, or "fursonas." These fursonas are a blend of human and one or more animal species, some of them mythological, such as dragons and griffins, but most are based on real animals, such as dogs, wolves, lions, bears, horses, and so on.

Many furries are casual hobbyists, but some really get into it to the point that they either make or commission to be made "fursuits." This is a costume of original design made to reflect the furry's fursona. Some of them are very elaborate, including things like moving wings or LED eyeballs, and can cost thousands of dollars.

The furry fandom began in the 1980s when a group of science fiction fans who enjoyed such characters began meeting in Los Angeles. One thing led to another, and organizers Mark Merlino and Rod O'Riley put together a convention in 1989 called Confurence. That conference ran until 2003, and it helped spur on a nationwide—and then international—growth in furry conventions. Currently, there are two furry conventions (furcons) in California: Califur, which is a revival of Confurence that is run by O'Riley and Merlino, is in Pomona and has about 1,300 attendees, and the larger Further Confusion is held in San Jose and has over three thousand attendees. BABScon in Burlingame also invites furries, but it's a mix of furries, sci-fi, and anime fans.

TALK LIKE A CALIFORNIAN

How can I talk like a Californian?

If you're not from California, you might get a little confused by some of the colloquialisms used in the state, especially by younger residents. Here are a few commonly used words and phrases. Not all are completely unique to the state, but many originated there or are commonly used.

- Bail: to abandon, quit, leave
- Baller: a rich, cool person
- Ballin': having a rich lifestyle
- Betty: a very good-looking woman, a "hot chick"
- Bust: a bad idea, a waste of time, or something dangerous

- Butthurt: upset, incensed
- Chi-chi (pronounced shee-shee): ritzy, posh, rich
- Civilians: used by Hollywood stars to refer to people who aren't Hollywood stars
- Dub: a $20 bill
- Flexin': showing off
- Gnarly: awesome, cool (sometimes shortened to gnar)
- Hella: very, really, a lot
- The Industry: refers to the entertainment industry (movies, television)
- Marinating: relaxing, chilling out, goofing off
- On heavy rotation: anything in large amounts
- Spot: to borrow
- Swole: being very muscular
- Turn up / turnt up: acting wild and crazy, possibly in a sexually promiscuous way / the state of being wild and crazy

Is such slang pervasive throughout the state?

The above terms are most prevalent in southern California, especially the Los Angeles area, but can be heard by a lot of youth everywhere. There is also some slang that is more common around the Bay, such as the below:

- Coo: a shortening of cool
- The cuts: the bad part of town
- Cutty: something that isn't right
- Dusty: undesirable
- Fasho: can be used variously to mean yes, okay, definitely, for sure, you're welcome
- Fucks with: doesn't refer to intercourse; rather, it means "I'm really close to someone" or "I really like someone/something"
- Giggin': having a wonderful time (usually refers to a good time while partying and/or dancing)
- Good looks: short for "good looking out," meaning "thanks for your time and help."
- On mommas: "I put that on my momma," which is a way of saying "I'm telling the truth"
- Slaps / Slapper: an adjective to describe a hip-hop or rap song, especially referring to a pleasurable bass rhythm
- Swoop: pick up
- Tryna: trying to
- Yadadamean: a shortening of "you know what I mean?"
- Yee: variation of "yes"

What's a "Valley Girl"?

A term that came into use in the 1970s and early '80s, it refers to a kind of debutante, particularly from the San Fernando Valley, who cares more about shopping and social status than more important things. Valley girls also talk in a distinctive way (see below). Valley girls were celebrated, in a sense, in the 1983 movie *Valley Girl,* starring Nicholas Cage, Deborah Foreman, and Elizabeth Daily. Frank Zappa sang about them in the identically titled song. The chorus went like this:

Always an unconventional songwriter, musician Frank Zappa (1940–1993) wrote "Valley Girl" to mock privileged young women in the San Fernando Valley.

> Valley Girl
> She's a Valley Girl
> Valley Girl
> She's a Valley Girl
> Okay, fine ...
> Fer sure, fer sure
> She's a Valley Girl
> In a clothing store
> Okay, fine ...
> Fer sure, fer sure
> She's a Valley Girl
> In a clothing store

What's "Valleyspeak"?

Valleyspeak was a way of talking commonly used among Valley Girls that is infused with such annoying phrases as "Oh, my God!," "fer sure," "barf me out," "grody," "so gross," "bitchin'," and so on. A distinctive inflection is used where the voice goes up at the end of a sentence. Thankfully, it's not used much anymore, although one does still hear a few of its phrases on occasion.

What are some other types of language one might hear in the state?

Because there is a large Hispanic community, you will not only hear Spanish but also Chicano English (a dialect of English) and Spanglish (a combination of Spanish and English).

ODDS AND ENDS

What is perhaps the strangest mascot at a California university or college?

That would probably be the University of California, Santa Cruz, Banana Slugs. One must really admire the humor of the student body for selecting a slimy, yellow forest floor creature. Back when the issue first came up as the university began to organize its sports program to the next level, becoming a Division III school in the NCAA, the administration chose the sea lion as the official mascot in 1980. The students, however, made the banana slug the unofficial mascot. For a few years, the school had two mascots, but the students finally won out in 1986, and they officially became Banana Slugs. In 2004, *Reader's Digest* declared it the country's best mascot, and in 2008, *ESPN* named it to its top ten list.

Which city boasts the world's largest skateboard?

The world's largest skateboard used to be at the Morro Bay Skateboard Museum in Marina Square (which, by the way, has a very cool collection of old skateboards and interesting facts about famous skateboarders of the past). It was surpassed in 2009, however, by one designed by Joe Ciaglia of California Skateparks and professional skateboarder Rob Dydrek of Los Angeles. Their wheeled beast is 36 feet, 7 inches long (11.14 meters), 8 feet, 8 inches wide (2.63 meters), and 3 feet, 7.5 inches high (1.1 meters). It was unveiled on the MTV series *Rob Dydrek's Fantasy Factory* and certified as the biggest by the *Guinness Book of World Records* the following year.

CALIFORNIA NOTABLES

ACTORS AND OTHER ENTERTAINERS

Which Californian was famous for his cartoon voices?

Anyone who loves Warner Brothers cartoons will be familiar with the late Mel Blanc (1908–1989), who was a San Francisco native. For Warner, he created the thilly thtyles of such characters as Bugs Bunny, Daffy Duck, Yosemite Sam, Porky Pig, Foghorn Leghorn, Speedy Gonzales, Marvin the Martian, Pepé Le Pew, and many more. He also performed for Hanna-Barbera, doing voices for the cartoon TV shows *The Jetsons* and *The Flintstones*. In addition, for Universal, Blanc was the voice of the inimitable Woody Woodpecker.

Which TV fitness guru proved you could escape from Alcatraz by swimming?

Born François Henri LaLanne in San Francisco, Jack LaLanne (1914–2011) proved you could do remarkable things if you led a healthy lifestyle of diet and exercise, including showing that one could swim to shore from Alcatraz Island while wearing handcuffs at the age of sixty-five.

LaLanne wasn't always so healthy. As a child, he was so addicted to sugar that he blamed his violent behavior on eating too much of it. He decided to change his ways by age eighteen with exercise and proper diet. As a businessman, he ran a bakery and a gym, training police and firemen. This work got him attention from a television producer who gave LaLanne his own fitness show, *The Jack LaLanne Show,* which ran from 1951 to 1985. Even into his nineties, LaLanne was in very good health until finally succumbing to pneumonia in Morro Bay.

Which famous martial arts expert was born in San Francisco?

Although many people think Bruce Lee (1940–1973) was born in China (his birth name was Lee Jun-fan), he was actually born in San Francisco's Chinatown. His father was an opera star and movie actor touring in the United States, and shortly after Bruce was born, the family went back to Hong Kong, even though the Japanese were threatening to invade the city. They did, shortly after the Lees returned, and Bruce's family stayed in Hong Kong during the occupation. Because he had a famous father and his mixed-race mother, Grace Ho, came from one of the wealthiest families in Hong Kong, Lee led a comfortable lifestyle after the war. However, he had trouble in school and often got into fights. His life was turned around when he started studying the martial arts discipline Wing Chun under master Yip Man.

Lee's parents still feared their son could get involved in the local gangs, so in 1959, they sent him to America, where he went to college and also became a martial arts teacher and founded the discipline of Jeet Kune Do. Surviving as a teacher and giving demonstrations of his skills, Lee had his first American acting role playing Kato, the butt-kicking sidekick to the Green Hornet on the short-lived (1966–1967) television show *The Green Hornet* (as the son of an actor, Lee actually had some movie roles as a child back in Hong Kong). He reprised the role in three crossover *Batman* episodes and also appeared in other television series, including *Ironside* and *Blondie*. While having bit parts in other films such as *Marlowe* (1969) and a repeating role in the 1971 series *Longstreet*, Lee branched out into choreographing fight scenes for Hollywood.

Lee is best remembered for his starring role in three feature films: *The Chinese Connection* (1972), *The Way of the Dragon* (1973), and, most of all, *Enter the Dragon*

Martial arts master Bruce Lee will forever be a legend for his skill, strength, and breakthrough work in TV and movies.

Why did Bruce Lee's son, Brandon, die so young?

Bruce Lee had two children: Brandon and actress Shannon. Born in Oakland, Brandon (1965–1993) followed in his father's footsteps, studying martial arts and making a career for himself in Hollywood. His most noted film, *The Crow* (1994), was also his last. During filming, the crew carelessly used a gun they thought only had blanks in it but actually contained one very real bullet. The gun was fired, striking Brandon Lee in the spine. He died on the table while surgeons tried in vain to save his life. To add to the tragedy, Lee died just before he was supposed to marry.

(1973). He died only six days before *Enter the Dragon* was released. The cause was a bad reaction to pain medications he was taking for back pain, which led to a lethal brain hemorrhage.

What California-born TV chef worked on top-secret projects during World War II?

Best known as the host of TV's *The French Chef* (1963–1973) and as the author of *Mastering the Art of French Cooking* (1961, 1970), Julia Child was born Julia McWilliams in Pasadena in 1912. After working in advertising in New York City, during the war she conducted top-secret research for the Office of Strategic Services and earned an Emblem of Meritorious Civilian Service. It was her husband, Paul Child, who introduced her to French cuisine. Julia was enchanted immediately, and she traveled to Paris to attend the Cordon Bleu. Wanting to share what she learned, she published the first volume of the two-volume guide to French cooking. This quickly led to her being offered a television show on National Educational Television. Child's honors include several honorary doctorates, including from Smith College, Brown University, and Harvard, an election as fellow of the American Academy of Arts and Sciences (2000), the French Legion of Honor (2000), and the U.S. Presidential Medal of Freedom (2003).

ACTORS AND ACTRESSES

Which of the *Friends* cast was born in Sherman Oaks?

Jennifer Anniston (1969–), who played Rachel Green on the long-running television sitcom *Friends* (1994–2004), is the daughter of actors John Aniston and Nancy Dow. She graduated from the New York School of Performing Arts and had several roles on stage and on screen but achieved fame with *Friends*. Interestingly, she was first considered for the role of neat-freak Monica Geller before she was chosen to play Rachel. After the show ended, she went on to star in several feature films, many of them romantic comedies.

Which actress comes from a prestigious line of actors and actresses that has been called one of the most famous theatrical families in America?

Coming from a long line of famous actors that included her grandfather John Barrymore and great-aunt and great-uncle Ethel and Lionel Barrymore, Drew's father, John Drew Barrymore, was also an actor, though less famous; her mother, Jaid, was also an actress. Drew, who was born in Culver City in 1975, started her career early by playing a little girl who meets a friendly alien in the blockbuster Steven Spielberg movie *E.T.: The Extraterrestrial* (1982). Since then, she has built a career as an endearing actress who has captured the hearts of many theatergoers. After a rough time as a teenager, when she struggled with alcohol and drugs, she emerged in the early 1990s to get roles in such films as *Poison Ivy* (1992), Woody Allen's *Everyone Says I Love You* (1996), and the horror hit *Scream* (1996). She continued to win bigger and bigger parts in such movies as *The Wedding Singer* (1998), *Never Been Kissed* (1999), *Charlie's Angels* (2000), *50 First Dates* (2004), and the acclaimed *Grey Gardens* (2009), which earned her a Golden Globe. Barrymore also founded the production company Flower Films, which released *Whip It,* a film she directed, in 2009.

Drew Barrymore comes from a famous acting family.

Who was the *Sea Hunt* star who later morphed his tough-guy persona into a hilarious role on the movie *Airplane!*?

Born in San Leandro, Lloyd Bridges (1913–1998) became famous as the star of the popular television series *Sea Hunt* (1958–1961), which was about a SCUBA diver's adventures at sea. The son of a movie theater owner who wanted him to be a lawyer, Bridges instead went to UCLA to study acting. He started his career on Broadway and also founded an off-Broadway theater, as well as producing, directing, and acting at Green Mansions, a theater in the Catskills. While he did appear in movies, his principal successes were on television. In addition to *Sea Hunt,* he had his own program, *The Lloyd Bridges Show* (1962–1963), as well as being in such series as *The Loner* (1965–1966), *Police Story* (1974–1975), *Joe Forrester* (1975–1976), *How the West Was Won* (1976–1978), and *Harts of the West* (1993–1994), and the miniseries *Roots, George Washington,* and *North and South Book II.* While noted for drama, Bridges generated

Who's the voice of the panda who learns Kung Fu?

The Santa Monica-born Jack Black (1969–) has found success as a comedian in numerous television and movie appearances, including the *Kung Fu Panda* franchise (three CGI-animated films) in which he plays the panda named Po who learns the secret of awesomeness in Kung Fu. In another animated feature, *Shark Tale* (2004), he voices a shark named Lenny who is a vegetarian and gets into trouble with his mobster shark dad.

Other starring comedic roles include *Shallow Hal* (2001) and *Nacho Libre* (2008), but he earned the most acclaim (and a Golden Globe nomination) for *School of Rock* (2003), in which he plays an unconventional music teacher. Black is himself a musician, and he formed the comedic rock group Tenacious D with his friend from Castro Valley, Kyle Gass (1960–).

guffaws in his roles in the movie spoofs *Airplane!* (1980) and *Hot Shots! Part Deux* (1993). He got a star on the Hollywood Walk of Fame in 1994.

Who is the nephew of director Francis Ford Coppola who has made quite a name for himself as an actor?

The winner of the Oscar for his role in *Leaving Las Vegas* (1995), Nicolas Cage (1964–) was born in Long Beach. He was born Nicholas Coppola, the son of August Coppola, who was a comparative literature professor and brother of the famous movie director. Getting his start in such films as 1983's *Rumble Fish* and *Valley Girl,* Cage developed a reputation over the years of finding eccentric character roles. He's played a gangster in *The Cotton Club* (1984), a thief in *Gone in Sixty Seconds* (2000), an adventurer in *National Treasure* (2004), and a caveman in *The Croods* (2013), among many other roles.

Which Angelino first gained fame as a child actor in the 1931 film *The Champ*?

Jackie Cooper (1921–2011) had a successful career as a child actor in Hollywood, and one of his most memorable performances was his role as Dink, the young son of an alcoholic boxer in *The Champ*. Later, while continuing work as an actor, director, and producer, Cooper was in the U.S. Naval Reserve, eventually attaining the high rank of rear admiral. More recently, fans might remember him as Perry White, the editor of *The Daily Planet* in the Superman movies that starred Christopher Reeve.

What Californian danced with the wolves?

Dances with Wolves (1990) was the movie that really made Kevin Costner a highly respected actor, director, and producer in Hollywood. Born in 1955 in Lynwood, Costner came from humble origins and went to school to study business. A chance meeting with actor Richard Burton convinced him to change courses and pursue his dream. His first break was in 1983's *The Big Chill*. If you don't recall him in the film, that's because all his scenes were cut out. Nevertheless, it did get him attention. Director Lawrence Kasdan cast Costner in the Western *Silverado* (1985). From there, his career took off with roles in *The Untouchables* (1987), *Bill Durham* (1988), and *Field of Dreams* (1989).

Who became famous for his television roles as first a befuddled father and then as a chemistry teacher-turned-meth dealer?

A Hollywood actor who was also actually born in Hollywood, Brian Cranston (1956–) first gained serious attention for his comedic role as a confused father with four very-hard-to-handle sons in the TV series *Malcolm in the Middle* (2000–2007), but as great as he was in that role, he amazed audiences and critics alike for his powerful portrayal of a desperate man driven to desperate measures in *Breaking Bad* (2008–2013), which won him (and the cast and directors and producers) five Primetime Emmys. *Breaking Bad* was about a chemistry teacher who discovers he has terminal cancer; he uses his knowledge of chemistry to start making and selling methamphetamines so that his family won't become impoverished. More recently, Cranston was nominated for an Oscar for his starring role in *Trumbo* (2015) about writers being blacklisted for their political beliefs.

Which actress gets to play opposite a bunch of geeky nerds in the TV sitcom *The Big Bang Theory*?

A Camarillo native, Kaley Cuoco (1985–) plays Penny on *The Big Bang Theory*, where the humor often comes from the fact that she's just a "normal" young woman who becomes friends (and lover) with brainiacs who work at CalTech in Pasadena. As an actress, Cuoco's career goes all the way back to the early 1990s as a child actress. She had a number of television roles, including in *8 Simple Rules* (2002–2005) in which she played Bridget Hennessey, as well as doing voice work on animated programs. Penny has, though, been her ticket to success.

Still often playing a tough guy, Clint Eastwood made his name playing Western gunmen and violent cops.

Which actor went from Spaghetti Westerns to mayor of Carmel-by-the-Sea?

Clint Eastwood (1930–) has certainly had a long and interesting career. Born in San Francisco, his early reputation was built on his tough-guy movies, including the Sergio Leone Westerns (they are called "Spaghetti Westerns" because they were directed by an Italian) *A Fistful of Dollars* (1964), *For a Few Dollars More* (1965), and *The Good, the Bad, and the Ugly* (1966). Eastwood was also very popular playing Harry Callahan in the "Dirty Hairy" movie franchise about a cop with few scruples when it came to killing crooks. While in his later career he continued playing the part movie fans loved in such films as *Pale Rider* (1985) and *Unforgiven* (1992), Eastwood also has stretched his acting muscles in the romance *The Bridges of Madison County* (1995), as a boxing trainer in *Million Dollar Baby* (2004), and as a war veteran in *Gran Torino* (2008). Also a director and producer, Eastwood was mayor of Carmel-by-the-Sea from 1986 to 1988.

Which former *Saturday Night Live* comedian was awarded a Mark Twain Prize for American Humor in 2011?

Comic actor Will Ferrell (1967–), an Irvine native, won the prestigious award that honored his work in television and film. The son of a school teacher and a former musician for The Righteous Brothers (Roy Lee Ferrell, Jr.), Ferrell was actually a very serious student and athlete in high school and college before he turned to comedy. He joined The Groundlings, a comedy group in Los Angeles where such SNL alums as Jon Lovitz and Laraine Newman also got their start. Ferrell was welcomed into the SNL cast in 1995, helping to boost the flagging show's ratings and becoming, in 2001, the ensemble's highest-paid member. He left in 2002 to dedicate himself to his movie career and the next year came out with the popular holiday comedy *Elf*. Other comedies followed, including *Anchorman: The Legend of Ron Burgundy* (2004) and *The Other Guys* (2010).

What Oscar-winning actress from L.A. started acting at age two and graduated from Yale University with a literature degree?

Jodie Foster (1962–) was born Alicia Christa Foster in Los Angeles (her siblings called her "Jodie," and she adopted the name for acting). Beginning with commercials and

---

What two-time Oscar winner once played a nun who could fly?

One of the quirkier television shows from the 1960s was *The Flying Nun*, which was about a nun whose habit hat was somehow capable of making her fly in strong winds. Pasadena-born Sally Field (1946–) played the starring role of the show, which ran from 1967 to 1970. Earlier, she was also well known for playing Gidget in the series of that name, even though it only lasted one season (1965–1966). Field went on to act in other television and movie productions, ranging from the humorous *Smokey and the Bandit* (1977) to her Oscar roles in *Norma Rae* (1979) and *Places in the Heart* (1984). Other movies in which she has had supporting or starring roles include *Steel Magnolias* (1989), *Mrs. Doubtfire* (1993), *Forest Gump* (1994), *Lincoln* (2012), and *Hello, My Name Is Doris* (2015). She also had roles in the TV series *ER* (2000–2006) and *Brothers and Sisters* (2006–2011).

working her way into television episodes and small TV parts, Foster gained great acclaim playing a young prostitute opposite Robert De Niro in Martin Scorsese's *Taxi Driver* (1977), for which she earned an Oscar nomination. She later won best actress Oscars for *The Accused* (1988) and *The Silence of the Lambs* (1991), as well as another nomination for *Nell* (1994). More recently, she has been in *Anna and the King* (1999), *Panic Room* (2002), *Nim's Island* (2008), and *Elysium* (2013), as well as directing *Money Monster* (2016) and *Charlie* (2016).

Was Luke Skywalker actually born in California? How about his sister?

Yes, he's not the Tatooine native you thought he was. Best known for playing the aspiring Jedi master in the first three "Star Wars" movies by George Lucas, Mark Hamill (1951–) was born in Oakland. After majoring in drama at Los Angeles City College and getting some small roles (as well as a solid recurring part on the soap opera *General Hospital* in which he played Kent Murray), Hamill got his break when Lucas tapped him to play the young hero in *Star Wars* (1977), which was later renamed *Star Wars, Episode IV: A New Hope*. He would reprise the role in *Episode V: The Empire Strikes Back* (1980) and *Episode VI: Return of the Jedi* (1983). Never able to exceed that early success, for the most part, Hamill nevertheless has been praised for voicing the Joker in *Batman: The Animated Series* (1992–1995).

Princess Leia Organa is also a Golden State native. Carrie Fisher was born in Beverly Hills in 1956 and is the daughter of singers Eddie Fisher and Debbie Reynolds. Her success as an actress has been a bit limited because of her struggles with bipolar disorder and drug dependency. She did act in such films as *Shampoo* (1975), *Hannah and Her Sisters* (1986), and *When Harry Met Sally* (1989), but, other than the "Star Wars" films, she is best known for the semiautobiographical novel *Postcards from the Edge* (1987), which she adapted herself into a successful screenplay.

Who played "Half Pint" on *Little House on the Prairie*?

The role of Laura Ingalls—or "Half Pint" as her father (played by Michael Landon) on the show called her—was played by Melissa Gilbert (1964–), who was born in L.A. *Little House on the Prairie* was a fam-

Mark Hamill starred in the first three "Star Wars" films and reprised his role as Luke Skywalker in *Star Wars VII: The Force Awakens*.

> ## Who are some famous movie action heroes from California?
>
> To name just a couple of the bigger stars, the Golden State is the home of action stars Dwayne Johnson, Liev Schreiber, and Vin Diesel. Diesel (1967–) was born Mark Sinclair in Alameda County and is popular for starring in the "Fast and Furious" franchise. Liev Schreiber (1967–) is a San Franciscan who has gained a large fan base for his role as Wolverine in the "X-Men" movies. And Dwayne Johnson (1972–), a former professional wrestler who went by the name The Rock, gained an audience in *The Mummy Returns* (2001) and *The Scorpion King* (2003).

ily drama set in America's pioneer days and ran from 1974 to 1983. More recently, her acting credits include everything from being the voice of Batgirl in *Batman: The Animated Series* (1992–1994) to being in the 2015 TV series *Secrets and Lies*. She has a star on the Hollywood Walk of Fame.

Where was Lara Croft born?

The actress who played the tomb-raiding Lara Croft is the native Angelino Angelina Jolie (1975–). Although she gained early fame playing sexy siren and action roles like in the "Tomb Raider" films, she also has gained respect as a talented actress, winning an Oscar for supporting actress in *Girl, Interrupted* (1999) and winning for a lead role in *Changeling* (2008). Jolie may also be recognized for voicing the character Tigress in the "Kung Fu Panda" animated features and for the fascinatingly complex part of the villainess in *Maleficent* (2014). Gaining headlines in social media for her marriage with Brad Pitt, what is more admirable is her humanitarian work; she devotes a third of her income to charities and has adopted several children from around the world.

Who is the actor who became known for bigger-than-life roles, such as Captain Ahab and General MacArthur, but, even more famously, Atticus Finch?

Gregory Peck (1916–2003) was born in La Jolla. With his deep voice and rugged good looks, he made a dashing leading man in heroic movies. He actually was studying medicine at UC Berkeley when he became interested in acting and traveled to New York City, where he started getting stage roles. His star rose quickly, and after his first big role in 1944's *Days of Glory,* he was nominated for an Oscar for *The Keys of the Kingdom* (1944). Other early successes followed, including the Alfred Hitchcock thriller *Spellbound* (1945) and the touching *The Yearling* (1946), for which he got a Golden Globe award and a second Oscar nomination. He would go on to notable roles as the title part in *Captain Horatio Hornblower R.N.* (1951), Captain Ahab in *Moby Dick* (1956), Sam Bowden in *Cape Fear* (1962), and his Oscar-winning part as Atticus Finch in *To Kill a Mockingbird* (1962). Stretching even more as an actor, he was in the horror film *The Omen* (1976) and played the horrifying Dr. Josef Mengele in 1978's *The Boys from Brazil.*

In what two productions did Gregory Peck appear in that were remakes of his earlier work?

Peck was in the 1991 remake of *Cape Fear,* playing a different part, and he was Father Mapple in the television miniseries *Moby-Dick* (1998).

Who went from such roles as a stoner to a gay politician in a diverse career that has, so far, won him two Academy Awards?

When he first gained the spotlight as wasted surfer dude Jeff Spicoli in 1982's *Fast Times at Ridgemont High,* who could have suspected that Angelino Sean Penn (1960–) would go on to such an amazing career? He earned critical acclaim for dramatic roles in such films as *Dead Man Walking* (1995), *Sweet and Lowdown* (1999), *I Am Sam* (2001), *Mystic River* (2003), and *Milk* (2008), winning Oscars for the last two of these.

Which actor started the Sundance Film Festival and has been a heartthrob for many since the 1970s?

The handsome, blond-haired, blue-eyed actor Robert Redford (1936–) has attracted the attention of women all over the world since he starred in such movies as *Butch Cassidy and the Sundance Kid* (1969), *The Way We Were* (1973), and *The Sting* (1973). A Santa Monica native, he next gained attention when his directorial debut, *Ordinary People* (1980), in which he also starred, won him an Oscar for directing. He also has an Oscar nomination for *Quiz Show* (1994) and was given an Academy Award for lifetime achievement in 2002. Redford founded the Sundance Film Festival, which is held in Park City, Utah, in 1978.

Who is the heartthrob who rose from *Growing Pains* to titanic proportions?

Yes, California can claim Leonardo DiCaprio (1974–) as one of its own. Born in Hollywood itself, the actor made most famous by playing the doomed lover Jack Dawson in the 1997 blockbuster *Titanic* got his start in a supporting role for TV's *Growing Pains* in 1985, as well as other television series such as *Roseanne* (1988). Not just another pretty face, DiCaprio worked hard to take on challenging roles early in his career, such as playing a mentally challenged man in *What's Eating Gilbert Grape* (1993). After his success in *Titanic,* though, he chose not to simply stick with romantic leading roles, taking a chance with 1998's *The Man in the Iron Mask* and working with director Martin Scorsese in *Gangs of New York* (2002). He moved to action thrillers with *Shutter Island* and *Inception* (both 2010), played a delusional J. Edgar Hoover in 2011's *J. Edgar,* was a villain in the Western *Django Unchained* (2012) and then returned to tragic romance in *The Great Gatsby* (2013). Although he won Golden Globes in 2005 for *The Aviator* and in 2014 for *The Wolf of Wall Street,* many thought DiCaprio was being snubbed for the Oscar. That changed in 2016 when he won an Academy Award for playing a betrayed frontiersman in *The Revenant,* which also won him a third Golden Globe.

What are some of actor Robert Duvall's most famous roles?

Robert Duvall was born in San Diego on January 5, 1931. A distant relative of Confederate general Robert E. Lee on his mother's side, he was the son of a navy admiral and grew up in Annapolis, Maryland. After serving in the army during the Korean War for a year, he studied acting on the G.I. Bill in New York City's Neighborhood Playhouse School of Theater, where his classmates included Gene Hackman, Dustin Hoffman, and James Caan.

Starting out as a child actor, Leonardo DiCaprio became a romantic lead in *Titanic* and won an Oscar for *The Revenant.*

Some of his early important roles include acting in the movies *To Kill a Mockingbird* (1962), *M*A*S*H* (1970), *THX 1138* (1971), *The Godfather* (1972), and *The Godfather: Part 2* (1974). Winning an Academy Award for playing Mac Sledge in 1983's *Tender Mercies,* he was also nominated for acting in *Apocalypse Now* (1979), *The Great Santini* (1980), *The Apostle* (1997), *A Civil Action* (1998), and *The Judge* (2015). He won Golden Globes for *Apocalypse Now* (1980), *Tender Mercies* (1984), *Lonesome Dove* (1990), and *Stalin* (1993), as well as three nominations. Duvall won a Primetime Emmy for *Broken Trail* in 2007 and a BAFTA in 1980 for *Apocalypse Now.*

What singer and TV host was responsible for many of America's popular television game shows?

Born in San Mateo and probably best remembered as the long-time host of *The Merv Griffin Show,* Mervyn Edward Griffin Jr. (1925–2007) started as a singer and had a hit with 1950's "I've Got a Lovely Bunch of Coconuts." He also acted occasionally, gaining some notoriety for open-mouth kissing actress Kathryn Grayson in the 1953 movie *So This Is Love.*

Not caring for movies much, he moved to television and hosted the game show *Play Your Hunch* from 1958 to 1962. After making a successful appearance as guest host of *The Tonight Show* before Johnny Carson took over, Griffin was given his own talk show from 1962 to 1986. Griffin found another successful career creating game shows, starting with *Jeopardy!* which first aired in 1964 (the memorable thirty-second song heard while contestants contemplate their final answers was written by Griffin). He also created *Wheel of Fortune* in 1975. He was inducted posthumously into the Television Hall of Fame in 2008.

What dog is said to have saved Warner Brothers Studios?

Warner Brothers was struggling financially in the 1920s, when a German Shepherd named Rin Tin Tin (1918–1932) came to the rescue. Rinny himself was rescued, along with his mother and littermates, from a bombed-out German dog kennel by U.S. Army Corporal Lee Duncan. (The name comes from the name of a French doll that was often given to soldiers for good luck.)

Duncan brought his dog back to Los Angeles and trained him to perform in dog shows, where the shepherd was noticed by someone from Hollywood, and the rest is history. After having to play a wolf in a few films, Rin Tin Tin was cast as himself and made a series of movies that did very well for the studio. And the dog was treated accordingly: he had a chauffeur, a valet, and his own chef. After he became too old to perform, he was replaced by Rin Tin Tin Jr. and then Rin Tin Tin III.

Who were the original hosts of *Jeopardy!* and *Wheel of Fortune*?

Art Fleming (1924–1995) was the host of the original *Jeopardy!* that aired from 1964 to 1975. Chuck Woolery (1941–) hosted the original daytime *Wheel of Fortune* from 1975 to 1981 but wasn't interested in the night version, which was taken over by former weatherman Pat Sajak (1946–) and cohost Vanna White (1957–). The daytime version went off the air, and the nighttime version became a huge commercial success.

Which famous starlet was born Norma Jeane Mortenson?

Before she became Marilyn Monroe (1926–1962), Norma Jeane Mortenson (baptized Baker) had a very rough childhood. Born in Los Angeles, she didn't know who her father was, and her mother was put in a mental hospital. She grew up in orphanages and foster care homes until she was sixteen. While working in a factory during World War II, she was discovered by a photographer who asked her to model for him for pin-ups. This led to movie contracts, first with Twentieth Century-Fox and then Columbia Pictures in the postwar years. She had minor roles at first and then began to make her way into lighthearted comedies such as *Monkey Business* (1952) and *Don't Bother to Knock* (1952). By 1953 she was gaining popularity with the comedy *Gentlemen Prefer Blondes* (which includes the show-stopping musical number "Diamonds Are a Girl's Best Friend") and the noir thriller *Niagara*. Another iconic moment involved Monroe standing over a subway grate in *The Seven Year Itch* (1955) to have her dress blow up all around her (the dress later sold at auction for over $5.6 million).

But Monroe was getting tired of playing the dumb blonde bombshell all the time, and she wanted to be something more. She took acting lessons at the Actors Studio in 1955 and founded her own Marilyn Monroe Productions to gain some measure of artistic freedom. MMP produced *The Prince and the Showgirl* (1957), and she would go on to get a Golden Globe for best actress for 1959's *Some Like It Hot*.

Monroe's personal life was on display almost as much as her silver screen persona. She had two very well publicized marriages: one to baseball star Joe DiMaggio and the other to famous playwright Arthur Miller. Both ended in divorce. Monroe was also frequently seen around the Kennedy family, and rumors flew around that she and President John F. Kennedy were having an affair. Monroe was found dead at her L.A. home. An overdose of barbiturates was determined to be the cause. While some conspiracy theorists claim it was a cover-up to protect the Kennedys (among other theories), a more likely explanation would be that Monroe had long been struggling with depression and she took too many pills either accidentally or on purpose.

A rare photo of Marilyn Monroe taking some time off in San Diego.

Even after her death, Marilyn Monroe's fame has remained solid, perhaps even grown. Sir Elton John wrote a famous song about her ("Candle in the Wind"), and her image is seen in artwork, collectibles, and even a giant statue that has toured everywhere from Palm Springs to points in Asia.

Which little darling of the Silver Screen later became a U.S. ambassador?

Shirley Temple (1928–2014)—later, Shirley Temple Black—was a hugely popular child star in the 1930s and 1940s. Born in Santa Monica, the little dynamo with curly hair could sing, dance, and just look adorable in films like *Bright Eyes* (1934), *Curly Top* (1935), *Wee Willie Winkie* (1937), and *The Little Princess* (1939). She became famous, too, for singing the songs "On the Good Ship Lollipop" and "Animal Crackers in My Soup." The sheet music for these songs sold hundreds of thousands of copies, and Shirley Temple merchandise was a booming business (and original merchandise from that era is now worth a small fortune). Even as she grew up, Temple continued to act in more mature roles, appearing, for example, in the 1948 John Wayne and Henry Fonda Western *Fort Apache*. She also briefly had a TV show, *Shirley Temple's Storybook* (1958–1959, 1960–1961) that was a children's story anthology.

After making some TV guest appearances, she left acting and turned to politics. Joining the Republican Party, she ran unsuccessfully for California's 11th district. She was active, though, in the Commonwealth Club of California and got noticed for her knowledge of affairs in Africa. Temple was asked by the Nixon Administration to serve in the United Nations General Assembly. She later was named Ambassador to Ghana (1974–1976) and Czechoslovakia (1989–1992).

Who is the former comic actor who became an acclaimed Oscar winner for *Philadelphia*?

Concord, California, native Tom Hanks broke into the big time with goofy comedies, first on the television sitcom *Bosom Buddies* (1980–1982), in which he played a man who had to dress as a woman in order to get an affordable apartment, and in movie comedies such as *Splash* (1984), *Bachelor Party* (1984), *The Money Pit* (1986), and *Dragnet* (1987). A romance movie that was well received, *Sleepless in Seattle* (1993) would be a rarity as Hanks began proving himself a gifted dramatic actor. A string of excellent movies would feature his gifts in performing arts, including *Philadelphia* (1983), *Forest Gump* (1984), *Apollo 13* (1995), *Saving Private Ryan* (1998), *The Green Mile* (1999), *Castaway* (2000), *The Da Vinci Code* (2006), *Captain Phillips* (2013), and *Bridge of Spies* (2015).

One of the most sought-after dramatic talents working in Hollywood today is Tom Hanks.

What hearththrob actor became famous for *High School Musical*?

Born in San Luis Obispo, Zac Efron (1987–) gained a wide following for the 2006 musical film in which he played Troy Bolton. He reprised the role in the 2007 sequel.

DIRECTORS

Who was the man behind the camera for two of American pop culture's most memorable films: *Gone with the Wind* and *The Wizard of Oz*?

Victor Fleming (1883–1949) was the director in both films. Born in La Cañada Flintridge, near Pasadena, he was one of the giants at MGM during the Golden Age of Hollywood. He learned about cameras while working in the photographic section of the army during World War I, which culminated with his being President Woodrow Wilson's chief photographer during the peace treaty signing at Versailles.

After starting work in Hollywood making silent films, some with Douglas Fairbanks, Fleming got a contract to work for MGM in 1932. Here, working with such stars as Clark Gable, Spencer Tracy, Hedy Lamar, and Judy Garland, he directed many films of note, including *Treasure Island* (1934), *Captains Courageous* (1937), *The Wizard of Oz* (1939), *Gone with the Wind* (1939), *Tortilla Flat* (1942), and *Joan of Arc* (1948).

Which L.A. producer was behind such films as *Jaws* and *Driving Miss Daisy*?

Richard Zanuck (1934–2012), a native of Los Angeles, had a long, successful career producing some of Hollywood's biggest hits of the 1970s and onward. The son of Darryl F. Zanuck (1902–1979), who was the head of production at 20th Century-Fox, the younger Zanuck followed in his footsteps, although his early career was challenging. After working his way up from the story department, he became president and was behind the production of *The Sound of Music* (1965). Despite that, he was blamed for later flops like *Dr. Doolittle* (1967) and fired by his own father. Zanuck got back up on the horse and found work at Warner Bros. as executive vice president.

In 1972 he partnered with producer David Brown (1916–2010) to create the Zanuck/Brown Company, which became the force behind the early movies by Steven Spielberg (1946–), including *Sugarland Express* (1974) and *Jaws* (1975). The company also produced *Cocoon* (1974), *Cocoon: The Return* (1988), and *Driving Miss Daisy* (1989) before closing its doors. Next up for Zanuck was his association on many films with director Tim Burton (see below). Together they made such hit films as *Big Fish* (2003), *Sweeney Todd: The Demon Barber of Fleet Street* (2007), and *Dark Shadows* (2012). Zanuck won an Oscar for his work on *Driving Miss Daisy,* and the Academy also awarded him the Irving G. Thalberg Memorial Award in 1991 given to creative producers whose body of work represents consistently high quality.

Who is the man behind the *Star Wars* franchise?

Oh, yes, the man who gave us the Force, Luke Skywalker, and Yoda is a California native, too: Modesto, to be exact. George Lucas (1944–) began making films of his own as a kid, practicing camera techniques while making up stories about World War II pilots and other adventures. He studied film, of course, at the University of Southern California, graduating in 1967 and quickly founding his own company, American Zoetrope. He was partners, interestingly, with Francis Ford Coppola, who is five years his senior. Even in his twenties, Lucas was fascinated by the technical aspects of filmmaking. His first feature film,

George Lucas changed sci-fi films forever when he released *Star Wars* in 1977.

THX 1138 (1971), was based on a student movie he made at USC, which starred Robert Duvall in a dystopian science-fiction thriller. While it received mixed reviews, Lucas did better with *American Graffiti* (1973), a fond tribute to Lucas's teen life in Modesto that is set in 1962.

The success of *American Graffiti* would be a feather in the cap of any young director, but it was *Star Wars* (1977) that would be Lucas's breakthrough. On a limited budget for a sci-fi space opera, Lucas and his team at Lucasfilm Ltd. developed innovative filmmaking techniques to get the effect they wanted, while also producing an enjoyable story that became a cultural phenomenon that is going strong today. Lucas followed it up with *The Empire Strikes Back* (1980) and *The Return of the Jedi* (1983).

During the 1980s, Lucas also collaborated with director Steven Spielberg (1946–) on the "Indiana Jones" movies about an adventurous archeologist who encounters paranormal phenomena while battling Nazis and other villains. *Raiders of the Lost Ark* (1981), *The Temple of Doom* (1984), and *The Last Crusade* (1989) were all big moneymakers. Harrison Ford starred in them all (and also played Han Solo in the *Star Wars* films). While follow-ups in *Star Wars* included *The Phantom Menace* (1999), *Attack of the Clones* (2002), and *Revenge of the Sith* (2005), as well as the Indiana Jones sequel *Kingdom of the Crystal Skull* (2008), these were not as critically well-received, yet they had good box office results.

Lucas became less involved in *Star Wars* as his attention was drawn more and more to the special-effects business through his company Industrial Light and Magic, which he founded in 1975 in Van Nuys but is now based in San Francisco. ILM has been a leader in computer-generated imaging and camera technology for decades and has had a huge influence on Hollywood films, especially in the fantasy and sci-fi genres.

Bowing out into semiretirement in 2012, Lucas sold both Lucasfilm and ILM to Walt Disney and announced he would only work on smaller-budget films. He was therefore only a creative consultant when *Star Wars* was reintroduced to fans in 2015 with *The Force Awakens*.

Out of whose creepy mind came such films as *Beetlejuice, The Corpse Bride,* and *Abraham Lincoln: Vampire Hunter?*

Tim Burton's (1958–) penchant for the mordant and bizarre goes back to his childhood, when he became an ardent fan of Vincent Price movies. Born in Burbank, he had a love of drawing and proved his talent while in the ninth grade when he entered a contest to create a poster for a garbage company; he won, and his design was used for the company's ads for a year. After attending the California Institute of Arts, the young Burton went to work for Disney as an animator. Here, his talent was quickly recognized, and he was even allowed to do his own short film for Disney. *Vincent* (1982) paid homage to Burton's hero, Vincent Price, and was about a boy who wanted to be just like the actor. Price even narrated it. Two years later, Burton made another quirky short, *Frankenweenie* (1984), which is a Frankenstein-like tale in which a dog takes the role of the monster. Burton remade it into a feature-length film in 2012. Paul Reubens liked *Frankenweenie* and selected Burton to direct *Pee-Wee's Big Adventure* (1985).

Thus began a long and definitely quirky career—sometimes as director, sometimes producer—that features such films (some blockbusters, others becoming cult favorites after their releases) as *Beetlejuice* (1988), *Edward Scissorhands* (1990), *Batman* (1989) and *Batman Returns* (1992), *The Nightmare before Christmas* (1993), *Ed Wood* (1994), *Mars Attacks!* (1996), *Sleepy Hollow* (1999), *Charlie and the Chocolate Factory* (2005), *Corpse Bride* (2005), and *Abraham Lincoln: Vampire Hunter* (2012).

SINGERS, MUSICIANS, COMPOSERS

What was unique about composer John Cage?

Born in Los Angeles, John Cage (1912–1992) was an *avant garde* composer who experimented with tape recorders, radios, record players, and the nonstandard use of musical instruments. He was a pioneer of electroacoustic music, which employed computer and other electronic sounds into compositions; Cage was also a leading voice in the genre of indeterminacy music, which was the idea to let the performer of a piece have much more freedom in interpreting a composition—sort of how freestyle jazz is done, only starting with a written piece of music.

What jazz musician and composer was noted for his unusual time signatures and his score for the movie *The French Connection*?

Born in Los Angeles, Don Ellis (1934–1978) was first turned on to jazz and big band music when he attended a Tommy Dorsey concert as a teenager, and he also enjoyed such greats as Dizzy Gillespie and Louis Armstrong. Graduating from Boston University with a degree in music composition, he played for the Glen Miller Band (Ray McKinley was conducting for the late Miller). After a stint with the U.S. Army, during which he played for the band, of course, Ellis settled in the Big Apple's Greenwich Village, got involved with *avant garde* jazz musicians, traveled in Europe, and became interested in Indian music when he met Harihar Rao as an ethnomusicology student at UCLA; he also experimented with Third Stream (mixing classical and jazz). Ellis then formed the Hindustani Jazz Sextet, which would perform at the 1966 Monterey Jazz Festival. With a contract with Columbia Records, the Don Ellis Band would be extremely popular, both among regular jazz enthusiasts and academics alike. He gained even more attention for writing the scores for *The French Connection* (1971) and *The French Connection II* (1975). Switching labels to Atlantic in 1977, Ellis was given the unusual task of writing new arrangements of the *Star Wars* theme song (by John Williams) and a second track from the movie, too, as well as composing more songs to fill a full album, which became *Music from Other Galaxies and Planets*. Ellis was already having heart problems at this time, and the following year, they caught up with him, and he passed away in Hollywood.

Which Grammy-winning singer used her talents to bridge the gaps between jazz, blues, and rock-and-roll music?

Born Jamesetta Hawkins in Los Angeles, Etta James (1938–2012) had a troubled life. She never knew her father, and her mother was gone so often that the child ended up in foster care. As many blues, gospel, and jazz singers have, James got her singing start in the choir at her church, soon becoming very popular there. At the tender age of fourteen, she met band leader Johnny Otis (1921–2012; a Vallejo, California, native, by the way), who helped her get her first breaks. He changed her name from Jamesetta to Etta James and renamed the group she had formed as the Peaches. The group had a 1955 hit with "Dance with Me, Henry," and they toured with Little Richard after that. Going solo, she had another hit in 1960 with "All I Could Do Was Cry," a bluesy, doo-wop tune, and, the same year, "My Dearest Darling." Signing with Warner Bros. Records, a label she stuck with

Etta James poses with her Hollywood Walk of Fame star in 2003.

through much of the 1970s, she continued to put out hits like "Something Got a Hold on Me" and "Tell Mama" and was a standard name on R&B Top 40 lists for years.

Toward the end of her career she had racked up six Grammy Awards, seventeen Blues Music Awards, and was in the Blues and Rock and Roll halls of fame. She passed away in Riverside due to complications from leukemia.

Which entertainment icon best known for her performance in *Cabaret* was also the daughter of a young girl who went to Oz?

The daughter of Judy Garland (Dorothy in *The Wizard of Oz*) and director Vincent Minnelli, Liza Minnelli (1946–) was born in Hollywood. She definitely had performer blood in her veins, and by her teen years, she was on stage and in nightclubs singing her heart out in New York City. Her first Broadway appearance was in the musical *Flora the Red Menace* (1965); it was not only her debut, it was also her first Tony Award performance. A few years later, she won an Oscar for the film version of *Cabaret* (1972), which is probably her best-remembered role. A second Tony came to her display shelf in 1978 for her performance in *The Act,* and three years later, she was applauded for costarring with

Who was the spunky Hispanic who rocked the radio with "La Bamba" and inspired a famous song after his death?

The tragically short life of Ritchie Valens (1941–1959) will always be remembered for the delightful, toe-tapping songs he wrote as part of the Chicano rock movement. Born in Pocoima, his young ears were filled with the sounds of flamenco, mariachi, R&B, and blues guitar music. His father encouraged him to learn to play the guitar and trumpet, and Valens also taught himself the drums. Joining a group called the Silhouettes at the age of sixteen, he was noticed by Del-Fi Records owner Bob Keane. Keane brought Valens to the studio, recording several singles, with "La Bamba" being the most successful. It sold over a million copies and was awarded a gold disc by the Recording Industry Association of America.

The fact that Valens died in a plane crash is made all the more creepy by the fact that he had a fear of flying ever since a freak, two-plane crash killed some of his high school friends. Nevertheless, the young talent got on board a small plane leaving from Fargo, North Dakota, that also had music sensation Buddy Holly aboard. It crashed mysteriously, killing Valens, Holly, J. P. "The Big Bopper" Richardson (of "Chantilly Lace" fame), and the pilot. Later, singer Don McLean wrote about the incident in his 1971 classic, "American Pie."

Dudley Moore in the movie comedy *Arthur*. Also nominated for a Tony for her role in *The Rink* (1983), Minnelli has had a successful career as a recording artist, too. Her well-known battles with drugs—in fact, she discussed it openly, along with her decision to go into rehab—Minnelli focused on concert performances when she was feeling well, including memorable performances at Carnegie Hall in Radio City Music Hall; she also toured with Frank Sinatra and Sammy Davis Jr. in the 1980s. More recently, she was inducted into the American Theatre Hall of Fame in 2000.

What famous rocker can say he is a founder of the rock bands The Byrds, CPR, and Crosby, Stills, Nash, and Young?

David Crosby (1941–) is a folk rock legend. Born in Los Angeles, he was definitely an integral part of the counterculture movement of the 1960s and early 1970s. Crosby was part of the Laurel Canyon songsters that included Joni Mitchell, Stephen Stills, and Cass Elliot. The son of Oscar-winning cinematographer Floyd Crosby, he attended Santa Barbara City College but dropped out to go to Greenwich Village, New York, where he would meet Bob Dylan. Dylan's publisher helped Crosby and the Byrds get their start with their demo disc, a version of Dylan's "Mr. Tambourine Man" that actually did better than the original. Crosby wrote the Byrds hit "Eight Miles High" and cowrote "Why" with Roger McGuinn. But Crosby's outspoken political diatribes during performances irked the other members, especially when they were playing at the 1967 Monterey Pop Festival (see also the chapter "The State of California: 1850 to the Present"). He was pressured to leave the Byrds, at which point, already friends with Stephen Stills, he joined what became Crosby, Stills, Nash, and Young (sometimes just Crosby, Stills, and Nash), which included Graham Nash and, sometimes, Neil Young. With this group, he penned such songs as "Guinevere," "Long Time Gone," and "Wooden Ships," the last of which he cowrote with Stills and Paul Kantner. Like pretty much all groups, CSN split apart, and the members went their separate ways. Crosby would perform solo and also with other greats of his day ranging from Joni Mitchell and Carole King to Jackson Browne and James Taylor. In 1996 he formed the group CPR, which includes his son, Pianist James Raymond, and guitarist Jeff Pevnar. This association lasted until 2004.

Though he didn't like to be thought of in that way, who was really the front man for The Grateful Dead?

The San Francisco-born Jerome John "Jerry" Garcia (1942–1995) achieved something few musicians in a group do: he was in The Grateful Dead for his entire professional career from 1965 until his death from a heart attack. His father was a professional musician, and his mother was an amateur pianist, so Jerry's first instrument was the piano. At the tender age of four, though, he lost most of his right-hand middle finger to an accident when his brother was chopping wood and Jerry wasn't careful when placing a piece of wood to be chopped. Then, the next year, his father drowned during a fishing trip. His mother took over running his father's bar, and Jerry went to live with his grandparents. It was there that he became interested in bluegrass and took up the banjo because his grandmother enjoyed it. He dropped out of school at age seventeen and served

briefly in the U.S. Army before returning to San Francisco, where he played folk and blues at local clubs while also teaching music and working as a salesman.

Garcia founded The Grateful Dead in 1965. However, the name originally was The Warlocks; he changed it the next year upon discovering there was already a group called The Warlocks. A textbook case of the right time (1960s) and place (San Francisco), the band's brand of psychedelic rock was perfect for the hippie culture at the time. Among their memorable hits are "Casey Jones" (1970), "Truckin'" (1970), "Friend of the Devil" (1970), "Uncle John's Band" (1970), "Ripple" (1970), "Sugar Magnolia" (1970), "Bertha" (1971), "Scarlet Begonias" (1974), "Fire on the Mountain"

Long-time guitarist and vocalist for The Grateful Dead, the late Jerry Garcia was one of the greats of his era.

> ## What California rocker had a Ben & Jerry's ice cream flavor named after him?
>
> Cherry Garcia is named after the Grateful Dead's Jerry Garcia. It is a sumptuous combination of cherries and chocolate chunks.

(1978), and "Touch of Grey" (1987). The Grateful Dead had a huge following of fans who called themselves "Deadheads." Garcia and his bandmates lived the high life, and the guitarist abused his health with drugs; he also had diabetes and sleep apnea, and his body finally succumbed in 1995, the year after he was inducted into the Rock and Roll Hall of Fame.

Which composer and musician from L.A. is noted for his quirky, rather satirical songs that have been featured in the *Toy Story* movies?

Randy Newman (1943–) was born in L.A., the son of an internist. While his parents weren't involved in music, Newman actually has many family members who are. These include grandfather Joey Newman, uncles Emil, Alfread, and Lionel Newman, and cousins Joey, David, and Thomas Newman, who were all composers of film and television scores, and his cousin Maria Newman, who is a musician and composer of classical music.

Turning professional at the green age of seventeen, Newman released his first single, "Golden Gridiron Boy," in 1962. It didn't do well, and he spent the next several years working his way through clubs and college shows until he found success with his first two albums: *Randy Newman* (1968) and *12 Songs* (1970). "Mama Told Me Not to Come" from *12 Songs* was recorded by Three Dog Night and became Newman's first big hit. In 1972, "You Can Leave Your Hat On" from the album *Sail Away* was covered by both Joe Cocker and Tom Jones. Newman's first hit that was on the airwaves with his own singing was "Short People" from *Little Criminals* (1977). "Short People," like many of his songs, was a satirical piece meant to mock how ridiculous prejudices are, but many people were offended because they took the fake jibes at short people at face value. He also had a minor hit with "I Love L.A." in 1983, a variation of which was used to promote tourism to the city.

Newman has received plaudits for his songs for television shows and movies. "You've Got a Friend in Me" for 1995's *Toy Story* was a sensation, and he wrote music for the two sequels, as well. He's also written scores for the films *Ragtime* (1981), *The Natural* (1984), *Seabiscuit* (2003), and many others, including the animated features *James and the Giant Peach* (1996), *Monsters, Inc.* (2001), *Cars* (2006), and *The Princess and the Frog* (2009), among others. He won a Grammy for the song "It's a Jungle Out There" (2003) for the TV show *Monk*. He's won, as of this writing, three Emmys, six Grammys, and two Oscars.

Which singer and songwriter started a career as a cheerleader and also served as a judge on TV's *American Idol*?

The daughter of concert pianist Lorraine Rykiss and a Jewish Syrian father named Harry Abdul, Paula Abdul was born June 19, 1962, in San Fernando. Starting off her career as a cheerleader for the L.A. Lakers, she became a skilled and sought-after choreographer and dancer. She did choreography work for The Jacksons and also is notable for coming up with the keyboard dance scene in the Tom Hanks movie *Big* (1988).

But Abdul also wanted to sing, and she took advantage of the height of the MTV era by combing her singing abilities with dance. She made a particular splash with the music video "Opposites Attract" (1989) in which she dances with an animated cat; she won a Grammy for the song. Several successful albums followed, including *Spellbound* (1991) and *Head over Heels* (1995). She went on to be a popular judge on the television contests *American Idol* and *The X Factor*.

Who was the hip hop artist known for singing "You Can't Touch This"?

Best known as M. C. Hammer (or simply Hammer), Stanley Kirk Burrell was born on March 30, 1962, in Oakland. He was an innovator in pop rap (making rap more palatable to a broader audience) and was the first to get a diamond album (for 1990's *Please Hammer, Don't Hurt 'Em),* getting attention in his music videos for wearing baggy "Hammer pants" in his dance numbers. Popular from the 1980s to the 1990s, some of his other albums include *Let's Get It Started* (1988), *Too Legit to Quit* (1991), *Inside Out* (1995), and *Look Look Look* (2006).

What other rap stars call California their place of birth?

Among the many artists who have come out of the Golden State are Dr. Dre (1965–), who was born straight outta Compton, Ice Cube (1969–), who is from Los Angeles, and Snoop Dogg (1971–), who was born in Long Beach.

Who is the former CCR musician who *Rolling Stone* considered to be one of the greatest guitarists and singers in rock history?

Berkeley native John Fogerty (1945–) was a founding member of the Blue Velvets, which was renamed the Golliwogs and, finally, by their better-known name, Credence Clearwater Revival. CCR had its heyday from 1967 to 1972, putting out such hits as "Born on the Bayou," "Proud Mary," "Who'll Stop the Rain," "Lookin' Out My Back Door," and "Down on the Corner." After the group broke up, Fogerty embarked on a solo career, trying country and Western songs with the *Blue Ridge Rangers* album in 1973. It didn't do well, and Fogerty's success was sporadic afterward. He had a Top 40 hit in 1975 with "Rockin' All Over the World" but didn't have another big hit until 1985's "The Old Man Down the Road." CCR was inducted into the Rock and Roll Hall of Fame in 1993, and in 1997 Fogerty earned a Grammy for the album *Blue Moon Swamp*. The next year, he was honored with a star on the Hollywood Walk of Fame.

How did an El Centro girl named Cherilyn Sarkisian become a pop diva?

Better known these days as Cher, she was born May 20, 1946, in a rather humble home run by her truck-driver father and a mother who occasionally acted and modelled. She was just sixteen when she dropped out of school, moved out of her house, and went to Los Angeles to find work as a dancer, singer, and actor. She got a break when she met Sonny Bono (1935–1998), who was working for record producer Phil Spector at the time. Sonny and Cher fell in love, got married, and Cher started a solo career. Because she suffered from stage fright, she asked her husband to join her on stage, and the pair became a singing duo. Their first big hit was 1965's "I Got You, Babe." Together, they became popular with the television show *The Sonny and Cher Comedy Hour*

Cher was actually once very shy as a performer, but her late husband Sonny Bono brought out the talent in her so that today she is a singing legend.

(1971–1974). Sadly, the couple divorced in 1975. They tried to reboot the show in 1976, but it was cancelled the next year.

A troubled, short-lived marriage to Gregg Allman of the Allman Brothers was compounded by a couple of failed albums in the late 1970s, but Cher made her comeback in the 1980s, more as an actress than a singer. She had feature roles in both the stage and film productions of *Come Back to the Five and Dime, Jimmy Dean, Jimmy Dean* (1982), *Silkwood* (1983), *Mask* (1985), *Moonstruck* (1987), and others. She won an Oscar and a Grammy for her performance in *Moonstruck*.

Cher would have ups and downs in her musical career, but the highs she hit were high indeed. Among her popular songs include "After All," "If I Could Turn Back Time," "I Found Someone," "Strong Enough," "Dark Lady," "The Shoop Shoop Song (It's in His Kiss," "Gypsies, Tramps and Thieves," "Save Up All Your Tears," "You Haven't Seen the Last of Me," and "Believe."

Is Weird Al Yankovic from California?

Where else would an accordion-player-turned-musical-parodist come from? Weird Al was born in 1959 in the town of Downey outside Los Angeles. Yankovic, who got the nickname "Weird Al" from college classmates, got his first big break on "The Dr. Demento Show" in 1976, when the doctor (Barry Hansen) played the song "Belvedere Cruisin'" from a tape that Yankovic had given him after Hansen had spoken at his high school.

While attending California State Polytechnic University as an architecture student, Yankovic worked as a disc jockey at the school's radio station and continued to work on songs that he'd submit to Dr. Demento. Some of his early spoofs include "My Balogna" (based on "My Sharona" by The Knack) and "Another One Rides the Bus" (a parody of Queen's "Another One Bites the Dust"). No pop act is safe from Weird Al, who has targeted everything from Michael Jackson ("Eat It," "I'm Fat") to Lady Gaga ("Perform This Way"). Most entertainers have taken the parodies in stride. The late Michael Jackson, for example, once said he was a big fan.

Weird Al, who has also appeared in movies and television, has won three Grammy Awards for best comedy album and a fourth Grammy for best concept music video ("Fat"). He recently announced he would no longer release albums but would, instead, publish new material exclusively online.

Musical satirist Weird Al Yankovic has been famously spoofing popular songs since the 1970s.

ARTISTS AND AUTHORS

Who was the photographer famous for his black-and-white photographs of the American West, especially Yosemite National Park?

Ansel Adams (1902–1984) was born in San Francisco and was initially thinking of being a pianist, but when his family took him to see Yosemite in 1916, he became enthralled with its beauty. His father gave him a Kodak Brownie box camera. The next year, he joined the Sierra Club. Thus began a career spanning over sixty years of beautiful nature photography, most of it in black and white. Adams founded Group f/64, too, who were San Franciscan photographers who enjoyed taking sharply focused, carefully framed photos that emphasized the beauty of the West.

What artist, landscape architect, and designer is often remembered for a table?

Los Angeles-born artist Isamu Noguchi (1904–1988) lived a productive life producing art that was often featured in public places and also for doing design work for choreographer Martha Graham. In the late 1940s, he began collaboration with other artists for the Herman Miller company designing furniture. The catalog of unique, forward-thinking furniture they designed is still considered the most influential catalog of modern furniture to come out of the twentieth century. Among the designs was the Noguchi table, which is still being produced for sale. Noguchi's art is honored and displayed today at the Noguchi Museum in New York City.

Which architect was in charge of constructing Hearst Castle?

A graduate of the University of California, Berkeley, Julia Morgan (1872–1957) is considered to be the first great woman architect from California. Born in San Francisco, she studied architecture at Paris's l'École

Nature photographer Ansel Adams is remembered for his breathtaking black-and-white pictures of Yosemite.

Nationale Superieure des Beaux-Arts. Returning to California, she assisted in the design of buildings for the University of California. She also designed the Hearst Greek Theatre and added decorative elements to the Hearst Mining Building. William Randolph Hearst obviously approved of her work because he chose her for the most ambitious project of her career: Hearst Castle (see "Central California and Agriculture"), which she worked on for nearly three decades. Among her other projects are the Oakland YWCA building, the Berkeley Women's City Club, and the North Star House in Grass Valley.

Morgan was awarded the American Institute of Architect's Gold Medal in 2014, the first woman to receive the honor, and she was inducted into the California Hall of Fame in 2008.

Did the cartoonist who created *Bloom County* come from California, too?

You guessed it, yes. Guy Berkeley "Berke" Breathed (1957–) was born in Encino, Los Angeles. His goofy comic strip was hugely popular in the 1980s. Featuring colorful characters such as Opus the penguin, Bill the cat, a rabbit named Hodge-Podge, a ten-year-old journalist named Milo Bloom, a Vietnam vet named Cutter John, and the scheming lawyer Steve Dallas, among others, the strip focused on a lot of political and social commentary and earned Breathed a Pulitzer Prize in editorial cartooning in 1987. The daily strip was discontinued by 1989, when Breathed switched to a Sunday-only strip called "Outland" that featured Opus and Bill. That one ended in 1995, followed by "Opus," which ran from 2003 to 2007. Breathed finally quit comic strips, declaring that the field made him a target for too many bitter attacks, and now he focuses on children's books.

Why is columnist Herb Caen so well remembered?

Herbert "Herb" Eugene Caen (1916–1997) was a longtime columnist for the *San Francisco Chronicle*. Although he was born in Sacramento, he became known as "Mr. San Francisco" for his "It's News to Me" column, which was all about that city; it vividly evoked his immense love of San Francisco and its people. The column first appeared in 1938, was interrupted when Caen served in the U.S. Army Air Forces during World War II and writing for the *San Francisco Examiner* from 1950 to 1958, and then his column reappeared in the *Chronicle* until his death.

Which novelist is noted for her literary journalism novels?

Joan Didion (1934–) was born in Sacramento and graduated from the University of California, Berkeley, with a bachelor's degree. She began her career working for *Vogue* magazine. The winner of the 2005 National Book Award for Nonfiction for *The Year of Magical Thinking*, she is noted for writing what is called creative or literary nonfiction, composing books that often focus on the culture of California. An example of this is her essay collection *The White Album* (1970), which is about 1960s and '70s California history and politics, and *Where I Was From* (2003), which is a signature blend of memoir, journalism, and history. Chaos and social and personal disintegration are frequent themes, sometimes concerning the political struggles of the world and sometimes on a more personal level, such as with *The Year of Magical Thinking* (2005), an account of her husband's, writer John Gregory Dunne's, death in 2003; *Blue Nights* (2011) is a similarly sad reflection of her daughter Quintana's death.

Which poet who was commonly associated with New England was actually born in California?

The Poet Laureate of Vermont and Pulitzer Prize-winning poet Robert Frost (1874–1963) was born in San Francisco, where his father was editor of the *San Francisco Evening Bulletin*. His family moved to Massachusetts in 1885 after his father died, and Frost would attend Harvard. From 1912 to 1915 they were in England, and the young, aspiring writer would meet such influential poets as Ezra Pound and Edward Thomas. Returning home in 1915 to keep distance from the war in Europe, he settled in New Hampshire and taught at Amherst College off and on during the 1920s and 1930s while publishing various poems and books. Frost's life would be marked by many personal tragedies: his father died of tuberculosis, his mother of cancer; several family members suffered from clinical depression, and all but two of his children died before the poet did. When he wrote about the pain of life, therefore, he knew what he was talking about.

From 1921 to 1963, he taught English at Middlebury College in Vermont, racking up Pulitzer Prizes for *New Hampshire: A Poem with Notes and Grace Notes* (1923), *Collected Poems* (1930), *A Further Range* (1937), and *A Witness Tree* (1943). Frost's mastery of poetry is not questioned today; his works have been lauded by his contemporaries and by later scholars alike who admired his command of colloquial English and his understanding of and empathy for average people and their personal struggles, of which he himself had many.

Who was the goofy cartoonist who inspired a fun and creative national contest?

San Francisco native Reuben Garrett Lucius Goldberg—Rube Goldberg (1883–1970)— was renowned as a cartoonist and came up with insanely and overly elaborate devices to perform simple functions, such as a contraption that took fourteen steps to swat a fly. Goldberg graduated with a degree in engineering from UC Berkeley, but after he got a job at the *San Francisco Chronicle,* he decided to stick with working for newspapers. It was after he moved to New York City, however, and began working for Hearst newspapers that he found his niche and his popularity. His popularity was at its height from 1922 to 1934, when his cartoons were syndicated. Among these were *Mike and Ike (They Look Alike), Foolish Questions, Lala Palooza, Boob McNutt, What Are You Kicking About?,* and *The Weekly Meeting of the Tuesday Women's Club*. His Rube Goldberg Machines appeared in strips featuring the character Professor Lucifer Gorgonzola Butts. A very productive artist, he had over fifty thousand cartoons to his credit.

Goldberg's granddaughter, Jennifer George, authored *The Art of Rube Goldberg: (A) Inventive (B) Cartoon (C) Genius* (2013) and runs Rube Goldberg, Inc., which has merchandise and licenses images by the cartoonist. More importantly, the nonprofit runs competitions for kids around the country that encourage them to be creative and inventive while making their own Rube Goldberg Machines. Students and teachers can get involved by visiting www.rubegoldberg.com.

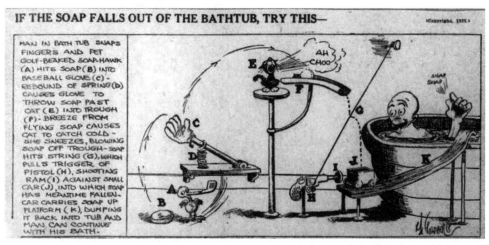

An example of a Rube Goldberg device, which is a comically, overly complicated machine designed to perform a simple task.

Who was named United States Poet Laureate in 2015?

Born in Fowler, Juan Felipe Herrera (1948–) is a poet, writer, teacher, performer, activist, and cartoonist. Often writing for children and young adults, Herrera is the son of migrant farm workers (in your face, Donald Trump). He won the Ezra Jack Keats Book Award in 1997 for *Calling the Doves/El canto de las palomas,* a bilingual memoir of his childhood. He won a National Book Critics Circle Award in 2008 for the poetry collection *Half the World in Light.* The next year saw him winning a PEN Open Book Award, a Guggenheim Fellowship in 2010, and in 2011 he was elected a chancellor of the Academy of American Poets. Governor Jerry Brown made him California's Poet Laureate in 2012, and in 2015 he became the first Chicano to be named U.S. Poet Laureate.

Who was the author who often wrote about the Chinese immigrant experience?

Maxine Hong Kingston (1940–) is a Stockton and, like a number of notable California authors, also a graduate of the University of California, Berkeley. A noted feminist who is also a professor emerita at her alma mater, Kingston won a National Book Award in 1981 for the story collection *China Men.* She also won a National Book Critics Award for the memoir *The Woman Warrior: Memoir of a Girlhood among Ghosts* (1976), a 1997 National Humanities Medal, an Asian American Literary Awards Lifetime Achievement Award in 2006, and 2013 National Medal of Arts, among other honors.

Which California author captured the vigor and grandeur of the West?

San Francisco native Jack London (1876–1916) is often remembered for such novels as *The Call of the Wild* (1903), *The Sea-Wolf* (1904), and *White Fang* (1906). He was not around for the California Gold Rush, but his sense of adventure drew him to Canada for the Klondike Gold Rush in 1897. Later, he started publishing short stories in publications such as *The Saturday Evening Post.* Among his other adventures abroad as a journalist, he was a war correspondent during the Russo-Japanese War in 1904. Returning to California, he purchased a farm he called the Beauty Ranch in Sonoma County. Much of his writings after 1910 were penned more for money than for any artistic desire and are considered much less important than his early work.

Known for his adventure novels, Jack London was famous for such books as *The Call of the Wild* and *White Fang.*

London passed away unexpectedly in his sleep at his ranch in 1916. Although a seemingly robust man, over the years he had suffered variously from scurvy, uremia, and addictions to alcohol and morphine. In addition to his books, his legacy is the Jack London Club, an animal rights group that protested cruelty to circus animals.

What was interesting about the writings of William Saroyan?

William Saroyan, who was born in Fresno in 1908 and passed away in his home city in 1981, was noted for writing about Armenian immigrants in California. This is to say, he wrote from experience, and did it well, winning a Pulitzer Prize for Drama for *The Time of Your Life* (1939), which also won a New York Drama Critics Circle Award. Some of his other important works include *My Heart's in the Highlands* (1939), *My Name Is Aram* (1940), and *The Human Comedy* (1943).

Which American author is perhaps the most quintessentially Californian?

John Steinbeck (1902–1968) was born in Salinas. Winner of the Pulitzer Prize for *The Grapes of Wrath* (see the chapter "The State of California"), many of his works are set in California, especially in Salinas Valley and the California coast. Among these are *Tortilla Flat* (1935), *Of Mice and Men* (1937), *Cannery Row* (1945), and *East of Eden* (1952).

ATHLETES AND COACHES

BASEBALL

Which California baseball slugger beat Hank Aaron's home run record?

Barry Bonds (1964–) had 762 home runs during his career. Born in Riverside, he played with the Pittsburgh Pirates (1986–1992) and the San Francisco Giants (1993–2007). The son of another major leaguer, Bobby Bonds, he surpassed Babe Ruth's homer record in 2006 and Aaron's record the following year. He was also a member of the 40-40 Club, as of 1996, which means he had over forty home runs that year (42) and stole forty bases.

Who is another power hitter in recent baseball history who also founded a charity for children?

Beloved in California for his years with the Oakland A's, Mark McGuire (1963–) was born in Pomona and had a stellar career. Although his homer record was broken by Barry Bonds, McGuire beat Roger Maris's 1961 homer record (62), and he won a silver medal playing for the 1984 U.S. Olympic baseball team. His career batting average was .263, with 583 homers and 1,414 RBIs. After his days with the A's (1986–1997), he played with the St. Louis Cardinals until 2001. He later became a coach for the Cardinals, Dodgers, and, as of this writing, the Padres.

Although forever associated with the New York Yankees, baseball great Joe DiMaggio was a native of Martinez, California.

Which renowned Yankee player was born in California and married Marilyn Monroe?

Joltin' Joe DiMaggio (1914–1999) will forever be a favorite among Yankee baseball historians, but did you know he was born in Martinez, California? He was one of nine children born to Sicilian immigrants. He went on to a major career, playing with the Yankees from 1936 to 1951, with the exception of the World War II years. With a .325 batting average, 361 homers, and 1,537 RBIs, he remains one of the all-time greats and was inducted into the Baseball Hall of Fame in 1955. Very popular with the fans, he also made the news marrying actress bombshell Marilyn Monroe in 1954, though she divorced him nine months later. They later became friends until her tragic death.

Who was one of the greatest hitters of all time?

Ted Williams (1918–2002) played for the Boston Red Sox, but he was born in San Diego. During a career that ran from 1939 to 1960 (with a break for World War II, during which he served in the Navy and Marines), Williams racked up 521 home runs, 2,654 hits, and 1,839 RBIs. Later in life, he managed the Washington Senators and Texas Rangers from 1969 to 1972 and helped raise millions of dollars for cancer research and treatment, the latter deed earning him a Presidential Medal of Freedom in 1991. Williams was inducted into the Baseball Hall of Fame in 1966, but he also was inducted into the Fishing Hall

---

Which baseball player got his name dropped in a Simon and Garfunkel hit song?

In the 1968 song "Mrs. Robinson" by the folk duo, which was made famous in the movie *The Graduate*, Joe DiMaggio gets a nod:

> Where have you gone, Joe DiMaggio?
> Our nation turns its lonely eyes to you.
> Boo hoo hoo!
> What's that you say, Mrs. Robinson?
> Joltin' Joe has left and gone away.
> Hey hey hey!
> Hey hey hey!

---

of Fame because of his contributions to sport fishing, including hosting a TV show on the subject.

Which baseball star is the only one to hit two grand slams in the same game at his home stadium?

Nomar Garciaparra (1973–), who is best remembered for his years with the Boston Red Sox, was born in Whittier. His notable achievement of two grand slams in a single game is matched only by twelve other players, and none of them did it at their own stadium. Garciaparra also played for the Chicago Cubs, the Dodgers, and the Athletics. A wrist injury forced him to retire in 2009 with a batting average of .313 and 229 home runs.

BASKETBALL

Who was the first NBA star to come out as gay?

While some retired players have come out of the closet, Jason Collins (1978–) was the first to do so while still actively playing. A Northridge native who went to Stanford University, he was not only the first in the NBA to announce he was gay, but he was the first of any major sport (football, baseball, and hockey included) to do so. Collins played with the New Jersey Nets from 2001 to 2008, then played for various other teams. He came out in the May 6, 2013, issue of *Sports Illustrated*.

Which coach was known as the "Wizard of Westwood"?

UCLA hoops coach John Wooden (1910–2010) is in both the College Basketball Hall of Fame and the regular Basketball Hall of Fame. He coached the Bruins' men's basketball team from 1948 to 1975, winning ten NCAA Championships (1964, 1965, 1967, 1968, 1969, 1970, 1971, 1972, 1973, and 1975).

Who's that surprisingly tall Asian-American basketball player?

Jeremy Lin (1988–), who was born in Torrance to Taiwanese immigrants, stands 6'3" (1.91 meters) tall and weighs 200 pounds (91 kilograms). He played for Palo Alto High School, but when no California college offered him a scholarship, he went to Harvard and played for them, graduating in 2010. His professional career started with the Golden State Warriors, and he has played variously for the Knicks, Rockets, Lakers, and Hornets.

FOOTBALL

Who is the four-time Super Bowl champion quarterback for the Patriots who might have been an MLB player?

Tom Brady (1977–) is a San Mateo native who has played for the New England Patriots since 2000, taking them to victories in Super Bowls XXXVI, XXXVIII, XXXIX, and XLIX. Brady is considered the greatest NFL quarterback since Joe Montana, and he was a fan of Montana as a young man attending San Francisco games at Candlestick Park. In high school, he was a talented baseball player and he was actually drafted in 1995 to play for the Montréal Expos, but Brady preferred to pursue football. In college, he was a backup quarterback for the Michigan Wolverines before making first string in 1998. Even so, when the 2000 NFL draft came along, no one really appreciated the hidden talents Brady possessed. New England took the young man, who proceeded to explode on the gridiron.

Which USC football star decided not to accept the Heisman Trophy?

Reggie Bush (1985–) has the unenviable sidebar note of being the first and, so far, only college football star to be forced to return the Heisman, which he had won in 2005 for gaining over 6,600 yards as a running back for USC. Born in San Diego, he attended high school in La Mesa. The Heisman Trust took his award away after accusing Bush of accepting $300,000 in cash and other gifts from a sports marketer, which is forbidden for college players to do. Despite this ugly chapter in his life, Bush has gone on to a successful NFL ca-

New England Patriots quarterback Tom Brady is a native northern Californian who was inspired to pursue the sport by watching Joe Montana play for the 49ers.

What incident involving the war in Afghanistan led to tragedy for a California footballer?

Army Ranger Pat Tillman (1976–2004), a Fremont native, played for Arizona State University (and was on their 1996 Rose Bowl-winning team, winning the Pac-10 Defensive Player of the Year) and then for the Arizona Cardinals as a safety. Tillman enlisted in the army shortly after the September 11, 2001, terrorist attacks and took part in Operation Iraqi Freedom in 2003. He then completed training to become a Ranger. On April 22, 2004, while in Afghanistan near the Pakistan border, Tillman was shot and killed. It later came out that he was shot, accidentally, by someone in his own unit. The military tried to cover up the fiasco, but the truth eventually came out. Since then, two books and a movie about the incident have come out: his mother wrote *Boots on the Ground by Dusk* (2008), and Jon Krakauer released *Where Men Win Glory: The Odyssey of Pat Tillman* the next year. Director Amir Bar-Lev made *The Tillman Story* (2010), which talks about what happened and the subsequent cover-up efforts.

reer and was on the winning Super Bowl XLIV New Orleans Saints team in 2009. He went on to play for the Dolphins and Lions and, beginning in 2015, is on the 49ers roster. Bush also gained some fame for dating TV reality show star Kim Kardashian.

Who is the Dallas Cowboy star from San Diego?

That would be Tony Romo (1980–). He is the grandson of Mexican immigrants, and his father was in the U.S. Navy and stationed in San Diego when Tony was born. Romo attended Eastern Illinois University, where he won the NCAA's Walter Payton Award for being the best player in the I-AA Division. Drafted by Dallas in 2003, he has been with the team ever since. He is the first Cowboy to pass for over 220 yards in his first eight starting games, and he has been on four Pro Bowl teams and has won several awards as passing and touchdown leader.

GOLF

Whose motto is "Grip It and Rip It"?

John Daly (1966–) of Carmichael made a splash in 1991, when he won the PGA Championship at Crooked Stick, Indiana; no one knew who the heck he was at the time. He has had somewhat of an up-and-down career since then, partly because of his problems with alcohol and gambling, but he won many fans over with his no-nonsense play characterized by his motto. Daly has also won the 1995 British Open, the 2001 BMW International Open in Munich, Germany, and the 2004 Buick Invitational in Torrey Pines, California. He is the author of the 2006 memoir *My Life In and Out of the Rough*.

What Hispanic American was the first and only golfer to be Rookie of the Year and Player of the Year in the LPGA the same year?

Born in Torrance, Nancy Lopez (1957–) has been called the greatest female golfer of her generation. Since turning pro in 1977 (and winning Rookie of the Year), she has won LPGA championships in 1978, 1985, and 1989 and was LPGA Player of the Year four times (1978, 1979, 1985, and 1988). Inducted into the World Golf Hall of Fame at the age of thirty, she won a total of forty-eight LPGA events before retiring in 2002. She married Ray Knight, who won the World Series while with the Mets.

Is Tiger Woods the greatest golfer of his generation?

That might be a matter for debate, though when Tiger Woods (1975–) was born in Cypress, his father encouraged his young son early on, and he became a child prodigy of golf. In fact, when Tiger was still shy of three years old, he appeared on *The Mike Douglas Show* and showed off his skills with the golf club.

Once he got on the pro circuit, it was as if Woods was unstoppable. He racked up the following titles as of 2016: four Masters (1997, 2001, 2002, 2005), four PGA Championships (1999, 2000, 2006, 2007), three U.S. Opens (2000, 2002, 2008), and three British Opens (2000, 2005, 2006). But his career hit a major bump in 2009, when it was revealed that he was having an affair. Divorced the following year, the personal setback and subsequent negative media attention had a bad effect on his performance on the links, and he has not won a major tournament since then (as of this writing).

Who might be considered Tiger Woods's biggest rival?

A likely candidate for that position would be Phil Mickelson (1970–). Born in San Diego, he turned pro in 1992 and has won Masters tournaments in 2004, 2006, and 2010. Mickelson, known as "Lefty" for obvious reasons, actually had a number of disappointing years in the beginning. Though clearly talented, it was a long time before he got to wear the green jacket and was consequently called "the greatest player never to win a major." He's been very successful in recent years, however, also winning the 2013 British Open.

Who was one of the greatest golfers to play the game?

San Diego native Mary Kathryn "Mickey" Wright (1935–) was inducted into the World Golf Hall of Fame in 1964 after a brilliant career that included thirteen

A child prodigy, Tiger Woods has been a wunderkind on the links during the 2000s.

> ## What is odd about Phil Mickelson being a left-handed golfer?
>
> While Mickelson plays golf using his left hand as the dominant one, he is actually right-handed in everything else he does. Why does he play golf with the other hand? Because when his father was teaching him the game, the young Mickelson mimicked his dad's movements, mirroring them, which resulted in his doing everything the opposite!

major championships. She won four Women's PGA Championships (1958, 1960, 1961, 1963), four U.S. Women's Opens (1958, 1959, 1961, 1964), three Western Opens (1962, 1963, 1966), and two Titleholders Championships (1961, 1962). In 1981 she was inducted into the Women's Sports Hall of Fame.

ICE SKATING

Who is the skater who captured the hearts of many Americans in the 1968 Winter Olympics?

Peggy Fleming (1948–) is still well remembered after winning the gold in women's figure skating in Grenoble, France. Born in San Jose, she also won five U.S. Championships, three World Championships, and a North American Championship. Her victory at the Olympics was especially poignant for America, however, which seven years earlier had suffered the death of all eighteen members of the U.S. figure skating team when their plane crashed in Belgium. The grace and beauty of Fleming's performance made her the country's sweetheart. A porcelain doll was designed to look like her, the U.S. Postal Service honored her with a stamp, and even Snoopy of the comic strip "Peanuts" had a crush on the skater. Retiring after the Olympics, Fleming became a television commentator, covering the sport for many years.

Which skater has won more U.S. national championships than any other American?

Michelle Kwan (1980–) was born in Torrance and has had a remarkable career in skating. Except for Finland's Sonia Henie (and tying American Carol Heiss), she has more world titles in singles competitions than anyone (1996, 1998, 2000, 2001, 2003); she won U.S. National Championships in 1996 and from 1998 to 2005; and she earned silver at the 1998 Olympics and bronze four years later. Retiring in 2006, she went to graduate school at Tufts University to earn a master's degree in international affairs, and she has worked as a goodwill ambassador for the George W. Bush and Barack Obama administrations, traveling everywhere from Russia and China to South Korea and Singapore.

What Californian picked up the reigns from Michelle Kwan in 2006?

Winning the 2006 U.S. championship, Sasha Cohen (1984–) of Westwood first gained attention when she finished just behind Kwan in the women's national championships of 2000. She qualified for the 2002 Olympic team but finished fourth. Cohen did better in 2006's games in Torino, Italy, standing on the podium with a silver medal around her neck.

TENNIS

Which Long Beach native made a splash with her victory against Bobby Riggs?

Billie Jean King (1943–) is one of the most successful tennis players in the sport's history. She's won thirty-nine Grand Slam ti-

After her retirement from a successful figure-skating career, Michelle Kwan became a U.S. ambassador.

tles, including six Wimbledons, four U.S. Opens, the French Open, and the Australian Open. In one of the most storied rivalries of the twentieth century, she played tennis champion Bobby Riggs (1918–1995) in what was called "The Battle of the Sexes" in 1973. Riggs had previously beaten Margaret Court (1942–), a former number-one player. It was a different story with King, though, who definitively beat him 6–4, 6–3, 6–3. Inducted into the International Tennis Hall of Fame in 1987, King further contributed to the sport by founding the Women's Tennis Association, the Women's Sports Foundation, and World Team Tennis.

What Californian beat the seemingly unbeatable Martina Navratilova?

Born in Palos Verdes, Tracy Austin (1962–) has the distinction, among others, of being the woman who gave champions Chris Evert and Martina Navratilova something to be humble about. Austin is the one who cracked Evert's 125-game clay court winning streak in 1979, as well as blocking her from getting a fifth U.S. Open title that year (she beat Navratilova in the semifinals). Thereafter, Austin would be a repeated thorn in the side of both these other tennis stars. Ranking number one in 1980, she won Wimbledon that year, and the next year she repeated her victory at the U.S. Open. She would win twenty-nine singles titles, but, tragically, a back injury cut her career short in 1983. Although she tried to make a comeback in 1988, she had to admit it was just no use and retired for good in 1989. A happy moment occurred a couple years later when, in 1992 at the age of thirty, she became the youngest person ever to be inducted into the International Tennis Hall of Fame.

What Olympian and Wimbledon champ was considered the *grand dame* of tennis?

Palos Verdes native Lindsay Davenport (1976–) enjoyed a long career with over fifty singles championships that included winning all four majors and a gold medal in the 1996 Olympics in the women's singles event. She won the Australian Open six times (1996–1999, 2001, 2005), the French Open in 1996, the U.S. Open in 1997, and Wimbledon in 1999, proving herself to also be versatile in playing on grass, clay, and concrete courts. Davenport became a pro when she was just fourteen, and she continued to play until 2006,

Serena (left) and Venus Williams are sisters who have both made history on the tennis courts of the world in singles and doubles.

when she became pregnant. She now has three daughters and one son and has settled down to family life in California with husband, Jon Leach.

Who are the dynamic sisters who have both won numerous majors in tennis?

Sisters Venus (1980–) and Serena (1981–) Williams were born in the city of Lynwood in the L.A. area, though their family moved to Florida when they were ten and nine, respectively, to train at the tennis academy in West Palm Beach run by Rick Macci. Venus was formerly ranked number one in the world, and Serena is ranked number one as of this writing (February 2016). They have each won four Olympic gold medals (three times while playing together in doubles), and Venus won the Australian and French Opens in 1998, while Serena won Wimbledon and the U.S. Open that year (1998 was definitely the year of the Williams sisters!)

WATER SPORTS

Who was the swimmer who made a career of big movie swimming pool extravaganzas?

Any fan of "aqua musicals" from the 1940s and 1950s will not fail to recall the inimitable Esther Williams (1923–2013). A Los Angeles native, she was a competitive swimmer in college, winning the AAU Championship in the 100-meter freestyle and winning three U.S. championships in freestyle and the breaststroke. She wanted to compete in the 1940 Olympics, but World War II put a stop to that. Instead, she performed at the San Francisco World's Fair that year, and it was there that an MGM scout found her. She debuted in *Andy Hardy Steps Out* (1942), starring Mickey Rooney, and that was followed by many movies with little plot but big, splashy numbers featuring Williams and lots of synchronized swimming and sparklers, such as *Ziegfeld Follies* (1946) and *Neptune's Daughter* (1949). She transitioned to nonswimming roles in the later 1950s but retired by 1961 to focus on being a mother while also endorsing swimwear.

Who was the Olympian diver who became a controversial model?

One of the most outstanding athletes of the 1980s was Greg Louganis (1960), who was a San Diego native. He won gold medals in 1984's L.A. games for platform and springboard diving and then repeated the performance in 1988 in Seoul, South Korea. The Seoul performance was particularly notable because he pulled it off after suffering a concussion in the preliminary dives. His wins made him the first diver to gold medal both events in successive Olympics. He was also the winner of five World Championships (three in springboard and two in platform diving) and six Pan American Game golds (three in each).

In 1995 Louganis announced that he was HIV positive and that he had been positive at the time he had injured himself in 1988. Paranoia about the virus that leads to AIDS was still intense back then, and even though any blood in the pool would have been quickly neutralized by the chlorine, Louganis was criticized by those who thought he put others at risk. The diver lost a lot of his commercial sponsors as a result, though Speedo kept him as a model and spokesperson until 2007. Now a spokesperson for HIV awareness, Louganis married his partner in 2013. He is a diving coach in Fullerton, California, and is a dog agility trainer, too.

Which two California women have both won twelve Olympic medals?

Natalie Coughlin (1982–), who was born in Emeryville and grew up in Vallejo and Concord, won five (two gold, two silver, one bronze) medals at the 2004 Olympics and another four personal medals and two team medals in 2008. This made her the first American woman to win six medals at a single Olympics. She also won a team bronze in the 2012 Olympic in London, bringing her total to twelve, tying her with Dara Torres (see below) and Jenny Thompson. A graduate of the University of California at Berkeley (her degree is in psychology), she was named NCAA Swimmer of the Year from 2001–2003.

Dara Torres (1967–) of Beverly Hills has the distinction of not only also winning twelve Olympic medals but also being the oldest swimmer ever to qualify for the Olympics (at age 41 for the 2008 games) and the first to qualify for five different Olympics. Her first Olympics was the 1984 games in Los Angeles, where she competed in the 4 × 100 meter freestyle relay at the age of seventeen; her last medals were at the 2008 Beijing games, where she won medals in two relays and in the fifty-meter freestyle.

Another interesting—though perhaps less admirable—achievement is that Torres was the first actual athlete to be on the cover of the *Sports Illustrated* swimsuit edition (1994). More interesting to many would be that she appears regularly on ESPN and other networks as a commentator.

OTHER SPORTS STARS

Which Californian is probably the most recognized name in skateboarding?

Tony Hawk (1968–) is a Carlsbad native who has greatly influenced the sport of vertical skateboarding, which is the specialty of using ramps and other inclines to perform tricks. The first person on record to successfully execute a 900 (two and a half spins while airborne), Hawk has one numerous competitions and turned skateboarding into a career, not just a hobby. He founded, in 2002, the extreme sport exhibition Boom Boom HuckJam and put his name on a series of skateboarding video games. Hawk has also appeared in movies and television and founded the Tony Hawk Foundation, which helps kids in low-income areas have recreational skateboard parks.

Californian Tony Hawk took skateboarding to the next level and was the first to execute a successful 900 (two and a half spins in the air).

Tony Hawk might be the best-known skateboarder to those outside that world, but who is considered even more influential by some?

It might depend some on whether you prefer vertical or street skateboarding, but the master of the latter is, unquestionably, Mark Gonzales (1968–). Gonzales is actually credited with inventing the street skateboarding style. He was a cofounder of the company Blind Skateboards and later formed another skateboard company, ATM Click.

Who's that skateboarder having fun on the television show *Life of Ryan*?

That's San Clemente native Ryan Sheckler (1989–), who took gold in the park skating competition at the 2003 X Games at the tender age of thirteen, when he was the youngest skateboarder to turn professional. He has toured with Tony Hawk (and appears as himself as a playable character on Tony Hawk video games) and starred in the MTV reality show *Life of Ryan* (2007–2009). Sheckler has continued to win at the X Games, although in the Street competition, not Park. He won the following: 2006 (silver), 2008 and 2010 (gold), 2011 (bronze), and 2012 (bronze).

Who is another skateboarder and snowboarder who benefited from some mentoring by Tony Hawk?

Although he's been an accomplished skateboarder, Shaun White (1986–) is perhaps better known for his snowboarding skills (and trademark long, red hair). He was born in

411

What boxer was nominated for a Grammy Award?

You probably guessed it: Oscar De La Hoya. Music has been an interest of his for years, and he even married a singer (Millie Corretjer). He recorded the CD *Oscar De La Hoya* in 2000 to good reviews. It includes songs written by the Bee Gees and Diane Warren.

San Diego, learning to ski, skateboard, and snowboard in the diverse environment of the southern part of the state. Taken under Hawk's wing, White blossomed in skateboarding, winning numerous X Games medals in vert. He also became an accomplished snowboarder in superpipe and slopestyle, garnering shelves full of X Games medals and then winning gold in the 2006 and 2010 Olympics in the halfpipe.

What handsome, charismatic boxer was known as "The Golden Boy"?

Although he was never a heavyweight—ranging from Super Featherweight to Middleweight during his career—Oscar De La Hoya (1973–) gained great popularity among fans around the world on a level usually reserved for the heavyweight title boxers. He was born in Los Angeles. Beginning his career in L.A. on the amateur circuit, he won the 1989 Golden Gloves and then gold at the 1992 Barcelona Olympics. He would go on to win titles in six weight divisions and was a huge audience draw, making promoters and cable television executives very happy. He finally retired in 2008 but was already running the Golden Boy Promotions company by that time. De La Hoya also was involved in the television reality show *The Next Big Champ* and the HBO boxing program *Boxeo de Oro*. Another business venture is his own clothing line.

Who is the soccer star known for sporting a pink headband?

Calling it just a small touch to assert a little of her own individuality into the game, the trademark headband is something Alex Morgan (1989–) likes to wear. Born in Diamond Bar, Morgan is known for her speed on the field, which made her a star at the University of California at Berkeley (she graduated in 2010 with a degree in political economy) and got her onto the 2009 U.S. National Team and the 2012 U.S. Olympics team. As of this writing, she plays for the Orlando Pride.

What NASCAR driver from El Cajon is considered one of the greats of his generation?

El Cajon native Jimmie Johnson (1975–), who is now retired from the sport, won five consecutive NASCAR races from 2006 to 2010, and he won a sixth title in 2013, putting him just behind greats Dale Earnhardt and Richard Petty.

Kerri Walsh (left) and Misty May-Treanor are shown here competing in Thailand in 2007. The duo have have won Olympic gold three times.

Who are the dynamic duo of beach volleyball who won three Olympic gold medals?

Misty May-Treanor (1977–) of Los Angeles comes from a family of athletes that includes professional tennis star Taylor Dent (her cousin), her baseball catcher husband, Matt Treanor, and her father, Butch May, who was on the 1968 U.S. Olympics volleyball team. May-Treanor started off with regular volleyball at Long Beach State, where she was on the 1998 NCAA championship team and named the MVP. Switching to beach volleyball, she partnered with Holly McPeak for the 2000 Olympics, placing fifth. May-Treanor then got a new partner, Kerri Walsh Jennings (1978–) of Santa Clara.

Jennings grew up in northern California and played basketball and volleyball at Archbishop Mitty High School in San Jose. She helped the volleyball team win three state championships. Her college career at Stanford was even more amazing. Jennings is only the second person in history to be a first-team All-American during all four years she was in college. The Cardinal won the Pac-10 four times and were in the Final Four three times, winning in 1996 and 1997, while she was at Stanford. Chosen MVP in 1996 of the Final Four and sharing the National Player of the Year spot in 1999, she turned pro and was on gold-medal World Championship teams in 2003, 2005, and 2007.

Pairing up with May-Treanor, the two proved nearly unstoppable and won Olympic gold in beach volleyball in 2004, 2008, and 2012.

413

BUSINESSPEOPLE

Who is probably the most prominent newspaper mogul to come from California?

Born in San Francisco, William Randolph Hearst (1863–1951) inherited control of the *San Francisco Chronicle* from his father, U.S. Senator George Hearst, and then built upon that to create a newspaper empire with publications in New York, Chicago, Los Angeles, Atlanta, and Washington, D.C. He also served in the U.S. House, representing New York's 11th District from 1903 to 1907, and made unsuccessful runs for New York City mayor and governor.

Hearst papers were known for their patriotic and effusive editorial style, and they are also notable for significantly developing the funny pages format. He branched out into radio stations and the movie company Cosmopolitan Productions. Also known for his lavish lifestyle, he famously had Hearst Castle constructed in San Simeon (see "Central California and Agriculture").

Who founded Apple, Inc.?

Two Steves from California did: Steve Jobs (1955–2011), who was born in San Francisco, and Steve "Woz" Wozniak (1950–), who was born in San Jose. There is no question that Apple has had a huge influence on the Digital Age.

Jobs was actually the son of a Syrian Muslim named Abdulfattah "John" Jandali, who was studying for his Ph.D. at the University of Wisconsin when he met Jobs's mother, Joanne Carole Schieble. Family problems involving prejudice against Muslims on Schieble's side and Jandali's family being upset that the baby was conceived out of wedlock led Schieble to flee to San Francisco, where she gave birth; she went on to marry Paul Reinhold Jobs, who adopted Steve. It was his adoptive father who taught the young Steve to work on electronics such as radios and TVs, which is how he became interested in the field. A rebellious teen with interests in both electronics and also in literature and philosophy, he became friends with with computer whiz Steve Wozniak when they were both working for Hewlett-Packard in 1971.

Together, their first little project was creating a device that hacked into telephone networks so they could make toll-free calls (Wozniak had been expelled from the University of Colorado at Boulder for hacking the university's system; he later attended UC Berkeley).

Which classic movie was based on the life of William Randolph Hearst?

Directed, produced by, and starring Orson Welles, *Citizen Kane* (1941) is considered one of the greatest films ever made and definitely Welles' masterpiece. It is, in part, based on the life of Hearst.

Wozniak was actually the brains who invented the Apple I computer, which was really just a hobbyist's toy. The Steves were trying to impress members of the Homebrew Computer Club in Palo Alto. But when the two started getting requests for the device, Jobs saw an opportunity for a business.

The business, Apple, was started from the Jobs home in Menlo Park (now a registered historic site). They came up with the Apple II and the company, joined by Ronald Wayne, began making real money with the help of investments from retired engineer Mike Markkula. After creating the flop Lisa computer, the company had a hit in 1984 with the debut of the Macintosh. Both men left the company in

The late Steve Jobs shows off the iPhone 4. Jobs was the face of Apple, though a lot of the brains behind the actual software came from Steve Wozniak.

1985—Wozniak because he didn't like doing management jobs and felt the company was going in the wrong direction, and Jobs because his own company's board fired him. Wozniak would pursue teaching and other business ventures, including the GPS technology company Wheels of WoZ; both men would eventually return to Apple, and Jobs cofounded Pixar Animation Studios, which was later acquired by Disney. Woz is still with the company, but Jobs passed away from complications caused by pancreatic cancer.

POLITICS, LAW, AND THE MILITARY

What professional quarterback later became a prominent Republican politician?

A Los Angeles native, Jack Kemp (1935–2009) played quarterback for the Buffalo Bills from 1962 to 1969, leading them to American Football League championships in 1964 and 1965. Earlier, he had also played for the Pittsburgh Steelers (in 1957), the Calgary Stampeders (1959), and the San Diego Chargers (1960–1962). He founded and was president of the AFL's player association.

His political career involved service in the U.S. House of Representatives from 1971 to 1989, representing different New York districts. Calling himself a "bleeding-heart conservative," he was a proponent of civil rights legislation while asserting that incentive-based systems to help people worked better than traditional social programs. Kemp felt that economic growth was more important than worrying about a balanced budget, and his type of logic gave credence to the boom years of the 1980s. The Kemp-Roth Tax Cut (Economic Recovery Tax Act of 1981) epitomized the Reagan years of a philosophy of trickle-down economics. During this time, he also was chair of the House Republican Conference (1981–1987). After an unsuccessful run for president in 1988, President George H. W. Bush appointed Kemp Secretary of Housing and Urban Development, a cabinet post he served in until 1993. He then made money as a public speaker; he was considered to be an obvious choice for the presidential nomination in 1996 but ended up as Bob Dole's running mate, losing to President Bill Clinton.

Was Richard Nixon also a native Californian?

Yes, the thirty-seventh president of the United States was born in Yorba Linda on January 9, 1913. The son of Quakers, he grew up in a modest home and became known as a very ambitious student and enthusiastic athlete (although his small size meant he sat on the bench a lot as a football player in school). Nixon graduated from Duke University School of Law and served in the U.S. Naval Reserve during World War II, serving in logistics in the Pacific Theater. He left active duty as a lieutenant commander in 1946 and retired from the Navy in 1953 as a full commander.

While on inactive duty, Nixon was elected to the U.S. House of Representatives, representing California's 12th district from 1947 to 1950. Next up was U.S. Senator for California for a term. Dwight Eisenhower picked Nixon as his running mate, making him vice president from 1953 to 1961. After losing to Kennedy (famously crashing during a 1960 debate when he looked nervous but Kennedy looked cool and calm on TV), he became senior partner in the New York City law firm Nixon, Mudge, Rose, Guthrie, and Alexander. He was only involved in politics in his efforts to get Republicans to gain seats in Congress.

Nixon returned to politics to campaign in the 1968 presidential elections. It was a strange campaign. President Johnson withdrew from campaigning, and when Robert F. Kennedy was assassinated, the race was between Vice President Hubert Humphrey and independent candidate George Wallace. Nixon edged out Humphrey by about a half million votes and won the White House.

As president, Nixon faced many international and domestic challenges. The Vietnam War would continue throughout his truncated presidency, but on a positive note, he made steps toward normalizing relations with China, signed two nuclear weapons treaties with the Soviet Union, and helped Israel win the Yom Kippur War. As home, he continued Johnson's policies on civil rights to integrate schools and initiated the coun-

What weapon bears Patton's name?

An excellent fencer, George Patton studied sword fighting in France, redesigned how the U.S. cavalry used the weapon, was the first U.S. Army officer to hold the title of Master of the Sword, and designed a sword more suited to thrusts than slashes—the Model 1913 Cavalry Sabre, also known as the Patton Sword.

try's first affirmative action plan. It was also during his administration that *Apollo 11* landed on the moon.

Many people forget Nixon's many accomplishments in light of the ignoble way his presidency ended in 1974. The "Nixon Tapes," as they were called, would reveal that he knew about the break-in at the Democratic National Headquarters at the Watergate complex in Washington, D.C. A culture of paranoia and dishonesty was revealed at the White House through the investigations of *Washington Post* journalists Bob Woodward (1943–) and Carl Bernstein (1944–). Nixon was impeached as a result, but before there could be hearings and a trial, he resigned his office, the first (and

Born in Yorba Linda, President Richard Nixon unfortunately ended his political career in shame when the Watergate case led to his resignation in 1974.

only, to date) U.S. president to do so. He was pardoned of any wrongdoing by President Gerald Ford (1913–2006; Nixon's former vice president) and passed away after suffering a stroke in 1994.

To learn more about the president and his life, it is well worth the visit to the Richard Nixon Presidential Library and Museum in Yorba Linda.

Why hasn't there been a Hispanic governor of California since it became part of the United States?

Actually, there *has* been a Hispanic governor since the state entered the Union in 1850. José Antonio Romualdo Pacheco Jr. (1831–1899), known as Romualdo Pacheco, was the state's twelfth governor, but he was only in office from February 27 to December 29, 1875. He also served as state treasurer (1863–1867) and lieutenant governor (1871–1875). He was named governor when Governor Newton Booth had to leave for Washington, D.C., having won a seat in the U.S. Senate. Pacheco had to step down less than a year later when his own second-in-command, William Irwin, won the next election. But don't feel sorry for Pacheco. He lived on a Mexican ranch for a couple of years and then served in the U.S. House of Representatives from 1877 to 1883 before returning to California to retire.

What general from San Gabriel commanded the 7th Army during World War II?

General George S. Patton Jr. (1886–1945) came from a military family, attended West Point, and was a remarkable fencer who participated in the 1912 Olympics pentathlon. During World War I, he fought with the U.S. Tank Corps in France. After this war, he continued his involvement in armored warfare. When World War II brought the U.S. into the conflict, he commanded the U.S. 2nd Armored Division in Europe. He led troops in northern Africa and then commanded the 7th Army during the invasion of Sicily. After being temporarily taken off active combat duty because of the bad public relations following his slapping of a soldier, Patton returned to the 3rd Army during the Normandy invasion, the Battle of the Bulge, and into Germany. After the war, he briefly served as military governor of Bavaria and of the 15th Army before dying in a car accident on December 12, 1945.

Who was the popular California politician who was almost president of the United States?

Born in Los Angeles, Adlai Stevenson II (1900–1965) was the Democrat Party's candidate for president in 1952 and 1956. He was the grandson of Grover Cleveland's vice president. A graduate of Princeton and Northwestern, Stevenson became an attorney, finding his way to Chicago, working for the Agricultural Adjustment Association and, during Prohibition, the Federal Alcohol Control Administration. He chaired the Chicago branch of the Committee to Defend America by Aiding the Allies from 1940 to 1941, was an attorney for the Secretary of the Navy, and then worked for the State Department.

The Democrat Party selected Stevenson to run for governor of Illinois in 1948, and even though he had no political experience, he won by proving himself an eloquent public speaker. As governor, Stevenson improved Illinois's highway system and reduced corruption in the police force. He also had the guts to veto a bill passed by the state legislature that would have made it illegal to belong to any group deemed "subversive" (this was during the Red Scare when Americans feared the Communists).

Stevenson ran for president twice against Dwight Eisenhower (losing twice), and in 1960, he lost the Democrat nomination to John F. Kennedy. President Kennedy appointed him to be ambassador to the United Nations, and he would remain in that post until his death from a heart attack in 1965.

Has there ever been a Californian on the U.S. Supreme Court?

Yes. Born in Los Angeles, Justice Earl Warren (1891–1974) served on the nation's highest court from 1953 to 1969 as chief justice. It was an important time for law at the time as the Civil Rights Movement was in full swing. The Warren Court, as it was called, was considered quite liberal regarding racial relations (it was perhaps no surprise that Warren was a graduate of the extremely liberal University of California, Berkeley), making rulings against school racial segregation in the landmark *Brown v. Board of Education* (1954) case.

Justice Earl Warren of Los Angeles served on the U.S. Supreme Court from 1953 to 1969.

Warren also chaired the Warren Commission, which investigated the President John F. Kennedy assassination in 1963. What you might not know about Warren is that he also was the governor of California for three terms (1943–1953).

SCIENTISTS, ENGINEERS, INVENTORS, AND EDUCATORS

What was Nobel Prize winner Luis Walter Alvarez noted for?

Luis Walter Alvarez (1911–1988) was a San Francisco-born physicist who won the 1968 Nobel Prize in Physics. This was the result of his work on a liquid hydrogen bubble chamber that he and his team used to take photographs of atomic particles and measure their interactions, which, in turn, led to the discovery of new particles and their resonances. This was just one of many impressive accomplishments, however. Working with his son, geologist Walter Alvarez (1940–), he came up with the Alvarez hypothesis, which was the first proposal that the extinction of the dinosaurs was the result of a large asteroid striking the earth. In addition, Alvarez was a contributor to the Manhattan Project (the team that developed the atom bomb during World War II), developed the transponder (a method of locating and identifying aircraft at a distance) and a landing system for aircraft, helped to isolate the radioactive isotope tritium, and developed an experiment to observe K-electron capture in radioactive nuclei.

Why was Hubert Howe Bancroft important to California history?

In a way, Bancroft (1832–1918) *was* California history. Born in Ohio, he moved to San Francisco in 1852 to become a book seller. Amassing a huge collection of publications, he started a publishing business in 1852, specializing in books and maps about the state and becoming an amateur historian. He published a handbook about the Pacific Coast in 1859. In addition to books about California, he created books on history about everything from Alaska to the Rocky Mountains down to Mexico and Central America.

Bancroft's growing private collection included government and church documents, periodicals, maps, pamphlets, and manuscripts, which he used as a resource for the books he published with help from a staff of researchers and writers (Bancroft's reputation suffered later in life when he was accused of not crediting his contributors for their substantial work). His *History of California* (1886–1890) was a seven-volume *tour de force* that became a standard reference for many years. Among his other books about the state are *California Inter Pocula* (1888) and *California Pastoral* (1888).

In 1905 Bancroft sold his collection of 60,000 books to the University of California, Berkeley, for $250,000 (he donated $100,000 to the university, too). This is now the Bancroft Library.

What is the name of the physicist noted for developing a commonly used transistor?

Born in 1936 in Santa Monica, Dr. Robert Bower is the inventor of the MOSFET (metal-oxide-semiconductor field-effect transistor), which is currently the most-often-used transistor in both digital and analog devices. Currently an emeritus professor at UC Davis, Bower was inducted into the National Inventors Hall of Fame in 1997 for his MOSFET.

Who is responsible for the technology used in many homes and factories to help clean the air?

The electrostatic precipitator, which is able to remove fine particulates out of the air, was invented by Frederick G. Cottrell (1877–1948), a chemist and a bit of a prodigy who was born in Oakland. Cottrell graduated from UC Berkeley at the age of nineteen. After teaching high school chemistry for a time, he resumed studies at the University of Berlin and Leipzig University and earned a Ph.D. in 1902 after studying under Nobel Prize winners Jacobus Henricus van 't Hoff and Wilhelm Ostwald.

Returning home, he began teaching at Berkeley, and it was while there that he researched how to remove harmful particles such as sulfuric acid mists from the air. The result of local manufacturing, the pollutants were harming the nearby wine and other agricultural industries. Cottrell came up with his electrostatic precipitator, which uses an electrical charge to attract and filter out contaminants from air blowing through the device. This became the model for air-cleaning machinery used in industry that also can be purchased today for home use.

In addition to this notable contribution to humanity, Cottrell founded the Research Corporation for Science Advancement in 1912. The RCSA funds scientific research that looks promising for revolutionizing various fields of study.

Who was the heroine whose true story was the basis for the film *Gorillas in the Mist*?

Another notable who was born in San Francisco, Dian Fossey (1932–1985) was a primatologist, anthropologist, and zoologist. Inspired by fellow anthropologist Louis Leakey, she studied gorillas in Rwanda, where she founded the Karisoke Research Center in 1967. But while there she became heavily involved in trying to keep mountain gorillas safe from poachers. The population was being decimated, either being killed outright or being captured for export to zoos. While poaching was illegal in Rwanda, it was not well enforced, and it was Fossey and her small team who managed to destroy

---

What might one say is a "note"-worthy fact about Ellen Ochoa?

Astronaut Ochoa is also a classically trained flutist and once played the flute for the Stanford Symphony Orchestra.

hundreds of traps and get numerous poachers arrested and imprisoned. She also opposed wildlife tourism in the area. It was this work that, many speculate, led to her murder in 1985, although no one was ever arrested for her death.

What Californian helped to invent the videotape recorder?

Charles P. Ginsburg (1920–1992), born in San Francisco, led a team of other inventors at the Redwood City-based Ampex Data Systems Corporation to invent the videotape recorder. He worked for Ampex from 1951 to 1986, with his greatest contribution being the development of using electromagnetic tape to record sound and images in a way that also allowed for the instant playback of such recordings.

Who was the first Hispanic woman to go into space?

Astronaut Ellen Ochoa (1958–) was born in L.A. and grew up in La Mesa. She studied physics at San Diego State University and completed a doctorate in electrical engineering in 1985 at Stanford. Ochoa became an expert in optical systems and is a co-inventor on three patents regarding such systems. She has also conducted research in automated space exploration systems. Joining NASA, her first mission as an astronaut came in 1993 aboard the space shuttle *Discovery*. She would go on three other missions (on *Discovery* and *Atlantis*), logging over a thousand hours in space. In 2007, she was named deputy director of the Johnson Space Center and was promoted to director in 2013, making her the first Hispanic woman to hold the prestigious post.

Was the first American woman in space also from California?

Yes, indeed. Sally Ride (1951–2012) was born in Los Angeles. A physicist by training, she was (as of 2016) the youngest American to fly into space, as well. Ride joined NASA in 1978 and was on two of the space shuttle *Challenger* missions, and she would serve on the committees that investigated both the *Challenger* and the *Columbia* disasters. Leaving NASA in 1987, she later taught physics at the University of California, San Diego. Ride passed away from pancreatic cancer in La Jolla.

Were any other astronauts born in California?

Gosh, yes! Other California astronauts include pilot Kevin P. Chilton (born in L.A.

Astronaut Ellen Ochoa is the first Hispanic woman to hold the office of deputy director of the Johnson Space Center.

in 1954), mission specialist Michael R. U. Clifford (born at Norton AFB in 1952), Michael Coats (Sacramento, 1946–), Frederick H. Hauck (Long Beach, 1941–), James D. A. van Hoften (San Francisco, 1944–), Michael J. McCulley (San Diego, 1943–), and Bryan D. O'Connor (Orange, 1946–).

Who was the inventor of the first working laser?

Theodore "Ted" Harold Maiman (1927–2007) was a Los Angeles native. He was working for Hughes Aircraft Company when he developed the first working laser, which was tested successfully on May 16, 1960. He did his undergraduate work at the University of Colorado and graduate work at Stanford, where he finished a Ph.D. in physics in 1955. He joined Hughes Aircraft the following year, where he worked on a maser project (microwave amplification by stimulated emission of radiation). Maiman was able to excite the frequency of the radiation used in masers to create the laser with the use of a synthetic ruby. For his work, he received numerous honors, including being inducted into the National Inventors Hall of Fame.

California Governors

Under Spain

Name	Years in Office
Gaspar de Portolá	1768–1770
Pedro Fages	1770–1774
Fernando Rivera y Moncada	1774–1777
Felipe de Neve	1777–1782
Pedro Fages	1782–1791
José Antonio Roméu	1791–1792
José Joaquín de Arrillaga (acting)	1792–1794
Diego de Borica	1794–1800
Pedro de Alberni (acting)	1800–1800
José Joaquín de Arrillaga	1800–1814
José Argüello (acting)	1814–1815
Pablo Vicente Solá	1815–1822

Under Mexico

Name	Years in Office
Pablo Vicente Solá (holdover from Spanish regime)	1815–1822
Luis Argüello (acting)	1822–1825
José María de Echeandía	1825–1831
Manuel Victoria	1831–1832
Pio Pico (twenty days)	1832–1832
José María Echeandía (in the south only)	1832–1833
Agustin Vicente Zamorano (in the north only)	1832–1833
José Figueroa	1833–1835
José Castro (acting)	1835–1836
Nicolás Gutíerrez (acting governor for four months)	1836
Mariano Chico (three months)	1836
Nicolás Gutíerrez (acting governor for three months)	1836–1836
Juan Bautista Alvarado (first revolutionary then constitutional governor)	1836–1842

Manuel Micheltoreña	1842–1845
Pio Pico; last Mexican governor of California	1845–1846
José María Flores (leader of government in the last days before surrender	1846–1847

UNDER THE UNITED STATES OF AMERICA

Name	Political Party	Years in Office
Peter Hardeman Burnett	Democrat	1849–1851
John McDougal	Democrat	1851–1852
John Bigler	Democrat	1852–1856
J. Neely Johnson	American	1856–1858
John B. Weller	Democrat	1858–1860
Milton Latham (served January 9–14)	Democrat	1860
John G. Downey	Democrat	1860–1862
Leland Stanford	Republican	1862–1863
Frederick Low	Republican	1863–1867
Henry Huntley Haight	Democrat	1867–1871
Newton Booth	Republican	1871–1875
Romualdo Pacheco (February to December)	Republican	1875
William Irwin	Democrat	1875–1880
George Clement Perkins	Republican	1880–1883
George Stoneman	Democrat	1883–1887
Washington Bartlett	Democrat	1887
Robert Waterman	Republican	1887–1891
Henry Harrison Markham	Republican	1891–1895
James Budd	Democrat	1895–1899
Henry Gage	Republican	1899–1903
George Pardee	Republican	1903–1907
James Gillett	Republican	1907–1911
Hiram Johnson	Progressive	1911–1917
William Stephens	Republican	1917–1923
Friend Richardson	Republican	1923–1927
C. C. Young	Republican	1927–1931
James Rolph	Republican	1931–1934
Frank Merriam	Republican	1934–1939
Culbert Olson	Democrat	1939–1943
Earl Warren	Republican	1943–1953
Goodwin Knight	Republican	1954–1959
Edmund G. "Pat" Brown	Democrat	1959–1967
Ronald Reagan	Republican	1967–1975
Edmund G. "Jerry" Brown	Democrat	1975–1983
George Deukmejian	Republican	1983–1991
Pete Wilson	Republican	1991–1999
Gray Davis	Democrat	1999–2003
Arnold Schwarzenegger	Republican	2003–2011
Edmund G. "Jerry" Brown	Democrat	2011–

Further Reading

Bakersfield. http://www.visitbakersfield.com/.

"The Best Golf Courses in California." *Golf Digest*. July 20, 2015. http://www.golfdigest.com/story/california-2015-2016-best-in-state-rankings.

Bishop, Greg, and Joe Oesterle. *Weird California: Your Travel Guide to California's Local Legends and Best Kept Secrets*. New York: Sterling, 2009.

"Braceros: History, Compensation." *Rural Migration News*. April 2006. https://migration.ucdavis.edu/rmn/more.php?id=1112.

Brownlow, Kevin, and John Kobal. *Hollywood: The Pioneers*. New York: Alfred A. Knopf, 1979.

Burns, John F., and Richard J. Orsi, editors. *Taming the Elephant: Politics, Government, and Law in Pioneer California*. Berkeley, CA: University of California Press, 2003.

CA.gov. www.ca.gov.

California Community Colleges Chancellor's Office. http://www.cccco.edu/.

California—Dream Big. http://www.visitcalifornia.com/.

California High Speed Rail Authority. http://www.hsr.ca.gov/.

"California Military History: California and the Second World War." http://www.militarymuseum.org/HistoryWWII.html. Accessed February 2, 2016.

The California State University. http://universityofcalifornia.edu/.

"California's Water: California's Water System." *Association of California Water Agencies*. http://www.acwa.com/content/california-water-series/californias-water-california-water-systems. Accessed March 10, 2016.

Discover Los Angeles. http://www.discoverlosangeles.com/.

Fresno Bee. www.fresnobee.com.

Grover, Joel, and Matthew Glasser. "L.A.'s Nuclear Secret: Part 1." *NBC 4*. http://www.nbclosangeles.com/investigations/LA-Nuclear-Secret-327896591.html. Accessed May 15, 2016.

Gustkey, Earl, *Great Moments in Southern California Sports*. New York: Harry N. Abrams, 1990.

Gutierrez, Ramon A., and Richard J. Orsi, editors. *Contested Eden: California before the Gold Rush*. Berkeley, CA: University of California Press, 1998.

Hart, James D. *A Companion to California*. New York: Oxford University Press, 1978.

Historic Monterey. http://www.historicmonterey.org/.

Hutchingson, W. H. *California: Two Centuries of Man, Land, & Growth in the Golden State*. Palo Alto, CA: American West Publishing, 1967.

Johnson, Paul C. *Pictorial History of California*. Garden City, NY: Doubleday, 1970.

Long Beach, California. http://www.visitlongbeach.com/.

Los Angeles Angels. www.losangeles.angels.mlb.com.

Los Angeles Clippers. www.nba.com/clippers/.

Los Angeles Conservancy. www.laconservancy.org.

Los Angeles Dodgers. www.dodgers.com.

Los Angeles Kings. www.lakings.com.

Los Angeles Lakers. www.nba.com/lakers/.

Los Angeles Times. www.latimes.com.

Martin, Philip. *Promise Unfulfilled: Unions, Immigration, and Farm Workers*. Ithaca, NY: Cornell University Press, 2003.

McNary, Dave, "Hollywood Continues to Flee California at Alarming Rate." *Variety,* March 5, 2014. Accessed at http://variety.com/2014/film/news/even-films-set-in-california-are-shooting-elsewhere-to-save-money-1201125523/ (April 11, 2016).

Mungo, Ray: *San Francisco Confidential: Tales of Scandal and Excess from the Town That's Seen Everything*. New York: Birch Lane Press, 1995.

Nagel, Charles E. "Sacramento Cholera Epidemic of 1850." *Golden Notes*. 4:1 (October 1957): 1–8.

Oakland Athletics. www.oakland.athletics.com.

Oakland Raiders. www.raiders.com.

Osmer, Harold, and Phil Harms. *Real Road Racing: The Santa Monica Road Races.* Harold L. Osmer Publishing, 1999.

Palm, Carl. *This Day in California History*. Austin, TX: Northcross Books, 2008.

Palm Springs California: Like No Place Else. http://www.visitpalmsprings.com/.

Pasadena Official Visitors Site. http://www.visitpasadena.com/.

Pinney, Thomas. *A History of Wine in America from the Beginnings to Prohibition*. Berkeley and Los Angeles: University of California Press, 1989.

Press, Skip. *Awesome Almanac: A Treasury of Facts and Fictions, Celebrities and Celebrations, and the Weird and Wonderful!* Walworth, WI: B&B Publishing, 1994.

Ripley's Ghost Towns and Other Adventures. http://www.ripleysghosttowns.com/.

Sacramento Kings. www.nba.com/kings/.

San Diego Chargers. www.chargers.com.

San Diego Padres. www.padres.com.

San Jose Sharks. www.sharks.nhl.com.

San Francisco 49ers. www.49ers.com.

San Francisco Chronicle. http://www.sfchronicle.com/.

San Francisco Giants. www.sanfrancisco.giants.mlb.com.

San Francisco Travel. http://www.sanfrancisco.travel/.

SFGate. http://www.sfgate.com/.

Sim, Nick, "This Is What Became of Michael Jackson's Private Neverland Theme Park." *Theme Park Tourist*. http://www.themeparktourist.com/features/20150720/30428/never land-untold-full-story-michael-jackson-s-lost-private-theme-park. July 23, 2015.

Starr, Kevin. *California: A History*. New York: Modern Library, 2007.

Sunset Magazine, http://www.sunset.com.

United States Department of Agriculture Economic Research Service. http://www.ers.usda.gov/.

University of California. http://universityofcalifornia.edu/.

Weird California. http://www.weirdca.com/.

Index

Note: (ill.) indicates photos and illustrations.

427

H

436

444